Contents

Preface to the second edition

In the eight years that have elapsed since the first edition was produced, there have been major changes in a number of fields, particularly in aspects of concrete technology, such as mix design and admixtures. These, together with an awareness of the need to stress certain areas, such as durability, and to rationalise others for ease of understanding, has led to a complete reappraisal of the book and the production of a new manuscript. It is hoped that the reader will find a reasonable balance between the science of materials and their detailed properties, and that most of the omissions of the earlier edition have been rectified.

The author is again indebted to many colleagues for valuable assistance in preparing and checking the new edition and to his mother for typing the manuscript.

Acknowledgements

We are grateful to the following for permission to reproduce copyright material:

The American Concrete Institute for Tables 3.4 and 3.5 from *Manual of Concrete Practice Part 1*; Edward Arnold for Fig. 4.32 from *Metallurgy for Engineers*; extracts and tables from BSS 449, 882, 1201, 1470, 1475, 4360, 4449, 4461, 4482, 4486, 4757, 5896, and BS CP 110, 1972, 'The Structural Use of Concrete', reproduced by permission of the British Standards Institution, 2 Park Street, London, W1A 2BS, from whom copies of the complete works may be obtained; British Steel Corporation for Figs. 4.28 and 4.31 from *Single Guide to Structure and Properties of Steel*; The Controller of Her Majesty's Stationery Office for Fig. 3.11 and Table 3.6 based on material from 'The design of normal concrete mixes'; Cement and Concrete Association for extracts based on the following: 'The determination of the proportions of aggregates approximating to any required grading', 'Basic mix method', 'Winter concreting'; Iliffe Scientific and Technical Books for Figs. 5.3 and 5.4 from *Plastics Materials*; John Laing Research and Development Limited for references made to the incorporation of polypropylene fibres in concrete for the modification of plastic and hardened properties; West's Piling and Construction for the mention of polypropylene fibres used in piling shells.

Chapter 1

Introduction

Recent years have seen the beginning of considerable changes in the construction industry and materials for construction are no exception. Traditionally, the use of building materials has been based, to some degree, on long-term experience rather than on intimate understanding and, as a result, generous allowances have been made against known modes of failure. This approach is not surprising if one appreciates the enormous complexity of materials, such as clay products or cements, even though they are made by basically simple techniques. Indeed, the success of the vast majority of materials and methods in the past is borne out by such terms as 'safe as houses' and the fact that old buildings are rarely demolished because of a condition of advanced deterioration. Developments which have occurred in materials and techniques have been based not so much on any inferiority in the traditional approach as on great technological advances in many fields which, together with rising prices, have forced the engineer and builder to consider very carefully other possible ways of achieving given standards of performance. At the same time, because larger buildings are often economically more viable than small buildings – and more dangerous if defects are present – attention has been paid to studies of the structural properties of materials. In particular, statistical laws have been applied to quantify the inherent variability of most materials and to arrive at sensible definitions of the word 'safe' in a given situation. Recently, published codes of practice typify the changes which are being made, while standards for materials reflect attempts to describe more accurately their relevant properties. An important requirement of codes of practice is that they should consider and allow for all modes of failure. There have been examples in recent times of problems arising because, owing to greater production control, property requirements of components, such as average strength, have justifiably been reduced. In some cases, this has led to adverse changes in other properties (perhaps durability) such that, although the component is satisfactory in respect of strength, it may not be able to fulfil its total requirements.

Changes of manufacturing techniques are by no means the only ones to affect the building industry. New products appear on the market continuously and the user must be able to make some judgement as to their suitability for his purpose.

1

This book attempts to provide an understanding, as well as a knowledge, of the performance of materials in a given situation. The most important single factor in determining properties is chemical structure which, in turn, depends on the atomic structure of the constituent elements. Materials may be classified according to the basic bond types which they exhibit. Siliceous and related materials form the largest group and are conveniently described under two chapter headings. Remaining chapters describe metals, organic materials and fibre reinforcement. In each case, a simple understanding of structure will allow a more accurate prediction of performance than would a much wider superficial knowledge which is not so based. This chapter is devoted entirely to the subject of atomic structure and forms the basis of remaining chapters.

Atomic structure

In much the same way as the structural properties and performance of a completed building depend on the individual units which it comprises and on the way these are assembled, so the behaviour of a single component, for example, a brick or steel beam, depends on the 'building units' which it contains. These units or atoms are entirely responsible for every property of the material whether it be physical, chemical or mechanical. Atoms are made up of still smaller units, the three main ones being protons, neutrons and electrons. These particles are important in their role as building units in atoms and, in some cases, are used to test materials. Table 1.1 shows their properties.

Many other sub-atomic particles have been discovered during recent research but they are of little consequence concerning the behaviour of bulk materials, since they are produced only by relatively rare sub-atomic interactions and are generally extremely short-lived – they soon revert to some combination of the more common particles. Atoms can be conveniently described in sections concerned first with the nucleus and then with the electron shells.

Structure and properties of the nucleus

This contains the protons and neutrons and, therefore, is by far the heaviest part of the atom. While it would be wrong to regard nuclear particles as completely motionless, they, nevertheless, occupy an extremely small space compared to that occupied by the atom as a whole. The protons and neutrons are held together by very short-range forces which disappear at separations greater than about 10^{-15}m. These forces are peculiar to nuclear particles – they are neither electrostatic nor gravitational in origin. The stability of nuclei stems from the fact that, when protons and neutrons come together, there is a small release of mass (M), this mass representing the 'binding energy' (E) of the nucleus. According to Einstein's equation $E = Mc^2$ where c is the velocity of light. A particularly stable

Table 1.1 Properties of the fundamental particles which comprise atoms

Particle	Charge (Coulomb)	Mass (kg)	Relative mass
Proton	$+1.602 \times 10^{-19}$	1.672×10^{-27}	1.000
Neutron	0	1.675×10^{-27}	1.002
Electron	-1.602×10^{-19}	9.109×10^{-31}	$\dfrac{1}{1836}$

unit is the proton-neutron pair and, in lighter atoms, the number of protons is often equal to the number of neutrons. The binding energy per nuclear particle tends to increase with nuclear size, reaching a maximum at element number 26 – iron (Fe). Thereafter, binding energy decreases, due to mutual repulsion of protons until, after lead (Pb), element number 82, nuclei are not fully stable. Hence, there are 82 basic types of stable element in the earth's crust, containing between 1 and 82 protons. Although, in some lighter atoms, the number of neutrons is equal to the number of protons, in heavier atoms, extra neutrons become essential to minimise proton-proton repulsion. In many elements (that is, atoms with a specified number of protons), a variable number of neutrons is possible: for example, carbon, which has six protons, may have six, seven or eight neutrons. The latter are known as isotopes of carbon and the relative quantities of each in naturally occurring carbon give an indication of their relative stability. In general, the neutron excess is only sufficient to stabilise the nucleus; if the excess becomes greater any than this, neutrons would tend to decompose, since free neutrons are not, in themselves, highly stable particles — they break up into protons and electrons.

Since the iron nucleus has the highest binding energy per unit mass, it is the most stable nucleus. Smaller nuclei have a tendency to grow (fusion) and larger nuclei tend to break up (fission). It may, therefore, be argued that all matter should eventually change to iron but, although theoretically this is the case, the stability of all 82 nuclei is, in practice, sufficiently great for rates of change to be infinitesimally small.

Nuclear power is, nevertheless, derived from the increase of nuclear stability that occurs on the fusion of light elements or the fission of heavy elements.

It is possible to change one element into another by nuclear physics – this might, for instance, be considered as a method of producing more useful or valuable elements from other elements but this could never be carried out on a commercial scale.

The use of materials must, therefore, be heavily geared to the existing balance of elements in the earth's crust. This balance is affected by relative nuclear stability but by other factors as well. The number of elements which are abundant in the earth's crust is quite small but these elements include oxygen, silicon, aluminium, iron, hydrogen and carbon.

Radioactivity

It has been established that 82 stable elements form the basis for virtually the entire range of materials used by man. However, a number of heavier elements do exist naturally and, in addition, it is possible to produce 'artificial' elements – that is, very large elements, or isotopes with an abnormal proton/neutron ratio. Such elements are described as radioactive, since they undergo changes in structure which eventually result in the formation of one or more of the 82 stable elements. It should be emphasised that radioactive changes in materials are relatively rare. Nevertheless, radioactivity does have a number of important applications in the construction industry and so a brief description of this type of behaviour is given.

The main cause of radioactivity is excessive nuclear size, resulting in disintegration by proton-proton repulsion. Since the proton-neutron pair is itself a highly stable group, heavy elements normally decay by rejection of a particle comprising such pairs – in fact two protons and two neutrons. This group constitutes a helium nucleus and is known as an alpha particle. These particles have a positive charge, due to the two protons which, combined with their substantial mass, causes them to be rapidly absorbed by normal materials. In consequence, they do not find application in construction.

A further cause of radioactivity is a proton-neutron imbalance, caused by an excessive number of neutrons – for example, when a heavy nucleus decays by emission of alpha particles to a new element which requires a smaller neutron excess for stability. Neutrons in this situation are converted into the more stable form of a proton and electron (known as a beta particle):

$$n \longrightarrow e^- + p^+$$

neutron   beta   proton
              particle

The beta particle is emitted – often at speeds up to 99 per cent of the speed of light, while the proton remains in the nucleus, improving the proton/neutron balance. It is quite common, therefore, for beta particles to be emitted by nuclei undergoing radioactive decay after they have emitted two or three alpha particles.

A further emission of energy in the form of short electromagnetic waves called gamma rays often accompanies alpha or beta particle emissions. The emission is due to the nucleus ending up in an 'excited' or high-energy state as the result of the decay process. Gamma rays are similar to X-rays and, although they damage human tissues, they are also useful for testing of materials, since they can penetrate materials as dense as concrete. A common source is the isotope of cobalt containing 33 neutrons:

$$_{27}Co^{60} \longrightarrow {}_{28}Ni^{60} + \text{beta particle} + \text{gamma ray}$$

In each case, the superscript refers to the nuclear mass and the subscript to the number of protons.

The most recent form of radioactivity to be discovered is neutron emission. Neutrons may be produced in a number of ways, for example, by bombardment of light nuclei with alpha particles:

$$_4\text{Be}^9 + {_2}\text{He}^4 \longrightarrow {_6}\text{C}^{12} + {_0}\text{n}^1$$

beryllium   alpha   carbon   neutron
             particle

Neutrons are particularly useful since, being uncharged, they can penetrate to the nuclei of atoms, unlike alpha or beta particles. In consequence, they are slowed down or 'moderated' by nuclear collision. Hydrogen has a much greater moderating effect on neutrons than any other element, since it has similar nuclear mass to the neutron (the neutron merely rebounds off heavier nuclei).

Half-life
The emission of radioactive particles occurs on a statistical basis and, as one particular element decays into another, the emission of the former material will decrease, since less of it remains. The relationship is exponential:

$$\frac{dN}{dt} = -\lambda N$$

where N is the number of particles at a time t and λ is a constant. The minus sign signifies that this is a decay process.

Separating variables and integrating:

$\text{Log}_e N = -\lambda t + C$ (C = constant)

If, when $t = 0$, $N = N_0$ this gives

$N = N_0 e^{-\lambda t}$

The time $t_{1/2}$ at which half the material $\frac{1}{2}N_0$ remains is called its half-life.

$$t_{1/2} = \frac{\log_e 2}{\lambda}$$

The term 'half-life' gives an idea of the useful life of a particular isotope. The emission of cobalt 60, for example, would decrease by 50 per cent over a period of about 5 years – its approximate half-life. Sources having half-lives in this region are often used – they correspond to a useful rate of emission combined with a reasonably long active life. Table 1.2 shows one means of decay of uranium into lead. Note that half-lives vary greatly.

Applications of radioactivity in the construction industry
The two main areas of use involve the absorption of gamma rays by materials, according to their density, and the detection of hydrogen using fast neutrons.

Gamma radiograph (BS 4408)   Concrete up to half a metre thick can be tested in this way. A small-diameter gamma source is placed in front of the structure to be photographed and an X-ray film enclosed in a flat cassette behind it (Fig. 1.1). Lead-intensifying screens are normally used in front of and behind the film.

Table 1.2 One means by which uranium can decay into lead

New name	Old name	Atomic no	Mass	Particles emitted	Half-life
Uranium 238	Uranium I	92	238	α	4.5×10^9 y
Thorium 234	Uranium X_1	90	234	β, γ	24.1 d
Protactinium 234	Uranium X_2	91	234	β, γ	1.17 m
Uranium 234	Uranium II	92	234	α	2×10^5 y
Thorium 230	Ionium	90	230	α, γ	8×10^4 y
Radium 226	Radium	88	226	α, γ	1622 y
Radon 222	Radon	86	222	α	3.82 d
Polomium 218	Radium A	84	218	α	3.05 m
Lead 214	Radium B	82	214	β, γ	27 m
Bismuth 214	Radium C	83	214	β, γ	20 m
Polomium 214	Radium C^1	84	214	α	1.6×10^{-4} s
Lead 210	Radium D	82	210	β, γ	22 y
Bismuth 210	Radium E	83	210	β	5 d
Polomium 210	Polomium	84	210	α, γ	138 d
Lead 206	Lead	82	206	Stable	—

y = years   d = days   m = minutes   s = seconds.

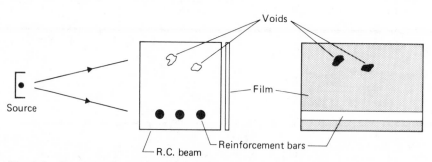

Fig. 1.1   Gamma radiography of reinforced concrete. Higher density areas produce lower transmission and, therefore, lighter areas on the film

These emit electrons when irradiated and they effectively make the film more sensitive. The gamma rays are not focused and, for maximum sharpness, the source should be as far as possible from the specimen, subject to obtaining satisfactory exposure times. The technique is particularly useful for examining grouting in prestressed concrete and for locating the position of steel.

Density measurement   This is a direct application of the effect of density of materials on their gamma-ray absorption. The density may be obtained by a transmission technique or by measuring back-scattered radiation. In the transmission technique, a source of gamma rays is placed on one side of the structure and a detector on the other (Fig. 1.2). The transmitted intensity decreases as density increases (Fig. 1.3). In the back-scatter method, the source is placed on the surface with the detector adjacent to it but shielded from direct radiation by a

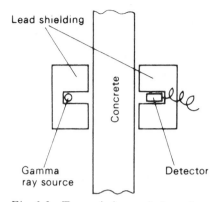

Fig. 1.2 Transmission technique for measurement of the density of concrete using gamma rays

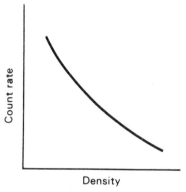

Fig. 1.3 The relation between transmitted intensity of gamma rays and density

lead screen (Fig. 1.4). The detector then measures back-scattered radiation, the detector response depending on the instrument geometry. The variation of response with density is shown in Fig. 1.5. Some instruments are so designed that the density of concrete occurs on the positive gradient portion and others so that it occurs on the negative gradient portion. The back-scatter method is particularly suitable for density measurement of structures with only one accessible surface, such as concrete slabs. Material between 50 and 100 mm from the surface contributes towards back-scattered radiation and corrections may be necessary if other materials lie within this region. There is also a tendency for different types of material to produce different density-response characteristics. Greatest accuracy is obtained by calibration of each material used.

The detection of gamma rays used for density measurement is usually carried out using a geiger counter, which is based on the ionising effect of the rays. The radiation enters a partially evacuated glass tube containing electrodes at a high dc voltage. When a radioactive particle enters the tube, it ionises the gas and causes a

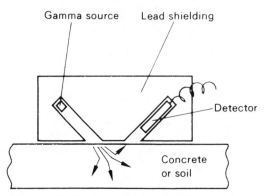

Fig. 1.4 Back-scatter method for density measurement using gamma rays

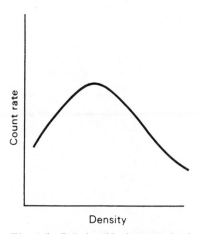

Fig. 1.5 Relationship between back-scattered gamma radiation and density

pulse of current which may be detected by a loudspeaker, or, when quantitative measurements are required, measured using a counter.

Fast neutrons The moderation of fast neutrons by hydrogen atoms provides a ready means for moisture content measurements in inorganic materials since, in these, moisture would be the only source of hydrogen. A generator is placed on the material and a detector which responds only to moderated or 'thermal' neutrons is positioned near it. The response of the detector will then be dependent on the moisture content of the material. Rapid, in-situ measurements can be made. For greatest accuracy, calibration graphs may be produced, using results obtained by conventional methods. In-situ measurements can be of great advantage, for example, in soil compaction where optimum moisture content depends on the compaction method, so that a small hand-compacted sample may have a different optimum moisture content from the correct value corresponding to compaction by machine. A further application is the measurement of binder content in asphalts, the binder consisting of hydrocarbons and, therefore, behaving in a manner similar to water.

Thermal neutrons may be detected using boron trifluoride tubes in which alpha particles are produced on irradiation.

$$_5B^{10} + {}_0n^1 \longrightarrow {}_3Li^7 + {}_2H^4$$

boron   neutron   lithium   alpha particle

Alpha particles are detected as previously.

Hazards of radioactive radiation

Although the advantages of the above techniques are evident, radioactive materials are potentially extremely dangerous, causing burning and destruction of living tissues when excessive doses are received. They should be stored in lead containers (or in paraffin wax or polythene in the case of fast neutron sources); clearly labelled; and handled with care, keeping out of direct line with the sources. When used regularly, a badge containing sensitive film should be worn by the operator and developed periodically. This will give the accumulated radiation received over that period and should be compared with permissible levels. Badges are, of course, no use in preventing severe exposure due to careless use of radioactive materials. All such sources are dangerous but fast neutrons are particularly harmful.

Electron shells – the Periodic Table

In practical terms, the behaviour of electrons which orbit the nucleus is far more important than behaviour of the nucleus itself, provided, of course, the nucleus is stable. The outer electrons, in particular, form the interfaces between atoms and determine every property of the material which the atoms are built up to form.

The electrons orbiting the nucleus, rather like the sub-nuclear particles, obey special laws which do not apply to materials in bulk. For example, the movement of electrons is usually associated with the production of energy in the form of electromagnetic waves and yet this could not apply to electrons in orbit around the nucleus. Such an emission would cause the electrons to spiral downwards into the nucleus as they lose energy. We find that the energy of an electron orbiting the atom is quantised – that is, it may take certain discrete values only – rather like the potential energy corresponding to the various steps on a staircase. The quantisation of the electron's energy gives rise to a number of orbits around the nucleus, the orbits of greater energy being further away from it. The electron shells are designated by the letters K, L, M, N etc. in order of increasing energy. The numbers 1, 2, 3, 4 etc. are also often assigned to electrons in these orbits. It has been found, in addition, that there are two other aspects of an electron's motion. First, although circular orbits (designated 's' orbitals) are possible, other shapes also occur, especially in higher energy orbits, and these more complicated orbital shapes form 'families'. For example, figure of eight ('p') orbitals are

Table 1.3 Types of electron orbit

Shell (no)	K 1	L 2	M 3	N 4
Shape permitted	s	s p	s p d	s p d f
No of sub-orbitals	2	2 6	2 6 10	2 6 10 14
Total electrons per shell	2	8	18	32

possible and there are three orbitals for any one energy content, corresponding to the three dimensions of space (Fig. 1.6). In M and larger shells 'd' orbitals are possible, the shapes of these being complex with five different possibilities. In the N shell and larger shells a still more complicated family of 7 orbitals ('f' orbitals) is possible and so on. (If it would appear, perhaps, unlikely that electrons could travel in these complex orbits, it may be worthwhile to comment that the orbits have, in fact, been calculated by considering the electron to be a wave rather than a particle. The wave-particle duality concept of matter is now well established and is essential to current explanations of atomic structure.)

The final aspect of the electron is 'spin' – the electron can spin in the clockwise or anti-clockwise direction in any one orbit.

Table 1.3 summarises the electron orbits and shows the total number of different orbits per shell. The numbers of sub-orbitals are all in multiples of two on account of the two spin possibilities of the electron.

Before the placing of electrons in shells can be considered, it is necessary to note that the sub-orbitals described complicated the energy situation – the more

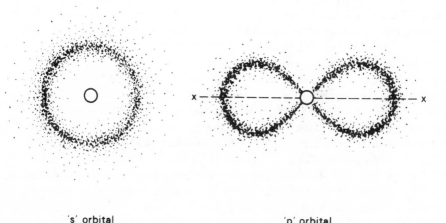

's' orbital   'p' orbital

Fig. 1.6 Charge clouds corresponding to 's' and 'p' orbits of an electron

complex orbital shapes correspond to higher energy. These energies are represented in Fig. 1.7 and it is evident that orbitals 3d and 4s; 4d and 5s respectively, have similar energy. Orbitals 4f (not shown) would clearly have greater energy than 5s – hence, it would be erroneous to consider that the outermost shells automatically correspond to greatest energies.

The build-up of the periodic table can now be considered and it is subject to several important conditions:

(a) The number of electrons in a stable atom must be equal to the number of protons in the nucleus. The corresponding negative and positive charges, therefore, balance.

(b) Only one electron is allowed in any one sub-orbital. This is known as Pauli's exclusion principle.

(c) The lowest, most stable, orbits fill first.

The initial formation of matter in the universe is likely to have involved the formation of stable nuclei, which would then gather electrons around them in orbits statisfying the conditions stated. Eighty-two stable atom types were formed in this way (Table 1.4), the simplest involving one proton and one '1s' electron – hydrogen. The first ten elements have the following configurations:

1. Hydrogen   (H)   1s
2. Helium   (He) $(1s)^2$ (i.e. two 1s electrons) K shell complete – inert
3. Lithium   (Li) $(1s)^2 2s$
4. Beryllium (Be) $(1s)^2 (2s)^2$
5. Boron   (B) $(1s)^2 (2s)^2 2p$
6. Carbon   (C) $(1s)^2 (2s)^2 (2p)^2$
7. Nitrogen   (N) $(1s)^2 (2s)^2 (2p)^3$
8. Oxygen   (O) $(1s)^2 (2s)^2 (2p)^4$
9. Fluorine   (F) $(1s)^2 (2s)^2 (2p)^5$
10. Neon   (Ne) $(1s)^2 (2s)^2 (2p)^6$ – L shell complete – inert

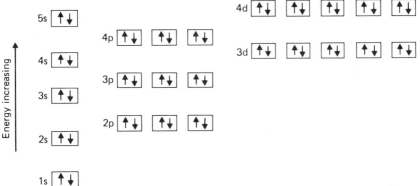

Fig. 1.7 Orbital energies of electrons. Note that for any one shell, the energy increases in orders s, p, d... The arrows represent the opposite spins of each pair of electrons

The build-up of electrons in elements of atomic number 11 (sodium) to 18 (argon) continues as would be expected, argon having the configuration $(1s)^2(2s)^2(2p)^6(3s)^2(3p)^6$. However, as indicated in Figure 1.7, the 3d sub-shell contains orbits of slightly greater energy than the 4s sub-shell, the latter, therefore, filling first, giving elements 19 and 20, potassium and calcium. The ten 3d orbitals fill subsequently, giving a familiar range of elements known as the transition elements. In element 36 (krypton), the 1s, 2s, 2p, 3s, 3p, 3d, 4s and 4p sub-shells are full, the 4d sub-shell filling after the 5s. Further complications occur as the f sections of the fourth and fifth shells fill, producing the lanthanides and actinides, respectively. The process could theoretically continue indefinitely, except that the nuclei of heavy elements are, as already explained, unstable.

It may be tempting at this stage to try to predict the properties of materials from the periodic table (Table 1.4). However, although some general rules regarding behaviour of the elements can be determined in this way, most practical properties of materials depend as much on the interaction of elements with one another as on their own basic properties, though the former follow from the latter. The most important basic property is the stability of each element formed. It is found that the most stable elements are those in which electron shells are complete. These elements are:

Atomic number	Element
2	Helium
10	Neon
18	Argon
36	Krypton
54	Xenon
86	Radon

It will be noticed that the last four correspond to completed 's' and 'p' sections of shells rather then full shells but this is due to the delayed filling of 'd' sub-shells explained above. Elements 4 (beryllium) and 12 (magnesium) are not inert, although they have complete 's' sub-sections, because there is still room for more electrons in those shells. The rule therefore, is that, when the outermost shell can accept no more electrons, the stability of the corresponding element reaches a maximum, the next heavier element being of much reduced stability. The periodic form of Table 1.4 reflects the variation in atomic stability. The most stable (inert) elements are referred to as Group 0. Groups 1A to Group VIIA, in turn, indicate increasing stability – for instance, in a Group VIIA element the electrons are held more powerfully to the nucleus than in the Group IA orbit of the same shell, since there are more protons in the nucleus of the former. The stability of elements in general decreases as they become larger, due to electron-electron repulsion – the same effect that produces relatively high energy states in the more complex 'd' and 'f' orbitals. The energy needed to ionise (or remove an electron from) argon is, for example, less than that needed to ionise helium, the most inert 'inert' gas. A further effect in heavy elements is that their density increases, since the electron shells are attracted more strongly towards the larger

Table 1.4 Periodic table after Mendeleev

	IA	IIA	IIIB	IVB	VB	VIB	VIIB	VIIIB	VIIIB	VIIIB	IB	IIB	IIIA	IVA	VA	VIA	VIIA	0
1s	1 **H** 1s																	2 **He** (1s)^2
2s / 2p	3 **Li** 2s	4 **Be** (2s)^2											5 **B** 2p	6 **C** (2p)^2	7 **N** (2p)^3	8 **O** (2p)^4	9 **F** (2p)^5	10 **Ne** (2p)^6
3s / 3p	11 **Na** 3s	12 **Mg** (3s)^2											13 **Al** 3p	14 **Si** (3p)^2	15 **P** (3p)^3	16 **S** (3p)^4	17 **Cl** (3p)^5	18 **Ar** (3p)^6
4s / 3d / 4p	19 **K** 4s	20 **Ca** (4s)^2	21 **Sc** (4s)^{2}3d	22 **Ti** (4s)^{2}3d^2	23 **V** (4s)^{2}3d^3	24 **Cr** 4s(3d)^5	25 **Mn** (4s)^2(3d)^5	26 **Fe** (4s)^2(3d)^6	27 **Co** (4s)^2(3d)^7	28 **Ni** (4s)^2(3d)^8	29 **Cu** (4s)^1(3d)^{10}	30 **Zn** (4s)^2(3d)^{10}	31 **Ga** 4p	32 **Ge** (4p)^2	33 **As** (4p)^3	34 **Se** (4p)^4	35 **Br** (4p)^5	36 **Kr** (4p)^6
5s / 4d / 5p	37 **Rb** 5s	38 **Sr** (5s)^2	39 **Y** (5s)^{2}4d	40 **Zr** (5s)^2(4d)^2	41 **Nb** 5s(4d)^4	42 **Mo** 5s(4d)^5	43 **Tc** 5s(4d)^6	44 **Ru** 5s(4d)^7	45 **Rh** 5s(4d)^8	46 **Pd** (4d)^{10}	47 **Ag** 5s(4d)^{10}	48 **Cd** (5s)^2(4d)^{10}	49 **In** 5p	50 **Sn** (5p)^2	51 **Sb** (5p)^3	52 **Te** (5p)^4	53 **I** (5p)^5	54 **Xe** (5p)^6
6s / 5d / 6p	55 **Cs** 6s	56 **Ba** (6s)^2	57 71	72 **Hf** (6s)^2(5d)^2	73 **Ta** (6s)^2(5d)^3	74 **W** (6s)^2(5d)^4	75 **Re** (6s)^2(5d)^5	76 **Os** (6s)^2(5d)^6	77 **Ir** (6s)^2(5d)	78 **Pt** 6s (5d)^9	79 **Au** 6s (5d)^{10}	80 **Hg** (6s)^2(5d)^{10}	81 **Tl** 6p	82 **Pb** (6p)^2	83 **Bi** (6p)^3	84 **Po** (6p)^4	85 **At** (6p)^5	86 **Rn** (6p)^6
7s / 6d	87 (7s)	88 (7s)^2	89 103															

Lanthanides (4f filling)
Actinides (5f filling)

The atomic number is indicated above each element. Subshells above or to the left of each element are complete. Lead (atomic number number 82) is the largest stable element

13

nuclei. Hence, heavy elements normally exist as denser materials than light elements.

Those elements in which a 'd' or 'f' section is filling behave quite differently from the others, since these elements do not achieve a stable state by loss of such electrons or by completely filling that particular sub-shell. They are, therefore, given the 'B' designation, the most important examples being elements 21 to 30. These elements are quite similar to one another in a number of respects, since they contain either 1 or 2 electrons in their outermost shell.

Excitation and ionisation

It is possible that, if energy is supplied to an atom, for example, by irradiation, electrons may be raised to higher orbits. This occurs in a discharge tube when the excitation is by electron collisions. When an electron returns to the ground state from a certain excited state, there will be an emission of the appropriate wavelength of light, the wavelength being shorter for a bigger jump. In a sodium discharge tube, for example, there is a substantial amount of the yellow colour of wavelength 589 nm which occurs when an electron jumps from the 3p level to the 3s level (that is, the ground state), hence the yellow colour of sodium lights. In some cases, excitation may take place to the extent that an electron completely leaves the atom causing it to be ionised. Ionisation also plays an important part in the operation of discharge tubes.

Bonding of atoms

Bonding is that process by which atoms become linked together, forming molecules.

As regards the atom, bonding occurs because it increases the stability (or reduces the energy) of atoms taking part. In some types of bond, the stable octet, which is characteristic of the inert elements, is obtained by the sharing or transfer of electrons. In others, the mechanism by which stability is increased is less straightforward.

From the point of view of the materials technologist, bonding is vitally important, since it is the only means by which cohesion, producing liquid and solid materials, can arise. In fact, it is true to say that, in any one lump of solid, there must be some rigid link between virtually every atom involved. In some cases, this link may be in the form of mechanical interlock between molecules although, without atomic bonding to form large molecules of complex shape, such interlock would clearly be impossible. The properties of all solid materials are derived from the properties of these bonds, although other effects often modify their strength.

When bonding unites atoms only in small groups, then the molecule would probably exist in the form of a gas at normal temperatures – for example, oxygen (O_2) and nitrogen (N_2). Each molecule in these examples comprises two atoms. As molecular size increases, the material is more likely to exist in liquid and, finally, in the solid form, especially if cooled, since weak bonding tends to occur between virtually all atoms and molecules, causing the liquid and then the solid state if thermal energy is low enough. Large molecules or groups of molecules often exist in the form of patterns known as crystals, the type and properties of these depending on the nature of the bonds which are involved. To summarise, we can say that, in gases, the molecules are largely unaffected by bonds between them, obeying the laws of motion which constitute the kinetic theory; in liquids there are bonding forces sufficient to produce cohesion but not rigidity; and in solids, atoms become rigidly orientated in relation to one another. In most solids, there is some degree of crystallinity. The strength of bonding in a solid can often be ascertained from its melting point, as well as by its mechanical strength. The strongest solids must be heated to very high temperatures before thermal energy can overcome the bonding effect.

Valency
This is the most important property of atoms in determining the nature of bonds formed and the elements with which they will combine. It will be recalled that, with the exception of the innermost (K) shell, the most stable atoms are those in which a stable octet occurs – a group comprising two 's' electrons and six 'p' electrons. Those atoms which have a small number of electrons in their outer shell will have a tendency to lose them and those in which the outer shell has a small deficiency will tend to gain them. The number of electrons by which an atom exceeds or falls short of an electron octet is described as its valency. Clearly no element can have a simple valency greater than 4, corresponding to half complete s/p sections, carbon and silicon being the most important examples. Group IA, IIA and IIIA elements have valencies of one, two and three, respectively, as have elements in Groups VIIA, VIA and VA, respectively. The valencies of elements in which 'd' sections are filling are much less well defined since, on losing the electrons in this section or gaining electrons to fill the section, inert elements are not obtained. Many of these elements may exhibit two valencies, for example, iron, Fe, number 26, may have valencies of two or three. Bonds are classified as primary or secondary according to strength.

Pimary bonds

Ionic bond
This occurs when, for example, an atom containing a single outer electron encounters another atom with a single electron missing in its outer shell. The electron in the former atom transfers to orbit the nucleus of the other atom. Hence, they have empty and complete shells, respectively. But the previously uncharged atoms will now be charged and, therefore, attract one another, coming together until this attraction is balanced by the repulsion of their respective electron clouds. If there are further atoms of each type available, the process will continue and a crystal will form. Common salt is an example (Fig. 1.8) – sodium has a single outer electron and chlorine has seven outer electrons. Similar reactions will take place between divalent elements, for example, calcium and

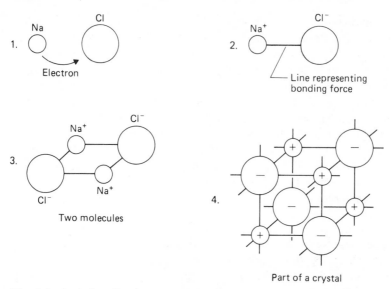

Fig. 1.8 Ionic bonding between sodium and chlorine forming common salt

oxygen (CaO); between divalent and monovalent elements in appropriate proportions, e.g. calcium chloride ($CaCl_2$), and so on.

It is important to appreciate that the bonding between the atoms results purely from their electric charges, hence, ionic bonding is non-directional and the crystal structure of the resulting compound is such as to minimise the distance between opposite charges and maximise the distance between like charges. The configuration of the ions depends on their sizes: there is a tendency for positive ions to be smaller than negative ions, for example, K^+ is smaller than Cl^-, although they both have the same number of electrons, because K^+ has two more protons in its nucleus and these attract the electrons more strongly. It is found that, if ions are of equal size, one positive can be surrounded by up to eight negative ions without the latter touching, giving an arrangement called the body-centred cubic crystal. As the size ratio decreases, however, fewer negative ions can pack around the positive ion without touching, hence, differing crystal structures are found. In sodium chloride, for instance, in Fig. 1.8, each ion has six near neighbours of opposite sign. In some ionic crystals, ion packing and valency requirements can result in solid materials having densities which are low compared to normal solid densities.

The presence of ions in water often interferes with the force between the ions of crystals so that many ionic compounds dissolve in water, producing a dispersions of ions.

Co-valent bond

This results when certain atoms come together so that one or more electrons orbit both nuclei and each atom has a stable octet for a part of the time. In methane, for example, four hydrogen atoms, each having one electron in its shell, approach a carbon atom having four electrons in its outer shell and each hydrogen electron encompasses both its own nucleus and the carbon nucleus. In return, the four electrons from the carbon atom each encompass a hydrogen atom. The arrangement is shown schematically in Fig. 1.9. The carbon-hydrogen bond is, in fact, very versatile, forming the basis of many organic materials. Some important examples are shown in Fig. 1.10. Note that it is possible for two, or three, electrons to orbit both atoms, as in ethylene (C_2H_4) and acetylene (C_2H_2), forming double and triple bonds, respectively. In both natural and synthetic organic materials, the carbon may form long-chain molecules, containing many thousands of atoms. The co-valent bond thus gives rise to fibrous materials. In contrast, many materials comprise very small molecules bonded in this way, for example, oxygen (O_2), nitrogen (N_2) and carbon dioxide (CO_2).

Another common feature of the co-valent bond is that, unlike the pure ionic bond, bond directions are well-defined, because orbits of bonding electrons must fit in with those of non-bonding electrons. This leads to great rigidity of which, perhaps, the most notable case is diamond. The bonding in diamond is pure co-valent, on account of the fact that only one element is involved and the 's' and 'p' orbitals in carbon are 'hybridised' or averaged to form four symmetrical bonds in the shape of a tetrahedron. The water molecule also contains bonds having well-defined directions and, when this bonding is extended to form ice, an increase of volume occurs as molecules reorientate to form further rigid 'hydrogen' bonds between them. This increase of volume on the freezing of water or the crystallisation of many salts is often the cause of extensive damage to porous building materials. It would be misleading to suggest that all bonds are either 'ionic' or 'co-valent' – many bonds are a combination of the two. For example, in water, each hydrogen atom shares its electron with the oxygen atom and the oxygen shares one electron each way, in reverse. However, since the oxygen contains more protons than the hydrogen, the electrons tend to spend most time

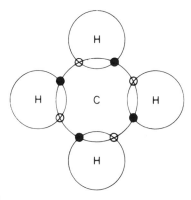

● Carbon electron

○ Hydrogen electron

Fig. 1.9   Co-valent bonding between carbon and hydrogen forming methane, CH_4

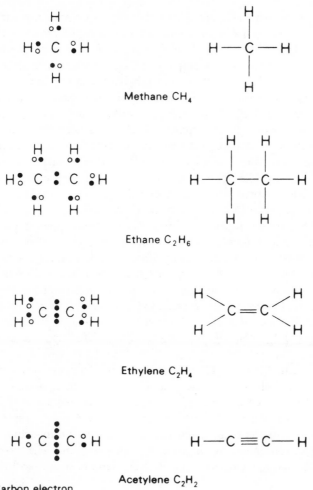

Methane CH₄

Ethane C₂H₆

Ethylene C₂H₄

Acetylene C₂H₂

● Carbon electron

○ Hydrogen electron

Fig. 1.10 Various ways of representing structure of some organic compound (i.e. formed from carbon). Note that, in each compound, hydrogen atoms attain two electrons and carbon atoms attain eight electrons

near to the more strongly charged nucleus, producing what is described as a semi-polar bond.

In silica, one of the earth's commonest materials, the bonding is partially co-valent, each silicon atom sharing an electron with each of four oxygen atoms. A tetrahedral shape is formed with silicon at the centre and an oxygen atom at each apex, each oxygen atom attaining stability by sharing another electron with a further silicon atom. The repeated tetrahedra form a crystal and, since the oxygen atom at each apex of the tetrahedron is bonded to two silicon atoms, the chemical formula is SiO_2. The structure of other common materials may be more complex, for example, anhydrous calcium sulphate (the basis of gypsum plaster) consists of a sulphate ion, SO_4^{--}, in which the sulphur (six outer electrons) shares two of its electrons with each of three oxygen atoms (each with six outer electrons), the two extra electrons which are necessary being borrowed ionically from the calcium which forms the Ca^{++} ion, as in Fig. 1.11. Note that the sharing between the sulphur and the oxygen is in one direction only since, with the two ionically borrowed electrons, the sulphur has eight electrons and has no need to borrow from the oxygen atoms. Each oxygen is, on the other hand, two electrons short and must, therefore, share with the sulphur. Such co-valency is known as co-ordinate co-valency. The one-way sharing often results in charged dipoles which, as in ionic compounds, tend to cause crystals to grow. The arrangement for calcium sulphate given above, however, does not, of course, constitute set gypsum plaster. On addition of water, the crystals reform to include water within their structure, hence, the plaster 'sets'. The formula for calcium carbonate ($CaCO_3$) is produced in a similar way to that of calcium sulphate. Various crystalline forms occur naturally and calcium carbonate crystals are also produced by the action of carbon dioxide on calcium hydroxide (slaked lime) in the presence of water. This is the action by which non-hydraulic building limes harden.

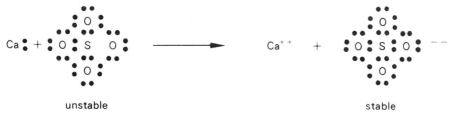

unstable   stable

Fig. 1.11   The formation of calcium sulphate from calcium, sulphur and oxygen

Metallic bond

When atoms of a single type and containing a few valence electrons approach one another, the electrons orbits may change to a nondescript nature – they move around the nuclei rather like a gas and cause an overall attraction between the positively charged remainders of the atoms and the electrons themselves (Fig. 1.12). Such bonding is clearly non-directional and the elections will, therefore, pack in tight patterns, resulting in crystals. An electric potential will cause an overal drift of the electron gas through the metal, constituting an electric current – hence, metals conduct electricity. The thermal conductivity of metals is also high, since electrons carry energy from one point to another by collision.

The great majority of elements form metals when they are present in the pure state – all those to the left of or below element numbers 5, 14, 33, 52, 85 (see Table 1.4). This is not so much an indication of the stability of metals as a result of the fact that ionic and co-valent bonds are not easily formed by these elements in the pure state. Indeed, many of these quickly combine with oxygen in ordinary atmospheres, producing more stable co-valent or ionic bonds. The occurrence of

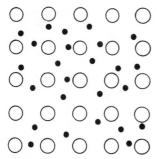

Fig. 1.12 Simple two-dimensional representation of a metal showing valence electrons forming a 'cloud' around symmetrically positioned metal ions

most of these elements as oxides or other compounds is an indication of their instability in metallic form. Tin (Sn), element number 50, can, in fact, change to a co-valent form simply by cooling, hence, it reverts slowly to a grey powder below 18 °C. There is probably some tendency to form co-valent bonds in most metals and, according to the extent of this, three different metallic crystal types may be formed. In all cases, however, the tight packing of atoms results in materials which are of much higher density in metallic form than their non-metallic counterparts. Although the metallic bond is not, in general, as strong as ionic and co-valent bonds, (actual bond strengths vary between about 10 per cent and 50 per cent of ionic/co-valent values, according to material), the density of packing of ions in metal crystals, combined with certain other properties considered later, result in metals being a most important bulk structural material.

van der Waals' bonds
In the bonds considered so far, the atoms have combined to produce a more stable arrangement by interaction of their electrons. In some cases, the materials produced were crystalline and, therefore, solid. In others, a stable arrangement was produced by formation of small groups of atoms, for example, oxygen O_2 or ethylene C_2H_4. It is commonly known, however, that the latter materials may be liquefied or even solidified if the temperature is lowered sufficiently. This can be explained by van der Waals' bonds. In any one molecule, the electrons in orbit around it produce small, instantaneous eccentricities of charge which cause neighbouring molecules to be attracted by it. Hence, this type of bond is operative between any adjacent molecules and, although it would, on average, have a strength of only about one per cent of ionic/co-valent bonds and it is easily overcome by thermal energy, it may produce a solid with a certain amount of strength, especially in the more 'polar' molecules. The softer plastics are examples of molecular chains made solid in this way (Fig. 1.13). van der Waals' bonds also are important in concrete and may be used to explain the phenomenon of creep. Colloidal properties of materials such as clay are similarly explained. Van der Waals' bonds are responsible for the solid nature of graphite – they cause the attraction between co-valent bonded carbon sheets. If the materials timber,

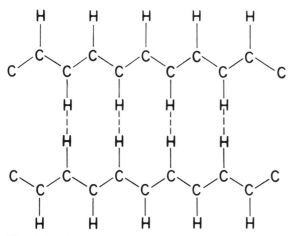

Fig. 1.13 Polyethylene (polythene) chains linked together by van der Waals' bonds (broken)

bitumen, paints and adhesives are added to the list, the importance of the bond may be appreciated. It may be argued that the bonds, which will solidify almost all non-crystalline, microcrystalline or fibrous materials manifest themselves in very different ways in the materials listed. The differences are, however, not as great as may at first be supposed. Essentially there are two groups – those which absorb water, including clay, concrete and, perhaps, timber and the remainder, which are imprevious to water. When water is absorbed into porous materials, it tends to cause swelling by being attracted to solid surfaces, reducing the effectiveness of the van der Waals' bonds. For this reason, there may be an initial increase in the strength of clay, concrete and timber if water is removed by heating. This is, however, followed by a decrease of strength at higher temperatures. Materials in the remaining group all lose strength immediately on heating.

Liquid state

In the gaseous state, atoms or molecules are in a condition of disorder, being more or less free to move as 'projectiles' in space, their velocity being dependent on temperature and the pressure exerted being the consequence of collisions with the walls of the containing vessel. The space occupied by the molecules of a gas is much larger than the size of the molecules themselves.

In a solid, there are rigid links extending throughout any one piece of material, resulting from chemical bonds or interlocking of molecules. Solids are, therefore, ordered structures, amorphous solids exhibiting short-range order and crystalline solids long-range order.

Liquids are intermediate in nature. Cohesion, which results from the tendency for molecules to bond with one another, causes molecules to come into contact with their neighbours but without forming rigid bonds. Hence, liquids are fluid and do not have strength, though their volume is comparable with that of the

21

corresponding solid that would be formed if thermal energy were decreased by cooling. The cohesive effect of liquids results in surface tension, which tends to cause liquids to assume the minimum possible surface area – spherical drops, if suspended in space. In addition, molecular affinity for most neighbouring solid materials results in capillarity, which may cause powerful attraction of liquids towards solids.

There is, strictly, no clear division between liquids and solids since, in glass, there are no well-defined bond directions or crystals, although, if glass is to be regarded as a liquid, it is certainly a very high viscosity liquid and can be treated, for practical purposes, as a solid. Bitumen and cellulose putties are also intermediate – they have short-term strength but flow under sustained stress. These are really examples of more complex groups of materials referred to as suspensions or dispersions, in which different types of material are intimately mixed.

The term 'suspension' generally refers to a solid dispersed in a liquid or gaseous medium. The particles are, however, relatively large (greater than $1\,\mu\text{m}$) and would separate with time or, alternatively, separation from the dispersion medium can be accelerated by centrifuging. When the dispersed particles become smaller – the order of $1\,\mu\text{m}$ or less – they are known as 'colloidal dispersions'. Examples are fog, smoke and clay, the dispersed phase and dispersion medium being, respectively, liquid/gas, solid/gas and solid/liquid. The properties of colloids depend very greatly on the particle size and shape, and on interactions between the dispersed phase and the dispersion medium. In true colloids, separation due to gravity does not occur: in fact, it can be observed under the microscope that colloidal particles are in a state of continuous random motion, known as 'Brownian' motion. Important examples of colloids in construction are clays and paints, and these will be considered in more detail under those headings.

Elastic deformation of solid materials

A solid material may be defined as one which is able to support some stress without plastic deformation, that is, a degree of elasticity exists. This does not, of course, preclude the possibility of time-dependent plastic movement known as 'creep', which occurs in a number of solid materials. By 'elasticity' is meant the ability of the material to return to its former shape on removal of the stress. It may be worthwhile to clarify, first, the molecular basis for elastic deformation and then to consider how, on overstressing materials, they deform further, causing eventual failure. It has been shown that, in most solids, there are bonds between virtually all atoms involved and that, in many cases, the atoms form regular arrays, as in crystals or fibres. The position of any atom in this array is determined by two influences – first, the bonding force holding it to other atoms and second, a force of repulsion which prevents atoms from approaching too closely. The situation between any two atoms is represented from an energy point of view in Fig. 1.14(a). Note that, although there is an energy release or decrease of energy

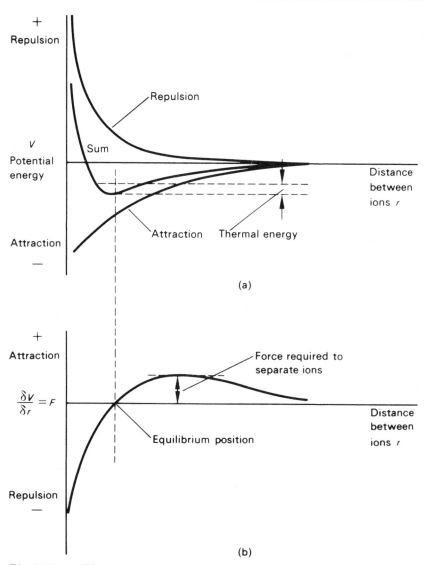

Fig. 1.14 (a) The potential energy of two ions as a function of their separation. The negative energy curve represents the metallic bonding tendency. The positive curve represents short-range repulsion;   (b) The force-distance curve obtained by differentiating curve (a)

due to the bonding force as atoms approach, there is an even greater *increase* of energy due to atom repulsion, if atoms approach too closely. Adding these energy curves gives rise to what is known as a 'potential well', the equilibrium position of the atom being at the lowest point of this well (Fig. 1.14(a)). The expansion of materials on heating is due to the fact that the sides of the well in Fig. 1.14(a) are not symmetrical. If thermal energy is added to the minimum equilibrium value, the atom vibrates, rather like a spring, between positions corresponding to the intercepts of its new energy value on the total potential energy curve. The new equilibrium position is midway between these points and atom separations increase, corresponding to expansion, as the material is heated. If heating continues, the positive thermal energy would eventually exceed the negative bond energy and melting would occur, as bonds become ineffective.

The elasticity of materials under stress is best visualised from the force/separation curve of Fig. 1.14(b), which is obtained by differentiating the net energy curve of Fig. 1.14(a). On applying tension to the material, the distance between atoms is increased, causing an increase in the bonding force corresponding to an increase of distance between atoms. Compression produces the reverse effect. There is, however, an important difference between tensile and compressive stresses. If a tensile force sufficient to separate the ions completely is applied (Fig. 1.14(b)), the bond and, hence, the material, will fail (tensile failure of this type is known as 'cleavage'). There is no such direct effect in compression, since greater compression simply causes greater repulsion of atoms. The stiffness or resistance to deformation of materials is determined by the slope of the force/separation curve at the equilibrium separation (Fig. 1.14(b)). Although the relationship is non-linear at this point, practically observed strains correspond to extremely small displacements on the scale shown, so that the non-linearity is not apparent and observed stress/strain relationships are usually sensibly linear. The elastic moduli of most materials in tension and compression are also equal, since there is no appreciable change of slope on tensile and compressive sides of the equilibrium position.

Plastic deformation of solid materials

The application of load to structural components results in stresses which can be categorised into three groups – compression, tension and shear. In atomic terms, their effects are quite different, since they place quite different loadings on atomic bonds. The effects may be visualised by consideration of a simple crystal under stress. To begin with, a metallic crystal is considered (Fig. 1.15).

Application of a compressive stress directly to the crystal merely reinforces the bonds and could not on its own, cause failure. It should be remembered, however, that a uniaxial compressive stress can be resolved into shear stresses of maximum value at 45° to the direction of the former and that it also induces tensile stress by Poisson's ratio effects.

Application of a tensile stress acts directly against atomic bonds though, to cause tensile failure, a large number of bonds would have to rupture at the same instant. Tensile stresses induce shear stress in the same manner as compressive stresses.

The effect of shear stresses in metals is different from tensile stresses, since plastic deformation can result, without total bond failure, ions merely swapping partners, as Fig. 1.16(b). Hence, the effect often occurs at lower stresses than would cause tensile failure, resulting in a distorted, though still intact, crystal.

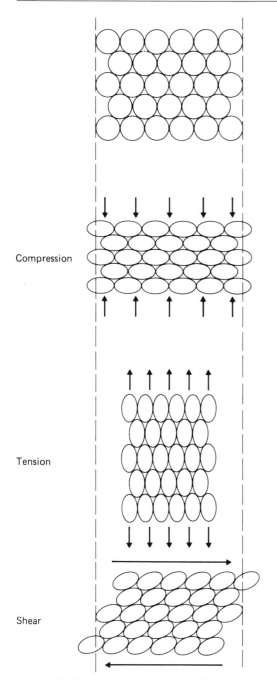

Compression

Tension

Shear

Fig. 1.15 Representation of elastic distortion caused by compression, tension and shear in a metal

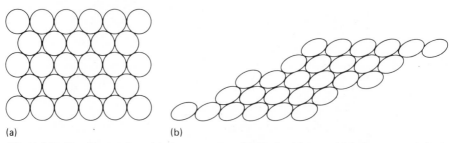

(a)   (b)

Fig. 1.16 Metal crystals: (a) Zero stress; (b) Under shear which has caused both elastic and plastic deformation. Each atom has slipped by one spacing

This ability for crystal planes to 'slip' gives metals the unique property of ductility. This important characteristic (together with the effects of imperfections in metal crystals which reduce their yield strength) is considered in more detail in Chapter 4.

Consideration is now given to ceramic crystals, which are represented by the arrangement of Fig. 1.17. The essential difference from metallic crystals is that adjacent ions are now oppositely charged and, generally, of different size. In pure tension or compression, the situation is not fundamentally different from that of metals but we find that, in shear, the ability of crystal planes to slide over one another is much reduced on account of the greater irregularity in the surfaces of possible slip planes and the more rigid bonding involved. Slip planes do exist in some ionic crystals and a possible plane is indicated in Fig. 1.17 but ductility is never exhibited in practice in ceramics which contain ionic or co-valent bonds, since they often contain amorphous (non-crystalline) areas and other imperfections which tend to cause fracture rather than plastic flow. These imperfections take the form of microscopic cracks or voids which amplify the stress at localised points and which, beyond a certain stress, propagate without plastic flow to cause rapid ('brittle') failure.

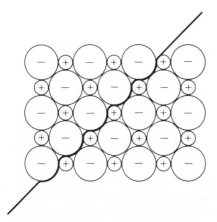

Fig. 1.17 Ionic crystal showing one possible slip plane. Note the increased irregularity of this plane compared to a similar one in a metal crystal (Fig. 1.16)

Imperfections and their effect on strength: Griffith's theory

A great many materials contain imperfections of some sort on a microscopic scale – these may originate from the formation process, as in many ceramics, or they may result from extensive working in metals. The effect of these imperfections, which may take the form of cracks or voids, is to concentrate an applied tensile stress at certain points in the material. The essential difference between ductile materials, such as pure metals and brittle materials, is that, in the former, plastic flow is possible, at least in the early stages of deformation, so that stress relief is possible in the areas which, as a result of imperfections, are under the highest stress. The stresses in the various rivets of a riveted connection are equalised by this process, the most heavily stressed rivets yielding and, therefore, allowing others to carry a share of the load. In brittle materials, plastic flow is not possible and the concentrated stresses tend to increase the size of the imperfection or flaw, leading to failure of the material as a whole. In consequence, observed failure stresses in bulk materials are usually many times lower than values which would be suggested by bond strengths. The plastic flow considerations given earlier would tend to predict, for example, that shear or tensile failure should not occur until very substantial strains are undergone, perhaps of 10 to 20 per cent, whereas, in practice, tensile failure strains in bulk ceramics are more typically about 0.0001.

Griffith proposed that the likelihood of propagation of a crack in a given material depends on the nature of the crack and on certain properties of the material. Since solids as well as liquids have surface energy (or tension), the propagation of a crack requires energy to be applied to the solid in order to create new surfaces. However, as the crack propagates, stress relief occurs in a triangular region above and below the crack, such that stored elastic energy is released in this part of the material. The energy released for a given additional length of crack is found to increase as the crack gets larger, since larger cracks produce a much greater area of stress relief, in much the same way as the area of a triangle of a given shape increases as the square on the length of its base. Griffith proposed that cracks would not propagate unless the length of the crack exceeds a critical length, so that the elastic energy released by its propagation is greater than the energy required to form new surfaces. If this length is exceeded, the crack could be referred to as 'unstable' since, once propagation were initiated by stress or impact, the energy required to continue propagation would be provided by the elastic energy released. The critical crack length depends on the type of material: in ceramic materials, it is much smaller than in pure metals because, in the latter, additional energy is needed to cause the metal to flow plastically at the crack tip. Hence, in metals, cracks usually reach observable sizes well before brittle fracture occurs whereas, in materials such as glass, even microscopic surface imperfections may exceed the critical length. The critical crack length decreases as the applied stress increases, since greater applied stress results in greater stored elastic energy. Hence, materials such as normal bulk glass can only be used safely provided the applied stress is small enough for the cracks which are already present to be below the critical value for that stress. The basic Griffith criterion for crack propagation from energy considerations is that:

$$f = \sqrt{\frac{2E\gamma}{\pi L}}$$

where f is the stress required to propagate a crack of length L in a material of elastic modulus E, having fracture surface energy γ per unit area (γ must be increased where extra energy is absorbed by plastic flow).

An alternative approach is to consider the extent to which a crack concentrates the stress. It has been found that the curvature at the tip (root) of each crack has an important influence on the resultant stress (Fig. 1.18). The stress f_R at the root is related to the applied stress f_A by the equation:

$$f_R = 2f_A \sqrt{\frac{L}{R}}$$

Where L is the crack length and R its root radius. If f_R is assumed to be the bond fracture stress and R is taken to be constant (R tends to have atomic dimensions in brittle materials – the order of 10^{-10} m), then:

$$f_A = \frac{k}{\sqrt{L}}$$

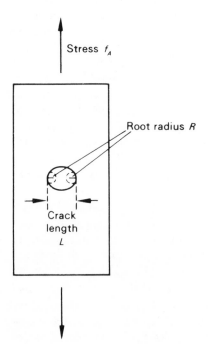

Fig. 1.18 Griffith's model for estimation of stress concentration due to a small crack in a brittle material

where k is a constant. Hence, this equation has a similar form to that obtained by energy considerations.

Crack widths vary in practice, obeying statistical laws, and the 'weak link' theory must be applied to brittle materials, the largest crack in a particular sample of material being the cause of failure. It will be noted that, as soon as cracks begin to propagate under stress, the stress concentration effect becomes more pronounced and failure can, therefore, be very rapid, the crack propagating at a velocity approaching that of sound in the material. The fracture strengths of brittle materials would also be expected to vary quite considerably, according to the size of the largest flaw in any one sample.

One consolation of the effect of flaws in concentrating stress is that some brittle materials are easily cut to size by the introduction of continuous flaws in desired positions, such that a small stress propagates a crack in the flaw direction. This is the principle of glass-cutting, though there is some skill in producing a *continuous* flaw with the cutter and, for reliable cutting, the glass surface itself should be free from additional flaws resulting from, for example, dirt or weathering.

Durability and fire resistance

The purpose of this chapter has been to establish a foundation upon which a study of the properties of materials can be based. It is found that chemical and thermal stability, as well as mechanical properties, tend to follow certain general rules. Solid materials do not decompose or deteriorate without the action of some definite agency – each form of deterioration involves the presence of another substance or energy source. Most forms of action involve at least one fluid medium. Fluids, which comprise liquids and gases, produce far greater reactivity when in contact with solids, since they produce greater areas of contact than solid/solid interfaces. Furthermore, in general terms, the more extended bonding in solid materials generally corresponds to lower reactivity. Of the natural fluid materials, water is the most important in relation to the stability of building materials. As well as being fluid, the polarity of the water molecule gives it considerable reactivity with other materials, particularly when other substances are dissolved in it. The deterioration of many building materials is due, at least in part, to the action of water.

The effects of temperature follow well-defined patterns. Increase of temperature corresponds to increased vibrational energy in solids and increased molecular velocity in fluids. Collisions between atoms, therefore, become more frequent and violent, resulting in increased reaction rates. Many deterioration processes are, therefore, greatly accelerated by increase of temperature. Some types of radiation, particularly ultra-violet, tend to energise surface layers of materials, accelerating changes, notably, the embrittlement of plastics. Many organic materials decompose under conditions of intense heat, giving flammable gases which, in turn, combine with oxygen, giving out heat and light. The process is, of course, that of burning but note that, in the strictest sense, solids do not 'burn': it is the gaseous products of thermal decomposition that constitute 'fire'. Removing the flame does not prevent the decomposition, although the flame does provide extra heat to increase further the solid temperature and, in this way, assists decomposition. Materials which have been subjected to high temperatures during manufacture will clearly be less susceptible to decomposition at temperatures below their former maximum, although damage can still result from stresses resulting from differentials of temperature within a structure or structural component.

Problems

1.1 Give, with reasons, the parts of the atom which are responsible for:
(a) chemical properties
(b) radioactive properties.

1.2 Explain why only two electrons are allowed to occupy sub-shell 2s, when six electrons are allowed in the sub-shell 2p.

1.3 In the periodic table, element 19 (potassium) contains one 4s electron while the 3d shell is empty. Explain the reason for this and name the lightest element which has:
(a) a complete 3d sub-shell
(b) a complete 5d sub-shell.

In what way are these two elements similar?

1.4 A gamma ray source used for density measurement has a half-life of 5 years. What would its useful life be if a count rate of not less than 25 per cent of the original value is essential for accurate readings?

1.5 The carbon isotope $_6C^{14}$, produced from carbon in the atmosphere by cosmic rays, has a half-life of 5680 years and is absorbed by living vegetation in which the level remains constant. It decays by beta particle emission. Calculate the age of timber in which the radiation emission has decreased by 5 per cent.

1.6 In the following series, in which thallium 210 disintegrates into lead, the atomic numbers and atomic masses are shown. What particles are emitted in the four changes?

	Atomic number	*Atomic mass*
Thallium	81	210
Lead	82	210
Bismuth	83	210
Thallium	81	206
Lead	82	206

1.7 What is an ion? Explain why ions of metals have radii smaller than the pure metal atom.

1.8 Explain the meaning of the terms 'atom', 'molecule', 'crystal' and 'polymer'.

1.9 Name two materials in which carbon is found naturally and two synthetic materials in which it occurs. Explain how bonding in these materials leads to their solid/liquid/gaseous nature.

1.10 Arrange in order the melting points of most plastics, ceramics and metals. Explain this in terms of chemical bonds.

1.11 Name two different types of material in which van der Waals' bonds are involved: compare their properties and give reasons for similarities and differences.

1.12 Discuss how the chemical bonding in a material affects the following properties:
   (a) strength
   (b) ductility
   (c) corrosion resistance
   (d) fire resistance.

1.13 Explain what is meant by disorder, short-range order and long-range order in materials. Classify crystalline solids, amorphous solids, liquids and gases in this way, giving examples of the first two categories.

1.14 Explain why the tensile strength of glass in bulk is much lower than that of glass fibres. If the theoretical strength of a particular type of glass is $7\,\text{kN/mm}^2$, the observed strength is $140\,\text{N/mm}^2$ and the root radius of cracks is $10^{-10}\,\text{m}$, calculate the crack length in the material.

References

1. R. T. Overman, *Basic Concepts of Nuclear Chemistry*. Chapman & Hall 1965.
2. 'Backscattering Method for Density Measurement using Gamma Rays', *Building Science*, Vol. 3. Pergamon, 1968.
3. R. A. Burgess, P. J. Horrobin and J. W. Simpson (eds), *Progress in Constructional Science and Technology* (gamma rays for density measurement), p. 193. Medical & Technical Publishing Co. Ltd, 1971.
4. BS 4408 Part 3: 1970, *Gamma Radiography of Concrete*. British Standards Institute.
5. R. Wormald and A. L. Britch, 'Methods of Measuring Moisture Content Applicable to Building Materials', *Building Science*, Vol. 3, No. 3. Pergamon, 1969.
6. K. L. Watson, *Materials in Chemical Perspective*. Stanley Thornes, 1975.

See also Bibliography

Chapter 2

Siliceous materials and ceramics

Silica (SiO_2), an oxide of silicon, is the most common compound in the earth's crust and it is not surprising, therefore, that it forms the basis of many building materials. Most clays contain a high percentage of silica. Fired-clay products are traditionally termed ceramics, although modern use of this term includes many other siliceous materials with similar properties, such as glass and mica, as well as some non-siliceous materials, such as metallic oxides used in electrical insulators and glazes.

Structure of silicates – minerals

These are based on the SiO_4 group which, in itself, is not stable because, although the silicon (tetravelent) is satisfied by means of one electron from each oxygen atom, making a stable octet in the silicon atom, each oxygen atom has a deficiency of one electron. The situation may be represented as in Fig. 2.1. The structure is, like silica, tetrahedral that is, each oxygen atom is at the vertex of a pyramid, the

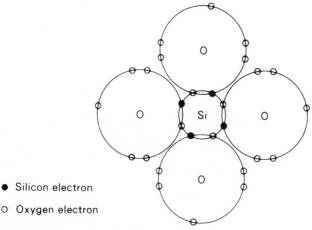

● Silicon electron

○ Oxygen electron

Fig. 2.1 Electron arrangement in the silicate unit. Each oxygen atom has only seven electrons

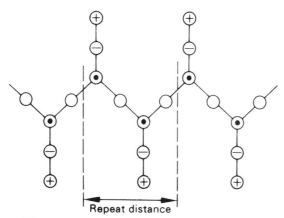

Repeat distance

● Silicon atom

○ Oxygen atom

⊕ Metal ion

Fig. 2.2 Silicate chain produced by sharing of base oxygen atoms

silicon being at the centre. Hence, four electrons are required and there is a tendency for the silicate units to form ionic bonds with metals by borrowing electrons from them. A large number of metals may combine in many different ways, producing the wide range of minerals which exists in the earth's crust. The silicate itself may form seemingly unrelated types of molecule. For example, two silicate tetrahedra may be linked by having a base oxygen atom in common. Figure 2.2 shows the production of a chain in this way. In the repeat distance shown, there are two silicon atoms and six oxygen atoms (four of which require an extra electron). Hence the formula will be, in its simplest form, $(SiO_3)^{--}$. The two minus signs represent two ionically borrowed electrons, provided by metals such as magnesium or aluminium which become bonded into the chain. These chains may also be linked by metals to make the ceramic solid. Double chains are possible, as in Fig. 2.3. There are four silicon atoms and eleven oxygen atoms in the repeat distance, six of which have one electron missing. Hence, the formula is $(Si_4O_{11})^{6-}$. These chains may be packed together in regular arrays by means of metal ions, when they produce crystalline forms which occur naturally as minerals. Alternatively, if the fibrous nature is retained, materials such as asbestos result. It is also possible for the silicate unit to form a sheet-like structure as in Fig. 2.4. The various forms for silicates are represented by models in Fig. 2.5.

Another material which is common in minerals is hydrated aluminium oxide (gibbsite) Al $(OH)_3$. In this compound, one Al^{+++} ion is ionically bonded to three $(OH)^-$ ions. A sheet structure is again formed, consisting of upper rows of $(OH)^-$ ions, then a layer of Al^{+++} ions (filling two-thirds of available gaps) and then a lower sheet of $(OH)^-$ ions, similar to the upper sheet, but displaced, so that

33

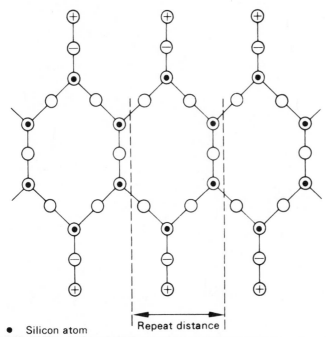

●   Silicon atom

○   Oxygen atom

⊕   Metal ion

Fig. 2.3 Formation of a double chain by sharing of base oxygen atoms. Hexagonal-shaped patterns are formed. Note that apex oxygen atoms (those above silicon atoms) must be bonded to a metal ion

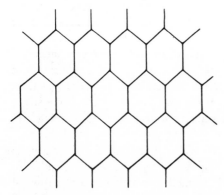

Fig. 2.4 Sheet structure resulting from repetition of the hexagonal-shaped units of Fig. 2.3

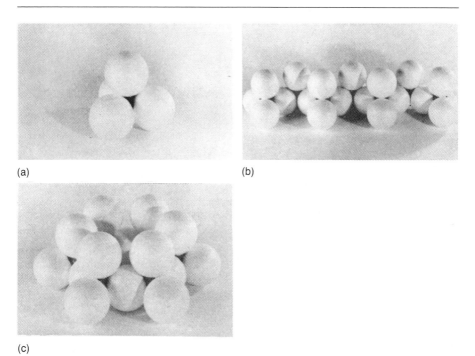

(a) (b)

(c)

Fig. 2.5 (a) Basic silicate unit. Dark sphere – silicon, light spheres – oxygen. All four oxygen atoms require one electron; (b) Silicate chain. The apex and side oxygen atoms require one electron; (c) Hexagonal silicate unit. This could form a double chain by repeating the hexagons in one direction of a sheet structure by repeating the hexagons in both horizontal directions

(a) (b)

Fig. 2.6 (a) Gibbsite sheet with upper layer of hydroxyl ions (dark), omitted to show aluminium ions (light) occupying two-thirds of available sites; (b) A complete gibbsite sheet showing how upper hydroxyl ions fit between lower ones

lower $(OH)^-$ ions fit between upper $(OH)^-$ ions (Fig. 2.6). Many minerals are formed when sheets based on silicon and aluminium come together. Each apex oxygen atom of the former replaces one $(OH)^-$ ion of the latter, producing a stable formation. Kaolinite, formula $Al_2(OH)_4Si_2O_5$, is a simple example (Fig. 2.7). Other minerals may form, for example, montmorillonite, when the upper sheet of the gibbsite layer is attached to a silicate sheet in the same way as the lower layer, producing $Al_2(OH)_2 2Si_2O_5$. These sheets tend to pack together by means of van

35

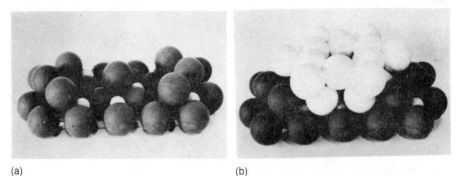

(a)   (b)

Fig. 2.7 (a) Gibbsite sheet with an upper hexagon of hydroxyl, ions removed;   (b) The apex oxygens of a silicate sheet (Fig. 2.5(c)) fitting into the hexagonal space shown in Fig. 2.7(a) and producing kaolinite

der Waals' bonds and may form many layers in some cases. Normally, the sheets are very small, due to strains imposed by the arrangement of the base oxygen atoms. These strains can be relieved by means of further metal atoms and the sheets then become bigger, forming the mica group of materials.

Properties of the silicates

In all these materials, co-valent and ionic bonds play an important part. Hence, there are no free electrons and the materials are good insulators of heat and electricity. Mechanically, properties depend on the particular structural forms. The crystalline forms, for instance, in minerals, are strong and rigid but have planes of weakness (cleavage planes), where bond densities are lower. The plate forms, if bonded by van der Waals' forces, tend to slip over one another easily, as in clay. They may also tend to absorb moisture. The fibrous forms have tensile strength in the fibrous direction but little strength in other directions. The basic structures of all silicates are very stable, so that they are unaffected by the atmosphere and many acids. This, together with high melting points, makes them a natural choice as building materials.

Clay and its properties

Clay is normally described as a soil of particle size less than 5 μm, (cf. 150 μm, the smallest BS sieve size for fine aggregate). Hence, clays need not, by definition, consist of minerals, although most clays contain a substantial proportion of mineral materials, so that a study of them will lead to an understanding of clay properties. The formation of kaolinite from silica and hydrated aluminium oxide has already been described, this being, in fact, one of the commonest minerals in clay. There are a number of others and many of these differ from kaolinite only in the arrangement of the silicon and aluminium-based platelets. Many properties of clays derive from the fact that they have a strong affinity for water, owing to a negative charge which exists on the surface of clay particles. Possible causes of this are:

1. An aluminium ion (trivalent) occupying the place of a silica ion (tetravalent). The silicate sheet would have one negative charge.
2. A divalent ion, e.g. magnesium, occupying the place of the aluminium ion in the alumina sheet.
3. Broken bonds, as at the edge of a sheet.
4. Adsorption of negative hydroxyl $(OH)^-$ ions to the clay surface.

The negative charge causes positive ions in the water to be attracted towards the clay surface, forming a double layer (Fig. 2.8) and water is, therefore, bonded to the surface. The state which the clay assumes depends on the relative magnitudes of the repulsion of adjacent surfaces, due to the double charged layer and the attraction of surfaces by van der Waals' forces. In most clays, the charged layer is insufficiently strong to prevent coagulation due to van der Waals' forces and the clay 'gels', taking up solid properties. An exception is, however, montmorillonite, which is hydrophilic, having a strong affinity for water. It absorbs large quantities, which prevent van der Waals' forces from causing coagulation of the particles. They can, therefore, remain in the liquid ('sol') form for long periods of time, if sufficient water is available. Montmorillonite is the main mineral in bentonite, an altered volcanic ash, which, within a certain range of moisture contents, behaves as a 'sol' on agitation, reverting to a soft 'gel' on being allowed to stand. In gel form, the material has a high resistance to water flow and has, therefore, been used for the stabilisation of soils during excavation at levels below the water table. The bentonite may be injected by grouting or excavation may take place through a slurry of bentonite which penetrates soil surfaces and gels, forming an impermeable film.

It is well known that there is an optimum moisture content for compaction of clay. This is evident from the above, since, when large quantities of water are present, the material will behave almost as a liquid while, at low moisture contents, bonding increases the stiffness of the clay so that air voids cannot be removed. Furthermore, the fact that the water is adsorbed – held to the clay – makes it difficult to drain saturated clay.

Soil stabilisation techniques

There are at least two methods of stabilising soil which depend on the principles given above.

The first, 'electro-osmosis' is a direct consequence of the presence of the negative charges on the surface of clay particles. The gaps between particles in a saturated clay will be filled with water containing positively-charged ions, as shown in Fig. 2.8. If a voltage is applied to the clay by means of electrodes, the positive ions in the water will be drawn to the negative electrode (cathode), carrying moisture with them. This phenomenon gives a simple, if expensive, means of draining saturated clay or silty soils. A further effect connected with

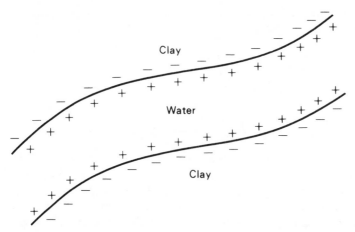

Fig. 2.8 The double layer formed at the surface of clay particles as a result of their negative surface charge

electro-osmosis in which colloidal particles move in the opposite direction (toward the anode) takes place simultaneously. This is known as electrophoresis and has been used for the injection of bentonite into soils. The bentonite then gels and stabilises the soil, forming a waterproof diaphragm. Alternatively, bentonite may be used in this way to waterproof walls and basements.

Another method utilises the fact that coagulation of sols can be obtained by the addition of a suitable salt in solution. This causes a contraction of the double layer of charge at the surface of particles, enabling them to approach more closely, so that van der Waals' forces cause coagulation.

The injection of salts into clays is not practicable, due to their low permeability, but coarser-grained soils, such as sands, can be consolidated by injecting a concentrated solution of sodium-silica, which can then be made to form a gel by injection of a solution of a salt such as calcium chloride.

Clay and related products

Many products used in construction are formed by heating naturally occurring minerals, such as clay or sand. Examples are clay bricks, blocks, tiles, pipes, terracotta, faience, sanitary ware and glass products. Materials with broadly similar properties or structure also exist naturally in the form of stones (many of which have been subject to heat at some stage in their history) and asbestos. These materials have a certain similarity in their properties and, hence, are considered as a group, but attention is first given to the effects of firing natural minerals.

The essential feature of most clays is that they contain a variety of intimately mixed minerals. The balance of the various types depends on the origin of the clay and widely differing properties result accordingly. On account of the predominantly very small particle sizes, substantial quantities of water are normally trapped in clays and this water may contain salts in solution. The firing process for clay products is heavily dependent on the diversity of mineral types, since clay products are invariably moulded before firing and are, therefore, required. to retain their shape during the process.

Heating causes certain minerals to fuse, while others remain solid, the overall effect being that bonding is extended throughout the whole unit without loss of shape. Total fusion could not be permitted unless the product were heated within its mould (and this would greatly increase manufacturing costs), while inadequate fusion would result in inferior strength and durability. The first minerals to fuse are normally metallic oxides and these act as fluxes, absorbing at the same time some of the salts present. On cooling, a 'glassy' matrix is formed, enclosing those particles which did not fuse. The process is known as vitrification, or, in some cases, sintering, according to the method used. The term 'glass' is given to any material in which extensive bonding occurs in such a way that crystals do not form. It may not be immediately obvious why, unlike most materials, the fused fractions of clay products do not crystallise on cooling. The reason is, again, based on the complexity of the fused portion, which contains a great variety of minerals. The bonds between them become directionally rigid on cooling but without orientation to form regular patterns. The structure can, hence, be regarded as a three-dimensional irregular array of molecular chains. Even where the range of minerals is restricted, as in ordinary 'glass' in which silica is the predominent mineral crystallisation is normally prevented unless the material is 'soaked' within a particular temperature range. This temperature usually corresponds to dull red heat in the region of 900 °C. Above that temperature, thermal energy is too great for crystallisation and below that temperature the liquid is too viscous to permit the organisation of atoms to form regular arrays. Hence, ordinary glass may be regarded as a super-cooled liquid, its transparency resulting directly from the absence of crystals, the boundaries of which would tend to scatter light. Most clay products are opaque because the degree of vitrification in them is very limited – it is only sufficient to bind the remaining solid material. Chemically, most ceramics are very stable, since the raw materials have been in existence over very long periods of time.

Clay bricks

The nature of clay varies greatly with depth and from region to region, and the manufacturing method and properties of the resultant unit vary accordingly.

Clay bricks may be classified in a number of ways, for example, as follows:

Staffordshire blue Bricks made from certain clays in this region are of dark blue colour and are usually of engineering quality.

Otterham mild stock An attractive yellow brick of low strength but good durability. The term 'stock' implies a locally-made brick.

The manufacture of bricks can be divided into the following stages: preparation of clay, moulding, drying and firing.

The first three stages can be taken together, since the preparation of the clay, the moulding process and the drying are interdependent and related to the nature of the raw material. The following methods are used:

Semi-dry process

This uses clays which have low natural plasticity. The clay is pulverised into a fine, granular material which is pressed in measured quantities into steel moulds, under progressively increased pressure. Indentations called 'frogs' are formed in one or both bed faces at the same time. Facings may be applied to one face and end of the brick, which would first be moistened. Facing materials may take the form of iron compounds, brick dust or sand. 'Rustic' bricks receive zig-zag scratches. Fletton bricks are made by the semi-dry process from Oxford clay shale, the name originating from the village near Peterborough where they were first manufactured. The semi-dry process accounts for over 50 per cent of the bricks manufactured in UK. The granular texture of the clay is often still evident after firing – it can be seen by inspection of fractured surfaces.

Stiff plastic process

The raw material is similar to that used in the above process, except that water is added to form a clot of stiff consistency. The brick is then pressed into shape. This method is used for the production of engineering-quality bricks, fractured surfaces being of relatively uniform texture. Both the semi-dry and stiff plastic processes result in products of accurate shape and dimensions.

Wire-cut process

Clays must be fairly soft and are rolled to a fine texture before moulding. The clay is then consolidated and extruded to dimensions which allow for shrinkage. The extrusion machine also produces perforations in the column of clay, which is finally cut to units of the correct thickness by tensioned wires. Perforated bricks, as they are often known, are usually dried before firing, since a fairly high moisture content, in the region of 20 per cent, is required for the extrusion of the clay.

Although these bricks are 'perforated' in the general sense, BS 3921 reserves the term for bricks in which the perforations occupy more than 25 per cent of the volume of the brick, such that the relationship between the strength of bricks and that of the brickwork may be different from that obtained with solid bricks. Bricks containing up to 25 per cent by volume of perforations – and these include most 'perforated' bricks in current use – are referred to as 'solid' bricks, since they can be treated in all respects as such.

Soft mud process

This uses soft clays obtained from shallower surface deposits. Breeze, town ash or other material may be added after mixing to improve the colour of the final product and/or to provide additional fuel for firing. The clay may be pressed into sanded moulds, either by machine or by hand, the latter process producing characteristic crease marks which result in the outstanding aesthetic appearance of handmade bricks. These bricks, having a high moisture content, must be dried before firing.

Three methods of firing bricks are now considered, the more common methods being described first.

Continuous kiln

Developed from the Hoffman kiln, continuous kilns comprise a series of chambers, normally forming an oval shape and interconnected by a series of ducts and flues. The heat was traditionally supplied in the form of coke, fed from above the chambers, but it now often takes the form of oil or gas. Bricks are loaded, dried, fired, cooled and unloaded from each chamber in rotation, the heat from those bricks which are in the cooling stage being used to dry and preheat those awaiting firing. The kilns are of relatively simple construction and form an economic way of firing bricks in large numbers. The total time in the kiln is usually about two weeks. Continuous kilns are, at present, the most widely used firing method.

Car tunnel kiln

Units are specially stacked onto large trolleys, incorporating a heat-resistant loading platform. The trolleys are then pushed end-to-end into a straight tunnel with a waist that fits the loading platform closely. As trolleys are progressively pushed through, the bricks reach the hottest part of the kiln, at which a temperature of about 1100 °C is attained. The fuel is in the form of gas or oil, supplied from above. The bricks finally enter the cooling zone and emerge from the other end. The firing time is relatively short and the complete process may take as little as one day in the case of bricks having a large area of exposed surface, for example, perforated bricks. Other types of brick heated at this rate would tend to 'bloat' and must, therefore, be fired more slowly.

Clamps

These are very large stacks of bricks built in open formations on a breeze base, in large open-ended enclosures – as many as a million bricks can be fired at once. The breeze is ignited and heats the bricks, assisted by fuel which is usually incorporated within the bricks themselves. The centre of the mass becomes red hot and some bricks are often overfired. Bricks near the edges of the stack are, conversely, underfired. The resulting product is, therefore, variable in shape, colour and strength, but the method is still used in a few areas because the bricks have an aesthetically pleasing appearance.

Effects of the drying and firing process

Drying implies the low-temperature stage of the heating process, in which free water is expelled from the clay. The process occurs whether or not bricks are subjected to a separate drying stage. Drying is carried out before firing, when the moisture content of the clay is high, such that bloating problems would occur if the green brick were subjected to the relatively high rate of temperature rise associated with firing. During drying, shrinkage occurs and the plasticity of the clay is reduced, as solid surfaces, previously separated by water, approach one another, increasing the strength of the van der Waals' forces.

During the early stages of firing (up to 300 °C), partially bound water is removed from the clay and, by 900 °C, carbonaceous material will have been oxidised and water of crystallisation expelled. There may also be phase changes or breakdown of the clay minerals. At this stage, gas formation should be complete and vitrification begins. The maximum firing temperature may be anywhere between 900 °C and 1400 °C, at which extensive vitrification may occur, depending on clay type. Temperatures above this value would cause collapse by fusion. At the vitrification stage, slight thermal expansion of the earlier stages is reversed and marked contraction occurs, as porosity is reduced. Hence, the shrinkage during firing increases with the firing temperature, for a given clay. For any one material and unit, there will be an optimum firing temperature, together with a maximum rate of temperature rise, if satisfactory properties are to be obtained.

If the firing temperature is too high, brittleness may result and shrinkage cracks may arise on cooling.

If the firing temperature is too low, vitrification will be inadequate and the unit will, therefore, be of low strength, high moisture movement and high salt content, since salts are absorbed into the glassy fraction of the brick if the temperature is high enough. Since firing at higher temperatures tends to produce coarser pores in the brick, underfired bricks will have lower frost-resistance than well-fired bricks (see Frost-resistance of porous materials).

When bricks are fired too rapidly, a vitrified surface skin may form, preventing the escape of gases which are formed internally. This may result in 'bloating', causing loss of strength and irregular shape in the fired unit.

The effects of the firing process vary widely, according to mineral types, and sophisticated methods may now be used to identify changes in particular compounds in the clay on heating. One such technique is differential thermal analysis (DTA), in which the heat input to the material is carefully monitored as the temperature rises. Phase or chemical changes are detected by a change in heat input, so that the origins of, for example, dimensional changes on firing can be obtained. By controlling such changes by variation of firing temperature or modifications to the raw material, the properties of the finished product can be modified or improved.

Properties of clay bricks to BS 3921

Although properties could be described under many different headings, the most important and representative ones are:

Compressive strength
Water absorption

Soluble salt content
Efflorescence
Frost-resistance
Expansion on wetting
Thermal expansion

Other properties, such as dimensions and appearance, may also be important but these are relatively easily assessed and do not greatly affect the stability or durability of the structure. Bricks are inherently variable, due to statistical fluctuations in the properties of the clay and the firing process and it is, therefore, essential that, in measuring properties, a sufficiently large number of representative samples be taken. Ideally, such tests should be conducted over an extended period of time: details of control chart techniques are given in BS 3921.

Compressive strength and absorption
BS 3921 requires that bricks are saturated before strength testing and, if they are to be laid frog upwards, the frogs are filled with mortar which should have reached a compressive strength in the range of $28\,N/mm^2$ to $42\,N/mm^2$ at the time the brick is tested.

Absorption may be measured by a five-hour boiling method or by a vacuum test, which give approximately equivalent results.

Bricks are classified as engineering class A if the average compressive strength is above $69.0\,N/mm^2$ and the absorption is not greater than 4.5 per cent, and engineering class B if the average compressive strength is above $48.5\,N/mm^2$ and the absorption is not greater than 7.0 per cent. Bricks for damp-proof courses should have an absorption not greater than 4.5 per cent. (If the absorption requirements of engineering bricks given above seem stringent, it may be worthwhile to comment that, since absorption figures are based on the mass of water absorbed compared to the mass of the brick, misleadingly low answers are obtained because of the differing densities of the two materials.) An absorption of 5 per cent would, for example, correspond to water-filled voids occupying over 10 per cent of the brick. Similarly, 20 per cent absorption, which would apply to weaker bricks, corresponds to nearly 40 per cent of the volume of the brick being occupied by water). Loadbearing bricks are classified with a number normally in the range 1 to 15, corresponding to compressive strengths in the range $7.0\,N/mm^2$ to $103.5\,N/mm^2$. The numbers are based on earlier Imperial equivalent strengths.

Soluble salt content
Salts of calcium, magnesium, potassium and sodium, notably sulphates, are associated with attack on cement mortars. However, since the likelihood and severity of attack depend greatly on the situation of the brickwork, maximum soluble salt content is given only in respect of 'special quality' bricks. The limits are 0.5 per cent for the sulphate radical, 0.03 per cent for the magnesium, potassium and sodium radicals, and 0.3 per cent for the calcium radical, since the

latter is found to be less harmful, probably due to the lower solubility of calcium sulphate. Barium carbonate may be added to the raw material to reduce soluble salt contents – it reacts with soluble sulphates, producing insoluble barium sulphate.

Efflorescence

A simple test is described in the standard, in which a visual assessment of efflorescence is made. Ordinary and special-quality bricks must develop no more than 'moderate' efflorescence when tested in this way. Bricks used internally are not subject to this requirement.

Frost-resistance

Theoretical aspects of frost-resistance are discussed in more detail later in the chapter, in the context of porous materials generally. A formerly-used term, 'saturation coefficient', which is a measure of the proportion of voids which are accessible to water, is not included in BS 3921, since it is now known to have little bearing on frost-resistance. One of three requirements must be satisfied for a brick which is to be considered 'frost-resistant'.

1. Evidence of frost-resistance of bricks in service in the proposed locality over not less than 3 years.
2. Satisfactory performance of sample panels of brickwork.
3. When evidence, as provided by the above methods, is not available, conformance with the engineering class B specification in respect of strength or water absorption.

Bricks of special quality are required to be 'frost-resistant' when assessed in this way and should be 'hard-fired'.

Expansion on wetting

Fired clay products of many types undergo a progressive irreversible expansion as moisture penetrates pores and is adsorbed onto internal surfaces. Over a period of years, this expansion may amount to over 1000×10^{-6}, especially in more porous bricks, though the movement of the brickwork is normally only about 60 per cent of this unless, for some reason, the mortar is expansive. The expansion roughly follows a negative exponential law, the rate of expansion depending on the condition of exposure. The time taken for 50 per cent of the movement to occur is typically given as one week, though it may vary considerably, according to brick type. Perhaps, surprisingly, soaking bricks before laying is not effective in reducing expansion. There is no British Standard test for moisture expansion but general recommendations are that clay bricks should not be used fresh from the kiln: a period of at least one week should be allowed before laying, unless bricks are known to have very small expansion. The *reversible* moisture movement of bricks is small, being less than 200×10^{-6}.

Thermal expansion

The coefficient of thermal expansion of clay brickwork is approximately 7×10^{-6} per °C, considerably less than that of most concretes, so that thermal movement is not normally a problem.

Refractory bricks

These are used where high temperatures are encountered, such as in furnace linings. They are formed from clays which are mainly silica and alumina, since the presence of metallic oxides found in many clays causes a reduced melting point on account of their action as fluxes.

Calcium-silicate bricks to BS 187

These are made by steam-autoclaving, under pressure, a finely divided mixture of sand and lime, the proportion of lime being between 5 and 10 per cent. A reaction occurs between the surface of the sand particles and the lime, producing a calcium-silicate hydrate, which 'glues' the sand particles together. The process takes about 12 hours, during which there is no change of size, so that dimensional tolerances are very good compared with clay bricks. Soluble salts or discolouration are not usually present, provided constituents materials are free from clay or organic impurities and, since the brick is of a light colour, pigments can be added, if desired, for facing purposes. BS 187 classifies strength as for clay bricks with a maximum mean value of $48.5 \, \text{N/mm}^2$ (compared with $104 \, \text{N/mm}^2$ for class 15, loadbearing clay bricks) and recommends uses for each grade. Hence, strengths are in general lower than in clay bricks and the mortar should be adjusted accordingly to avoid cracking of bricks. Bricks other than class 2 or those to be used under permanently damp conditions are generally required to have drying shrinkage not more than 400×10^{-6}. The moisture movement and thermal movement of sand-lime bricks are higher than those of clay bricks and they should not be saturated before laying, rendering or plastering. Joints in brickwork are recommended every 7 m or so. Differential thermal movement may cause cracking if, in large lengths, they are bonded to clay brickwork. Although calcium-silicate bricks are suitable for all normal purposes, their chemical resistance is not as good as that of clay bricks and slight deterioration has been known to occur over periods of years in polluted atmospheres, due to the action of atmospheric sulphur dioxide on the calcium-silicate bonding agent.

Use of bricks

A brick must be suited to the purpose for which it is intended. Environments may vary between dry, warm air, as in interior use, and permanently damp and, possibly, aggressive soils when used below damp-proof courses or in earth-retaining walls. Even a correctly selected brick may be unsatisfactory if used improperly. For example, calcium-silicate bricks, laid wet, will tend to shrink if used internally and may then crack, especially if the mortar used is too strong. Since clay bricks undergo an irreversible expansion on wetting, while concrete structures tend to *shrink* with time, brick panels in concrete structures must have movement joints. Otherwise, spalling of bricks may occur. In general, as with other materials, bricks should be stored in conditions similar to those of use but it is especially important to avoid rain and frost during storage.

Ideally, in order to ascertain the suitability of a brick for a certain purpose, a panel of brickwork may be constructed and exposed in similar conditions for at least 1 year but, failing this, a good guide can be obtained from the requirements for special-quality bricks, provided sampling procedures are satisfactory. Variability from batch to batch is important and an assessment of the likely variability of bricks should be made by carrying out tests or batches selected at random over an extended period.

Loadbearing brickwork
Considerable progress has been made concerning the behaviour of bricks and mortar in brickwork, leading to the possibility of multi-storey brickwork structures, lateral stability usually being provided by carefully designed and constructed systems of crosswalls. The main problem is that of testing large units under the various possible stress systems which could be encountered in a wall. What are, at the moment, necessarily large safety factors in brickwork will reduce as quality control in brick production improves and the nature of loading stresses is increasingly understood.

Larger units
Although experimental variations in size of bricks have not produced a satisfactory appearance, several newer types of unit have been produced, a notable example being perforated or hollow building blocks that obviate the need for a cavity. These give a wall of increased stability with lower erection costs. The perforations produce similar thermal performance to a cavity brick wall, although damp-proofing properties are not so good. One disadvantage of such units is that, when they are used instead of a cavity wall, the whole wall is then of dense clay material, which is more expensive and of considerably inferior thermal properties to the now established clay brick outer-leaf and insulating-block inner-leaf construction. Experiments have been made with complete brick panels, mortar joints being obtained by pressure grouting of pre-assembled bricks. Such panels are, however, difficult to handle unless reinforced and would only be suitable for large-scale modular types of construction.

Other fired-clay products

Although the use of preformed plastic and concrete units has increased tremendously in recent years, many different types of fired-clay products are still used and accepted as first-rate materials. They have the advantage that they have been proved by use in buildings over many years. Although only clay roofing tiles and pipes are described here, the range of fired-clay products is extensive, including, as well as the above, sanitary ware, glazed porcelain tiles, flooring tiles, terracotta (unglazed clay units used for decorative or architectural purposes) and faience (glazed decorative units). The products to be described are similar in composition and manufacture to clay bricks, though it may be worthwhile to indicate the chief criteria on which individual units may be judged.

Clay tiles for roofing to BS 402

The first requirement is durability, since exposure of roofing tiles is much more severe than that of clay units in vertical surfaces, tiles being of necessity much thinner as well. The most severe conditions are those in which rain in winter months is followed by frost: the temperature of horizontal surfaces can decrease very rapidly on clear nights, causing rapid freezing of absorbed water. The durability of clay tiles is, therefore, generally measured by water absorption – a limit of 10.5 per cent average is required by BS 402 – though comments made below on frost-resistance of porous materials must still apply. It has been found, in the past, that machine-made tiles often had a shorter life than handmade tiles, since they had a greater tendency to laminate. Modern manufacturing methods may reduce this tendency and the use of handmade tiles is now decreasing, owing to the difficulty in obtaining labour at reasonable cost. It seems likely however, in view of the aesthetic properties of handmade clay tiles, that these units, which have first-class durability, will continue to be made available for high-quality applications. Other requirements of BS 402 include minimum transverse strength and limits on their longitudinal curvature.

Clay pipes

The continued use of clay pipes, perhaps like tiles, reflects their proved reliability in use. Modern plastic jointing methods have reduced fixing costs and allow greater movement of pipes. Salt glazing has been largely replaced by ceramic glazing or by vitrifying pipes, since, during the salt-glazing process, hydrochloric acid is emitted in gaseous form into the atmosphere, causing pollution. The British Standards for clay pipes (BSS 65 and 540) do not require any type of glazing and this is due to the comparatively smooth abrasion-resistant surface which is produced by modern manufacturing methods. Water absorption is of little consequence, except where aggressive fluids are encountered, since pipes are not normally subject to frost attack.

BSS 65 and 540 give dimensional tolerances and loads for pipes of 'standard' strength and 'extra' strength. A pressure test is specified, with two classes, corresponding to surface and underground pipes. The latter also require an impermeability test. Alkali- and acid-resistance are also specified.

Stones for building

These may be natural stones or reconstructed stone. Since the latter involves use of an artificial binder, it is described under the general heading of concrete. While the use of stone as a structural material has decreased in recent years, wide use is still made of it as a decorative finish in flooring and cladding. A stone which is suited to its purpose, and correctly formed and applied, achieves extremely good effect and durability. Natural stones may be broadly classified according to origin.

Igneous
This is rock which is formed from a molten material known as 'magma'. Those formed by the earth's crust are coarse-grained with large crystals of minerals such as felspar, as in granite. Rapid cooling as, for example, when volcano lava solidifies, produces a finer structure, such as basalt. Both granite and basalt are very hard with no natural bedding planes and are hence difficult to work but, when used for simple shapes, e.g. kerb stones, have produced units of excellent durability. Porosity and moisture movement are negligible, due to the crystalline forms of these stones. Their high silica content also means that they are unaffected by environmental pollution. These properties, together with advances in mechanical cutting and finishing, make granite a popular material for use in thin sections, in cladding of buildings. Other modern applications of granite include use as an aggregate for high-strength concrete and, in ground form, in abrasion-resistant surfaces. There are granite quarries in most parts of Britain, with the exception of the South East, where sedimentary rocks predominate.

Sedimentary
These consist of small particles of either igneous rocks, such as quartz or felspar, or fragments of decayed animal or vegetable matter, cemented together by materials such as silica, calcium carbonate, clay or iron oxide. They may be broadly classified as sandstones or limestones, corresponding to grains of silica and calcium carbonate, respectively. Sedimentary stones have natural bedding planes across which bonding is weak and which, on exposure, tend to admit water, causing flaking in polluted atmospheres. Hence, the bedding planes are best laid horizontal. This is quite possible where loadbearing stone blocks are used but may be impossible where thin sections are required, as in cladding. For this reason, the use of sedimentary stones for cladding is relatively uncommon.

Sandstones The silica – often pure quartz – is cemented together with iron oxide, silica, calcium carbonate or clay. The iron oxide is responsible for the brown colour of some sandstones. The best type of sandstone is that which is cemented by silica, the resulting product being strong and durable, for example, Dunhouse stone from Durham. Calcareous sandstones are strong but less resistant to atmospheric pollution, since the calcium carbonate may be dissolved by the combined action of sulphur dioxide and carbon dioxide. Clay-cemented sandstones are of low durability. Most sandstones are found in Northern England and Scotland, where they are used extensively as aggregates for concrete.

Limestones These are based on calcium carbonate. This may occur in the form of a sediment deposited by living matter. It is then fine-grained as, for example, in chalk, where the calcium carbonate is present as the crystalline form, calcite, finely divided to give a soft rock in Southern England but more crystalline to give a hard limestone in Northern England, Ireland and Scotland. Alternatively, it may consist of a precipitate from solution or of marine life cemented together. In some cases, the sediment occurs in the form of rounded grains – oolites – for example, Ancaster stone and Portland stone. Portland stone also contains large fossils. As would be expected with any massive deposit of sedimentary rock, the properties of the stone vary with depth. One particular feature of limestones is their low coefficient of thermal expansion – approximately $4 \times 10^{-6}/°C$, compared with granite, which has a coefficient of expansion of $11 \times 10^{-6}/°C$. Some limestones contain significant quantities of dolomite, which has the formula $CaCO_3MgCO_3$. Such stones are known as magnesian limestones.

Metamorphic

This is a rock or clay the structure of which has been changed by heat or pressure, increasing its crystallinity. There are two important types used in building: marble, which is normally imported and slate, found mainly in North Wales, Northern Ireland and Northern Scotland.

Marble   This can be considered as limestone with various other materials, such as iron, incorporated and recrystallised by the action of heat. The impurities give rise to the attractive colouring of the stone, purer varieties being white. Although more resistant varieties may be used externally, as a limestone, it has poor resistance to atmospheric pollution and soon loses its polish, so that it is used mainly as a decorative material for internal uses.

Slate   This is formed by modification of clay by pressure to shale and then, by heat, to slate. The stone has pronounced thin laminations which are the reason for its use as a roofing material. Being derived from minerals found in clay, slates have extremely good resistance to weathering and pollution. Over a period of time, however, delamination takes place, causing disintegration. This may occur in less than 10 years with some imported slates. Some Lake Districk 'slates' are, in fact, obtained from sedimentary rocks with thin bedding planes. Slates have also been used successfully as damp-proof courses. Roofing slates are covered by BS 680, which specifies an absorption of not more than 0.3 per cent after 48 hours' boiling, together with a wetting and drying test. Slates to be used in conditions of severe exposure to atmospheric pollution should satisfy a test for resistance to sulphuric acid. The use of slate in roofing has decreased in recent years, owing to the considerable craft skill which is necessary in forming and dressing them. It is now possible that the development of machines for this purpose may result in much wider use of this material which, in common with handmade clay tiles, has considerable aesthetic value.

Selection of stones for building

When used internally, selection may be based primarily on aesthetic effects, although ease of cleaning and abrasion-resistance will also be important, especially for flooring. Externally, some types of stone can be so expensive to maintain in polluted city atmospheres that their use is restricted to 'prestige' building. Some varieties of stone – especially limestone – have, to some degree, a self-cleaning effect, due to dissolution of the surface by water. The effect is, however, not always satisfactory, since, over a period of time, considerable erosion can take place and sheltered parts of the building are not cleaned in this way. Granites stay clean for longer periods of time but are more difficult to clean one dirt has accumulated. Limestones form hard films of calcium sulphate on exposure to polluted atmospheres, although this film may flake off, due to differential thermal movement with the background or by crystallisation of salts underneath it. Care should be taken when using stones of different types. Sandstone, in particular, may be affected by magnesium sulphate solution produced by the effect of pollution on magnesium limestone or cast stone. Since even stone from the same quarry may vary as new beds are uncovered, the assessment of the suitability of a stone should be based on weathering tests on newly-quarried samples. When severe exposure is anticipated, for example, as in copings, freezing tests are essential. Further tests on the effect of salts present in background brickwork or atmosphere should also be carried out, although it is now common practice to coat the back of stone with bitumen if the stone is to be used against brick or concrete. Where sedimentary stones are bedded in mortar, crystallisation damage can be reduced by use of fairly weak porous mortar from which evaporation of water occurs preferentially. Hence, salts may be drawn into the mortar, reducing damage to the stone. The surface layers of such mortar would inevitably deteriorate, though decay could be retarded by use of a sulphate-resisting cement and, when it occurs, it is relatively easy to repoint mortar joints. Table 2.1 shows some well-known stones which are representative of their type, together with properties.

Frost-resistance of porous materials

Although the mechanism by which frost causes damage to porous building materials has been the subject of extensive study, the precise mode of deterioration is still not fully understood. It is known, however, that the vulnerability of materials to frost cannot be determined directly from simply-measured properties, such as porosity, absorption, coefficient or even permeability. The lack of correlation between porosity and frost-resistance is easily explained, since sealed pores in most materials could not absorb water and would, therefore, play no role in frost attack. To appreciate how a permeable, highly-absorbent material may be frost-resistant, it is necessary to consider the factors affecting the formation and stability of ice crystals in porous materials.

It is found that water in smaller pores is prevented from freezing by surface (capillary) forces, which cause powerful attraction between the water and the pore sides. Ice is, therefore, most likely to form in larger areas where surface forces are less important. Since the surface of most exposed structures cools most rapidly, ice is most likely to form at the surface, in large pores just beneath the

Table 2.1 Properties of some typical natural building stones

Group	Type	Name	Compressive strength (N/mm^2)	Density (kg/m^3)	Absptn (per cent)	Example
Igneous	Granite	Dartmoor Granite	130	2650	0.1	Waterloo Bridge
Sedimentary	Oolitic	Portland Stone	40	2200	4	St Paul's Cathedral
	Magnesian	Anston	30	2100	7	Houses of Parliament
	Sandstone	Woolton	60	2400	5	Anglican Cathedral, Liverpool
Metamorphic	Slate	Kirkstone Slate	130	2700	0.1	Lake District villages

surface or in imperfections, such as cracks. As the temperature of internal areas is reduced, water tends to be drawn towards surface regions where ice has already started to form, in preference to freezing within internal pores. It is found that, in materials containing only large pores, water is quickly drawn to the surface where it freezes. Such materials are frost-resistant, even though they may have quite large absorption coefficients. The most frost-susceptible materials are those which contain a fairly fine pore structure. In such materials, there may be a progressive build-up of ice in surface regions as the temperature falls. Damage may be caused if ice crystals grow just beneath the surface, in cracks or even due to pressures caused by the resistance of finer pores to movement of water. Very fine pores would not contribute to damage, since water in them would not be removed except at very low temperatures and would not freeze while inside such pores. It appears that pores having sizes in the range 0.01 mm to 0.1 mm are chiefly responsible for frost damage in weather conditions prevailing in the UK. Sealed pores may relieve some of the pressures caused by movement or freezing of water, while large pores which empty at an earlier stage may be able to accommodate water from finer pores as it moves towards the surface. This is particularly the case in air-entrained concrete where the air bubbles which would not normally fill with water are able to accept gel water in the concrete as it freezes. It has been found, in support of the arguments given above, that engineering bricks contain relatively coarse pores, as do most sandstones, and that both materials have high resistance to frost. Conversely, limestones and fletton bricks, which have a finer pore structure, are much more vulnerable to frost. A fairly common mode of failure in fletton bricks is spalling of the facing, due to the formation of ice lenses in less vitrified regions just below the dense surface skin, while another common occurrence in brickwork generally is the extrusion of small columns of ice from cracks within bricks or at mortar joints. It also follows that, whereas strength and absorption in bricks correlate fairly well, the same would not apply to strength and durability, with the possible exception that bricks having very high strength are usually durable. In other strength ranges, it is possible for weak bricks to be durable, while fairly strong bricks (up to approximately 50 N/mm^2) may have low durability. As explained above, durability depends on pore structure rather than on the presence or absence of pores.

It is clear that the frost-resistance of bricks or stones as individual units cannot be considered in isolation from the masonry units into which they are built. Bricks and stones are almost invariably laid in a bed of cement mortar and, in the case of brickwork, in particular, the brick/mortar interface plays an important part in the performance of the behaviour of the overall panel, since interface areas are very large. If the panel is to be weather-proof, it is essential that the mortar have low absorption and that capillary paths are not formed between the brick and the mortar. An important factor affecting behaviour of the mortar joints is the 'suction' of bricks, which is related to their absorption. Weaker bricks, such as flettons or stock bricks, are normally of medium to high suction, so that a good bond is normally formed between brick surfaces and the mortar. There is a tendency, however, when laid in dry weather, for the brick to draw excessive quantities of moisture from the mortar, resulting in a poor bond between the bed face of bricks and the rapidly-stiffening mortar layer. In the longer term, mortar may not hydrate sufficiently to become impermeable. This tendency may be overcome by dampening (not soaking) high-suction bricks or by use of lime in the mortar, which helps to resist the suction of the bricks. Low-suction bricks, such as engineering bricks, will require a slightly stiffer mortar and, to ensure adequate bond, the cement content should be higher or lime should be added. In the absence of adequate bond between mortar and brick faces, very large quantities of water can be drawn into the structure through the capillary paths formed.

Since frost attack only occurs in masonry which has admitted water, it is evident that the risk of damage is, in all cases, much reduced when masonry is designed and constructed so as to avoid the admission of water. This involves, for example, the use of damp-proof courses in all work in contact with the ground, damp-proof membranes behind earth-retaining walls, good eaves projections on the roofs of dwellings and the use of copings on parapet or free-standing walls. The durability of brickwork is increased by avoiding raked joints and using weather-cut and struck pointing in exposed situations. The use of very strong pointing materials is, however, not recommended: it may result in the face of the brickwork or stonework carrying a disproportionately large fraction of the load, leading to spalling of external horizontal edges of the brick or stone.

Glass

Modern scientific progress has brought with it new materials and methods but, as a glazing material, glass has remained unchallenged and seems likely to continue to dominate this field into the foreseeable future. Raw materials are plentiful and cheap, and glass has unrivalled abrasion-resistance, light-transmission properties and resistance to weathering or chemical attack.

Ordinary glass is based on silica – silicon oxide – which, in crystalline form, exists in a tetrahedral array, as described in Chapter 1. It has been explained that, if silica is cooled at normal rates from the liquid, an amorphous structure results. This may be regarded as a heavily and randomly distorted form of the crystalline structure. Although silica forms the basic network of glass, it is not used in the pure form because its melting point is too high – in the region of 1700 °C. Instead, the silica network is modified by compounds such as sodium carbonate, which, at high temperatures, decomposes to sodium oxide and then combines with part of the silica, forming sodium disilicate, thereby interrupting some of the rigid silicon-oxygen links. Hence, 'soda-glass', as the material is known, melts at a much lower temperature, in the region of 800 °C. Unfortunately, soda-glass is water soluble and a further network modifying compound, calcium carbonate, is added to stabilise the glass. The approximate composition of a typical soda-lime glass is:

SiO_2	75 per cent
Na_2CO_3	15 per cent
$CaCo_3$	10 per cent

Smaller amounts of other materials may be added as follows:

Manganese dioxide to remove coloration due to iron in the sand.
Oxides of aluminium and magnesium to improve chemical stability.
Lead to improve surface lustre or, in larger quantities, to produce a high-density glass resistant to X-rays.
Borax to produce glass having very low thermal movement – such glasses are highly resistant to thermal shock.

Manufacture of glass

The raw materials are mixed, in the correct proportions, with a quantity of scrap glass, 'cullet', and heated to about 1500 °C. The cullet melts first and permits reaction and fusion of the remaining ingredients at temperatures below the melting point of pure silica. The liquid is then cooled to a temperature of 1000 to 1200 °C, at which its viscosity is sufficiently high for forming. The most important processes are as follows.

The flat-drawn process
The glass is drawn upwards on a metal grille known as a 'bait', the sheet engaging with rollers which prevent its waisting. The glass is annealed to relieve cooling stresses and then cut to size. This type of glass contains slight ripples but is

economical, and was formerly used in domestic dwellings, offices and factories. It has now been largely replaced in the UK by float glass.

Rolled glass

The glass is drawn off in a horizontal ribbon on rollers and is then annealed. Such glasses do not give clear vision but can be given textured or patterned finishes. Wire may be incorporated, producing 'Georgian glass', a material with higher fire-resistance and increased safety against injury from impact. Wired glass is widely used in roof-lights and low-level glazing.

Float glass

This glass is optically flat and is produced by drawing it along the surface of molten tin in a bath. It is now used for general glazing purposes, as well as mirrors, shop windows and other situations where clear, undistorted vision is essential.

Strength of glass

The strength of any glass unit is determined largely by the effect of any surface imperfections it may contain. An indication of maximum tensile strength is obtained by tests on very thin glass fibres which are sensibly free of flaws and which may withstand stresses of up to $3000 \, N/mm^2$. The tensile strength of bulk glass, as measured by flexural tests, may vary between 20 and $200 \, N/mm^2$, according to its surface condition. The highest strength is obtained immediately after manufacture, though strengths are still variable. Strength reduces on aging, as surface imperfections are increased, whether by chemical attack or simply mechanical abrasion, glass which has weathered for some years being much weaker than new glass. For this reason, old glass is more difficult to cut and more likely to fracture due to movement or fixing stresses.

Toughened glass

The surface flaws in glass can be removed chemically but toughening can be carried out more simply by heat treatment. Sheet glass is heated uniformly until just plastic and then cooled by air jets. The outer layers contract and solidify and then, as inner layers try to follow, they throw the outer layers into compression, tending to close the microscopic cracks. In this way, the overall strength of the glass can be increased several times and impact strength may increase sevenfold. Figure 2.9 shows the approximate stress distribution in a sheet of toughened glass. On bending, the compressive stress on one face reduces and failure occurs only when this has been reversed to the normal tensile limit. If the surface is broken, the stress distribution becomes unbalanced and the material shatters into fragments. Hence, cutting or edge working are not possible and it must be ordered to size. Toughened glass has widened the application of glass to include solid glass doors, large windows and suspended glass curtains. Very large areas of

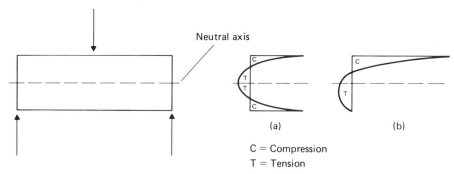

Fig. 2.9 Simple representation of the stresses in a sheet of toughened glass subject to bending: (a) No load; (b) Under load. Failure does not occur until the tensile strength at the lower surface is exceeded

glass are more conveniently suspended from a structural frame, since, when used in this way, the weight of glass itself contributes considerably towards stability. Large sheets may be joined by square metal plates at their corners, gaps being filled with transparent plastic material. Additional stability may be achieved by means of stiffening fins which may also be of glass. Such glass curtains are, themselves, an architectural feature and have been used as complete faces of two-storey buildings.

Thickness and weight

Although the thickness of ordinary glass was traditionally measured in terms of its mass per unit area, thickness is now given directly, the common sizes being 3 and 4 mm thick. The thickness of glass for ordinary glazing should increase with wind load and glass area. Square sheets should be thicker in general than rectangular sheets since, for a given area, there is less restraint at the centre of a square sheet of glass. The thickness of toughened glass also depends on other factors, such as the impact loading it is likely to have to withstand.

Thermal conductivity – double glazing

Glass, being composed largely of silica, has a thermal conductivity similar to a dense clay brick (approximately 1.0 W/m °C). The resistance of single glazing to heat loss is due to the surface resistances of the glass rather than to its own ability to restrict heat flow. Double glazing, similarly, depends on the four surface resistances of the two glass sheets. The most efficient types of thermal double glazing are those in which the cavity is factory-sealed, either by doubling up and sealing the sheet of glass itself or by using plastic sealing strips between two sheets. These types reduce greatly the risk of condensation in the cavity. A thermal double-glazing unit need not have a large cavity to be effective: a 5 mm cavity is satisfactory, having a U value of approximately 3.4 W/m² °C. The optimum size is 20 mm (U value 2.9 W/m² °C), while the U value of double glazing with cavities larger than 20 mm remains approximately constant. Vertical single glazing in conditions of average exposure will have a U value of approximately $5 \text{ W}/\text{m}^2 \,^{\circ}\text{C}$.

Thermal movement

This varies between $5.6 \times 10^{-6}/\,^{\circ}\text{C}$ for high-silica glasses, such as borosilicates, to $9 \times 10^{-6}/\,^{\circ}\text{C}$ for lead crystal. The former will, therefore, be more resistant to thermal shock. Thermal movement takes place in glazing, and glazing compounds should have the ability to allow this movement. Fracture of windows often follows when fixing tacks contact the edge of the glass. In a suspended glass assembly, the sheets expand downwards, so that a flexible jointing material should be provided at the base and around door frames. Damage may also result from solar radiation, which produces differential movement between the centre of the glass and its perimeter, which is shaded from the sunlight by the glazing compound. This is particularly the case with heat-absorbing glasses. The stresses which result are most likely to cause failure when the edge cover is about 30 mm, since smaller cover reduces the differential and larger cover increases the area of cool edge-glass to meet the tensile stress produced. Risk is minimised by reducing edge cover as far as possible; by using dark, heat-absorbing frames; by avoiding insulating materials in direct contact with the glass in the case of cladding; and by avoiding edge flaws in the glass, which usually initiate fracture. Toughened glass has, of course, greater resistance to damage by solar radiation. Coloured toughened glass panels are available with a layer of glass fibre and a vapour barrier bonded directly behind them, giving a U value of about $1.0 \text{ W}/\text{m}^2 \,^{\circ}\text{C}$.

Light and heat transmission

The direct transmission of light depends on the angle of incidence, as well as the glass thickness, but a maximum value of 90 per cent may be assumed in normal glazing. Glass tends to absorb infra-red radiation, so that corresponding heat transmission is about 80 per cent. Thin metallic layers can be included in the glass during manufacture and these reduce the transmitted heat by some 30 per cent, though light transmission properties are also affected. Such glasses are useful where solar radiation is a problem, as in roof lights or large areas of glazing. In air-conditioned buildings, they reduce the cooling requirement and, hence, the plant size and, in other buildings, they improve standards of thermal comfort.

Durability

Glass is unaffected by the atmosphere and by most acids, with the exception of hydrofluoric acid. Alkalis, which occur in cement or chemical paint strippers, attack glass and destroy the smooth surface and light transmission properties.

Table 2.2 Sound-level reduction in single and
double glazing (openable windows)

Type and thickness of glazing	Reduction (dB)
3 mm single glazing	20
12 mm single glazing	22
3 and 4 mm double-glazed window with absorbent in 200 mm cavity	31

Sound insulation

The sound-reduction properties of glazing are typical of those of a thin panel or membrane. Resonances occur at low frequencies, the insulation improving towards high frequencies. High-frequency insulation is, however, reduced by the 'coincidence effect'. In double glazing, the cavity size required for effective sound reduction is about 200 mm, much larger than that for best thermal-insulation properties. To be satisfactory, it is extremely important that air paths through glazing should be prevented. The use of different thicknesses of glass in the two sheets and an absorbent material in the cavity increases the sound insulation. Typical sound-reduction values at medium frequencies for opening windows are given in Table 2.2.

Asbestos

Asbestos exists in many different forms but is essentially a siliceous material with the fibrous molecular structure already described. It is, in fact, the only naturally-occurring inorganic fibre. Being a mineral, it has extremely good durability and chemical resistance, and can be heated to high temperatures without melting or burning. Most uses derive from these properties, together with its high strength in the direction of the fibres. There are three main types of fibre, chrysotile, crocidolite and amosite.

Chrysotile has the formula $Mg_3Si_2O_5(OH)_4$ and it contains small amounts of aluminium, iron and sodium. It has good heat-resistance and, being resistant to attack by alkalis, is very suitable for use with Portland cements, as in asbestos-cement products.
Crocidolite (blue asbestos) contains more iron than chrysotile and has greater strength and acid-resistance.
Amosite contains relatively long, stiff fibres, having excellent heat resistance, and is very suitable for insulating boards.

Embrittlement of asbestos fibres may begin at temperatures as low as 300 °C, due to loss of water on crystallisation but degradation is gradual and some strength may be retained at temperatures up to 1700°C. Fusion is complete at 2000 to 2500 °C.

Health hazard

It is unfortunate that asbestos particles may seriously affect the health of those who are in prolonged contact with the material. Inhalation of fibres may produce a disease of the lungs known as 'asbestosis', related lung cancer or a rare disease called mesothelioma. It is likely that crocidolite represents a particular hazard and, for this reason, the fibre has not been imported by manufacturers into the UK since 1970, though it is quite common in existing buildings and may still be imported in the form of manufactured goods. Stringent regulations now apply in areas where asbestos dust may be present. These require the provision of respirators, protective clothing and exhaust ventilation. Special storage and waste-disposal facilities are necessary in particular situations. In general, hand tools produce less dust than power tools. Another hazard occurs in demolition work if asbestos has been used for insulation purposes. The most harmful type, crocidolite, may be recognised by its blue colour (chrysotile and amosite are generally white and brown, respectively) unless paint has been applied but great care is necessary when dealing with the material in any form. The cheapness and inertness of asbestos are, nevertheless, such that it is still an important constructional material.

Asbestos cement

This material is formed from a mixture of short fibres, Portland cement and water, built up in layers to form sheets which are moulded and cured. Alternatively, silica and lime may be added during manufacture, the mix then being steam-autoclaved. Such types are also covered by the British Standards given below. It is used to form a wide variety of products, many of which are used externally, having a life of at least 40 years. During this time, however, impact strength decreases due to embrittlement (which also produces an *increase* in flexural strength). Some softening of the surface may also occur, due to the action of pollution on the cement. Life can be prolonged by painting, an alkali-resistant primer being essential. Since products are brittle, fixings must allow a certain amount of movement and must not cause localised stresses around them. Asbestos cement is commonly used in rainwater goods, many types of pipe, cisterns, conduits and troughs. In sheet or tile form, asbestos cement is available in the fully-compressed or semi-compressed states. Full compression results in high density – typically $1800 \, kg/m^3$, and high bending strength – typically $22.5 \, N/mm^2$. Semi-compressed forms have densities of approximately $1450 \, kg/m^3$ and bending strengths of $16 \, N/mm^2$. Fully-compressed products may have smooth finishes on both surfaces, while semi-compressed sheets have only one smooth surface. Pigments can be included for colouring, and treatments or coatings may be applied to smooth surfaces for such purposes as preventing fungus growth, providing attractive appearance or protecting against acid attack. The resistance of roofing products to external fire is given as 'P 60', as defined in the current edition of BS 476, Part 3 (corresponding to 'Ext. S. AA' in BS 476, Part 3, 1958), signifying that the material passes a preliminary ignition test and that fire does not penetrate in less than one hour. There is, however, a tendency for asbestos cement to shatter under the intense heat of an internal fire, so that roofing or cladding should be protected by lining sheets or panels in conjunction with insulation. All tiles and sheets for external uses are required to comply with permeability and frost requirements. Specifications for the various sheet materials are covered by BS 690.

Flat sheets may be used for such applications as side claddings, partition and ceiling linings, and infill panels in curtain walling, fully compressed sheets being used where high-quality surface finish or impact-resistance is required. Fully-compressed sheets may also be used as shuttering for concrete, though account should be taken, when fixing, of the fibre direction in the sheet, since strength is lower at right angles to the fibre direction. In greater thicknesses (up to 25 mm), the material may be used for window sills, window boards and bench tops.

Corrugated sheets have the advantage of increased rigidity for a given sheet thickness, so that they are particularly suited to roofing and cladding of larger industrial and agricultural buildings.

Sheet can also be used in the form of slates for roofing, producing a very even covering of highly uniform colour. Slates are centre-nailed and the fully-compressed form, which are of lower weight and thickness than semi-compressed slates, are additionally restrained by copper disc rivets at the tail of each tile. Efflorescence can be a problem initially if the uncoated sides of slates become wet.

Low-density insulating boards and wallboards to BS 3536

Insulating boards have a density of not more than $900 \, kg/m^3$ and thermal conductivity not more than $0.175 \, W/m \, °C$. They may be used as surface membranes in roofs, walls, ceilings, partitions and ducting, or as protection to structural steel.

Wall boards are tougher than insulating boards, having densities in the range 900 to $1450 \, kg/m^3$ and thermal conductivity not greater than $0.36 \, W/m \, °C$. They may be used where greater mechanical resistance is required, such as on doors or as overlays for floors.

Sprayed asbestos

Although sprayed asbestos has been extremely effective as a means of providing fire-protection to structural steelwork and concrete, its use has now virtually ceased on account of the health hazard it poses. The former British Standard, BS 3590, has been withdrawn and protection is now provided by the preformed insulating boards and wallboards described above. It is advisable to seal or replace any existing sprayed asbestos coatings to minimise the dust hazard.

Problems

2.1 Describe how their basic molecular shape is responsible for properties of pure silica, mica, clays and asbestos.

2.2 Explain the following properties of clays:
(a) their slippery nature when wet
(b) their cohesive nature when uniformly damp
(c) the tendency to compact most efficiently at a certain moisture content
(d) their shrinkage and increased strength on drying
(e) the difficulty involved in draining them.

2.3 Tests carried out on a certain type of brick of average length 220 mm and average width 106 mm showed that its average compressive load was 1830 kN. After 5 hours boiling in water, the average mass increased from 2.94 to 3.05 kg. Use BS 3921 to classify the brick.

2.4 A brick is required for use in a parapet wall where appearance is important and where severe exposure is likely. Describe some simple tests which could be made to ascertain its suitability.

2.5 What do you consider to be the prospects of brickwork in the future? Give suggestions as to what developments will be necessary to ensure maximum potential.

2.6 Suggest possible modes of failure in a brick wall or pier. Explain why the mortar does not have to be as strong as the bricks themselves. (See also Ch. 3.)

2.7 Give four possible sources of sulphates in brickwork and explain how they may affect:
(a) the bricks
(b) the mortar.

2.8 Discuss the deterioration of building fabrics due to crystallisation.

2.9 Discuss the relative properties and uses of limestone and granite.

2.10 What properties of glass cause it to be regarded as a supercooled liquid? Describe the inherent weakness in glass and explain how it may be overcome.

2.11 Discuss how the structure of asbestos is responsible for the following properties:
(a) tensile strength
(b) resistance to fire
(c) resistance to heat conduction.

Give applications of the material based on each property.

2.12 Describe how, by appropriate design and use of glass and asbestos, a timber-framed glazed door could be made resistant to radiant heat and flame-penetration.

References

1. Herman Salmang, *Ceramics*. Butterworths, 1961.
2. R. N. Young and B. P. Warkentin, *Introduction to Soil Behaviour*. Macmillan, 1966.
3. *Fullers' Earth Products*. Fullers' Earth Union Ltd, Redhill, Surrey.
4. L. Casagrande, *The Application of Electro-osmosis to Practical Problems in Foundations and Earthworks*. HMSO, 1947 (National Building Studies Paper No. 30).
5. National Brick Advisory Council, HMSO, 1950 (Paper No. 5).
6. BRE Digests on bricks, stones, asbestos, cement etc.

7. H. O'Neill, *Stones for Building*. Heinemann, 1965.

8. D. B. Honeybourne, *Laboratory Freezing Test for Natural Building Stone*. BRS Miscellaneous Paper No. 3, 1965.

9. *Glass*. Technical information from Pilkington Bros. Ltd, St Helens.

10. *Asbestos*. Technical information from Turner Asbestos Cement Ltd.

Relevant British Standards

BS 65 & 540: Part 1: 1971. *Clay drain and sewerpipes, including surface water pipes and fittings.*

BS 187: 1978. *Calcium silicate (sandlime and flint lime bricks).*

BS 402: Part 2: 1979. *Clay plain roofing tiles and fittings.*

BS 680: Part 2: 1971. *Roofing slates.*

BS 690: *Asbestos cement slates and sheets.*

BS 3536: Part 2: 1974. *Asbestos insulating boards and asbestos wallboards.*

BS 3717: 1972. *Asbestos-cement decking.*

BS 3921: 1974. *Clay bricks and blocks.*

BS 4036: 1966. *Asbestos cement fully-compressed flat sheets.*

Chapter 3

Cement and concrete

Concrete is a mixture of aggregates, cement and water. On mixing, the latter two materials form a matrix which encloses and fixes the aggregate, producing strength. Other materials may be used instead of, or as well as, the above (e.g. additives – substances added during manufacture of cement, or admixtures – substances added during mixing of the concrete). It is important that properties of all constituent materials are understood in order to predict the likely performance of hardened concrete. Hence, these materials are discussed first.

Cements

The vast majority of cements used for concrete are hydraulic, that is, they set solely by chemical reaction with water. Portland cements are most widely used, although two other types – high-alumina and super-sulphated cement – are also worthy of mention.

Portland cements

These were first so named owing to the similarity to Portland stone of concretes made with them. There are many types of Portland cement produced by variants in raw materials or in the manufacturing process. The most common type is known as 'ordinary Portland cement'.

Manufacture of ordinary Portland cement

The basic raw materials for ordinary Portland cement are clay or shale and calcium carbonate, in the form of chalk or limestone (Most clays consist chiefly of silica, SiO_2, abbreviated 'S', alumina, A_2O_3, abbreviated 'A' and some iron oxide, Fe_2O_3, abbreviated 'F'.) The materials, in approximate proportions 80 per cent calcium carbonate and 20 per cent clay or shale, are finely ground, mixed and heated together to a temperature of 1400 to 1500 °C in a rotary kiln, which is inclined slightly so that, on rotation, the material passes gradually from one end to the other. The kiln is heated by powdered coal, injected at the lower end. As the constituents pass down the kiln, the temperature rises, causing dehydration of raw materials by 400 °C. The calcium carbonate decomposes to form calcium oxide, (abbreviated 'C') by about 900 °C and, as the temperature increases further, the compounds dicalcium silicate (C_2S), tricalcium aluminate (C_3A) and tetracalcium aluminoferrite (C_4AF) are formed. The latter materials fuse together and further reaction between them, C_2S and free lime produces a fourth compound, tricalcium silicate (C_2S).

The C_3A and C_4AF form the matrix and the other two compounds occur as crystals within the matrix. On cooling, a clinker is formed. Figure 3.1. shows a sample of such clinker, ground, polished and etched, crystals of C_2S and C_3S being visible against the glassy background of C_3A and C_4AF. About 5 per cent of gypsum is added and the two are ground together to form a fine powder, which is Portland cement. The properties of the four chief compounds in cement are as follows:

Tricalcium aluminate (C_3A)
This combines rapidly with water and is, therefore, chiefly responsible for the initial setting, the rate of setting of the cement being controlled according to the amount of gypsum present. Considerable heat is evolved (870 J/g) and the solid hydrate material is also chemically attacked by sulphates. It has little cementing value but behaves as a flux during manufacture, enabling C_2S and C_3S to form at lower temperatures. It constitutes about 10 per cent of ordinary Portland cement.

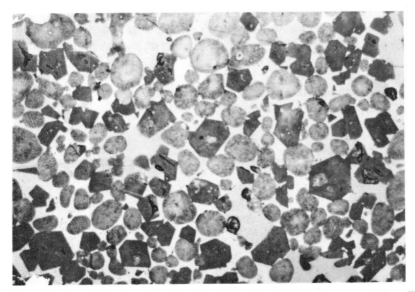

Fig. 3.1 Magnified view of etched polished section of Portland-cement clinker. The dark angular material is tricalcium silicate, the rounded lighter material, dicalcium silicate, and the lighter background, tricalcium aluminate. Some darker background material is visible. This is tetracalcium aluminoferrite

Tetracalcium aluminoferrite (C_4AF)
This is the only compound in cement containing iron, hence, the quantity produced depends only on the iron content of the clay. Ordinary Portland cement contains about 10 per cent of C_4AF. The hydration of the compound is controlled, as with C_3A, by the gypsum present, a slow set occurring with heat evolution of 420 J/g. The material contributes little to long-term strength but is expensive to remove and, like C_3A, is valuable as a flux during manufacture of the cement. It is responsible for the grey colour of cements.

Tricalcium silicate (C_3S)
This hydrates quickly on adding water, with high heat evolution (500 J/g). It occupies between 30 and 60 per cent by weight of Portland cement. It is mainly responsible for early strength (for example, at seven days).

Dicalcium silicate (C_2S)
This hydrates slowly with a heat evolution of 260 J/g. It occupies between 15 and 35 per cent of ordinary Portland cement. It is largely responsible for the ultimate strength of the cement.

Factors affecting the properties of Portland cement (BS 12)

Modern construction methods often involve exacting specifications for concrete and it is, therefore, of prime importance that the properties of the cement used be known and that they be as consistent as possible. The nature of the raw materials for cement (including coal used for firing) is such that there is an inherent difficulty in producing uniform quality, since variations are bound to occur, to some degree, from day to day as well as on a long-term basis. However, a considerable amount can be done to minimise variations in cement properties and, when these do occur, it is usually possible to ascertain them either by private testing or by contacting the cement manufacturer on a day-to-day basis, if necessary. The properties of cement are affected chiefly by its chemical composition and its fineness.

1. Chemical composition
The relative proportions of the four compounds already described depend on the relative proportions of the four constituent compounds, calcium oxide, silica, alumina and ferrite which, in turn, depend on the relative proportions of clay and limestone, and the balance of minerals within the clay. Bogue has produced equations which enable the quantities of the four compounds to be calculated:

per cent C_4AF = 3.04 (per cent F)
per cent C_3A = 2.65 (per cent A) − 1.69 (per cent F).
per cent C_2S = 8.60 (per cent S) − 3.07 (per cent C) + 5.10 (per cent A)
      + 1.08 (per cent F)
per cent C_3S = 4.07 (per cent C) − 7.60 (per cent S) − 1.43 (per cent F)
      − 6.72 (per cent A)

Note that the C_4AF, the only compound containing iron, is determined completely by the percentage of F. The percentage of C_3A is determined by the alumina content but with a deduction due to the alumina taken up by the C_4AF. The C_2S and the C_3S equations are more complex but note that, on adding the equations:

per cent C_4AF + per cent C_3A + per cent C_2S + per cent C_3S =
per cent F + per cent A + per cent S + per cent C (approximately)

The Bogue equations are useful, since the results of a normal chemical analysis of cements give the percentages of calcium oxide, silica, alumina and ferrite. They also enable the effect to be determined of variations in the relative proportions of limestone and clay. For example, if the calcium oxide content increases by 1 per cent, silica would decrease by about 0.7 per cent, alumina by 0.2 per cent and ferrite by 0.1 per cent, so that the change in C_2S is $8.60 \times (-0.7) - 3.07 \times (1) + 5.10 \times (-0.2) + 1.08 (-0.1) = -10.2$ per cent. A similar increase of C_3S occurs and these changes will have a significant effect on the properties of the cement. Hence, it is essential that the balance between limestone and clay be very carefully controlled.

Other methods of chemical analysis, such as microscopic examination of etched, polished sections of cement clinker, enable the compounds in cement to be measured directly.

British Standard 12 lays down limits for the proportion of calcium oxide to the silica, alumina and ferrite; and for combustible or acid-soluble impurities and magnesia (magnesium oxide) which may cause expansion (unsoundness) of cement paste on hydration. If free lime in crystallised form in the cement clinker is present, this could also lead to unsoundness and, since this is not easy to distinguish from the large quantity of chemically combined lime in cement, a separate soundness test for it is required by BS 12. The expansion of a pat of hydrated cement after a period of boiling is measured, boiling being essential to accelerate hydration of the lime. (This test does not detect magnesia, hence, the separate requirement for the latter.) An excess of gypsum could also cause unsoundness, so that BS 12 specifies limits for this, depending on the percentage of tricalcium aluminate present.

The chemical composition of cement affects also the setting time and strength of cements, but, since other factors also are involved, BS 12 measures these properties directly rather than in terms of the four main compounds described above. (In any case, results using the Bogue equations, which are based on equilibrium between the four compounds in crystallised form, are subject to errors, since the compounds C_3A and C_4AF, which were formerly liquid, do not crystallise completely. There is always a proportion of 'glass' in the cement clinker and this affects the proportions of C_2S and C_3S.) An initial and final setting time are defined empirically using a cement paste of standard consistency. The initial setting time should not be less than 45 minutes for ordinary Portland or rapid-hardening Portland cement, a period related to the time after mixing required for placing, compaction and finishing of concrete. The final setting time should not be more than 10 hours. Strength tests on mortar cubes in compression are described. Alternatively, if suitable aggregates are available, 100 mm concrete cubes may be used for the compression test.

2. *Fineness*
The hydration of cement is a process which involves penetration of water into cement particles to produce a cement 'gel'. Hence, a finer ground cement will hydrate more quickly and produce earlier strength. At the same time, more gypsum is essential to combat the extra C_3A revealed by the greater surface area of cement particles. Since, on drying, cement gel shrinks, finer cements will correspondingly exhibit greater initial drying shrinkage at an early age. Final strength and shrinkage values are, however, similar to those of ordinary Portland cement. Fineness is measured by the term 'specific surface', the average surface area of cement in m^2/kg. It is obtained according to BS 12 by measurements of the permeability to air of a compacted cement bed of standard thickness, a finer cement being less permeable. Ordinary Portland cement is required to have a specific surface of not less than $225 \, m^2/kg$; rapid-hardening Portland cement, not less than $325 \, m^2/kg$.

Other types of Portland cement

Rapid-hardening Portland cement
This is covered by BS 12, being essentially different from ordinary Portland cement only in respect of fineness and strength requirements. It attains a strength approximately 50 per cent higher than ordinary Portland cement at three days, though long-term strengths are similar. Accompanying the rapid early strength gain is a considerable evolution of heat so that rapid-hardening Portland cement is often used in cold weather to assist in development of maturity. However, on the same account, it should not be used in mass concrete, where the heat concentration would cause a reduction in strength due to thermal stressses.

Ultra-rapid-hardening cements, which are very finely ground, are also on the market, the same arguments as above applying but to a greater degree. In addition, such a high degree of fineness in the cement tends to reduce workability and, therefore, there will be some loss of strength if the water content of the concrete is increased to compensate.

Extra-rapid-hardening Portland cement
This consists of rapid-hardening Portland cement with approximately 2 per cent of calcium chloride. However, on account of the corrosive effects of the latter when used in reinforced or prestressed concrete, this cement is no longer available.

Low-heat cement (BS 1370)
This contains relatively small percentages of the compounds C_3S and C_3A which have the greatest heat evolution. BS 1370 requires a heat output of not more than

250 J/g by 7 days and 290 J/g by 28 days. The rate of gain of strength is lower but this cement has an ultimate strength similar to that of ordinary Portland cement and is suitable for mass construction where heat concentration must be avoided. Concretes of high cement content must not, of course, be employed – they would negate the effect of the low-heat cement. Its fineness, as required by BS 1370, must not be less than $275\,m^2/kg$ in order to ensure satisfactory strength development. Note that, due to the small amount of C_3A, sulphate resistance of this cement is greater than that of ordinary Portland cement.

Sulphate-resisting Portland cement (BS 4027)

Sulphate attack is due primarily to the effect of sulphates in solution on C_3A. (See 'Hydration of cement'.) Hence, the sulphate resistance of a cement will improve as the quantity of C_3A decreases, a maximum content of 3.5 per cent being specified in BS 4027. This can be achieved by addition of iron ore to the raw materials so that more C_4AF is produced and the alumina is used up in this way instead of forming C_3A. In other respects, sulphate-resisting cement is similar to ordinary Portland cement, although minimum fineness is $250\,m^2/kg$. Note that even concrete made with sulphate-resisting Portland cement may be attacked physically by sulphates if porous, since, on drying, crystallisation will take place inside the concrete, causing expansion and disruption. Hence, the use of sulphate-resisting cement is no substitute for the production of dense, non-porous concrete.

Portland blast-furnace cement (BS 146)

This consists of Portland cement clinker and gypsum, ground together, with up to 65 per cent of quenched blast-furnace slag, which contains lime, silica and alumina. The hydration of the Portland cement initiates that of the latter, producing a strength progression similar to that of ordinary Portland cement, though early strengths may be lower, so that adequate curing is essential. Portland blast-furnace cement has a higher sulphate resistance than ordinary Portland cement, hence, its use in sulphate soils and for construction in or near the sea. A low-heat form of Portland blast-furnace cement is available and is covered by BS 4246. The heat output and strength development are similar to those of low-heat Portland cement.

White cement

This is made using china clay, which contains very little iron, the latter being responsible for the grey colour of ordinary cement. White Portland cement is one of the most expensive Portland cements, since there are few geographic locations where china clay is found, and modifications to the method of firing and grinding are required. In the absence of C_4AF, other fluxes may be used to assist in manufacture. The cement conforms to BS 12, though long-term strength is likely to be lower than that of ordinary Portland cement. White cement is used for the production of white or coloured concrete.

Hydrophobic Portland cement
This is ordinary Portland cement to which a small percentage of ground-in water repellent, such as oleic acid, is added. Such cements can be stored for a considerable time in damp atmospheres without subsequent deterioration. On mixing, the acid coating breaks down and behaves as an air-entraining agent but mixing time should normally be about 25 per cent longer than for ordinary Portland cement. Early strength development of concretes using such cements is slightly reduced.

Cements other than Portland cements

High-alumina cement (BS 915)
The cement was first developed in France, in response to the need for a concrete which would resist attack by sulphates. It is made by heating a mixture of limestone or chalk and bauxite (aluminium ore) in a special furnace, heated by powdered coal to a temperature of about 1600 °C. This causes complete fusion of materials. Cooling produces a clinker which is ground to give a cement with slightly lower specific surface than that of ordinary Portland cement.

The predominant compound in high-alumina cements is CA (monocalcium aluminate), though compounds with other proportions of calcium oxide and alumina also exist, together with small proportions of iron, silicon, titanium and magnesium oxides.

On hydration of the cement, the chief compound produced is calcium aluminate decahydrate, CAH_{10}. Setting is not rapid (BS 915 requires an initial setting time of not less than two hours). However, once setting commences, strength development is much quicker than with Portland cements, the final set being not more than two hours after the initial set, the required strength of mortar cubes at 24 hours being 41 N/mm^2 minimum. Figure 3.2 shows comparative strength developments of a concrete mix with gravel aggregate, using various Portland cements and high-alumina cement at a water/cement ratio of 0.6.

There is considerable heat evolution so that water immersion or spray is necessary during the early stages to prevent excessive temperature rise. Alternatively, this heat could offset the effect of placing the concrete in sub-zero temperatures. The shrinkage of high-alumina-cement concrete is similar to that of ordinary Portland-cement concrete.

If the temperature of high-alumina cement hydrate is allowed to rise above about 25 °C in the presence of high humidity, the CAH_{10} becomes unstable, changing gradually into C_3AH_6 (tricalcium aluminate hexahydrate) and AH_3 (aluminium hydroxide), and this process may occur at any stage in its life. These changes are accompanied by the formation of small pores in the cement, so that the resulting hydrate has, consequently, decreased strength and increased permeability. The process is known as conversion but the reduction in strength can be avoided if some unhydrated cement is still present during conditions of conversion, so that pores are filled with new hydrates as they are formed. The loss

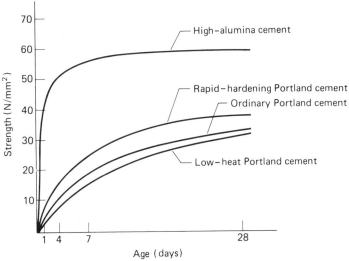

Fig. 3.2   Strength development of gravel-aggregate concretes using various cements at a water/cement ratio of 0.6

of strength depends also on the rate of conversion, rapid conversion resulting in a strength loss of 40 to 45 per cent and slow conversion (which may occur in normal environmental conditions) resulting in a strength loss of about 35 per cent. It is quite likely that concrete which is allowed to overheat during the first 24 hours could convert relatively rapidly at this stage.

A further problem resulting from conversion is that high-alumina-cement concrete becomes more susceptible to chemical attack and, particularly, sulphates or alkalis, which might be leached out of neighbouring materials. Hence, high-alumina cement, which for a number of years enjoyed widespread use in precast units of all kinds, is now withdrawn from structural use in the UK.

A variety of other applications exists for high-alumina cement, based predominantly on the superior chemical resistance of the material. As a precaution against the effects of conversion, concretes of low water/cement ratio are, nevertheless, recommended, careful attention being paid to compaction. Although high-alumina cement requires a water/cement ratio of about 0.5 for complete hydration, values below this do not lead to reduced strength, since there is chemical bonding between hydrated and unhydrated parts of cement grains. Also, at any given water/cement ratio, less free water will remain after hydration.

A further important use of high-alumina cement is as a refractory cement since, on desiccation by heat, a ceramic bond is developed which is retained at temperatures of up to 1300 °C. The cement is used in lightweight concrete for flue linings.

Mixtures of high-alumina cement and ordinary Portland cement   The setting time of such mixtures is reduced to a degree dependent on their proportions, a very rapid 'flash set' taking place when between 30 per cent and 80 per cent high-alumina cement is used. This is thought to be due to rapid setting of the Portland cement fraction owing to chemical combination of its retarder, gypsum, with calcium aluminate hydrates from the high-alumina cement. The ultimate strength of such pastes increases with the percentage of high-alumina cement but ultimate strengths are lower than those of ordinary Portland cement, unless at least 75 per cent high-alumina cement is used. Mixtures may be useful when a very rapid set is required, for example, in sealing leaks and for making rapid fixings into masonry, but mixing of these cements is not generally recommended.

Super-sulphated cement (BS 4248)
This is made from granulated blast-furnace slag, calcium sulphate (hence the name) and a small percentage of Portland cement clinker which behaves as an activator. The cement is highly resistant to sulphates and has a low heat output so that it may be used in mass concrete even in tropical conditions. The ultimate strength is similar to that of ordinary Portland cement. Water/cement ratios less than 0.4 should not be used, since the cement has a high water requirement. Richer mixes than would be required with ordinary Portland cement are, therefore, essential for a given strength and workability. Super-sulphated cement is not suitable for steam curing since this retards its strength development. It must be stored dry. The cement is no longer manufactured in the UK, since sulphate-resisting Portland cement is more competitive in cost.

Hydration of Portland cement

This is a complex and gradual process involving the reaction of water, initially with surface layers only of the cement, to form a hydrated matrix, further hydration continuing by the movement of water through this matrix. (An indication of the very slow penetration of water into cement is given by the fact that cement clinker may, before grinding, be stored in bulk in the open air with no significant deterioration.)

Eventually, all voids in the cement paste may become filled with cement hydrate, provided the water/cement ratio is sufficiently low. The chief compounds which contribute to strength in Portland cements are C_2S and C_3S. They combine with water as follows:

$$2(2CaOSiO_2) + 4H_2O \longrightarrow 3CaO.2SiO_2.3H_2O + Ca(OH)_2$$
$$\text{tobermorite gel}$$
$$\text{and} \quad 2(3CaOSiO_2) + 6H_2O \longrightarrow 3CaO.2SiO_2.3H_2O + 3Ca(OH)_2$$

(In these equations, the full formula for calcium silicates has been used to enable the equations to be balanced.) Note that calcium hydroxide is produced in each case – in the form of smooth, parallel, platy crystals. It would be wrong to regard these reactions as a complete description of hydration of the calcium silicates. Various compounds in the C-S-H system are possible, depending on ratios of constituents, prevailing conditions and time, the various products possibly having quite different crystal structures. The products exist in the form of extremely small crystals connected together to form a solid matrix and known as a 'gel', implying that there is no long-range order as in, say, metallic crystals. The actual form of the gel depends on a number of factors, such as composition of the cement grains: crystals may exist as fibres up to 2μm in length, as a honeycomb ('reticular') network, or as flattened or grainy particles. In each case, the dimensions are very small and a characteristic of cement gel is its consequent very high specific surface (about $200\,000\,m^2/kg$ compared with approximately $300\,m^2/kg$ for unhydrated ordinary Portland cement). The term 'tobermorite gel' has been used to describe the calcium silicate hydrates, since tobermorite is the nearest naturally occurring mineral to cement gel but, in general, it would be inaccurate to use this term as a description of hydrated calcium silicates, owing to the various forms of the latter.

The hydration of C_3A is modified by the gypsum added during manufacture. Calcium sulphoaluminate (ettringite), which has a high sulphate content, is first formed but, as more C_3A dissolves, the concentration of the sulphate radical decreases and, eventually, a calcium aluminate monosulphate hydrate is formed. There may, in fact, be a sudden emission of heat some hours after hydration begins, if, when all the gypsum is consumed, there is some remaining tricalcium aluminate which will hydrate quickly. The monosulphate will revert to ettringite in the presence of sulphates, causing expansion and disruption of the hardened cement.

C_4AF also forms a calcium aluminate hydrate, the iron forming a separate compound.

Water in hydrated cement
It is clear from the above that water exists, chemically bound, in hydrated cement, mainly in the form of calcium silicate and calcium aluminate hydrates. However, this is not the only water involved with the cement gel since the latter, owing to its very high specific surface, adsorbs water strongly. The spaces in which this water exists are known as 'gel pores' and occupy about 28 per cent of the total gel volume. Hence, although, in theory, a given mass of cement requires only 25 per cent approximately of its mass of water for complete hydration, in practice, adsorbed water in the gel is not available for hydration and fully hydrated cement gel corresponds to a water/cement ratio of about 0.42. Therefore, at low water/cement ratios, hydration can never fully occur. This is, however, not necessarily a disadvantage from a strength point of view, since the bonding in unhydrated cement particles is more powerful than that in the cement gel and there is also strong bonding between hydrated and unhydrated parts of a cement particle such that, in normal concrete, strength increases even as water/cement ratios decrease to values as low as 0.25, provided full compaction is achieved. It might be thought at first that, in saturated concrete, cement pastes of low water/cement ratio would be able to hydrate using 'external' water, available during curing, but this may not be possible, since cement hydrate expands by

about 114 per cent of its former volume – hence, it must occupy at least some of the space previously occupied by the water and there may, therefore, be insufficient room for the hydration products when low water/cement ratios are used. For example, 1 g of cement (relative density = 3.15) occupies about 0.318 ml before hydration and, therefore, after hydration approximately:

$$0.318 + 0.318 \times \frac{114}{100} = 0.68 \, \text{ml}$$

For this reason, 0.362 ml of water, corresponding to a water/cement ratio of 0.36, will be required to provide the space for expansion (though this is insufficient to cause complete hydration). At water/cement ratios over 0.36 correspondingly, there will be extra space around the cement gel, known as capillary pores, and it is through these that water for further hydration passes. Capillary pores must contain water if hydration is to continue and, since a paste of 0.42 water/cement ratio will contain capillary pores, complete hydration cannot take place unless extra water is available during curing to fill them. Full hydration, in fact, requires a water/cement ratio of about 0.5 or greater.

The rate of hydration of cement decreases exponentially with time and, even in the presence of ample water, it is doubtful whether the process ever reaches completion, since continued hydration depends on penetration of ions through the hydrated gel to the unhydrated cement kernel. At water/cement ratios of about 0.7, depending on the fineness of the cement, the capillary pores remain interconnected and continuous, even in fully hydrated cement, so that the resulting concrete is permeable. At a water/cement ratio of 0.4, on the other hand, the cement paste becomes largely impermeable at an age of about 3 days. The effect of increasing water/cement ratio on the porosity and permeability of mature concrete is illustrated in Fig. 3.3. The effect of water/cement ratio may be summarised as follows:

water/cement ratio below 0.23: insufficient water for complete chemical combination.

water/cement ratio 0.23–0.36: sufficient water for chemical combination but hydration does not take place fully because:

(i) there is insufficient water for gel pores to fill (unless further water is available during curing)
(ii) there is insufficient space for the cement gel.

water/cement ratio 0.36–0.42: hydration may take place completely only if extra water is available during curing (see Fig. 3.4).

water/cement ratio 0.42: there is sufficient water for hydration and gel pore water but, in practice, since capillary pores must contain water for the hydration process to continue, a value of 0.5 is necessary unless water is available during curing. At water/cement ratios over 0.7, the cement paste remains permeable indefinitely.

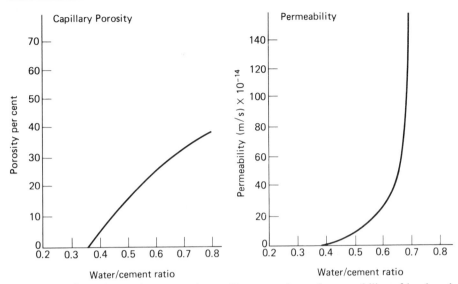

Fig. 3.3 Effect of water/cement ratio, capillary porosity and permeability of hardened cement paste. Permeability rises rapidly when there are sufficient pores to produce continuous capillaries in the cement paste

Strength of hardened cement paste

The atoms within each platelet or fibre of cement gel are, of course, bonded by co-valent or ionic bonds as in clay platelets. For the cement to have strength, however, these platelets themselves must be bonded together. The bonding here is thought to be of two types – van der Waals' bonds, due to the very small distances between platelets or fibres, and further 'primary' bonds also. The former are responsible for the strong adsorption of water and the latter are essential to limit the swelling of hardened cement paste which tends to occur on adsorption of water. Without the existence of these primary interparticle bonds, cement would disintegrate like clay on soaking in water. The primary bonds are responsible to a large degree for the strength of cement paste but the van der Waals' bonds are important in explaining moisture movement, thermal movement, shrinkage and creep of concrete.

The low tensile strength of cement paste relative to its compressive strength is explained using the same arguments as for ceramics, together with the fact that, in the damp or wet state, the internal pressure exerted by adsorbed water tends to assist tensile stresses and oppose compressive stresses. As a consequence, the tensile strength of cement products is lower when they are wet.

Aggregates for concrete

Aggregates are used in almost all concretes because they reduce the cost of the

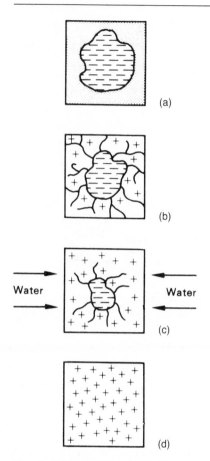

Fig. 3.4 Hydration of cement as a water/cement ratio of 0.36, assuming extra water to be available during curing (the process would take some years to complete); (a) Unhydrated cement and water; (b) Hydrated cement containing capillary pores. Unhydrated cement kernel; (c) Extra water required to fill capillary pores so that hydration can continue; (d) Cement completely hydrated

material considerably but also because they often result in an improved product. For example, shrinkage and thermal movement of most concretes are less than those of neat cement paste and properties such as abrasion-resistance are often better. In a typical 1:2:4 mix using aggregates of relative density 2.5, about 75 per cent of the total volume is occupied by fine and coarse aggregates and, in lean-mix concrete, this figure may be as high as 85 per cent.

Types of aggregate

The great majority of aggregates used for concrete are obtained from natural sources, either in the form of rock which is crushed or gravel which may be crushed or simply screened (i.e. large sizes removed) before use. In any particular area, only one type of aggregate usually occurs locally and, due to high costs of transportation of aggregate, normal concrete will be made with this type.

Natural aggregates are now briefly classified petrologically, since there are some important properties which are specific to the various groups. The simplest means of classification is according to the mode of formation of the rocks concerned.

Rocks which were at one time molten are described as igneous. Examples are granite and basalt, and the flint group of aggregates is igneous in origin, the rock being broken up and often worn smooth by glacial action. When fine particles become cemented together over a period of time, the resultant rock is described as sedimentary, limestone and sandstone being of this type. Limestone has several characteristic properties – it results in a concrete with a relatively low coefficient of thermal expansion and also excellent fire-resistance. Abrasion-resistance, conversely, is not generally as good as that of other aggregate types. Sandstones vary greatly according to source, some sandstones being of high strength but others being less strong and exhibiting significant moisture movement, which is not found in aggregates generally. Where stones have been formed or modified by heat and pressure, a metamorphic rock is produced. The most important of these is marble, which is formed from limestone and is widely used for its decorative effect, for example, in terrazzo flooring.

Artificial aggregates may be manufactured from natural or waste materials and their use, mainly in the form of lightweight aggregates, is rapidly increasing. They are described under the heading of 'Lightweight concrete'.

Aggregate properties and their effect on the properties of concrete

Density

Aggregate densities may vary within wide limits, according to the type of material. Some lightweight aggregates have densities below $500 \, \text{kg/m}^3$, while others, such as magnetite, have solid densities of over $7000 \, \text{kg/m}^3$. In general, natural aggregates having solid densities in the region of $2600 \, \text{kg/m}^3$ are most widely used, the former finding application where low- or high-density concretes are required.

The solid density of aggregates is now described by the term 'relative density' (formerly, specific gravity), which is the ratio of the density of the aggregate to that of water. It is often quite important to have an accurate knowledge of aggregate density – for example, it affects the yield of a mix which is batched by weight and, in some types of concrete, the theoretical density of the compacted material must be calculated. Reference will, therefore, be made to the three definitions of relative density which arise according to the treatment of voids in the aggregate. An aggregate particle has been drawn three times in Fig. 3.5, the pores to which water has access being represented, for simplicity, as a single

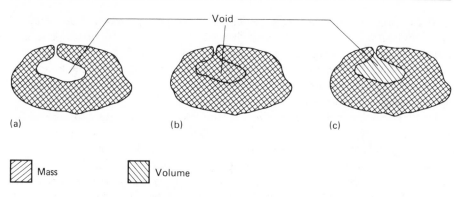

Fig. 3.5 Representation of three methods of measuring relative density of aggregate: (a) Apparent; (b) Saturated, surface dry; (c) Oven-dry

enclosure in the particle. The definitions are:

$$\text{Apparent relative density} = \frac{\text{Mass of dry aggregate}}{\text{Solid volume of aggregate}}$$

$$\text{Saturated surface dry relative density} = \frac{\text{Mass of aggregate} + \text{water in pores}}{\text{Volume of aggregate including pores}}$$

$$\text{Oven-dry relative density} = \frac{\text{Mass of dry aggregate}}{\text{Volume of aggregate including pores}}$$

The apparent relative density is highest, since permeable voids are, in effect, treated as external to the aggregate. The term is used for the calculation of theoretical dry density in tests for lean concrete for road-bases. The saturated, surface-dry state is normally used for mix design purposes. The lowest value resulting from the 'oven-dry' formula would be used to predict the density of the hardened concrete in the dry state.

Maximum size

Aggregates are classified as coarse aggregate if they are largely retained on a 5 mm mesh sieve and fine aggregate if the majority pass a 5 mm sieve. The term 'sand' is normally reserved for fine aggregate resulting from the natural disintegration of rock. The maximum size of aggregate to be used in concrete is governed mainly by the dimensions of the structure for which it is required. As a general rule, the largest size of aggregate should not exceed 25 per cent of the minimum dimension in the structure, particular care being taken with heavily reinforced concrete. In most constructional engineering and building applications, the normal maximum aggregate size is 20 mm, while in roads it may be 40 mm, and larger still in mass construction, such as dams. In the latter, occasional large lumps of rock or masonry known as 'plums' are included in addition to the mixed concrete, though these should not occupy more than about 30 per cent of the total volume of concrete. Since increasing the maximum size of aggregate reduces the surface area of aggregate to be bonded in a given volume, the cement and water requirement for a given strength may be reduced, producing a more economical mix. In mass concrete, this will reduce the heat production of the concrete though, above about 40 mm maximum size, concretes tend to become weaker, due to failure of the now heavily stressed bonds between aggregate and cement paste. The fine aggregate should also be 'matched' to the maximum size of coarse aggregate: for example, a fine aggregate with fine grading combined with a large coarse aggregate may lead to a concrete of low cohesion.

Shape
This may vary between 'rounded' (implying water-worn material) to 'angular' (material with clearly-defined edges, produced by crushing). Particles between these extremes would be classed as 'irregular', that is, having rounded edges. In normal concretes, angular material tends to produce concrete of lower workability but higher strength for a given water/cement ratio. In high-strength concrete, workability is not affected in this way – some angular aggregates may produce higher workability than rounded aggregates. Other possible shapes include 'flaky' and 'elongated' but the non-isotropic and relatively high specific surface of these detracts from their value as aggregates for concrete.

Surface texture
The two extremes are 'rough' or 'honeycombed' textures, which will provide an extremely good key to cement, and 'glassy' surfaces which do not form a strong bond with cement. Intermediate possibilities are 'smooth' or 'granular'. Although rougher surfaces will tend to reduce workability, they also tend to result in increased strength – subject, of course, to the aggregate being itself satisfactory in other respects.

Crushing strength
There is little advantage in using rich concrete mixes containing weak aggregates, since clearly the latter, which generally have low 'E' values, will take only a small stress under load, the cement paste being thus overstressed and failing at low loads. Similarly, a high-strength aggregate, such as crushed granite, would be best utilised where a high-strength concrete is required: the extra cost of such materials would be of little benefit in the medium-strength range. A guide to the suitability of a particular aggregate from the strength point of view may be obtained by inspection of crushed concrete cubes made with that aggregate. If a significant number of fractured aggregate particles is visible (say, more than about 25 per cent), then it is likely that improved strength would be obtained with stronger aggregate. In practice, there is, of course, the question of availability of stronger material and it may be more economical to provide more cement per unit volume in a mix than to transport stronger aggregates over considerable distances.

Grading

This term is used to describe the relative proportions of various particle sizes between the nominal maximum aggregate size and the smallest material present, which passes a 150-μm sieve. The object of grading aggregates is to produce concrete with satisfactory plastic properties (workability, cohesion and resistance to bleeding), as well as satisfactory hardened properties (strength, voids content, durability and surface finish), using as little cement as possible. The importance of grading may be illustrated by referring to an opposite extreme, for example, concrete made with marbles of a single size. If marbles were packed perfectly into a given volume, they would occupy a maximum of 74 per cent of the total volume. Supposing such a figure to be unlikely in practice, take a value of 70 per cent. This would imply voids of 30 per cent, requiring this total percentage of water/cement mortar to occupy them. Assuming a water/cement ratio of 0.5 and relative densities of 1 and 3 respectively, 0.33 parts by volume of cement would correspond to $0.5 + 0.33 = 0.83$ parts by volume of mortar. Hence, the percentage cement and water to occupy, say, 30 parts of void would be:

$$30 \times \frac{0.33}{0.83} = 11.9 \text{ parts cement and 18.1 parts water}$$

By volume, the mix would be

70:11.9:18.1
aggregate : cement : water

By mass, the mix would be approximately:

175:35.7:18.1 assuming relative density of aggregate = 2.5

This implies an aggregate/cement ratio of about 5:1 which does not represent an extremely rich mix and, assuming the cement fully hydrates, this should produce a non-porous concrete. Such a mix would, however, be totally unsuitable for concrete because:

(a) The cement paste would bleed (that is, the cement particles would settle out of the water, due to their relatively high relative density
(b) it would be impossible to obtain a finish on the concrete surface
(c) the large areas of neat aggregate and cement would cause severe shrinkage, movement and loading stresses at interfaces

A graded aggregate will tend to overcome these problems to a degree dependent on the type of grading. Hence, a well-graded aggregate will, by ensuring that there are no large volumes of neat cement paste, produce a cohesive but workable concrete, resistant to bleeding and with satisfactory strength. In a well-graded aggregate, the voids between particles of a given size are filled by particles which are slightly smaller, voids left by these being filled in the same way until the particles of smallest size are reached. The absence of an intermediate size will tend to mean that, for a given strength and workability, more finer material than necessary will be required, with consequent increases in cement and water contents to coat the extra surface. Perhaps, the exception here occurs with 10 and 5 mm sizes. It is found that 20 mm particles leave gaps of approximately 3 mm and that, by omission of the 10 and 5 mm sizes, known as 'gap grading', workability may be increased for a given water content. Gap-graded concretes have been used for such purposes as sea-wall construction, the larger stones resisting the continued abrasion of the sea. With gap-graded aggregates, there is an increased tendency for segregation, especially in the case of lean, wet mixes ('segregation' being the term used to describe settlement of coarse material to the bottom of the concrete, mortar rising towards the top). Where there is an excess of sizes in the range 10 to 5 mm, the mix will tend to be 'harsh', with increased friction, lower workability and increased air voids, if there is insufficient finer material in the mix. Figure 3.6 shows four grading curves for 20 mm aggregates, as found in Road Research Note 4, which, from experience, have been found to produce satisfactory concrete, together with a typical gap-graded curve. The lower curves correspond to coarser gradings and would be suited to mixes of high cement content, which tend to be more cohesive. The upper curves would be suited to mixes of lower cement content.

From the above, it is apparent that close control over aggregate grading is essential if best use is to be made of material and it is now common practice to obtain aggregates in two or more sizes rather than in 'all-in' form. The latter may

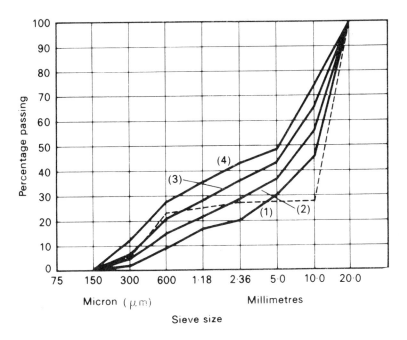

Fig. 3.6 Four grading curves for 20 mm aggregates, given in Road Note 4, together with a 'gap-graded' curve (indicated by the dotted line)

be of use in low-strength concretes but, wherever concrete of consistent strength durability, colour and texture is required, use of two or more sizes is a major contribution, provided gradings are checked periodically. Use of, for example, 20–10 mm; 10–5 mm aggregates and fine aggregate means that size proportions from 20–5 mm are closely controlled and of constant ratio to fine aggregate. Materials in this form will be more expensive, requiring separate stockpiles and extra supervision and testing but, for a given characteristic ('minimum') strength, a lower average strength of concrete should be acceptable, so that the concrete is more economical. BS 882 gives the grading requirements of all the forms of aggregate given above. Figure 3.7 shows the four 'zones' into which fine aggregates may be classified. There is overlap on all sieve sizes except the 600 mm size, which is, therefore, the most important size in establishing grading. Zone 1 is the coarsest. Owing to the high specific surface of Zone 4 fine aggregate (into which 'builders' or 'soft' sands often fit), BS 882 suggests that trial concrete mixes should be made to ascertain suitability in a given mix. Similar arguments apply to the coarser Zone 1 fine aggregates. For coarse aggregates, there is no zonal classification, because the number of sieve sizes involved is smaller. Although the grading curves given form sound guidelines for the production of good concrete,

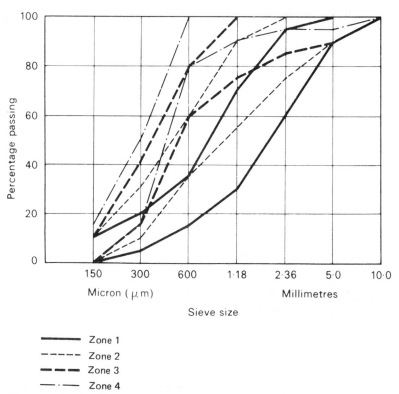

Fig. 3.7 Grading zones for fine aggregates for concrete

it is nevertheless possible, by careful design, to produce satisfactory concrete with aggregates having other gradings. In these cases, however, the need cannot be over-emphasised for trial mixes to ascertain suitability, together with a high degree of quality control.

Quality

This term manifests itself primarily in two ways:

1. *Silt* This may be defined as material composed of particles passing a 75 μm sieve. Owing to its high specific surface, its presence requires additional water for a given workability. Also, since such materials are often of a clayey nature, they decrease the bond between aggregate and cement, reducing the strength of concrete.
2. *Organic impurities* Such materials, being acidic, reduce the alkalinity of cement paste which is essential for its hydration, thereby affecting setting time and strength.

Moisture

Almost all aggregates contain some moisture, the important requirement for batching of aggregates being to establish whether this water will contribute to workability or whether water additional to the quantity based on the mix design will be necessary, due to absorption of aggregates. There are four possible states in which an aggregate may exist. (Fig. 3.8)

1. Oven-dry: implying that, on heating to 105 °C, there would be no loss of weight. This state rarely occurs in practice.
2. Air-dry: there is no free moisture and surface layers of aggregate are dry. This state occurs in upper parts of aggregate stockpiles in dry weather.

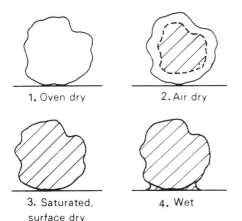

1. Oven dry   2. Air dry

3. Saturated, surface dry   4. Wet

Fig. 3.8 The possible states that an aggregate may be in with respect to moisture content

3. Saturated, surface dry: this is the 'ideal' state for an aggregate for concrete, since it requires no alteration to mixing water.
4. Wet: surplus moisture is present. This is the most common state.

(1) and (2) will require extra water to be added at the mixer, especially in the case of lightweight-aggregate concretes, since these aggregates are highly absorbent. (4) will require a deduction of water at the mixer equal to the total free moisture present in the batch of aggregate. Fine aggregate normally holds greater amounts of free moisture than coarse aggregate since, in a given mass, there are more points of contact between the larger numbers of particles involved. Water is held at these points by capillarity.

Design and specification of concrete mixes

The object of mix design is, by systematic analysis of properties of materials and knowledge of how they affect concrete properties, to produce batch quantities for a given volume of concrete, such that the properties of both the fresh and hardened materials are as required for the specific purpose, as economically as possible. The most important properties of fresh concrete are workability and cohesion, while those of hardened concrete may include strength, durability, colour, surface texture, density or other properties. It must be emphasised that the materials for concrete are such that mix design methods rarely produce the exact properties required of the concrete and trial mixes should be made in all cases in order to obtain the best performance. Best results will be obtained by a combination of both techniques, the design stage being used to give an indication of batch quantities. Results of trial mixes may also be extremely useful for future purposes, as they provide information on the effect of variation of batch proportions on properties of the concrete. Mix design, implying step-by-step determination of ratios or batch quantities for a specific purpose, is still relatively uncommon in this country. More common and widely used by the ready-mixed concrete industry are standard or 'prescribed' mixes, that is, mixes in which cement, aggregate and, possibly, water content are specified for each volume required. Such mixes may be satisfactory for many purposes, provided a sufficient range is available. Many companies rely partly on the skill of the batcher-man to judge correct workability, so that water figures, where given, are not always adhered to, especially where moisture is present in aggregates. Table 3.1 shows some prescribed mixes in the BS Unified Code of Practice 110 'The Structural Use of Concrete'. Such mixes are often used for 'normal' concretes, since they obviate the need for design, while still allowing some prediction of strength and durability. A step further still from designed mixes are nominal mixes (e.g. '1:2:4; medium workability'), in which no characteristic strength is specified and quality control is minimal. These mixes are only suitable for small quantities of slightly stressed concrete such as footings or raft foundations in domestic buildings. It will be apparent, therefore, that designed concrete mixes will be used either where carefully controlled or special properties

Table 3.1 Prescribed mixes for ordinary structural concrete (CP 110). Weights of cement and total dry aggregates in kg to produce approximately 1 m³ of fully compacted concrete together with the percentages by weight of fine aggregate in total dry aggregates. The grades represent characteristic 28-day cube strengths (five per cent failures), though cube testing is not required for prescribed mixes

Concrete grade	Nominal max. size of aggregate (mm)	40		20		14		10	
	Workability Limits to slump that may be expected (mm)	*Medium* 50–100	*High* 100–150	*Medium* 25–75	*High* 75–125	*Medium* 10–50	*High* 50–100	*Medium* 10–25	*High* 25–50
7	Cement (kg)	180	200	210	230	—	—	—	—
	Total aggregate (kg)	1950	1850	1900	1800	—	—	—	—
	Fine aggregate (per cent)	30–45	30–45	35–50	35–50	—	—	—	—
10	Cement (kg)	210	230	240	260	—	—	—	—
	Total aggregate (kg)	1900	1850	1850	1800	—	—	—	—
	Fine aggregate (per cent)	30–45	30–45	35–50	35–50	—	—	—	—
15	Cement (kg)	250	270	280	310	—	—	—	—
	Total aggregate (kg)	1850	1800	1800	1750	—	—	—	—
	Fine aggregate (per cent)	30–45	30–45	35–50	35–50	—	—	—	—
20	Cement (kg)	300	320	320	350	340	380	360	410
	Total aggregate (kg)	1850	1750	1800	1750	1750	1700	1750	1650
	Sand Zone 1 (per cent)	35	40	40	45	45	50	50	55
	Zone 2 (per cent)	30	35	35	40	40	45	45	50
	Zone 3 (per cent)	30	30	30	35	35	40	40	45
25	Cement (kg)	340	360	360	390	380	420	400	450
	Total aggregate (kg)	1800	1750	1750	1700	1700	1650	1700	1600
	Sand Zone 1 (per cent)	35	40	40	45	45	50	50	55
	Zone 2 (per cent)	30	35	35	40	40	45	45	50
	Zone 3 (per cent)	30	30	30	35	35	40	40	45
30	Cement (kg)	370	390	400	430	430	470	460	510
	Total aggregate (kg)	1750	1700	1700	1650	1700	1600	1650	1550
	Sand Zone 1 (per cent)	35	40	40	45	45	50	50	55
	Zone 2 (per cent)	30	35	35	40	40	45	45	50
	Zone 3 (per cent)	30	30	30	35	35	40	40	45

in the concrete are required or where large quantities of concrete will be used. In the latter, the cost of mix design and quality control will be regained by the more economical mix specifications they make possible.

Selection of materials

This must be a compromise between the ideal for the particular purpose, the materials readily available and the relative costs. For example, there is a wide range of cements on the market and, although ordinary Portland cement is the cheapest, there may well be a reason for using a 'special' cement, perhaps, if early or very early strength is required, where ordinary Portland cement would induce thermal stresses, or where extra heat would be advantageous, such as in winter concreting. It may, on the other hand, be worth considering the use of a modified ordinary Portland-cement mix as an alternative to special cements. There is often little choice in selection of aggregates, since locally available materials are usually far cheaper than 'imported' aggregates. However, the use of lightweight aggregates is increasing and their use may be considered. Admixtures may also be of benefit in particular situations, although a very wide range of concrete mixes can be produced without them and their use constitutes another possible source of error, particularly in view of the very small dosages normally required.

Preliminary tests on materials

1. Cements

Ordinary and rapid-hardening Portland cements are covered by BS 12, though modern cements give strength results significantly above minimum requirements in the standard. These increases are allowed for in current design methods and other variations can be easily detected in trial mixes. Cement testing is extremely important, however, as a part of quality control, although the tests of BS 12 are not site tests and require skilled personnel for their execution. Cement manufacturers are, however, normally willing to supply details of their cement properties.

2. Aggregates

The following tests are important, the first three acting as a guide to the overall suitability of a given aggregate and the fourth enabling the water content of the mix to be accurately calculated. The latter test should also be carried out regularly during production and the other tests at intervals or when there is cause for doubt. Relative densities of aggregates and bulk density of coarse aggregate may be required by some design methods. BS 812 describes methods for these.

(*a*) *Grading* A grading curve for the aggregate is obtained using the BS standard sieves, ranging from the nominal maximum size of the aggregate to 150 μm. It is essential to obtain a representative sample of aggregate – a poorly produced stockpile may itself contain segregated sizes, larger sizes tending to be at the

Table 3.2a Details of a sieve analysis of 0.5 kg of a fine aggregate. Comparison of the per cent passing column with Fig. 3.7 shows that the aggregate is a zone 2 aggregate. From below, the fineness modulus = 2.62

Sieve size	Amount retained (g)	Cumulative amount retained (g)	Per cent retained	Per cent passing
10.0 mm	0	0	0	100
5.0 mm	0	0	0	100
2.36 mm	85	85	17	83
1.18 mm	65	150	30	70
600 μm	65	215	43	57
300 μm	170	385	77	23
150 μm	90	475	95	5

Sum of percentages retained = 262.

Table 3.2b Details of a sieve analysis of 5 kg of 20 mm coarse aggregate. The sum of percentages retained is equal to 260 and this together with the four smaller sieve sizes not used here makes the total percentage retained for fineness modulus calculations = 660. Hence, fineness modulus = 6.60

Sieve size (mm)	Amount retained (kg)	Cumulative amount retained (kg)	Per cent retained	Per cent passing
37.5	0	0	0	100
20	0	0	0	100
10	3.25	3.25	65	35
5	1.50	4.75	95	5
2.36	0.25	5.00	100	0

bottom. Several samples should be taken and mixed, and then divided, either by quartering, or by a riffle box to give a quantity suitable for sieving. The aggregate should be dry and too large a quantity will give false analysis due to 'blinding' of sieve apertures by particles. Table 3.2 shows gradings of a typical fine and 20 mm coarse aggregate, indicating the method for calculating fineness modulus. Figures 3.9 and 3.10 show the Road Note 4 and Cement and Concrete Association methods of proportioning these aggregates to give the grading curves of Road Note 4. The Road Note 4 method is convenient for two aggregate sizes: gradings of available materials are presented on the two vertical axes, respective sieve sizes joined by lines, and then the gradings from Figure 3.4 indicated. The grading which fits best can be ascertained, bearing in mind the properties of these gradings already described. It is rare (and also unnecessary) for gradings to conform exactly to 'ideal' gradings and it is always possible to adjust mix proportions if gradings do not match closely those required. The grading shown

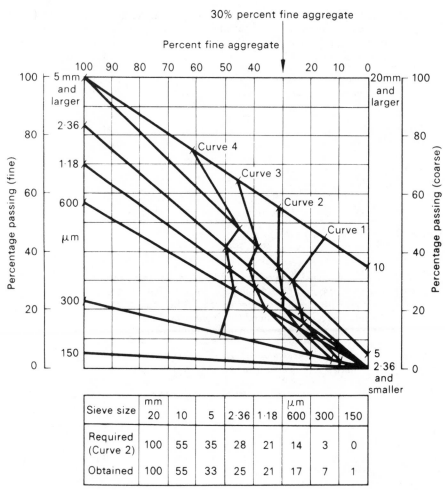

Fig. 3.9 Road Note 4 method of combining fine and coarse aggregates to conform to a given grading curve. In this case, curve 2 of Fig. 3.6 has been used, resulting in 30 per cent aggregate being required

by way of example is intentionally a rather poor fit. A ratio of 30:70, fine:coarse aggregate has been chosen, though this is slightly richer in fine particles and will tend to lead to a mix of lower workability. If this proves to be the case in a trial mix, the problem could be remedied by slightly increasing water and cement content, while keeping the water/cement ratio constant. The alternative method of combining aggregates shown (Fig. 3.10) is particularly useful where three sizes of aggregate are to be combined (e.g. when the coarse aggregate is obtained in single sizes), since proportions of fine, medium and coarse material can be read off directly from intercepts on the vertical axis. It is advisable, however, to calculate resultant gradings using the ratios obtained in order to compare with

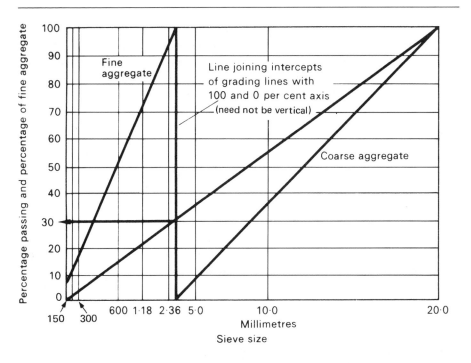

Sieve size	mm 20	10	5	2.36	1.18	μm 600	300	150
coarse	100	35	5	0	0	0	0	0
fine	100	100	100	83	70	57	23	5
70% coarse	70	24·5	3·5	0	0	0	0	0
30% fine	30	30	30	24·9	21·0	17·1	6·9	1·5
obtained	100	54·5	33·5	25	21	17	7	1
required (curve 2)	100	55	35	28	21	14	3	0

Fig. 3.10 Cement and Concrete Association method of proportioning aggregates. The sieve-size scale is obtained from the percentage-passing data of the required grading, working backwards from the diagonal line which then represents the required grading. To obtain straight lines for gradings of given aggregates, draw the steepest reasonable lines

that required. If a mix is lean or likely to segregate, it is better to use more fine aggregate to decrease the possibility of undersanded parts in the mix. Yet another alternative is to calculate the quantity of fine aggregate required as a part of the mix design procedure, using its fineness modulus (see below), though this has the disadvantage that the aggregate grading cannot be fully described by any single number.

(*b*) *Silt test* This is mainly a problem in relation to fine aggregate and a rapid assessment of silt content can be obtained by a field settling test. A sample of aggregate is shaken in a measuring cylinder containing salt solution. On allowing it to stand, the silt settles slowly as a distinct layer above the aggregate, the salt in solution helping to flocculate silt particles which otherwise might stay in suspension. If the result is greater than 8 per cent by volume, the material is suspect. BS 812 describes a more accurate method for determination of silt content by weight and this should be used if in doubt. Where excessive silt is present, the aggregate should be rejected or, if this is not possible, the cement content should be adjusted and trial mixes made to test suitability of the concrete. The cleanliness of coarse aggregate can be ascertained by visual inspection or, in cases of doubt, by a decantation method.

(*c*) *Organic impurities* The test described in BS 812 is based on the effect of organic impurities on the pH value of a standard cement paste. Almost immediately after mixing, the calcium hydroxide liberated in solution in concrete raises its pH to a strongly alkaline value (12.40 or above, in the case of the standard mortar paste). On the pH scale, 0 is concentrated acid, 7 neutral and 14 concentrated alkali. Organic impurities, for example, topsoil, if present in significant quantities, will reduce the pH value of the concrete and, hence, affect setting and strength properties. In the test described in BS 812, the cement is first checked with a standard sand, first clean, then contaminated to ensure that the particular cement in use gives the pH value required with the clean sand and then a sufficient reduction on contamination. In the 1973 edition of BS 882, the BS 812 test is not required as evidence of quality, due to difficulties in its interpretation. When in doubt, concrete cubes should be made.

(*d*) *Moisture content* In the case of aggregates containing free moisture, it is the free moisture only which is required, since absorbed water will not affect the properties of the concrete. This is determined most commonly by one of the following methods:
  (i) Oven-drying method. This is a direct and simple way of determining moisture content. Results may be determined very quickly by use of microwave ovens. These would give total moisture content, since microwave ovens cause evaporation of absorbed, as well as surface, moisture.
 (ii) Siphon can (BS 812). This is based on the principle that a given mass of aggregate containing free water will occupy a larger volume than a dry aggregate. The volume of each is obtained by displacement of water in a specially designed can, suitable for site use. A sample of dried material is, however, necessary. If the free moisture content of the aggregate is required, this sample should be surface-dry only. If the total moisture content is required, it should be oven-dry. This test relies heavily upon constant relative density of material from sample to sample.
(iii) Chemical method. A rapid value can be obtained by mixing a sample of the damp aggregate with an excess of calcium carbide in a pressure vessel. The

calcium carbide reacts with the moisture, producing a gas the pressure of which is proportional to the quantity of moisture present. The moisture content reading will correspond to a value somewhere between the free and total moisture content, depending on the degree of crushing of the material.

It is most important to note that moisture content often varies from one part of an aggregate stockpile to another, as well as with time. Great care should be taken in obtaining a representative sample, especially when the final sample is small, as in method (iii).

In the case of absorptive aggregates, the absorption coefficient would also be required.

3. *Quality of water* (*BS 3148*)

This is important, since contaminated water may lead to impaired performance of the hardened concrete. As a general rule, if water is suitable for drinking, then it is likely to be suitable for making concrete. If there is any doubt, it is advisable to carry out the setting time and strength tests of BS 12, using samples of the water in question and also distilled water for comparison. The standard indicates that a strength reduction up to 20 per cent in the former is acceptable.

Although sea water is suitable for ordinary concrete, since the effect of salt in the normal concentrations found is slight, it is not recommended for reinforced concrete, owing to the increased corrosion risk, or for high-alumina-cement concretes. A further problem of sea water is the increased likelihood of efflorescence resulting in unsightly salt deposits, particularly if drying is concentrated at certain positions in the structure. Many salts are also hygroscopic and, therefore, tend to perpetuate dampness at positions where they build up.

Examples of moisture content corrections

(a) Non-absorptive aggregates. Calculate corrected batch masses of aggregate and water for a concrete mix if given quantities are:

coarse aggregate – 1300 kg
fine aggregate   – 500 kg
water   – 150 litres

and the fine and coarse aggregates content 5 per cent and 3 per cent moisture, based on wet weight, respectively.

1300 kg of coarse aggregate contains $3/100 \times 1300 = 39$ litres water and, therefore, only 1261 kg of coarse aggregate. Hence, use $1300 \times 1300/1261 = 1340$ kg of coarse aggregate.

500 kg of fine aggregate contains $5/100 \times 500 = 25$ litres water and, therefore, only 475 kg of fine aggregate. Hence, $500 \times (500/475) = 526$ kg of fine aggregate. These contain $1340 \times 3/100 + 526 \times 5/100 = 40 + 26 = 66$ litres water. Therefore, water to be added at the mixer $= 150 - 66 = 84$ litres.

(b) Repeat the above example, assuming the aggregates have absorption coefficients of 5 per cent and 10 per cent by weight of dry material, fine and coarse, respectively. In this case, the given batch quantities of coarse and fine aggregates would be based on the saturated surface dry (SSD) condition. The corresponding quantities of dry and damp aggregates are:

Dry   *Damp*

coarse aggregate $1300 \times \dfrac{100}{110} = 1182 \, \text{kg}$ $1182 \times \dfrac{100}{97} = 1219 \, \text{kg}$

fine aggregate $500 \times \dfrac{100}{105} = 476 \, \text{kg}$ $476 \times \dfrac{100}{95} = 501 \, \text{kg}$

The water absorbed is based on the dry materials.

$$= \frac{10}{100} \times 1182 + \frac{5}{100} \times 476 = 142 \text{ litres}$$

The water content is based on the wet materials.

$$= \frac{3}{100} \times 1219 + \frac{5}{100} \times 501 = 62 \text{ litres}$$

Corrected batch quantity of water is

$150 + 142 - 62 = 230$ litres

Note   The total mass of material

$= 1219 + 501 + 230$
$= 1950 \, \text{kg}$

This equals the sum of the original batch quantities.

Determination of batch quantities

This is based on the required properties in relation to the results of preliminary tests on, or assumed properties of, materials. There are four quantities which must be determined for a given volume of concrete; those of water, cement, coarse aggregate and fine aggregate. These quantities are designed to give an average strength which will be higher than the characteristic strength by a margin that depends on the quality control and other factors (see 'Statistical analysis as an aid to quality control and design').

It is widely acknowledged that the strength of fully compacted concrete, as determined by concrete cube tests, is determined largely by the free water/cement ratio, that is, the quantity of free water in the mix relative to that of cement, by weight. Figure 3.11 shows typical strength/water/cement ratio curves for ordinary Portland and rapid-hardening Portland cement concretes, manufactured using uncrushed aggregates based on information given in the DoE method of mix design. As a guide, when crushed aggregates are used, the cube strength will be increased by about $6 \, \text{N/mm}^2$, though the difference may be

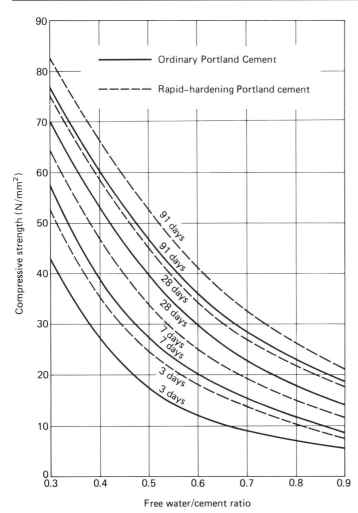

Fig. 3.11 The relationship between the compressive strength of concrete and free water/cement ratio (uncrushed aggregates). Based on DoE method of mix design (Crown copyright material from the Building Establishment 'Design of normal concrete mixes' by permission of the Controller, HMSO).

slightly increased in high-strength concretes and slightly reduced at low strength. A further constraint on water/cement ratio is durability, typical maximum values being indicated in Table 3.3. Clearly, the lower of the two values corresponding to strength and durability requirements must be adopted.

While most mix design methods involve the estimation of free water/cement ratio, there are a number of ways of tackling the remaining stages. Road Note 4, for example, was based on the principle that, for a given water/cement ratio, aggregate size and grading, higher aggregate/cement ratios will reduce workability, since there is more material to 'wet'. Aggregate/cement ratios were given in

Table 3.3 Maximum water/cement ratios for
concrete to be durable in various types
of structure and environment

Type of construction	Climate	
	Severe	Normal
Bridge decks	0.45	0.50
Thin sections in air exposed to weather	0.50	0.55
Moderate sections; road slabs	0.55	0.60
Concrete protected from weather	—	—

Table 3.4 The water content required for a given workability of concretes, air-entrained
and non-air-entrained (American Concrete Institute). Contents given to the
nearest 5 kg

Slump in mm	Water requirement in kg per m^3 of concrete					
	Non-air-entrained			Air-entrained		
	10 mm agg.	20 mm agg.	40 mm agg.	10 mm agg.	20 mm agg.	40 mm agg.
25–50	205	185	160	180	165	145
75–100	225	200	175	200	180	160
150–175	240	210	185	215	190	170
Approx. entrapped air (per cent)	3	2	1	—	—	—
Approx. entrained air (per cent) – moderate exposure	—	—	—	8	6	4.5

tables for a given workability, water/cement ratio aggregate size, type and
grading. The main limitation of the method was that there were only four
'standard' overall aggregate gradings for each size of aggregate used (Fig. 3.6)
and this was rather inflexible when dealing with mixes of differing cement content
and workability.

More recent methods of mix design have been concerned with actual batch
quantities per cubic metre rather than with aggregate/cement ratios. The mix
design method of the American Concrete Institute, for example, utilises the fact
that the water content per cubic metre of concrete depends mainly on aggregate
size and workability. Free water contents are given in Table 3.4, which also

Table 3.5 The relationship between bulk volume of rodded coarse aggregate and the volume of concrete produced as a function of maximum size of coarse aggregate and fineness modulus of fine aggregate (American Concrete Institute)

Maximum size of aggregate (mm)	Ratio	bulk volume of rodded coarse aggregate / volume of concrete produced		
		Fineness mod. fine agg. = 2.4	Fineness mod. fine agg. = 2.6	Fineness mod. fine agg. = 2.8	Fineness mod. fine agg. = 3.0
10		0.50	0.48	0.46	0.44
20		0.66	0.64	0.62	0.60
40		0.76	0.74	0.72	0.70

includes values corresponding to air-entrained concrete. Although the table is based on angular aggregates, no distinction is made between crushed or uncrushed aggregates, adjustments being made, as necessary, at the trial mix stage. The cement content per cubic metre is then found from the relationship:

$$\frac{\text{cement content}}{\text{per cubic metre}} = \frac{\text{free water content per cubic metre}}{\text{free water/cement ratio}}$$

Bulk volumes of coarse aggregate per cubic metre of concrete are also specified (Table 3.5), depending on the fineness modulus of the fine aggregate. Note that smaller maximum sizes require more fines whereas, in the case of very fine aggregates (i.e. low fineness modulus), smaller quantities of fines are required. Again, there is no distinction between crushed and uncrushed material, the adjustment being automatic, since angular coarse aggregates will have a lower bulk density. Hence, in the relationship:

$$\frac{\text{batch mass of aggregate}}{\text{per cubic metre}} = \left\{\begin{array}{c}\text{bulk volume} \\ \text{per cubic metre}\end{array}\right\} \times \{\text{bulk density}\}$$

the batch mass of an angular coarse aggregate would be reduced. The fine aggregate content is determined by subtracting the volumes of the cement, aggregate and water from one cubic metre, allowing as necessary for entrapped or entrained air, as in Table 3.4

The DoE method of mix design works along similar lines to obtain batch masses of water and cement per cubic metre of concrete, except that distinction is made between the water content required for crushed and uncrushed aggregates (Table 3.6). The concrete density is then estimated graphically on the basis of assumed relative densities for cement and water, and the measured relative densities of aggregates. The aggregate mass is obtained by subtraction:

$$\frac{\text{batch mass of aggregate}}{\text{per cubic metre}} = \text{density} - \left\{\begin{array}{c}\text{mass of water} \\ \text{per cubic metre}\end{array} + \begin{array}{c}\text{mass of cement} \\ \text{per cubic metre}\end{array}\right\}$$

Table 3.6 Approximate free-water contents (kg/m³) required to give various levels of workability (DoE method of mix design*)

Slump (mm) V-B (s)					
Maximum size of aggregate (mm)	Type of aggregate	0–10 >12	10–30 6–12	30–60 3–6	60–180 0–3
10	Uncrushed	150	180	205	225
	Crushed	180	205	230	250
20	Uncrushed	135	160	180	195
	Crushed	170	190	210	225
40	Uncrushed	115	140	160	175
	Crushed	155	175	190	205

* Crown copyright material from the Building Research Establishment *Design of normal concrete mixes* by permission of the Controller, HMSO.

The fine aggregate proportion of the total aggregate is obtained from graphs as a function of water/cement ratio, workability, zone classification of fine aggregate and maximum aggregate size. The effect is similar to that of the ACI method, fine aggregate content increasing with reducing maximum aggregate size, reducing cement content and coarser fine aggregates. The DoE method has the possible advantage that the fine aggregate content is increased as workability increases for a given water/cement ratio, thereby reducing the risk of segregation at high workability. The ACI method indicates, however, that the coarse aggregate contents of Table 3.5 may be respectively increased or reduced up to 10 per cent for correct workability concretes.

Examples are now given illustrating the use of each method, water/cement ratios being 'given' information in order to avoid the difficulty arising from the fact that the ACI method bases strength on cylinders rather than cubes.

Obtain batch quantities for one/cubic metre of concrete (non-air-entrained) to have free water/cement ratio 0.5 and slumps of (a) 40 mm (b) 100 mm, using 20 mm crushed coarse aggregate of bulk density 1650 kg/m³, zone 2 fine aggregate (fineness modulus 2.6) and ordinary Portland cement. Relative densities of aggregate and cement are 2.6 and 3.15, respectively.

DoE method (reference to tables and graphs in the DoE method is required).
(a)
Water content = 210 kg/m³
Cement content = 420 kg/m³
Wet density = 2340 kg/m³
Aggregate content = 1710 kg/m³
Fine aggregate content

$$= \frac{36}{100} \times 1710 = 616 \, kg/m^3$$

(b)
Water content = 225 kg/m³
Cement content = 450 kg/m³
Wet density = 2320 kg/m³
Aggregate content = 1645 kg/m³

$$\frac{41}{100} \times 1645 = 674 \, kg/m^3$$

Batch quantities per cubic metre
Cement   420 kg
Water   210 litres
Fine   616 kg
Coarse   1094 kg
            2340 kg

Batch quantities per cubic metre
Cement   450 kg
Water   225 litres
Fine   674 kg
Coarse   971 kg
            2320 kg

ACI method

(a)

Water content $185 \, kg/m^3$
Cement content $370 \, kg/m^3$
Coarse aggregate 0.64×1650
                    $= 1056 \, kg/m^3$

Volumes of materials:

Cement $\dfrac{370}{3.15 \times 1000} = 0.117 \, m^3$

Water $\dfrac{185}{1000} = 0.185 \, m^3$

Coarse Aggregate $\dfrac{1056}{2.6 \times 1000} = 0.406 \, m^3$

Air   0.020
                 0.728

Abs. Volume of
fine aggregate $= 0.272 \, m^3$
Mass of
fine aggregate $= 0.272 \times 2600$
                  $= 707 \, kg/m^3$

Batch quantities per cubic metre
Cement   370 kg
Water   185 litres
Fine   707 kg
Coarse   1056 kg
           2318 kg

(b)

Water content $200 \, kg/m^3$
Cement content $400 \, kg/m^3$
Coarse aggregate 0.64×1650
                    $= 1056 \, kg/m^3$

Volumes of materials:

Cement $\dfrac{400}{3.15 \times 1000} = 0.127 \, m^3$

Water $\dfrac{200}{1000} = 0.200 \, m^3$

Coarse Aggregate $\dfrac{1056}{2.6 \times 1000} = 0.406 \, m^3$

Air   0.020
                 0.753

Abs. Volume of
fine aggregate $= 0.247 \, m^3$
Mass of
fine aggregate $= 0.247 \times 2600$
                  $= 642 \, kg/m^3$

Batch quantities per cubic metre
Cement   400 kg
Water   200 litres
Fine   642 kg
Coarse   1056 kg
           2298 kg

A significant difference between the DoE and ACI methods is that water content in the latter is always lower, presumably reflecting differences in the respective aggregate gradings. Corresponding cement contents are in consequence, also lower. The differences would be allowed for in trial mixes, which would lead to more accuracy in water content than either method could predict.

It is noticeable that when, in the DoE method, workability is increased, the fine aggregate content is also increased, and the coarse aggregate content reduced.

In the ACI method, the latter is unchanged at the higher workability (although the method allows an adjustment to the coarse aggregate content at different degrees of workability, as necessary), hence, since the higher-workability concrete contains more water and cement, the fine aggregate content is actually reduced, in contrast to the increase resulting from the DoE method. The resulting cohesion may be low although, again, corrections could be made at trial-mix stage. The differences in density between the two methods arise partly from a 2 per cent air allowance in the ACI method. Note that, in each case, the mix of higher workability has lower density, since the water content is higher.

Trial mixes

These are a most important part of the mix-design procedure. Initial trial mixes may be made in small quantities, for example, using a 20 kg sample of concrete. Water should be added until, by visual inspection, the workability is correct. The workability and cohesion should then be determined and adjustments made as necessary. For example, if the workability is correct but the mix is harsh, the proportion of fine aggregate should be increased, possibly increasing the water content slightly to maintain workability. If, on the other hand, the cohesion is good but the workability is too high, then the water content should be reduced, the cement content reduced, such that the water/cement ratio remains constant. An increase in the mass of fine aggregate, such that its volume increase is equal to the volume reduction of cement, could then be made to maintain cohesion. Cubes should also be made to check the strength of the mix. Having corrected mix proportions, a full-size trial mix could be made, placed and compacted, using plant and techniques to be employed in production, since these inevitably affect the properties and performance of concrete. A density determination of this concrete would then give an accurate indication of the volume yield of the mix. This mix could be used for a temporary structure or, perhaps, as foundation concrete.

Modern trends in mix-design procedures

The above methods of mix design contain a number of inherent disadvantages. For example, the water/cement ratio, as determined by strength requirements, depends on the type of coarse and fine aggregate used, and errors introduced by use of standard graphs, such as Fig. 3.11, can be considerable. Again, it has been shown that satisfactory concrete can be made without the need for aggregates to conform to grading curves, as in Fig. 3.6, and fineness modulus also is an insufficient description of the grading properties of fine aggregate. These problems all relate to aggregates and, in practice, it may take time to apply effectively general rules for design to particular aggregates. Since, in a given district, aggregates are obtained from a small number of sources, a logical approach to mix design might be to produce design graphs for a particular aggregate type and workability, enabling batch quantities per cubic metre to be

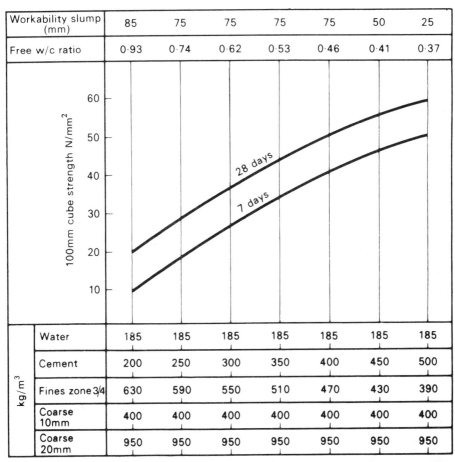

Workability slump (mm)	85	75	75	75	75	50	25
Free w/c ratio	0·93	0·74	0·62	0·53	0·46	0·41	0·37
Water	185	185	185	185	185	185	185
Cement	200	250	300	350	400	450	500
Fines zone 3/4	630	590	550	510	470	430	390
Coarse 10mm	400	400	400	400	400	400	400
Coarse 20mm	950	950	950	950	950	950	950

Fig. 3.12 Mix design chart, by P. L. Owens, for concrete of medium workability using 20 mm quartzite aggregate. Note that quantities of water; for 10 mm and 20 mm aggregates are constant. As the cement content increases, the sand content decreases, such that the total volume of materials remains constant. The strength graphs are obtained experimentally

read off directly. Such design graphs would take time to produce but, once in existence, would obviate the need for the above, more approximate, methods of mix design. A typical graph by P. L. Owens is shown in Fig. 3.12. Trial mixes will still be necessary, as cement and aggregate properties may vary, but results obtained should be closer to those required, without extensive testing of aggregates and time spent on 'rational' methods of mix design. There will always be a place for such techniques but they could be employed in the production of such graphs for each aggregate type so that time taken by the engineers in designing mixes is minimised. Such schemes have already been used but the main problem in adopting them for general use is the establishment of a suitable commercial basis for their operation.

Properties of fresh concrete

It should be appreciated that the properties of hardened concrete are closely related to those of the freshly mixed, plastic material, so that it is of great importance to be able to measure and control the latter. Furthermore, if, by means of tests, the concrete is found to be unsuitable for its purpose, it is far easier to reject a mix before it has set and hardened, and easier still if the failure can be detected by tests before placing.

The most important terms relating to fresh concrete are workability and cohesion. Workability is defined as that property of concrete which determines its ability to be placed, compacted and finished, though particular emphasis is placed on the process of compaction. The cohesion of a concrete mix is a measure of its resistance to segregation, that is, the separation of particle fractions of different sizes. High cohesion also facilitates the production of a high-quality surface finish.

Additionally, a method of measuring the air content of fresh concrete and a method of analysing fresh concrete are considered.

Workability

Workability must be controlled within fine limits if concrete of consistent quality is to be produced. If the workability (and, therefore, the water content) is too high, the concrete will be more prone to segregation in the fresh state and, in the hardened state, the quality will be impaired. Too low a workability will make compaction difficult, with increased risk of air voids – it should be noted that 5 per cent of entrapped air will lead to a strength reduction of about 30 per cent. The workability of concrete must be matched to the techniques of compaction, placing and finishing, and should result in concrete of uniform composition and maximum density for the particular mix used. Since workability is a complex property involving interplay between the quantity of water in the mix, the volumes of constituents and internal friction due to particle abrasion, its measurement must be made empirically, and mixes of different proportions but of similar workability may give different results to a particular test. The workability categories, extremely low, very low, low, medium and high, can only act as a guide when specifying concrete and some reliance must be placed upon trial mixes. During production, however, workability tests provide a simple means of quality control. A further point is that, due to absorption of water by cement (and aggregates, if absorbent), workability may decrease rapidly after mixing. To compare results, therefore, tests should be carried out at a standard time after addition of the water and, preferably, just before placing.

Slump test

This is still the most widely used test, due to its simplicity and convenience. Concrete is placed and compacted in four layers by tamping rod, in a firmly held slump cone (Fig. 3.13). On removal of the cone, the difference in height between

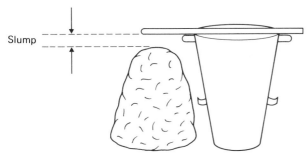

Slump

Fig. 3.13 The slump test

the uppermost part of the slumped concrete and the upturned cone is recorded in mm as the slump. Less cohesive mixes, for example, lean mixes, tend to give a greater or shear, or even collapsed, slump and aggregate type also affects the result at given workability, so that allowances may have to be made. Dry mixes often give no slump at all and, in this case, another test should be used.

Compacting factor test

A sample of the mix is allowed to fall through two hoppers into a cylinder, thereby compacting itself to a degree dependent on its workability. The contents of the cylinder are weighed and then the same volume of fully-compacted concrete is weighed. The compacting factor is then calculated from:

$$\text{compacting factor} = \frac{\text{weight of partially compacted concrete}}{\text{weight of fully compacted concrete}}$$

A value near unity indicates a workable mix, while a value of, for example, 0.70 would indicate a dry mix. The compacting-factor test is useful for drier mixes, although these tend to hang up in the hoppers. The problem of richness also applies, richer mixes compacting more easily for a given compacting factor. The apparatus is also more bulky than the slump-test apparatus and most forms require separate weighing equipment, so that it is not as commonly used as the slump test.

V-B consistometer

A slump test is first carried out, using a slump cone fixed on to a small vibration table. Then a weighted transparent plastic disc, held in a vertical guide, is allowed to rest on the surface of the slumped concrete. The vibrator, in the form of an electrically-operated eccentric rotor under the table, is then operated and the time in seconds for the disc to fall, such that the concrete wets its whole circumference, is recorded. This is then the consistency of the concrete in 'V-B degrees'. The V-B test is suitable for dry mixes and, particularly, those which are to be compacted by vibration, since the test itself involves vibration of the concrete. A possible disadvantage of the V-B apparatus is that it requires an electric power supply (normally 3 phase).

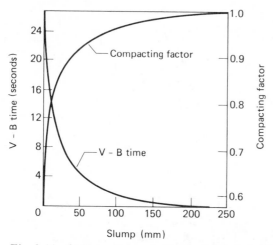

Fig. 3.14 Comparative results for the three workability tests. The V-B test is suitable for very low workability, the compacting factor test for low/medium workability and the slump test for medium/high workability

Comparative results of the above workability tests are shown in Fig. 3.14. The approximate form only is indicated, that actually obtained being dependent on richness of mix, and type and grading of aggregate. The graph, however, indicates the reasons for the suitability of each test as given above. In practice, having decided from the above arguments which type of test is to be used, it is normal to use that method only, since it is not easy to correlate results from different methods and, in any case, these do not assist in quality control – an important use of workability tests.

Cohesion

Although, perhaps, not of such importance as workability, there will be an optimum degree of cohesion for each concreting situation. The need for adequate cohesion has been explained but it should also be understood that a concrete which is unnecessarily cohesive will also be unnecessarily expensive, since the extra-fine material incorporated will increase the water and, hence, the cement requirement at a given strength level. There is no BS test specifically for the measurement of cohesion but the appearance of concrete after a slump test will give some indication. Alternatively, a simple test which may be carried out is by trowelling, say, 15 kg of concrete on a flat, non-absorbent surface. The degree of cohesion is assessed by the ease with which a smooth surface finish is obtained when trowelling to a thickness of about 75 mm. High cohesion is only necessary when the concrete may be dropped from some height during placing or when there are relatively large areas of finished concrete to be produced – as, for example, in thin slabs or slender columns.

Analysis of fresh concrete

An apparatus to analyse concrete mixes accurately and quickly – preferably within a few minutes – would be of great benefit in many types of concrete production. It would detect errors in batching equipment or in its operation and act as a further means of control, allowing action to be taken, if necessary, before placing. The main problem is that of obtaining sufficient accuracy quickly. The method described in BS 1881, for example, is slow and requires a knowledge of the relative densities of the aggregates. Perhaps, the most important aspect of the analysis of fresh concrete is that of measuring the cement content, since the free water content can usually be inferred with reasonable accuracy from the workability, especially if details of aggregate properties are known. A number of schemes have been developed in which cement is separated from the remainder of the concrete and either weighed or detected chemically. In one commercially-operated system, for example, concrete is placed in a vertical 'elutriator' column and the fine material is washed out by a controlled upward flow of water. A known proportion (say 10 per cent of the fine material) is then washed through a 150 μm sieve and allowed to settle into a collecting vessel. After siphoning excess water to a predetermined level, the vessel and contents are weighed and the cement content obtained from a calibration graph. Once calibrated, a result can be obtained within 5 minutes although, in such a method, any silt in the aggregate will lead to an over-estimated cement content. A correction can be made by repeating the test with clean aggregate. Such methods permit the measurement of cement content to within about 20 kg/m^3 of the correct value, at a 95 per cent confidence level, provided concrete is tested within about two hours of mixing. Where longer delays are envisaged, the use of an appropriate quantity of retarder will delay hydration and, hence, increase accuracy.

Where an accurate and rapid indication of water content is required, nuclear techniques, involving the moderation of fast neutrons by water, have been employed but this technique is, at the present time, of a specialised nature. A further, though slow, alternative is oven-drying.

Compaction of concrete

Although a detailed treatment of the methods of compaction is outside the scope of this book, a number of important points are summarised here.

The approximate effect on strength of under-compaction has already been briefly stated, though it may be added that the relationship between strength s and porosity p is of approximately negative exponential form:

$$S = S_0 \, e^{-kp}$$

k being a constant and S_0 the strength at zero air voids. Constant k takes a value of about 8 in order that 30 to 35 per cent strength loss occurs in the 5 per cent voids. Note that the first one per cent of air voids leads to the largest per cent loss of strength – about 9 per cent. Hence, the need to eliminate as much air as possible will be appreciated, although air contents in the region of 1 per cent are considered normal. Conversely, over-compaction will also lead to strength loss, particularly at surface layers, due to the effect of water rising to the surface of concrete, especially in lifts of some depth. What might be regarded as the exception to this effect is revibration, in which concrete is subjected to further compactive effort some time – perhaps in the region of 2 hours – after placing. If, for instance, external vibrators are operated at this stage, an increase of strength and improvement in surface finish may be obtained. The former is probably due to the extra consolidation achieved, together with removal of any plastic cracks, while the latter is due to removal of further air by the second application of vibration.

Prolonged agitation of concrete is in no way detrimental, provided full compaction is finally achieved. However, workability reduces steadily from the time of adding the mixing water and delays of well over 2 hours may, especially in hot weather, make full compaction very difficult to achieve. Any extra water added (other than the small amount to replace evaporation) will reduce strength according to the water/cement ratio rule.

Entrapped or entrained air in concrete

The former term refers to air voids present due to insufficient compaction and the latter to air intentionally included in the form of very small air bubbles as a workability aid or to improve frost-resistance. The total air content of a fresh mix can easily be obtained by an apparatus based on Boyle's law and shown in Fig. 3.15. A sealed vessel containing a sample of the compacted concrete is

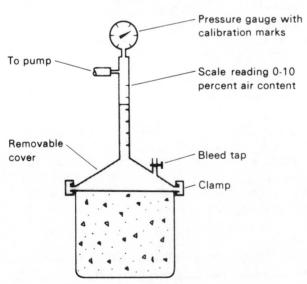

Fig. 3.15 An apparatus for measurement of the quantity of air in freshly mixed concrete

pressurised to a standard pressure, normally about 2 atm. The air in the concrete is the only compressible medium and the percentage of air in the contents, measured by the reduction in the volume, can be read off directly from a calibrated scale. It is important to attempt to simulate the compaction of the concrete in the actual structure when using this test. This method also fails to detect water-filled voids in the concrete which, on drying out, would become air voids. The presence of such voids could be detected by density methods – from cubes (although, again, compaction as in the structure is not likely) or by in-situ methods, for example, radioactive techniques.

Curing of concrete

This is the process in which, by means of moisture in the concrete, the material matures, increasing in strength and decreasing in porosity. The process is in no way dependent on air, so that, once setting is complete, ideal curing conditions are those in which the concrete is completely saturated. Temperature is also important. The ideal curing temperature for ordinary Portland cement concrete is in the region of 10 °C – higher temperatures lead to a more rapid hydration but a less favourable crystal structure. In the case of rapid-hardening Portland cement, the optimum temperature is lower, in the region of 5 °C. However, temperatures of up to 25 °C do not significantly reduce long-term strength. At temperatures lower than these respective values, strength development is slow, due to reduced hydration rates. Curing should continue until the material has sufficient strength to resist shrinkage cracking. Thin sections, in particular, tend to dry out very quickly as soon as protection is removed. High water/cement ratio concretes are permeable and will, therefore, be most seriously affected in this way, especially as they also exhibit high shrinkage. Even in mass concrete, a short curing period may cause problems, since, on exposure, surface layers may dry and shrink, while inner layers continue to hydrate, resulting in surface cracking. It is clear from the above that the curing method and precise curing period will depend on the type of structure and its situation but, ideally, the concrete should be kept moist, if necessary by artificial means, for at least seven days and, after this, thermal shock or rapid drying due to, for example, solar heat, should be avoided. In the case of exposed concrete slabs, curing may be achieved by covering with sacking which should be kept damp, or with polythene sheeting, which is effective in retaining moisture. Concrete road bases are effectively sealed by plastic sheeting or by coating with bitumen emulsion or other curing compound, although cracking may still occur, due to temperature variations. Formwork for structural concrete protects it from temperature changes and drying, and should be left in position as long as possible. Cements with a high heat output present a problem, since temperatures within formwork may rise 20 °C or more above the ambient temperature. The use of low-heat cements is recommended where this is likely to happen but, in any case, if formwork is left in position as long as possible, sudden stresses, due to cooling and evaporation, will be minimised. There is often a temptation to spray with cold water a surface found to be warm on removal of formwork, but this may be disastrous, due to the thermal shock and consequent surface stresses it produces. Sprayed curing membranes may be used but a period of 1 to 3 hours must first be allowed for surface moisture to evaporate before they are applied.

Curing in hot weather

Hot weather will exaggerate some of the problems already mentioned. Owing to evaporation, the quantity of mixing water may have to be increased to produce the required workability at the time of placing, which may have to be carried out more quickly, due to more rapid hydration of cement and consequently decreased setting time. A warm, dry atmosphere may cause plastic cracking due to surface evaporation. Such cracks, which do not normally penetrate more than about 50 mm, may be retrowelled but steps must then be taken to conserve all possible moisture in the concrete. The use of a low-heat cement or lean mixes will reduce the extra heat due to hydration. Aggregates form the main bulk of the concrete, so that, if these are stored in large stockpiles, the diurnal temperature variation in them and, hence, the concrete, will be minimised. In general, concreting thin, exposed sections above about 30 °C in low humidities should be avoided.

Curing in cold weather

Freezing of concrete before it is fully cured may result in a substantial reduction in strength and durability and, if freezing occurs before it sets, concrete is rendered virtually useless. Concrete can be safely exposed to frost once it reaches a compressive strength of 2 N/mm^2 (provided it is not saturated) and, once frost-resistant, hydration will continue, though at a reduced rate, down to temperatures of approximately -10 °C, since water in smaller pores does not freeze until much lower temperatures. The rate of strength gain depends, in a complex way, on the grade of concrete, the temperature and the time after placing. The term 'maturity' has been used previously where temperature, measured above the datum -10 °C, is multiplied by the time after placing in hours to give an index of the degree of hydration and, hence, strength development but it is found that concretes of a given maturity so defined are weaker if cured at temperatures below 10 °C than those cured at higher temperatures. A 0 °C datum, conversely, leads to a low estimate of strength of concrete cured near freezing point. More complex formulae have been suggested but pre-hardening times are probably best expressed empirically, Table 3.7 indicating typical values of minimum pre-hardening times for various grades of concrete at curing temperatures in the range 5 °C to 20 °C. It is noticeable that pre-hardening times increase greatly for lower grades of concrete at lower temperatures. If concrete is likely to be saturated, larger values are necessary and concretes below Grade 20, which

Table 3.7 Minimum pre-hardening times for various grades
of concrete at curing temperatures in the
range 5° to 20 °C (from Ref. 8)

Characteristic strength at 28 days N/mm^2	Minimum prehardening time at stated curing temperature in hours			
	20 °C	15 °C	10 °C	5 °C
20	24	32	46	71
25	22	30	42	65
30	20	27	38	59
40	17	23	33	50

have water/cement ratios over 0.7, may never be frost-resistant. The periods may, in general, be reduced by about 25 per cent if rapid-hardening Portland cement is used and by a further 25 per cent if calcium chloride is included also.

In all types of concrete, full compaction is necessary if maximum frost-resistance is to be provided. When concreting is being carried out in cold weather, measurements of concrete temperature, using a thermometer in the concrete, protected by a metal sheath, should be made periodically, so that maturity can be estimated. The following steps will assist in obtaining the required maturity:

1. Use a rapid-hardening or high-alumina cement, an admixture such as calcium chloride or a higher-strength mix requiring a lower pre-hardening time.
2. Heat the aggregates and/or water to increase the initial temperature of the concrete.
3. Use insulated formwork. The best insulator is a layer of trapped air. This may be obtained, for example, by tarpaulin over an airspace on slabs, or formwork with a backing of an insulating material.
4. Enclose the structure in a temporary heated covering, for example, polythene sheeting on scaffolding.

If the concrete relies on its own heat, together with insulated formwork for protection, thin sections will be far more difficult to deal with satisfactorily since they are, in general, of greater surface area for unit mass. Such types of construction should be avoided in very cold weather unless satisfactory maturity before freezing can be ensured.

Steam curing

The object of steam curing may be to accelerate strength development or simply reduce the time for precast products in the mould. It can be carried out at low or high pressures.

Low-pressure steam curing

Steam at a temperature of 55 to 80 °C is passed through chambers containing the units for a period of about 12 hours. The final strength of units is only slightly lower than that obtained ultimately by normal curing but it is important that the temperature be increased in a controlled manner. Temperatures over 50 °C should be avoided during the first two hours and a delay of 2 to 5 hours before steam curing is beneficial. A possible explanation of the problem is that the vapour pressure of water in any trapped air in the concrete rises rapidly with temperature, causing disruption if heating is carried out too quickly. Concretes containing finer cements or high water/cement ratios are most seriously affected.

The 12-hour strength of a steam-cured concrete may be three to four times that obtained by normal curing and large precast panels cured in this way can often be handled at the age of one day. The product formed has a chemical structure similar to that of hydrated cement paste. Low-pressure steam curing of concrete cubes is becoming increasingly used for obtaining rapid estimates of the 28-day strength of concrete.

High-pressure steam curing (autoclaving)

This is quite different from the method described above, the units being heated in pressure vessels, at a pressure of about eight atmospheres to approximately 180 °C. The addition of finely-ground silica increases the strength by a reaction similar to that which occurs in the manufacture of calcium-silicate bricks, the lime being provided by the hydrating cement; in particular, the tricalcium silicate. As in low-pressure steam curing, the rise of temperature should be gradual.

The specific surface of the resulting hardened paste is much lower than that of normally cured cement paste and the hydrate should be regarded as microcrystalline rather than in 'gel' form. As a result, drying shrinkage and moisture movements are smaller, due to reduced quantities of adsorbed water. Hence, the concrete is more durable than normally cured concrete and its resistance to sulphate attack is greater. High-pressure steam curing produces normal 28-day strength in about one day but is not suitable for reinforced concrete, since bond strength is reduced. Precast concrete blocks are often cured in this way.

Steam curing by either process cannot be carried out on high-alumina cement which, in any case, develops strength rapidly under normal curing. The high cost of cement in the latter is balanced by the cost of steam-curing apparatus and power in the former.

Properties of hardened concrete

These are described under the headings of strength, elastic modulus, shrinkage and moisture movement, carbonation shrinkage, creep, impact, fatigue, thermal properties, fire resistance and durability.

Strength

The strength of cement bound materials in compression, tension and shear follows the same general pattern as in other 'ceramic' type materials, such as stone or fired-clay products. Concrete contains many imperfections in the form of pores, voids and cracks which, combined with its heterogeneous nature, lead to stress concentrations at localised points in the material, in spite of a 'uniform' applied stress. The stresses in tension are especially amplified according to Griffith's theory (see Ch. 1) and, in consequence, tensile strength is only approximately 10 per cent of compressive strength. Indeed, it is likely that even compressive stress may eventually cause failure by crack propagation, if only due to Poisson's ratio strains, which occur in the plane at right angles to the direction of application of stress. The cracks may propagate at stresses which are relatively small compared to the ultimate stress, whether the concrete is loaded in tension or compression, but development of these cracks is normally arrested at low stresses and they are, therefore, referred to as 'stable cracks'. At a later stage, and particularly in tension, the energy released by crack propagation becomes greater than the work required to form new crack surfaces and cracks propagate rapidly, leading to failure. In most concretes, the aggregate is harder and stronger than the cement paste and, in the case of a vertically applied stress, for example, this would result in greater stresses above and below aggregate particles. Cracks in many cases, therefore, propagate between aggregate particles, the nature and variability of which have an important effect on the strength of the concrete as a whole.

As a result of its low tensile strength, concrete is generally reinforced in areas where tensile stresses arise, although some tensile or flexural strength is, nevertheless, assumed in such situations as unreinforced road slabs, ground-floor slabs and foundations.

Factors affecting strength

Consideration has already been given to a number of factors affecting strength, though it may be appropriate to elaborate on some aspects of this information.

Water/cement ratio

As far as mix proportions are concerned, this is the most important factor affecting strength for given materials, lower water/cement ratios leading to higher strengths. The effect may be broadly considered as the same as that of compaction, higher water/cement ratios resulting in a more porous cement paste and, hence, lower strength. The situation is complicated, however, by the fact that strength continues to increase, subject to the achievement of full compaction, down to water/cement ratios as low as 0.1, compressive strengths in the region of 300 N/mm^2 having been achieved, using cement 'compacts'. The cement, in these cases, is largely unhydrated, the hydrated components merely filling voids and forming thin 'glue lines' around each cement grain. The

Table 3.8 Strength ratios for concrete at various ages

Age days/months	1	3	7	28	2	3	6	12
Strength ratio	0.15	0.45	0.67	1.00	1.10	1.16	1.20	1.24

strength-water/cement ratio relationship is, in fact, approximately logarithmic in the normal strength range, the log of strength increasing uniformly with reduction in water/cement ratio. Illustrating this point, the strength of concrete is increased by 25 per cent by reducing the water/cement ratio from 0.6 to 0.5 and further 25 per cent increases would be obtained by further reductions to 0.4 and 0.3. Clearly, when the added advantage of high durability is considered, there would seem to be great advantage in producing powerful compaction methods for concretes of low workability and low water/cement ratio.

Though of comparatively minor importance, it is also found that, at a given water/cement ratio, concretes of lower cement content (and, hence, lower water content) tend to be slightly stronger – presumably because they contain less of the relatively weak cement paste per unit volume. This further reinforces, on economic grounds, arguments already given for lean concrete mixes of very low workability.

Age

After an initial period of about 12 hours, the strength of concrete increases rapidly with time, the rate of hardening thereafter reducing, the strength approaching its long-term value exponentially. Correlations between strength at different ages are important, since they often form the basis of 28-day, or later, strength prediction, by testing at early ages. Typical age factors are shown in Table. 3.8. The relationship between 7- and 28-day strengths has been the subject of particular interest, the general working guide being that 28-day compressive strength is 50 per cent greater than 7-day strength. Substantial deviations from this rule can, however, occur: for example, where the hydration process occurs rapidly, the 28-day strength will show a smaller percentage increase over the 7-day strength, a rise of less than 30 per cent being possible. Situations causing smaller increases would include the use of fine cements, high curing temperature or high-strength concrete. Conversely, increases between the two ages may be greater than 50 per cent when lean mixes are employed or when curing temperatures are low.

Curing

Curing may influence the strength of concrete both from the point of view of the time for which it is applied and the effectiveness of the method used. While it is accepted that continuous saturation represents the ideal condition for all concretes, the effect of loss through curing depends very much on the type of mix

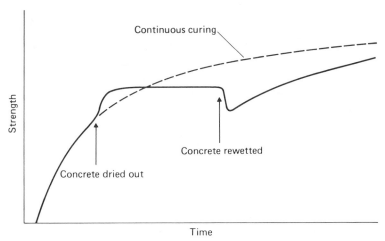

Fig. 3.16 Effect of discontinuous curing on the strength development of concrete (assuming no shrinkage damage)

used and on the type of structure. In strength terms, for example, poor curing would be less damaging to mass concrete than to thin sections, which could dry out more quickly. When concrete is allowed to dry out, further bonds are formed in the cement-paste fraction, so that the concrete strength can increase quite rapidly (Fig. 3.16) Thereafter, since hydration can no longer proceed, strength development is arrested. On rewetting, there is a rapid strength loss caused by the absorption of water, followed by a recovery such that, in the long term, provided shrinkage damage has not occurred, the strength approaches the value that would be obtained by continuous curing. The effect of curing method depends on the water/cement ratio of the concrete: sealing moisture in, for example, by polyethylene sheeting, is adequate in concrete mixes of water/cement ratio over 0.5 – these contain ample water for hydration. Saturation is more important with concretes of low water/cement ratio, since these mixes may become self-desiccated. This is particularly important in the early stages of curing: for example, capillary pores in a concrete of 0.4 water/cement ratio may be discontinuous by the age of 3 days, so that curing after this time may not greatly assist strength development, even if it does delay shrinkage. With weaker mixes, curing should be carried out for longer periods, since an impermeable matrix takes longer to form in these.

Methods of testing for strength

These may be classified as destructive and non-destructive, the former providing the basis for most design and production aspects of structural concrete, despite the fact that destructive testing, as well as non-destructive testing, must be regarded, in general, as an indirect way of ascertaining concrete strength. The basic problem of destructive tests is that it is rarely economical to carry out full-scale in-situ tests, while the problem of non-destructive tests is that they measure some property other than strength, thus requiring correlation information. Nevertheless, factors of safety in structural concrete design have decreased progressively in recent decades, reflecting the measure of confidence which can be attached to destructive testing in particular, together with increased understanding of correlations and improvements in the quality of concrete. There are also many situations in which non-destructive testing has made an important contribution, particularly when assessing the strength of concrete in connection with remedial treatment.

Destructive tests

(a) *Cube test* This is the most common type of destructive test for concrete in the UK, owing to the cheapness of cube moulds and the comparative simplicity of manufacture and testing of cubes. Carefully obtained samples of the concrete mix are placed and compacted in steel moulds, with machined inner surfaces. Bonding with the steel is prevented by coating with release agent. The surface of each cube is covered with a rubber mat with identification marks, or the entire mould sealed. After 24 hours, the cube is removed and cured under water at about 20 °C, until testing. The cube is then placed between the platens of a compression testing machine, trowelled face sideways, and the load is applied such that the stress increases at a given constant rate until failure. The maximum load is recorded. The compressive strength of concrete, as recorded by the cube test, may be affected by the following factors:

1. The size of cube. 150 mm cubes, for example, fail at stresses approximately 5 per cent lower than those of 100 mm cubes. This would be consistent with the 'weak link' theory, since the larger quantity of material present in a large cube is more likely to contain a very weak region. Whatever the explanation, the effect illustrates the earlier affirmation that the strength of concrete depends on the method of test. One possible advantage of large concrete cubes is that, since they contain a larger sample of concrete, there should be less variability in cube results and this effect is obtained in practice. The effect is more important when larger aggregates (say, 40 mm) are employed, for which 150 mm cubes are always recommended.
2. Test results for cubes depend on their moisture condition, a cube dried just before testing giving a higher strength. Hence, since the 'wet' state is the most reproducible condition, cubes should always be tested wet.
3. Decreasing the loading rate gives lower cube strengths, due to the increased contribution of creep to failure. While the effects of, for example, doubling or halving the BS loading rate of 15 N/mm^2/minute are probably less than 1 per cent, extremely high loading rates – for example causing failure in 1 μs – could double the failure stress and very low loading rates would give significant strength reductions.

4. Low results will be obtained if there are stress concentrations at the surface of the cube. These may be due to particles of loose material on the cube surface, or irregularities in the surfaces of the loading platens, because of wear. The machine must stress all parts of the cube surface equally. To this end, it is most important that the upper platen of the testing machine, which is located on a ball seating, should lock on loading, so that the concrete cube is evenly stressed, even if its elastic modulus varies from place to place or if the cube is not exactly centrally placed. Failure to lock would result in preliminary failure of the weaker or most heavily stressed areas of the concrete cube. It is found that best results are obtained if the ball seating of the testing machine is not lubricated with a high-pressure lubricant. Correct and incorrect failure of concrete cubes is illustrated in Fig. 3.17. The ability of the machine to load correctly can be ascertained by use of, for example, a rectangular aluminium prism, with strain gauges attached to its four faces. On stressing such a prism in the machine, equal stresses should occur on the four faces. The concrete cube should, of course, be centred in the machine to minimise eccentricities in loading arrangement.

The machine itself should also be checked for accuracy in calibration of loading. The existing British Standard for testing machines (BS 1610) deals with load calibration but does not cover possible eccentricities in loading, such that a 'Grade A' machine may still be unsatisfactory in this respect. A standard which covers this important requirement is essential if true description of a machine's accuracy is to be obtained. An effective way of checking the overall performance of a compression machine is by reference testing in which matched pairs of concrete cubes of various strengths are tested on the machine in question and on a carefully verified standard reference machine. Any defect in the machine is then revealed by discrepancies in test results for each pair. If expensive in terms of pessimistic estimates of strength, it is, perhaps, fortunate that unsatisfactory machines tend to give low rather than high test results.

The 45° planes of Fig. 3.17 would suggest a shear failure in the concrete, the shear stress being of maximum value in these planes when uniaxial stress is applied. However, the stresses in the cube are not uniaxial, since the platen surfaces, themselves, provide considerable frictional lateral restraint to the cubes, as illustrated in Fig. 3.18. This is confirmed by the decrease in cube strength obtained by inserting rubber pads above and below the cube, thereby decreasing

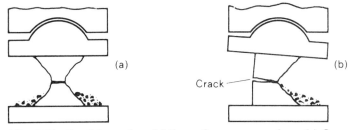

Fig. 3.17 Possible modes of failure of a concrete cube: (a) Correct; (b) Incorrect

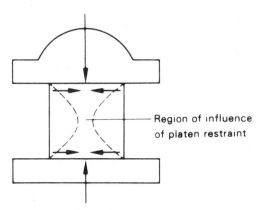

Region of influence
of platen restraint

Fig. 3.18 Stresses caused by platen restraint on a cube during testing

restraint and resulting in a quite different mode of failure. If this is the case, the pyramid shapes could correspond to the regions of influence of the platen restraint, actual failure being in tension as a result of stresses induced in the remainder of the cube, according to the Poisson's ratio of the concrete. In any case, the observed compressive strength of concrete has been estimated to be as much as double that in the actual structure for this and other reasons, for example, curing conditions. Hence, it is very difficult to correlate closely cube strength and structure strength. The use of prisms or cylinders (as in the USA) would reduce the effect of platen restraint but such shapes are more costly to produce. The main value of the cube test is *not* in attempting to obtain directly the strength of the structure, but the test may be useful in the following ways:

1. As a means of quality control. Assuming cubes are reliably made, cured and tested, cube variations will be indicative of variations in the concrete from which they are sampled. Hence, they provide a means of detection of changes in materials or errors in methods.
2. A minimum or 'characteristic' cube strength is the normal way of specifying concrete strength, rather than attempting in-situ measurements on the structure itself. The required cube strength for a given structure is decided upon by experience or from codes of practice.

(*b*) *Compressive testing of cores drilled from the concrete* Cores, although expensive to obtain, allow visible examination of concrete for segregation or voids and provide a direct means of measurement of the in-situ concrete strength. The end faces must be accurately flat, parallel and at right angles to the cylindrical core axis and this is normally achieved using a thin high alumina cement capping. The failure stress is affected by the shape of the core, measured stresses being multiplied by a constant, dependent on the length/diameter ratio, to produce the equivalent strength of a core in which this ratio is 2:1. To compare with cube test results, a further factor of 1.25 is employed, since failure stresses in cubes are substantially increased by the effect of platen restraint, as described earlier.

(*c*) *Direct tension testing*   In situations where concrete is to be subjected to tensile stress, some form of tensile test is preferred to compression testing, since there is no unique relationship between compression and tensile test results, the effect of aggregate type, in particular, depending on whether tensile or compression tests are used. While a pure tensile test might be regarded as the ideal from which other types of tensile behaviour could be deduced, direct tension testing is, at present, rare, since relatively elaborate means of gripping the test specimen are necessary. The methods involve the use of glued end pieces, the casting of concrete around a metal anchorage frame or the gripping of specimens by plates, relying to some extent on friction. Results obtained indicate that the ratio between uniaxial tensile strength and 100 mm cube strength varies from 0.08 at cube strengths in the region of 20 N/mm^2 to 0.05 at cube strengths of 60 N/mm^2. The absence of a British Standard test for direct tension testing reflects the difficulty in adopting this type of testing for routine commercial purposes.

(*d*) *Indirect tension test (cylinder splitting test)*   In this test, cylinders which are typically 300 mm long and 150 mm in diameter, are loaded in a compression tester with their cylindrical axes horizontal, stress concentrations being avoided by use of hardboard or plywood strips about 12 mm wide (Fig. 3.19). The successful operation of the test requires careful alignment of the cylinder (or use of a jig) and packing strips should be used once only to ensure uniform bedding, especially in the case of weak concretes, for which plywood is the more suitable material. Except near the packing pieces, a tensile stress is induced in concrete on the vertical plane and the tensile strength f_T at failure is given by:

$$f_T = \frac{2P}{\pi DL}$$
where P = load at failure
D = diameter of cylinder
L = length of cylinder

The strength measured in this way is similar to direct tensile strength for values in the region of 2 N/mm^2 but, in the case of high-strength concretes,

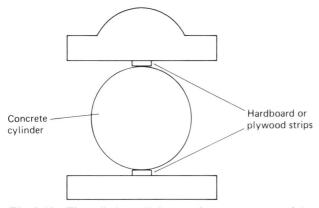

Concrete cylinder

Hardboard or plywood strips

Fig. 3.19   The cylinder-splitting test for measurement of the tensile strength of concrete

113

indirect tensile strength may be in the region of 25 per cent higher than direct tensile strength.

A most convenient aspect of the indirect tension test is that it can be carried out on a compression tester and this advantage, combined with the fact that results are more consistent than those from other tension tests, has led to its adoption as the standard test for concrete used in concrete pavements in the UK. The DoE method of mix design, for this reason, includes a section on design for indirect tensile strength as measured in this way.

(*e*) *Flexural test* The test described in BS 1881 uses a two-point loading system on a 100×100 mm or 150×150 mm beam, as shown in Fig. 3.20, which produces a constant bending moment between loading rollers.

Assuming that normal bending theory applies the extreme fibre stress at failure is given by

$$f_T = \frac{wl}{bd^2}$$

where l = length of beam between supporting rollers
$\quad w$ = load at failure
$\quad b$ = breadth
$\quad d$ = depth

provided failure occurs between the loading rollers. The stress measured in this way corresponds to the weakest portion of concrete in the central third of span but stresses based on the flexural test are, nevertheless, approximately twice the failure stresses measured using tension tests on similar concrete. A contributory factor to this difference is probably that the neutral axis of the beam moves upwards during the test, increasing the proportion of the cross section which carries tensile stress. BS 1881 describes an 'equivalent cube' test which can be carried out on the broken ends of the beam after failure. These ends, which are not damaged in the flexural test, are loaded in compression between auxiliary platens 100 or 150 mm square, appropriate to the width of the beam and give an

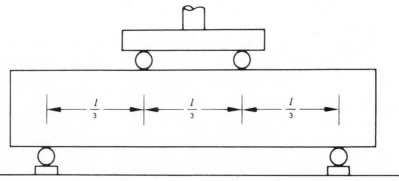

Fig. 3.20 Apparatus for measurement of flexural strength of concrete, showing two-point loading system

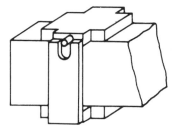

Fig. 3.21 Equivalent cube test for measurement of 'cube strength' of a broken part of a concrete beam

indication of the cube strength of the concrete (Fig. 3.21). Results are normally about 5 per cent higher than a normal cube-test result, due to the contribution to strength of the concrete outside the auxiliary platens.

Perhaps, the main limitations of the flexural test stem from the fact that either a special machine or a compression-machine attachment are necessary for its execution and the variability of results is somewhat greater than that produced by the indirect tension test.

Non-destructive tests
Although three of the methods of non-destructive testing described measure stiffness rather than strength, they are included in this section because their object is normally strength or quality determination. Further comments are made on the significance of elastic moduli obtained in the section which follows under that heading.

(*a*) *The Schmidt rebound hammer*   This is a small, portable instrument containing a spring-loaded plunger. When pressed against a well-restrained concrete surface, the plunger is forced into the instrument, loading a spring to a point where a mass is released and, under the energy of the spring, hits the end of the plunger. The mass rebounds to a distance dependent on the hardness of the material against which the plunger rests. The rebound distance is recorded by a marker and may be related to strength for a given material by means of cube results. The distance of rebound depends on the inclination of the hammer, use on soffits, for example, giving higher readings due to the assistance of gravity on the rebound. Since the area of contact of the plunger with the surface is only a few square millimetres, a large number of readings (for example, twenty) is essential to average-out local variations in the concrete. Trowelled surfaces are best avoided and, to ensure adequate restraint and avoid the risk of damaging the concrete, readings should not be taken near to arrises. The test is unreliable at ages greater than three months since, by this stage, progressive carbonation may have resulted in a hardened surface layer. The simplicity and convenience of the instrument make it a useful means of checking the strength progression of in-situ concrete.

(*b*) *Electrodynamic method*   This is based on the principle that the resonant frequency of a concrete beam depends on the velocity of compression waves

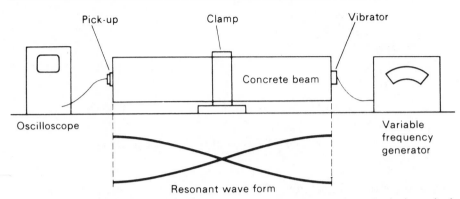

Fig. 3.22 Determination of the elastic modulus of concrete by an electrodynamic method

through it, which, in turn, depends on the modulus of elasticity of the concrete. The simplest form of resonance, shown in Fig. 3.22, occurs when the wavelength (λ) equals twice the length of the beam (l). If the frequency (f) of applied mechanical vibrations is varied until the pick-up response is a maximum, then the velocity (v) of the waves is given by:

$$v = f\lambda$$
$$= 2fl$$

If the beam is assumed to approximate to an infinitely long, thin rod, then v is related to E, the elastic modulus by the equation:

$$v = \sqrt{\frac{E}{\rho}}$$

where ρ = the density of the concrete.
Therefore $E = 4f^2l^2\rho$.

For a given aggregate, there is a correlation between elastic modulus and strength, although E, as measured by the electrodynamic method, increases as moisture content increases – such a change decreasing strength. The application of this method is limited by the fact that it must be carried out on small beams – it is not an in-situ test. It is, nevertheless, useful for repeated tests on a single specimen to measure, for example, the effect of curing conditions on concrete properties.

(c) *Ultrasonic pulse velocity* Pulses of ultrasound, usually having frequencies in the region of 150 kHz, are passed through a concrete structure by means of transmitting and receiving transducers and an accurate indication of the time taken is obtained using electronic circuitry. In more modern instruments, the equipment is extremely simple to use, the time in microseconds being displayed digitally. There are three possible modes of use, direct transmission, semi-indirect transmission and indirect transmission (Fig. 3.23). The most satisfactory method is direct, since the strongest signal is received in this way. When,

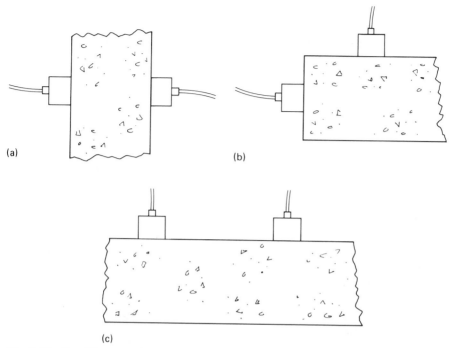

Fig. 3.23 Possible transducer arrangements in ultrasonic testing of concrete: (a) Direct; (b) Semi-direct; (c) Indirect

however, access to opposite surfaces is not possible, the other two methods can produce useful information, though the transmission path is less well defined. The pulse velocity, once obtained, can be used to find the elastic modulus of the concrete (E) from the formula:

$$E = v^2 \rho \left[\frac{(1 + \sigma)(1 - 2\sigma)}{(1 - \sigma)} \right]$$

where v = pulse velocity
ρ = density of the concrete
σ = Poisson's ratio for the concrete.

The use of the formula requires a knowledge of the Poisson's ratio for the concrete, so that there is an increasing tendency to interpret the pulse velocity directly.

The following aspects of concrete quality can be checked:
(i) Variations in concrete quality.
   In-situ strength variations due to, for example, inconsistent batching, can be easily located using direct or indirect transmission methods.
(ii) Construction faults.
   Areas of honeycombing can be detected, since ultrasonic pulse velocities depend on the degree of compaction. In columns, for example, compaction

117

planes may be detected, together with possible weak areas towards the top of lifts, where water contents are often higher.

(iii) Concrete deterioration.

Ultrasonic pulse velocities are affected by fire damage; by progressive deterioration as occurs, for example, in high alumina cement concrete; or by cracks. To detect the latter in a concrete slab, for example, the indirect method may be used, transmission times between selected grid points being measured.

Precautions. The ultrasonic pulse velocity through steel is approximately 6 km/s, compared to 4 km/s for normal concrete, so that effective pulse velocities are increased when a significant quantity of steel is present in the transmission zone. It is preferable to avoid zones of influence when taking readings, though correction factors can be applied if reinforcement details are known. Reinforcement running at right angles to the direction of transmission has a relatively small effect and bars of diameter less than 10 mm can also be ignored. Pulse velocity also increases with moisture content, so that standardisation of curing and testing condition is important when producing correlations between cube strength and in-situ pulse velocity.

(*d*) *Other tests* A number of other methods of assessing strength have been suggested, for example, pull-out tests on bolts cast into the concrete to a depth of 75 mm, or measurement of penetration of steel probes fired into the concrete. In each case, the property measured and strength can be correlated, surface effects not being so important as in, say, the rebound hammer test. The specialist equipment required has, however, limited the extent of use of such tests.

The extent of testing of concrete

As with other aspects of quality control, the extent of testing of concrete depends on the quality and quantity of concrete to be produced. When small quantities of concrete only are produced, it may be considered better to provide an extra safety margin in terms of cement content rather than worry about testing. Such practice is, however, open to grave errors which may pass unnoticed unless some check on quality is made and, in any case, many specifications require a certain cube strength, requiring cubes to be made. If a detailed check on strength development is required, E values by the electrodynamic or pulse velocity methods may be obtained at frequent intervals, being correlated with cube strengths periodically. Such methods may also be used to predict likely strengths at 7 and 28 days. Alternatively, accelerated curing techniques enable prediction of these strengths to be made within 24 hours of placing of the concrete.

Other tests described may be useful if, for any reason, the quality of concrete is in doubt. If, for example, cube-test results are unsatisfactory, rebound hammer readings could be taken on the in-situ concrete (provided, of course, the hammer is calibrated) and, if this also gives unsatisfactory results, a final decision on removal of concrete could be taken after cutting and testing cores.

Statistical analysis as an aid to quality control and design

It is now widely accepted that statistical techniques are necessary to rational-ise design of building elements, since any one component will have inherent variations of a statistical nature, so that one can never be absolutely certain of its ability to perform its task. Instead, an acceptable probability of failure is decided upon and, as far as possible, components are designed upon such a basis. In this way, safety margins for different types of component can be matched, bearing in mind the importance of that component, so that economic designs are produced without undue danger of 'weak links' in the chain. Such methods also may be applied to other materials, for example, steel, timber and bricks.

Evaluation of cube results
If a graph is plotted relating the frequency with which a certain cube strength occurrs to cube strength for concrete of a particular type, it will be of the form shown in Fig. 3.24. The average strength is obtained by dividing the area in half by a vertical line and it will normally be close to the peak of the graph. The

% below given strength	0	0	0	2	8	20	40	62	82	94	100	100	100	100	100	100	100	100	100	100	100	A
	0	0	2	4	8	12	18	26	36	46	56	66	74	80	86	90	94	96	98	100	100	B
No. below given strength	0	0	0	1	4	10	20	31	41	47	50	50	50	50	50	50	50	50	50	50	50	A
	0	0	1	2	4	6	9	13	18	23	28	33	37	40	43	45	47	48	49	50	50	B
No. of cubes/interval	0	0	0	1	·3	6	10	11	10	6	3	0	0	0	0	0	0	0	0	0	0	A
	0	0	1	1	2	2	3	4	5	5	5	5	4	3	3	2	2	1	1	1	0	B

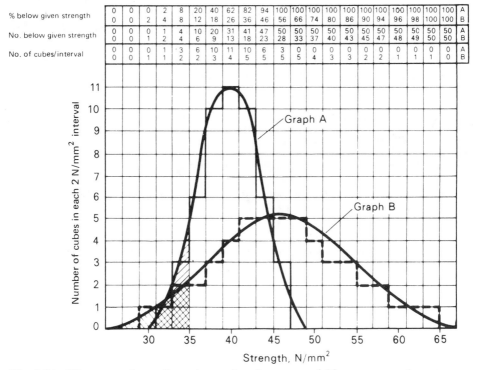

Fig. 3.24 Histograms drawn from the results of two sets of fifty concrete cube tests. Graph A represents good quality control and Graph B poor quality control. The total area under each graph is the same. Also, the area under each curve to the left of the 35 N/mm² line is the same, implying equal numbers of results beneath this strength. Curve B is, however, indicative of a greater probability of very low cube results than curve A

variability of the cube results is represented by the width of the graph. Graph B clearly represents concrete which is more variable than that of Graph A. Variability is normally measured by the term standard deviation, s. For a set of n results, of values $x_1, x_2, \ldots, x_i, \ldots, x_n$ of average value $\bar{x}$, s is given by:

$$s = \sqrt{\frac{\Sigma(x_i - \bar{x})^2}{n-1}}$$

Also, since, in some cases, larger results may be expected to have larger variations, the coefficient of variation v is defined as:

$$v = \frac{100s}{\bar{x}}$$

Hence, if for a given type of measurement, s is proportional to $\bar{x}$, then v will be constant.

If, as indicated above, a characteristic strength is specified for a concrete, implying a certain probability of failures or, in the case of cube results, a certain percentage of failures, then the average of cube strength is not the only information of importance. In Fig. 3.24, the area to the left of a given line relative to the whole area indicates the proportion of results below that strength level. The total areas of Graphs A and B are equal, since 100 per cent of results must lie somewhere. The two curves have been so drawn that the areas below a strength of $35 \, \text{N/mm}^2$ are equal and the probability of finding a cube result below this strength is in each case 8 per cent, that is:

$$\frac{\text{area of graph below } 35 \, \text{N/mm}^2}{\text{total area of graph}} \times 100 = 8 \text{ per cent}$$

Note, however, that Graph A achieves this probability with:

(a) a lower average strength than Graph B ($40 \, \text{N/mm}^2$ compared to $46 \, \text{N/mm}^2$)
(b) fewer very low cube results than Graph B.

'A' represents better quality control than 'B' and this will cost more, but the concrete corresponding to Graph A will require less cement than that corresponding to Graph B, so that, provided sufficient quantities of mix A are used, the reduction in the cost of cement will more than offset the extra cost of better quality control. Furthermore, a structure made with mix A will be safer than that made with mix B because the probability of very low cube results is reduced.

It is clear from the above that an assessment of probability of results below a certain value depends on the areas of the histogram type of graph shown. The process can be simplified by plotting the percentages of results falling below each strength on a special non-linear scale against strength. The result is a straight-line graph (see Fig. 3.25). Having drawn the graph, the percentage of results falling below any strength can be read off directly. (Note that 0 and 100 per cent values are not drawn on the y-axis, since probabilities, in each case, are zero.)

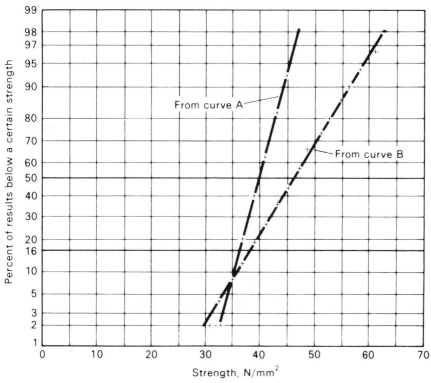

Fig. 3.25 The results of Fig. 3.24 plotted such that a straight-line graph is obtained. In each case, the standard deviation can be obtained by subtracting strengths corresponding to the 50 per cent and 16 per cent lines. For example, Graph A corresponds to a standard deviation of $40.0 - 36.5 = 3.5 \, \text{N/mm}^2$

Alternatively, if the standard deviation and average of results are known, the (characteristic) strength, below which a percentage of results falls, can be assessed from a 'k factor' given by:

$$A = C + k \times s$$

| average | characteristic | k factor | standard |
| strength | strength | | deviation |

A table of k factors for various percentage failures is shown in Table 3.9. For example, the mix of Graph A has an average strength of $40 \, \text{N/mm}^2$ and $s = 3.5 \, \text{N/mm}^2$. To find the strength below which 5 per cent failures occur, use $k = 1.64$. Hence:

$$C = A - 1.64s$$
$$= 40 - 1.64 \times 3.5 = 40 - 5.74$$
$$= 34.26 \, (34.3) \, \text{N/mm}^2$$

This value can be checked from the 5 per cent line on the graph.

This type of technique enables a target mean strength (T) to be established when designing a concrete mix, based on a required characteristic strength C,

121

Table 3.9 A table of *k* values
for various values of
percentage failures

Number of failures permitted	k factor
16	1.00
10	1.28
5	1.64
2	2.05
1	2.33

with a given failure rate defining a certain value of k. Some idea of the standard deviation is essential in order to find T in the equation $T = C + ks$. In the case of new plants, this may be made suitably large and then reduced when cube results give a direct value of s.

The initial value of s chosen normally depends on the strength of concrete produced. To some degree, weaker concretes are likely to have lower standard deviations, since it is impossible to obtain negative cube strengths (that is, the coefficient of variation, v, is constant). On the other hand, high-strength concrete mixes normally require careful control and, in any case, cube results above the ceiling strength for a given aggregate type are extremely unlikely. Hence, standard deviations may decrease at high strengths. These arguments are reflected by the recommendations of BS CP 110 for initial ks values. For grades 7, 10 and 15, the margin is taken to be two-thirds of the characteristic strength, hence the margin increases with strength. For concretes of grades 20, 25 and 30, a margin of $15 \, N/mm^2$ is specified and for high-grade concretes a lower margin (not less than $7.5 \, N/mm^2$) may be used. In the DoE method of mix design, the initial standard deviation is taken to be $8 \, N/mm^2$ for concrete of grade 20 or above, decreasing proportionately with concrete grade below this strength. These values may be compared with the requirements of BS CP 110 given above, which are based on 5 per cent permissible failures ($k = 1.64$). The minimum recommended value for s when at least 40 cube test results are available is $4 \, N/mm^2$ for concrete of grade 20 or above, again decreasing proportionately at lower strengths. High- or low-strength concretes often give skew distribution curves for the reasons given above, so that characteristic strengths obtained by the use of the formula may not correspond to those measured directly from graphs of the type given in Fig. 3.25. Generally, calculations result in low values of characteristic strength for low-strength concretes and high values for high-strength concretes.

Statistical methods are of greatest value when large quantities of concrete are continuously produced, as on large sites or in the case of ready-mixed concrete. In these situations, it is an advantage to monitor the concrete continuously, using cube tests, results of such tests being plotted so as to make clear the trends in average strength and standard deviation, as soon as possible. A simple way of achieving this is to plot results on a graph, as shown in Fig. 3.26. Control

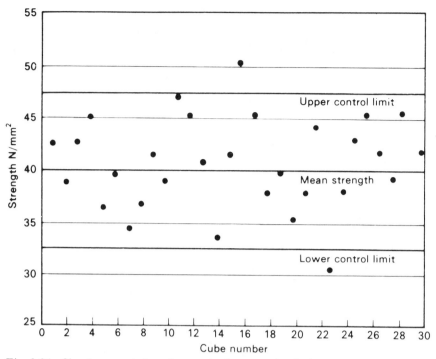

Fig. 3.26 Simple control chart for monitoring progress during production of concrete. The target strength in this case is $40\,\text{N/mm}^2$ and the anticipated standard deviation is $4.5\,\text{N/mm}^2$, with a permissible failure rate of 5 per cent. The first thirty cube results are shown and these indicate satisfactory performance, since only one result is below the lower control limit and there are approximately equal numbers of cubes on each side of the mean strength line

limits of $T \pm ks$ are included and, as well as the general trend of results, low or high results are immediately apparent. A more sophisticated method is the use of cumulative sum techniques. For example, if the target mean strength is $35\,\text{N/mm}^2$ and cube results are 31, 39, 32, 34, 37 N/mm^2, the differences are -4, $+4$, -3, -1, $+2$ and the cumulative difference is $-2\,\text{N/mm}^2$, which means that the average strength as given by the above five results is slightly below that required. By means of a continuous plot of this value as new results are obtained, steps can be taken to rectify any sudden change in average strength. Similar procedures can also be used with standard deviation values, differences between the results being compared to the average expectable difference for the given s value. If accelerated curing techniques are being used to predict 28-day strength, a similar graph can be drawn for accumulated differences in corresponding cube results, changes being made in the correlation graphs, as necessary.

If, for any reason, a change in mix proportions is found to be necessary, this can be effected by altering cement content, using a graph which relates strength to cement content or, if such a graph is not available, by altering the cement content on the basis that an increase of 6 kg of cement per cubic metre will increase the average strength by about $1 \, \text{N/mm}^2$ and vice versa. If the standard deviation alters, the change should be multiplied by the k factor concerned and the cement content then changed as above. For example, if, with a k factor of 2.0, the standard deviation increases to 4.5 from $4.0 \, \text{N/mm}^2$, the average strength must be increased by $2 \times 0.5 = 1 \, \text{N/mm}^2$, requiring 6 kg extra cement per cubic metre. In all cases, the cause of changes should be investigated and, if necessary, remedial measures taken. A very high cube result should be regarded with suspicion – it increases the standard deviation and, hence, causes a reduction in characteristic strength. The question may well be asked, 'Why aren't all the cube results as good as this?'

Compliance testing

There are practical difficulties in implementing characteristic strength requirements, since characteristic strength as defined in BS CP 110, for example, requires an analysis of large numbers of concrete cubes, representing very large volumes of concrete. Therefore, while the term is satisfactory in checking the overall progress of work, an additional and simpler basis must be provided by which each batch of concrete can be judged. There is always the possibility, for instance, of a poor batch in an otherwise satisfactory scheme and an additional means is required by which such concrete can be identified and removed, if necessary. Such testing is known as 'compliance testing' and is well illustrated by the testing plan given in BS CP 110, in which:

(a) the average strength determined from any group of four consecutive cubes must exceed the specified characteristic strength by not less than 0.5 times the current margin
(b) each individual result must be greater than 85 per cent of the characteristic strength

If clause (a) is not complied with, then all concrete represented by the cubes is put 'at risk'. If clause (b) is not satisfied, the concrete put at risk is confined to that concrete represented by that cube. Concrete which is 'at risk' is not automatically rejected and removed but becomes subject to the engineer's judgement and may, depending on the degree of deficiency, be subject to further testing or, after consideration of the situation in which the concrete is used, it may be accepted.

To illustrate the operation of these compliance clauses, consider concrete having a mean strength of $30 \, \text{N/mm}^2$ and standard deviation $5 \, \text{N/mm}^2$. Taking the k factor for 5 per cent failures of 1.64, the current margin, ks is $5 \times 1.64 = 8.2 \, \text{N/mm}^2$. Hence, the characteristic strength is $30 - 8.2 = 21.8 \, \text{N/mm}^2$. If this is exactly the characteristic strength required, the probability of individual cube results below 85 per cent of $21.8 \, \text{N/mm}^2$ (or $18.6 \, \text{N/mm}^2$) is represented by a k factor of $(30 - 18.6)/5 = 2.28$. This corresponds to a failure rate of 1.1 per cent: hence, 1.1 per cent of cubes representing concrete just satisfying the characteristic strength requirement would fail compliance clause (b). The standard deviation of means of 4 is $5/\sqrt{4} = 2.5\,\text{N}/\text{mm}^2$. The reference strength for clause (a) is $21.8 + \frac{1}{2}(8.2) = 25.9\,\text{N}/\text{mm}^2$.

The percentage of random means of 4 falling below this strength is given by a k factor of $(30 - 25.9)/2.5 = 1.64$. Hence 5 per cent of means will fail clause (a). However, most batches of concrete are judged 4 times by clause (a) in which *overlapping* groups of 4 are checked and experience shows that this increases the risk of non-compliance to an estimated 13 per cent, depending on the degree of overlap of non-compliant groups, if concrete just meets the characteristic strength requirement. That such a proportion of concrete should be at risk might appear unreasonable when concrete satisfies the characteristic strength requirement but the basic problem is that of identifying, by means of small samples, defective concrete. If more positive discrimination is required against concrete which has a higher failure rate than 5 per cent based on the characteristic strength, with a high acceptance rate of concrete with less than 5 per cent failures, then more rigorous testing schemes would be necessary, involving larger sampling rates and, therefore, greater cost. It may be added that concrete suppliers would be unlikely to supply concrete of characteristic strength just equal to requirements, since any adverse change in quality control or material would then result in an unacceptable characteristic strength. In practice, therefore, concrete suppliers tend to aim at strengths somewhat above the minimum value. If, for example, as in the ready-mixed industry, characteristic strength is based on $k = 2$, representing 2.3 per cent permissible failures, the mean strength from the above example would be $21.8 + 2 \times 5 = 31.8\,\text{N}/\text{mm}^2$. When judged from BS CP 110, the failure rate of random means of 4 would correspond to a k value of $(31.8 - 25.9)/2.5 = 2.36$ or slightly less than 1 per cent. Hence, perhaps, 4 per cent of concrete would be at risk compared with 13 per cent previously, the compliance clause of BS CP 110, therefore, encouraging the supplier to increase the mean strength slightly above the minimum acceptable level.

Elastic modulus

The elastic modulus of concrete is important from two points of view. First, it determines the resistance to deflection of concrete structures. Since many structural components have to satisfy deflection criteria – concrete beams, for example – those manufactured from concrete of high 'E' value would deflect less and would be preferred. Secondly, and conversely, high stiffness concretes generate higher stresses when movements, such as thermal movement or shrinkage, are restrained. From such standpoints, low stiffness concretes would be preferable, although these would naturally be less satisfactory from the first standpoint.

The elastic modulus of concrete is, of course, equal to the gradient of the stress/strain graph, although complications arise because the graph is non-linear (Fig. 3.27). The departure from linearity for stresses of up to 50 per cent of ultimate is small but, thereafter, the elastic modulus decreases, due to the

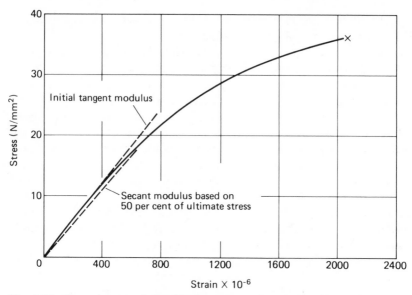

Fig. 3.27 Stress/strain relationship for concrete in compression

combined effects of microcracking and creep. Commonly stated values of elastic modulus are initial tangent modulus and secant modulus based on 50 per cent of ultimate stress. Since the electrodynamic test described earlier is based on very small stresses, it approximates to the former, while the latter, which is usually 5 to 10 kN/mm² lower, is more realistic for predicting deflections in structural members. Possibly, even lower values may be appropriate where concrete is stressed locally to failure, as in shrinkage cracking.

Stress/strain curves in tension and compression are essentially similar, except that failure values are much reduced in tension.

For a given type of aggregate, the elastic modulus and strength of concrete correlate well, although the relationship is not linear and it also depends on age. The elastic modulus of a concrete can be expressed in terms of the volume fractions and E values of the separate components, quite high values being obtained when volume fractions of aggregate are high, (as, for example, in dry lean concrete) even when the cement paste fraction is of relatively high water/cement ratio and the concrete is, therefore, of low strength. Hence, decreasing porosity of the cement paste fraction, whether by increasing age, at least during the curing period, or by decreasing water/cement ratio, generally increases strength more than elastic modulus. The relationship employed in BS CP 110 is, for example:

$$E_t = 9.1(f_{cu})^{0.33}$$

where E_t is the initial tangent modulus assumed in design in kN/mm² and f_{cu} is the characteristic cube strength in N/mm². It will be evident that the failure strain of concretes will increase as design strength or maturity rise.

Shrinkage

In general usage, the term 'shrinkage' denotes any contraction, irrespective of cause, but in the context of concrete 'shrinkage' is used to denote contraction due to loss of moisture.

Concrete, effectively cured, has a tendency to expand slightly as it matures. The expansion is, however, small – long-term values of 100×10^{-6} being typical – and, on drying, it is quickly reversed, shrinkage of over 2000×10^{-6} being possible in cement mortars. Shrinkage can, in fact, occur while concrete is still plastic, if substantial water loss takes place. Plastic cracking will consequently occur, as briefly described under 'Curing of concrete'.

When hardened concrete is dried for the first time, a particularly large contraction occurs, followed by smaller expansions and contractions on subsequent wetting and drying cycles, respectively. The effect is shown in Fig. 3.28 and it is also evident that subsequent movements reduce in magnitude. The origin of these movements lies in the cement-gel component of the concrete. The expansion on wet curing is caused by the adsorption of water into the gel pores, which are extremely small, about 0.15 μm in diameter. The pressure of this water swells the gel and, hence, the concrete. When the concrete dries for the first time, some of the gel water is removed and, consequently, the gel contracts, new bonds tending to form, as gel surfaces which were previously separated by water come together. Hence, shrinkage results in a temporary increase of strength, provided restraint does not lead to cracking. If the concrete is re-wetted, water access is reduced and, therefore, the shrinkage cannot be reversed. Repeated wetting and drying cycles then produce progressively less movement, as the cement gel gradually stiffens and water access becomes more limited. These movements are referred to as 'moisture movements' to distinguish them from the initial larger movement for which the term 'shrinkage' is reserved. Since the cement-paste

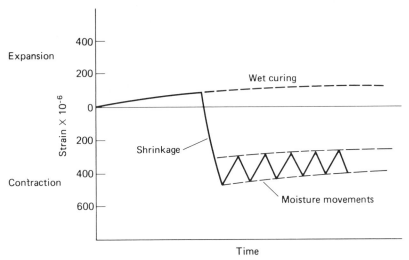

Fig. 3.28 Shrinkage and moisture movements in concrete

Table 3.10 Approximate long-term
shrinkages of concrete
as a function of
water/cement ratio and
aggregate/cement ratio

Long term shrinkage for given W/C and
$A/C \times 10^{-6}$

A/C	W/C		
	0.4	0.6	0.8
4	500	1000	segregates
6	300	500	700
8	200	300	500

fraction is the 'active' component of the concrete in respect of shrinkage, those concretes containing larger proportions of cement paste, particularly of high water/cement ratio, shrink most. Table 3.10 shows approximate figures for long-term shrinkage using inert aggregates.

These figures may be compared with the failure strain in tension of concrete which is in the order of 100×10^{-6}, depending on strength. Hence, all concretes represented in the table would fail if shrinkage in them were completely restrained. Such failures may occur within one month in the case of ordinary Portland cement concretes but failure periods may be halved if rapid-hardening Portland cement or high-alumina cement is used. The rate of shrinkage depends on the porosity of the cement gel but, in general, approximately half occurs within one month of casting. The aggregate may also affect shrinkage, concretes employing smaller aggregates shrinking more because water requirements are increased. Also, whereas most aggregates restrain movements of the cement paste, some are moisture susceptible – certain sandstones, for example – and shrinkage of concretes employing these will, in consequence, be increased.

In order to limit shrinkage damage, the following guidelines should be followed:

1. Do not use excessive cement and water content – BS CP 110, for example, specifies a maximum of 550 kg of cement per cubic metre of concrete.
2. Where concrete is restrained, it is particularly important to provide contraction joints.
3. Cure concrete until its tensile strain capacity is sufficient to accommodate shrinkage.
4. Avoid rapid drying out, which may cause differential shrinkage problems.

Carbonation shrinkage

This is not a true shrinkage, since it occurs when calcium hydroxide crystals in the cement near the surface of the concrete, which are stressed due to cement shrinkage, dissolve in carbonic acid, which is present because of carbon dioxide in the atmosphere and water in the concrete. Calcium carbonate is formed, crystals being deposited in pores so that the compressive stress formerly acting on the calcium hydroxide crystals is relieved, with corresponding reduction in volume. Carbonation shrinkage requires moisture and, therefore, increases to some degree at higher humidities. At humidities above about 50 per cent, however, carbonation cannot continue beneath the surface of the concrete, since the pores are blocked by moisture. Therefore, at high humidities, carbonation shrinkage falls off. The pore-blocking action also results in higher surface strength, lower permeability and lower moisture movement in carbonated concrete, though the strength effect is small, occurring only at the surface. In a good-quality concrete, carbonation should not reach depths of more than 10 mm from the surface, although, in the case of lightweight or other porous concretes, substantially increased penetration may occur. It is, of course, important that concrete around reinforcement is not carbonated, since the protection of the reinforcement from corrosion depends on the alkaline environment provided by the calcium hydroxide. The depth of carbonation of concrete can be easily ascertained by spraying phenolphthalein onto a freshly-broken surface, non-carbonated areas turning pink.

Creep

This may be defined as time-dependent strain resulting from sustained stress. Such strains tend to build up over a period of months, and even years, in concrete under service stresses but they can also make a significant contribution to failure strain when samples are quickly loaded to failure, as in routine resting. A typical graph of creep against time is shown in Fig. 3.29. It is noticeable that both creep

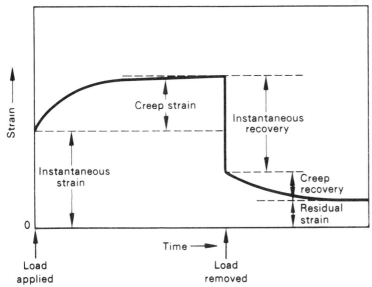

Fig. 3.29 Creep and creep recovery in concrete

129

strain and creep-recovery strain tend to limiting values after a time, approximately 30 per cent of ultimate creep strain occurring in two weeks.

The residual strain in the concrete is associated either with continued hydration or with permanent changes to the structure resulting from stress.

The origin of creep probably lies, to a large extent, in the water contained in the cement gel, since it is much reduced in desiccated concretes. The exact mechanism has been the subject of much debate, theories including the effect of 'viscous shear' in the cement gel, the movement of adsorbed water in the gel and microcracking. The effect, in all cases, is, however, a release of stress in the most heavily stressed areas – typically associated with larger-aggregate particles in the cement paste. The term 'specific creep' or creep per unit stress is used for comparison of different types of concrete, ultimate values in the region of 100×10^{-6} per N/mm^2 applied stress being typical for normal concrete loaded at the age of 7 days. Specific creep is increased in weaker concrete, although actual creep in a concrete member manufactured from such a concrete would not be greatly different from that of a stronger member, since working stresses would be lower. Creep also increases if finer cement is used; if the concrete is loaded at an earlier age; if the moisture content of the concrete is higher; or if the load is applied under drying conditions. Creep increases with applied stress, being roughly proportional to stress at low stresses. At stresses above 75 per cent of ultimate, however, the concrete will eventually fail.

The effects of creep in concrete structures must be considered from two points of view. First, in any prestressed component, creep will reduce the prestress and, hence, reduce the load-carrying capacity of the member, unless further prestress is applied after the bulk of creep has occurred. The creep in such situations is roughly equal to the shrinkage. Also, differential creep in massive structures may cause cracking: for example, in mass concrete when internal regions become warm due to cement hydration, the stresses are relieved by creep. The temperature reduces subsequently and the now more mature concrete is able to creep less under the tensile stresses caused by cooling, hence, cracking may occur. Conversely, creep may, in many situations, relieve stress caused by, for instance, non-uniform loads and, therefore, reduce the danger of cracking.

Thermal properties and fire-resistance

It need hardly be mentioned that, owing to the moisture in concrete, it is not possible to quote a coefficient of thermal expansion, as would be possible, for example, for steel. When concrete is heated, water diffuses from gel pores into capillary pores and the concrete as a whole tends to lose weight. Hence, an initial expansion may be offset by the consequent moisture change, which may take some considerable time to complete. A further effect which influences expansion is the decrease of surface tension of water with increase of temperature. This results in a further expansion of concrete due to the reduction of the compressive effect of water in capillary pores. This capillary effect is greatest at humidities of about 50 per cent since, at high humidities, capillaries are full of water and there are fewer water/air interfaces while, at low humidities, they are almost empty. The expansion coefficient of concrete also depends on that of the aggregate used. As far as it is possible to quote an 'average' value, normal concretes have coefficients of thermal movement around $11 \times 10^{-6}/°C$ which, fortunately, is similar to that of steel, so that relative movement in reinforced concrete is usually insufficient to destroy the steel/concrete bond. Some aggregates – for example quartzite – may, however, have coefficients of $13 \times 10^{-6}/°C$ or more, while that of limestone concrete is in the region of $8 \times 10^{-6}/°C$.

The thermal conductivity of concrete is dependent on its density (Fig. 3.30), though it is also affected by aggregate type and moisture content. Generally, dry, dense concrete has a thermal conductivity of about 1.2 W/m°C – about that of clay brickwork – so that neither of these materials is effective as an insulating material unless used in great thicknesses. When saturated, conductivity may be up to 15 per cent higher.

The fire-resistance of concrete depends on its thermal conductivity, since concrete of low conductivity will heat up more slowly. Hence, lightweight concretes tend to have better fire-resistance than dense concretes.

To some degree, damage in fire is caused by temperature gradients which tend to cause spalling of surface layers. This is particularly true in the case of siliceous aggregates and flints. The effect can be exacerbated by the expansion of any moisture in the concrete. Limestone resists fire well, probably largely due to the fact that calcination is strongly endothermic, hence, the temperature of the

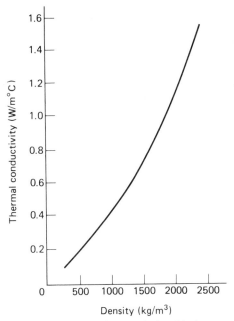

Fig. 3.30 Approximate relationship between the density and thermal conductivity of dry concrete. The exact relationship depends on aggregate type

concrete does not rise so rapidly. In addition, the low thermal expansion of limestone concretes will reduce differential stresses. In the Building Regulations, limestone is classed with lightweight aggregates from the point of view of fire-resistance.

When the temperature of concrete rises, the cement paste is also affected. Breakdown begins at about 300 °C, 50 per cent of strength is lost between 450 °C and 600 °C, depending on aggregate type and, by 800 °C, the concrete is virtually useless. Many concretes undergo permanent colour changes during fire, the above temperatures corresponding to pink, grey and buff, respectively, so that some tentative visual assessment can be made of fire damage.

For effective resistance to fire, adequate cover to reinforcement is essential since reinforcement, once exposed, can rapidly transmit heat. Unlike mild steel, the strength loss to concrete is irreversible and quenching by water may add to the damage caused by the fire itself.

Impact strength

Although the impact strength of concrete may be regarded as 'low', in the sense that under impact small loads can cause considerable damage, the stresses in concrete at which failure occurs under impact are considerably higher than when failure is caused by low loading rates, this rule already having been given under testing of concrete for strength. In many situations, concrete has to withstand impact, whether by chance during service or by design, as in pile caps. Ability to withstand impact is determined by measuring the total energy absorbed at failure resulting from standard blows. After high initial energy absorption caused by local damage, the energy imparted to the concrete during impacts decreases and then, prior to failure, energy absorbed rises as cracks multiply and propagate. Impact strength generally correlates well to tensile strength, stronger concretes absorbing less energy per blow, since they behave more elastically, but requiring considerably more impacts to cause failure.

Fatigue

In some structures, such as concrete machine bases, floors and roads, stresses fluctuate continuously, with the result that failure is often attributable to fatigue. Damage is progressive, a network of cracks building up in the concrete, and the deterioration is readily monitored by ultrasonic equipment. There is no well-defined endurance ratio such that resistance can be guaranteed below a certain stress, irrespective of the number of stress reversals applied. For this reason, endurance ratios based on 10^7 stress reversals are often given and, in addition, the amount of variation of stress is an important factor, higher stress variations causing earlier failure. Taking a concrete slab, for example, the number of cycles to failure for loads varying between zero stress and half ultimate static strength would be in the region of 10^6. If the variation of stress were reduced (for example when a proportion of the stress comprises the steady stress imposed by self-weight) this number would, however, be substantially increased. It will be appreciated that, since factors of safety generally above 2 are used, very large numbers of stress reversals are normally required for fatigue failure in structures unless, for some reason, stresses exceed the design level.

Durability of concrete

The decay of concrete may be the result of two basic mechanisms, physical attack and chemical attack, and, in almost all cases, water will be involved at some stage. For example, crystallisation and frost damage both involve the admission of water to the concrete, while most aggressive chemicals are only active in aqueous solution, since it is in this state that they are ionised.

The arguments determining the extent of damage by frost and crystallisation are much the same as those given for bricks and stones in Chapter 2, although the permeability of concrete can, of course, be controlled by regulation of water/cement ratio and aggregate type. The damage occurs when water contained in capillary voids freezes, water in gel pores remaining liquid well below its normal freezing point. Water tends to be drawn from capillary voids towards the surface of the concrete where, on freezing, it creates pressures which may exceed the tensile strength of the material. These pressures may be reduced when, by use of air-entraining agents, microscopic air bubbles are well distributed in the concrete, such that no capillary void is more than about 150 μm from a bubble. The bubbles are normally empty, even in saturated concrete, and do not increase the permeability or water absorption of the concrete. The quantity of air required is about 9 per cent of the volume of the mortar and, when expressed as a percentage by volume of the concrete, it, therefore, depends on aggregate size, concretes employing large aggregate having less mortar per unit volume than those employing smaller aggregates. Damage produced by frost is progressive, each freezing cycle causing further break-up, surface layers being worst affected. Hence, frost-resistance is normally ascertained by freeze/thaw tests, in which concrete can be subjected to freezing and thawing cycles relatively quickly. As an indication of the rate of deterioration, 50 freeze/thaw cycles would reduce the compressive strength of concretes of 0.4, 0.6 and 0.8 water/cement ratio by approximately 10 per cent, 20 per cent and 60 per cent, respectively. 100 cycles would cause 30 per cent, 70 per cent and 100 per cent reductions, respectively. It will be appreciated that fully exposed concrete, even in the UK, must be manufactured using low water/cement ratios if long service is to be achieved.

Crystallisation damage is similar to frost damage in so far as it is related to the permeability of the concrete. The damage tends, however, to be much more localised, being found mainly in areas where drying can readily occur. The worst situation is probably where one section of the concrete is kept permanently damp, other sections being able to dry. Salts in solution are drawn by capillarity to the drying area and deposited at the point where water evaporates. For example, in marine structures, the most susceptible area is likely to be around high-water mark. Many salts are also hygroscopic and, therefore, help maintain dampness in positions where they accumulate, increasing the susceptibility of concrete to frost attack.

Sulphate attack

The effects of some acids and sugar on concrete are mentioned elsewhere (see 'Organic impurities' and 'Admixtures for concrete') but the most common form of chemical attack is caused by the presence of sulphates in the soil or ground water (see 'Cements' for details of the chemical effect). The resistance of cements to sulphate attack increases in the order: ordinary Portland cement, Portland blast-furnace cement, low-heat cement, sulphate-resisting cement, super-sulphated cement and high-alumina cement. When in doubt, tests for sulphates should be carried out, especially in clay soils; BS 1377 gives methods for these. The sulphates from a measured sample of dried soil or ground water are extracted using barium chloride, which forms an insoluble precipitate of barium sulphate. Alternatively, an ion exchange method may be used. Quantities of sulphates are measured in the form of total SO_3, expressed as a percentage of the original oven-dry weight for soils or in grammes per litre for ground water. Increased resistance to sulphates is obtained by use of concretes of low water/cement ratio which are relatively impermeable to water. When concreting in a heavily sulphated soil (over 2 per cent for example), sulphate-resisting Portland or super-sulphated cement should be used, with a cement content of about $370 \, kg/m^3$ and a water/cement ratio not exceeding 0.45, in conjunction with an inert protective coating. Less aggressive conditions, for example, 0.5 per cent sulphates, would allow the use of sulphate-resisting or super-sulphated cements with about $330 \, kg/m^3$ of cement and a water/cement ratio not exceeding 0.5. Low-heat or Portland blast-furnace cement should only be used where sulphate contamination is slight (say, 0.5 per cent or less). Ordinary and sulphate-resisting Portland cements should not be used with ground waters of pH less than 6. Super-sulphated cement can, however, be used down to pH 3.5 provided the free water/cement ratio does not exceed 0.4.

Alkali aggregate reaction

This occurs when sodium and potassium oxides in the cement react with certain siliceous components of some aggregates, such as opal and tridymite, forming a calcium alkali-silica gel. An expansion ensues which can cause disruption and disintegration of the concrete. Some carbonates have also been known to produce a similar effect, though deterioration due to either cause is rare in the UK. The effect, which is similar to the pozzolanic effect used in the production of calcium-silicate bricks, can be controlled by incorporating a proportion of very fine aggregate of the type which is attacked in this way (passing a 150 μm sieve). The aggregate appears to combine with the alkalis present without the disruptive effect which occurs when particles of larger aggregate react. Tests are necessary to ensure that a sufficient quantity of the finely-divided aggregate is incorporated. Alternatively, the problem may be overcome by the use of cements of low-alkali content or, possibly, by incorporating a proportion of ground granulated blast-furnace slag.

Surface treatments

There are many proprietary treatments designed to reduce permeability and/or increase surface hardness and, hence, improve the wear resistance and durability of concrete.

Typical compounds, which are applied in solution, are magnesium fluosilicate, zinc fluosilicate and sodium silicate. These stabilise calcium compounds, forming fluorides or silicates which fill the pores in the concrete, increasing surface hardness and reducing permeability. They act on only a few millimetres of concrete at the surface and should be regarded as a form of remedial treatment rather than a substitute for high-quality concrete, which should have inherent hardness and impermeability. Other surface treatments include oils, resins and bitumen, and these might be adopted when the concrete will be in contact with, for example, highly aggressive soils or chemicals.

Protection of steel

The principles by which steel in concrete is protected are given elsewhere, though it may be summarised here by stating that reinforcement depends for its protection on the alkaline environment of the concrete. It is important that it be at a sufficient depth below the surface, particularly where the concrete is subject to wetting and drying. Over a period of time, surface layers 'carbonate', that is, calcium hydroxide in the concrete reacts with carbon dioxide in the atmosphere, producing calcium carbonate. This reaction decreases the alkalinity of surface layers and corrosion of the steel could ensue if carbonation reached the reinforcement. The operation of the cover-meter depends on the magnetic effect of steel (Fig. 3.31) and enables the depth of reinforcement to be determined to within about 20 per cent accuracy for a range of sizes of reinforcement. The thickness of cover necessary depends on the grade of concrete and the severity of exposure. BS CP 110 requires cover of not less than 15 mm for high grades and

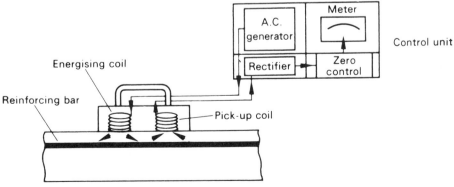

Fig. 3.31 Cover-meter for location of the depth of reinforcement

this value increases for lower grades or severe exposure, being 60 mm for grade 40 concrete in concretes exposed to sea or moorland water.

Admixtures for concrete

These may be defined as materials, other than cement, aggregates and water, which are added at the mixer. The term 'additive' normally denotes a material incorporated with the cement during manufacture. There is a large number of admixtures on the market which play a significant role in concrete production but they must not be regarded as substitutes for good design and production techniques.

Only very small quantities of admixtures are normally required, so that great care should be taken to ensure uniform distribution throughout the concrete mix. Admixtures should be added to the mixing water and thoroughly dispersed before use. A number of the more commonly used admixtures are described below.

Accelerators

The most common of these is, at present, calcium chloride, which acts mainly upon the calcium silicates in Portland cements, resulting in more rapid hydration and, hence, an increased rate of heat output which, in turn, further accelerates strength development. Calcium chloride is most active in rich concrete mixes using finer cements. Substantial strength improvements can be obtained between the ages of 1 and 7 days, especially in cold weather: for instance, 3-day strength may be doubled at 2 °C, especially if advantage is taken of the slight plasticising action of calcium chloride. Long-term strengths are similar to those of ordinary concrete. Calcium chloride also reacts with the tricalcium aluminate in the cement, reducing the setting time such that, when used in proportions of over 3 per cent by mass of cement, a flash set occurs which has proved useful for the short-term plugging of leaks. There are many other salts which also accelerate the strength development of concrete, though the use of many of these is prevented by side effects: for example, sodium chloride reduces long-term concrete strength. Calcium chloride has itself a most important side effect – its use increases the danger of corrosion to steel reinforcement, since it depresses the pH value of the cement, increases its electrical conductivity and, in sufficient quantity, destroys the passivating effect of the OH^- ions present. There is some uncertainty as to what proportion of chloride ions is necessary to induce corrosion, 1.5 per cent by weight of anhydrous calcium chloride being initially permitted by BS CP 110, with the exception of prestressed concrete, for which chlorides were not permitted. It now seems likely, however, that lower total chloride contents may be necessary to avoid corrosion, especially when sulphate-resisting cement is used, since chlorides reduce sulphate resistance. BS CP 110 now limits total chloride ion contents to 0.1 per cent by weight of cement in prestressed concrete or heat cured concrete containing embedded metal. When concrete is made with sulphate-resisting or supersulphated cement the limit is 0.2 per cent. When concrete containing embedded metal is produced with other cement types the limit is 0.4 per cent ion content. The shrinkage of concrete is also increased by addition of calcium chloride and this may be a further factor in inducing corrosion, if subsequent cracking allows carbonation to penetrate as far as reinforcement. Calcium chloride should not be used with high-alumina cement.

More recently, investigations have been carried out into non-chloride-based accelerators, examples being calcium formate and soluble nitrites, benzoates and chromates. These work on similar lines to calcium chloride but have shown a much lower tendency to cause corrosion of steel. They are, however, more expensive than calcium chloride-based accelerators.

Retarders

These operate chiefly on the tricalcium aluminate in the cement, which is responsible for setting. They are normally based on sugars, tartaric acid, ligno-sulphonates and carbohydrate derivatives. The degree of retardation depends on the dose but retardation up to 10 hours is most common, in which case the concrete should be of normal compressive strength by the age of three days. In some cases, long-term strength can be increased, due to the formation of an improved gel structure and it is also quite common for retarders to act as water reducers, resulting, again, in improved long-term strength. Great care is necessary with dosages, which are often very small. A substantial overdose can completely destroy the setting properties of the concrete, this in fact being the basis of one of the uses of retarders, for instance, when delivery of ready-mixed concrete is delayed by breakdown of the transport vehicle. The most important uses are to maintain workability during large pours and to prevent rapid setting, with its concomitant problems in hot-weather concreting.

Workability aids

These admixtures operate by means of electrostatic charges attaching themselves to cement grains and imparting a negative surface charge, so that the grains repel one another. Cement 'flocs' are, in consequence, avoided and free water increased, so that workability rises. Lignosulphonates and hydroxylated carboxylic acids both have plasticising effects, though refinements or derivatives are required to avoid excessive retardation. The increased workability itself may be utilised; the water content may be reduced at constant workability to give increased strength; or, as is common in the ready-mixed concrete industry, water and cement contents may be reduced, resulting in a more economical concrete. Excessive doses of ordinary workability aids tend to cause retardation and air-entrainment of the concrete.

In recent years, the demand for highly fluid, self-levelling, self-compacting, though cohesive, concretes has led to the development of 'super-plasticisers'. These, though more expensive than those described above, can be used in higher dosages without the side effects previously mentioned. The commonly used materials are sulphonated melamine formaldehyde condensate and modified lignosulphonates. These can typically increase slump from 75 mm to over 200 mm, without segregation, provided the original mix is cohesive, for example, suitable for pumping. The increase of workability is maintained for a short time only – between 30 and 60 minutes – so that, in the case of ready-mixed concrete, it is added on arrival at the site. The long-term strength, shrinkage, creep and durability of super-plasticised concrete do not appear to be significantly altered. Flowing concrete may be used to save on manpower, where access is difficult, with congested reinforcement, for rapid pumping of concrete or underwater concreting using tremie pipes. Alternatively, water reductions up to 30 per cent may be made at normal workability, producing high-strength concrete without the need for high cement contents.

Air-entraining agents

Microscopic air bubbles (of size less than 1 mm) can be generated within concrete, either by reducing the surface tension of the mixing water or by use of dispersing agents, which work on the same principles as plasticisers. Examples of the former are neutralised wood resins or soaps, while lignosulphonates are a common dispersing agent. Air contents of up to 30 per cent can be obtained in this way although, for most purposes, content in the region of 5 per cent is required. The amount of air entrained depends on mix proportions and workability, more workable concretes tending to result in higher air content, while fine mixes entrain less air, probably since the fine material 'competes' for the water with the air. Air-entraining agents reduce internal friction in fresh concrete, since the air bubbles act as a low-friction aggregate. Hence, for a given workability and cohesion, water and fine-aggregate content can be reduced. As would be expected, the entrainment of air causes a loss of strength, 4 per cent of air typically producing a 20 per cent strength loss, if no adjustment in mix proportions is made. If, however, water and fines content are reduced, at least some of this loss can be avoided and, in the case of leaner mixes, it may be possible to maintain full strength.

Air entrainment may be used for the following purposes:
1. To improve resistance to frost and de-icing salts. A substantial improvement is obtained, such that current specifications for concrete roads in the UK stipulate an air content of 4.5 per cent in the top 50 mm of the concrete.
2. To act as a workability aid and to prevent bleeding or segregation. The cohesion of a harsh mix may be improved or very good cohesion may be produced from an average mix where placing conditions might lead to segregation or a high-quality surface finish is required.

Waterproofing agents

These may either have a pore-filling action or introduce a hydrophobic layer in capillaries which prevent water access. Examples of the former are silicates of sodium, aluminium and zinc, while the latter include calcium and aluminium stearates. These also entrain air, though they are useful for reducing the absorption of mortars for renderings. As far as concrete in general is concerned, however, it is generally considered preferable to achieve impermeability by means of well-designed and placed ordinary concrete rather than by use of admixtures.

Pozzolanas

This term embraces a variety of materials which contain a chemically active (amorphous) form of silica, examples being volcanic ash, blast-furnace slag and, perhaps most important, 'fly ash' or pulverised fuel ash – a fine ash of specific surface normally in the range 250 to $450 \, \text{m}^2/\text{kg}$, obtained from electrostatic precipitators at coal-fired power stations. These materials increase the cohesion and resistance to bleeding of fresh concrete but, more important, after slow early strength development, they may increase long-term strength, reducing permeability and increasing resistance to sulphates and alkaline aggregate reaction. The improvements result chiefly from chemical combination of the finely-divided silica with lime released by the cement. Some pore-filling action is, however, also involved. Since the cost of pfa is approximately half that of cement, it is now being increasingly used in part replacement (typically 30 per cent) of cement, especially in mass concrete where low early heat output is an advantage. Since the composition and quality of pozzolanas varies from place to place, trial mixes are essential to determine suitability. (Blast-furnace slag is, strictly, not a pozzolana: it has inherent hydraulic properties, the lime only activating these.)

Other types of concrete

High-strength concrete

Concretes of high strength are now widely used in a number of applications, for example, precast products or prestressed members. Using methods already described, it is quite possible to obtain cube strengths as high as $70 \, \text{N}/\text{mm}^2$ at 28 days. Higher values can be obtained, however, by appropriate selection of materials and slight modification of these methods, giving 28-day strengths up to $80 \, \text{N}/\text{mm}^2$, which may be regarded as the 'ceiling strength' for concretes using ordinary Portland cement. Rapid-hardening Portland cement may give strengths up to $90 \, \text{N}/\text{mm}^2$ at 28 days but the long-term strength will be similar to that of ordinary Portland cement.

Aggregates for high-strength concrete should be strong, for example, granite or flint, and preferably of angular shape with a rough or granular surface texture, as is obtained by crushing natural rock. Hence, crushed granite is commonly used. Crushed flint, on the other hand, is not as suitable, since crushing produces smooth, glassy surfaces which do not key well to cement paste.

It is well known that the water/cement ratio is the most important factor in determining strength of concrete. Therefore, to make high-strength concrete, the water/cement ratio should be low, in the range of 0.30 to 0.45. However, the effects of aggregate type and workability on strength at a given water/cement ratio are more pronounced than at medium strengths, so that a design code must include all three parameters in obtaining a certain strength. To illustrate the effect of workability, it is almost impossible to obtain a strength over about 65 N/mm^2 at 28 days at medium workability. Decreasing the workability, at constant water/cement ratio, hence, making the mix leaner (and cheaper), will increase this figure towards those given above, provided compaction can be achieved at the very low workability that ensues. The reason for this, perhaps, rather surprising fact, is probably that, in leaner mixes of a given water/cement ratio, there is less excess moisture in a given volume, hence, fewer potential voids, with the associated strength reduction. Alternatively, the water content may be reduced after placing, for example, pressed paving slabs in which water/cement ratios are reduced to values of about 0.3 by application of pressure after compaction. The technique is limited, however, to precast goods of suitable size and shape.

High-alumina cement

High-alumina cement has been used widely in high-strength concrete on account of its rapid strength development. This cement develops 70 to 90 per cent of its long-term strength within 24 hours of mixing, hence, it is useful where very tight schedules have to be kept or in repairs where disruption is involved. The high cost of this cement is, however, a disadvantage. Design of mixes may be carried out as with Portland cements, the resulting concrete being slightly more workable, due to the slightly lower specific surface of high-alumina cement. The use of high-alumina cement in structural concrete in the UK is now restricted by building regulations, due to the effects of conversion.

Failure of the concretes mentioned above is due to cracking in the cement mortar at places where the stresses are most concentrated – perhaps, where aggregate particles are closest, since there is no chemical bonding between aggregate and cement. Much higher strength may, therefore, be obtained by using unground cement clinker instead of aggregate, since, as already stated, there is a chemical bond between hydrated and unhydrated parts of cement particles. Hence, if cement is mixed with its clinker at a very low water/cement ratio, perhaps 0.1, the whole mixture will become chemically bonded. Compaction under high pressure is essential for such dry mixes but strengths of over 300 N/mm^2 have been obtained in this way. The less hydrated cement present, the stronger will be the product, since the 'aggregate' has an E value about four times higher than the hydrated cement. High-alumina cement is used in this way, producing a concrete which is very expensive but with high abrasion and chemical resistance as required, for example, for some types of floor surface.

Lean concrete

Sometimes known as dry lean concrete, this material may contain as little as 5 per cent cement by weight. It is normally used for road-bases, being compacted by heavy or vibrating rollers, so that workability may be much lower than is normally possible for concrete. In fact, the correct water content of lean-mix concretes is obtained by compaction tests at various values as for soils, the optimum moisture content (i.e. moisture content at which density is a maximum) being used. For gravel aggregates, the value is approximately 6 per cent total by weight of dry materials, corresponding typically to approximately 4.5 per cent free water, assuming an aggregate absorption of 1.5 per cent. Trial mixes may be designed using the strength-free water/cement ratio graph of Fig. 3.11, extrapolating slightly, if necessary. If, for example, the strength requirement results in a free water/cement ratio of 0.86, the cement content (by weight of dry materials) would be:

$$\frac{4.5}{0.86} = 5.2 \text{ per cent}$$

The aggregate content would, therefore, be $100 - 5.2 = 94.8$ per cent (oven-dry). This gives mass ratios of:

Cement	Aggregate	Free water
5.2	94.8	4.5

The aggregate and water batch quantities will need to be adjusted according to the absorption and moisture content of the particular aggregates used. The fine aggregate content employed is normally between 35 and 40 per cent of the total aggregate. This is rather higher than in normal concrete, in order to avoid the possibility of under-sanded parts of the mix, with consequent segregation, and to obtain a sealed surface. The maximum aggregate size may be either 20 or 40 mm, depending upon local availability. As regards strength, the Department of Transport Specification for Road and Bridge Works requires the 28-day compressive strength of concrete cubes compacted to refusal to be more than 10 N/mm^2 but less than 20 N/mm^2, when lean concrete is used in road-bases. The lower limit ensures that the lean concrete has sufficient strength to resist stresses due to traffic loading, while the upper limit is intended to prevent the formation of widely-spaced cracks in the road-base, which tend to result in reflection cracking in the bituminous surfacing. It remains to be seen whether the upper limit, which is of recent introduction, has the desired effect, since there are other factors which influence crack distribution in the road-base. Since the Department of Transport's strength specification applies to cubes compacted in a particular manner, there is an additional requirement that the dry density of the in-situ road-base, as measured by the sand replacement method, is at least 95 per cent of the theoretical dry density calculated from the relative densities of the constituent materials. The dry density of a sample of concrete is equal to the mass, *excluding* that of any water, divided by the volume of its constituents, *including* that of the water. In calculating theoretical density, perhaps, the best approach is to consider the aggregate fraction as oven-dry, dividing its mass by the *apparent* relative density, to obtain its absolute volume, treating all water as free water.

In recent years, considerable interest has been shown in the use of rolled lean concrete in the construction of dams, on account of the low heat of hydration, low shrinkage and potentially rapid construction that is possible with such material. The lean concrete acts as a structural fill in conjunction with an impermeable upstream face and may offer significant overall cost advantages compared with conventional gravity structures.

Lightweight concretes

These may have dry densities between $400 \, \text{kg/m}^3$ (aerated) and $1800 \, \text{kg/m}^3$ (structural lightweight concretes) compared to 2200 to $2600 \, \text{kg/m}^3$ for normal concrete. They may have the following advantages:

1. They produce lower foundation loads and are particularly useful in upper storeys of tall buildings.
2. They may be placed in higher lifts than dense concrete.
3. They improve the thermal performance of buildings by reducing their thermal inertia.
4. They have better fire-resistance than dense concrete.
5. Lightweight aggregates are often produced from waste products, hence, they are reasonably cheap.
6. Fixings may be made more easily than with dense concrete, for example, good fixings can be made into most types of lightweight concrete with cut nails.

As concrete density decreases, strength follows the pattern based on the law given earlier, relating voids to strength. However, the strength can vary considerably for a given density, according to both the structure and surface characteristics of the aggregate particles. Elastic modulus may be as low as 50 per cent of that of dense concrete having a similar strength, especially in the very low-density concretes, reflecting the reduced stiffness of lightweight aggregates. Shrinkage and creep are, on this basis and on account of higher cement paste contents for a given strength, also increased. Lightweight concrete may be broadly classified into three types – 'no-fines', lightweight aggregate and aerated concretes.

No-fines concrete

As the term implies, this type of concrete contains only coarse aggregate normally graded between 20 mm and 10 mm. The material produced has an open texture such that, when used in walling, a good key is provided for plastering internally. Externally, no-fines concrete is normally protected from rain by rendering, although the material has inherent low permeability, since pores are too large to permit capillarity. The upper strength limit is about $15\,N/mm^2$ but the shrinkage and moisture movement are considerably less than those of normal concrete, due to the discontinuous nature of the cement paste fraction. No-fines concrete may be made using natural or lightweight aggregates, the former being stronger but denser. Correct batch quantities are best obtained by trial mixes, the water content being so chosen that each particle of aggregate is well coated with cement grout. Too little water reduces cohesion and too much causes the cement grout to segregate at the base. Wetting aggregates before use is the best way of obtaining a consistent water content.

Lightweight aggregate concrete

Although naturally-occuring lightweight aggregates have been used (e.g. volcanic cinders and sawdust), the majority of aggregates are manufactured from denser materials, such as clay or slate. They are covered by BS 877 (foamed slag aggregates) and BS 3797 (other types of aggregate). Some examples are as follows.

Foamed slag This is blast-furnace slag, cooled quickly by using water. On crushing, an angular, rough material is produced, giving concrete of strength up to $40\,N/mm^2$ at 28 days.

Expanded clay, shale or slate This process is based on the fact, already mentioned under 'Clay bricks', that rapid heating of clay causes bloating, due to expansion of trapped gases. The clay is heated in the form of small rolled lumps, the basic shape being retained after firing. Alternatively, a mixture of clay and colliery shale is heated, ignition taking place and producing a fused clinker. Crushing the clinker produces an angular material. These aggregates may be used to give strength up to about $45\,N/mm^2$ at 28 days.

Expanded pulverised fuel ash (pfa) The ash, which is obtained as a waste product from power stations, is mixed with water and powdered coal to form nodules. Sintering causes ignition and the nodules expand into hard, spherical particles. The material produces concretes of high strength/density ratio with strength up to $55\,N/mm^2$, together with fairly low shrinkage.

Design of lightweight aggregate concrete mixes

The method of absolute volumes is not easy to apply, since aggregates are highly absorbent. For a given aggregate type, however, there is a fairly well-defined relation between water/cement ratio and strength. Ratios are often quoted in volumes for lightweight materials, masses for weight-batching being obtained from bulk densities. Water added at the mixer should be corrected according to:

1. the absorbed water in aggregates (deduct value)
2. the absorption of the aggregates (add value).

There is more justification in lightweight than dense concrete for final correction of water at the mixer to produce correct workability, since the above corrections are substantial and may vary considerably from batch to batch. Natural fine aggregate used in place of lightweight fine aggregate increases strength and workability, and reduces shrinkage, but also increases the density of the concrete.

Precautions In view of the increased shrinkage of lightweight concrete, it is important to allow adequate contraction and movement joints in structural concrete. A further most important consideration from the point of view of durability is that carbonation in lightweight concrete often reaches depths of 15 mm or more, so that reinforcing steel must have substantially increased cover. It has been demonstrated, however, in recent years, that, by appropriate modifications to design and practice, both reinforced and prestressed lightweight concrete can be successfully employed.

Aerated concrete
This is concrete containing bubbles of gas, produced either by means of an air-entraining agent or chemically, for example, approximately 0.2 per cent aluminium powder by weight of cement. If fine sand only is used as an aggregate, concretes of extremely low density (for example, 400 kg/m^3) may be produced. The material, however, behaves rather like ordinary concrete of high cement content, having high shrinkage and moisture movement. These may be reduced by high-pressure steam curing, and this material is used widely for precast blocks and partitions where the very low densities and thermal conductivity obtainable are beneficial. The housing market is now heavily geared to the use of these blocks as a result of the tightening of the Building Regulations regarding thermal-insulation standards of domestic dwelling. Much higher rates of work can also be achieved, since one block can, in volume terms, correspond to as many as 7 standard bricks. Aerated blocks must, however, be kept dry before use, as they have very high absorption and wet blocks are much heavier to handle.

Mortars

These may be defined as mixtures of sand, binder such as lime or cement, and water, used for jointing or surfacing. The plastic properties of mortars are of considerable importance: they must combine good cohesion with high workability and adequate suction to the background. (It should be emphasised that mortars do not bond chemically to the background, they 'key' on to the material by absorption of mortar into surface layers. Hence, a porous or open texture provides the best grip.) The strength of mortars is not normally required to be high. In renderings, the mortar should be strong enough to resist shrinkage cracking and sufficiently impervious to resist frost damage. When used for jointing, the mortar should be weaker than the units to be joined, so that, if relative movement occurs, cracking will occur in the mortar joints rather than in the units themselves. Furthermore, since mortar joints are normally thin, failure in them due to shear is unlikely and walling units may have strength as much as five times grater than the mortars used in them. On the other hand, brickwork normally has a strength between 25 and 40 per cent that of the strength of the bricks used, as determined by the test of BS 3921 (these facts reflect the type of test used on bricks, mortar and brickwork). One of the most likely modes of failure in brickwork with a large slenderness ratio is buckling caused by tensile stresses due to eccentricity of load. Lateral loads may contribute to this kind of failure.

Choice of mortar mix

This is determined by the type of brick or block used and the conditions under which the work is to be carried out. The richest mix in common use is 1:3 cement:sand, by volume, this being most suitable for engineering bricks or other high-strength units, though the mortar may be used with bricks or blocks of lower strength in positions which are susceptible to damp, such as below dpc, in parapet walls or in free-standing walls. More suitable for general use, however, are 1:6 and 1:9 mixes, the former being preferred for construction in winter weather or for more exposed situations. At the lean end of the spectrum, 1:12 mixes may be used for internal partitions. In all cases, the mortar must be able to absorb small movements of the structure without being so permeable that weathering damage occurs. In exposed situations, these requirements often result in high-strength bricks as essential, even though loading may be slight, since mortars leaner than about 1:6 often weather badly, especially where there are sulphates present or saturation is possible.

Plasticisers in mortars

The cohesion in mortars needs to be far greater than that in ordinary concrete mixes, since high resistance to bleeding is required, in spite of high water content and workability. This cohesion or 'fattiness' was traditionally achieved by the use of lime in mortar: in fact, in many cases, the lime also acted as the cementing agent. The use of lime mortars is now declining, although a brief description is given here, since lime mortars have certain attributes. Hydrated lime (calcium hydroxide) is obtained by heating calcium carbonate to form calcium oxide and then adding water:

$$CaO + H_2O \longrightarrow Ca(OH)_2 + heat$$

If an excess of water is added, lime putty is produced, and this was formerly popular because it could be stored in tubs on site for considerable periods of time. If, however, the quantity of water added is chemically correct according to the above equation, a powder is produced which may be marketed in bags and lime is now more commonly used in this form. Ordinary (non-hydraulic) limes set by combination with carbon dioxide in the atmosphere:

$$Ca(OH)_2 + CO_2 \longrightarrow CaCO_3 + H_2O$$

Hence, such limes set gradually by exposure to the atmosphere, the surface layers hardening first. Limes containing impurities (for example, magnesium carbonate, obtained in dolomitic limestone) are known as hydraulic limes and these limes harden to some extent without the need for carbonation by the atmosphere. Hydraulic limes may be used without cement, mixes being typically 1:2 or 1:3 lime: sand by volume, though non-hydraulic limes are predominantly used at present, their overriding function being as plasticisers.

The main attribute of lime is its ability to give a highly-cohesive mortar which also adheres well to the surfaces of the brick or block. The likelihood of capillary paths between brick and mortar joint is, therefore, reduced, particularly in the case of stronger, lower-suction bricks. The quantity of lime to be used in a mortar decreases as the cement content rises, since cement itself has some plasticising action. Typical lime content (by volume) is as follows:

Cement	Lime	Sand
1	$\frac{1}{4}$	3
1	1	6
1	2	9
1	3	12

Perhaps, the most commonly used plasticisers at present are the liquid admixtures based on water-reducing and air-entraining agents already described. Both lower water and higher air content result in increased cohesion, and the entrained air, combined with an effectively reduced water/cement ratio, gives the mortar better frost-resistance than its lime-plasticised counterpart of similar cement content. Liquid plasticisers also obviate the need to store and batch a further bulk material, though mortars so produced do not have quite the fattiness of lime mortars and are, in consequence, slightly less resistant to bleeding.

Yet another means of obtaining the necessary plastic properties in mortars is by the use of masonry cements (BS 5224). The cement fraction of these is much more finely ground than in ordinary cements and the addition of inert mineral plasticisers and air-entraining agents contributes to cohesion.

Precast concrete

Precast concrete products, in the form of building blocks, paving slabs and similar units, have been in existence for some time but recent years have seen a considerable increase in the size and variety of products manufactured. The reasons for these developments are as follows:

1. The increase in modular types of construction and system building has led to a demand for large numbers of identical units, such types of unit being most economically produced by means of closely-controlled factory production techniques.
2. Advances in mechanical plant have allowed a greater degree of automation.
3. Developments in prestressing and post-tensioning techniques have enabled large structural units for buildings, roads and bridges to be manufactured in precast form.
4. By compacting dry concrete mixes, using powerful compaction machinery or vacuum techniques, cement content and, hence, costs, can be reduced for concrete of a given strength.

Problems

3.1 The table shows the chemical composition of five cements which are ordinary Portland cement, rapid-hardening Portland cement, sulphate-resisting Portland cement, white Portland cement and low-heat Portland cement.

Compound (per cent)	Cement A	Cement B	Cement C	Cement D	Cement E
C_3S	57.5	55.9	33.0	45.3	29.7
C_2S	15.9	23.8	35.0	26.9	41.9
C_3S	8.5	13.0	9.4	2.0	2.1
C_4AF	6.7	1.0	10.0	16.9	18.0

Identify each cement. What cement might, on the basis of the above figures, be used in place of:
(a) sulphate-resisting cement
(b) rapid-hardening Portland cement?

Why, in the second case, would the use of the substitute be unlikely?

3.2 A chemical analysis of a cement gives the following composition:

	Per cent
SiO_2	23.3
Al_2O_3	5.2
Fe_2O_3	2.6
free CaO	66.3

By use of the Bogue equations, give the likely properties of this cement.

3.3 Describe what is meant by conversion in high-alumina cements and how adverse effects caused by it can be minimised. Discuss the use of high-alumina cement for precast products.

3.4 Give three important tests which should be carried out on an aggregate in order to assess its suitability for use in high-quality concrete.

3.5 For a cubic metre of particular lightweight concrete mix, the masses of fine and coarse aggregate required are 395 kg and 850 kg, respectively. The aggregates have absorption coefficients of 4 and 10 per cent and total moisture content of 10 and 5 per cent, fine and coarse, based on wet weight, respectively. Calculate corrected batch quantities for the aggregates and the correction to be made in water added at the mixer.

3.6 Explain the meaning of the following terms applied ιo mixes:
(a) nominal
(b) standard
(c) designed

and discuss the situations in which they might be used.

3.7 Use the DoE method of mix design to produce batch quantities for 50 litres of concrete to the following specification:

Cement	Ordinary Portland
Aggregates	Fine – zone 2, uncrushed, relative density 2.6
	Coarse – uncrushed, relative density 2.6
Compressive strength	$35 \, N/mm^2$ at 28 days (5 per cent defectives): no previous results available.
Workability	30 to 60 mm slump.

Use three sizes of aggregate in turn, 10 mm, 20 mm and 40 mm, and comment on the cement and water content in each case.

3.8 Use the DoE method of mix design to produce batch quantities for 20 litres of concrete to the following specification:

Cement	Ordinary Portland
Aggregates	Fine – zone 3, crushed, relative density 2.7
	Coarse – 20 mm, crushed, relative density 2.7
Indirect tensile strength	$3.0 \, N/mm^2$ at 28 days; (1 per cent defectives): no previous results available
Workability	30 to 60 mm slump.

3.9 Use the DoE method of mix design to produce batch quantities for 50 litres of concrete, as in Question 3.7, using 20 mm aggregate, except that 4 per cent of entrained air is to be included. Compare quantities with those resulting from Question 3.7 and comment.

3.10 Use the method of the American Concrete Institute, together with the graph of Fig. 3.11, to calculate batch masses for an air-entrained concrete mix with 25 to 50 mm slump, to have a 28-day mean strength of $45 \, N/mm^2$, using ordinary Portland cement with a relative density of 3.15; 20 mm coarse aggregate with a rodded bulk volume of $1800 \, kg/m^3$, relative density 2.7; and fine aggregate with a fineness modulus of 2.4, relative density 2.6.

3.11 In concrete practice, the addition of extra water to a mix just before placing is quite a common occurrence. Discuss the effect of water content adjustment on:
(a) the plastic properties
(b) the hardened properties of concrete.

3.12 Define 'maturity' of concrete. Some codes of practice restrict the placing of concrete at a temperature of 5 °C or less on a falling thermometer. Give the reasons for this and methods by which concrete could be protected from the possible consequences.

3.13 Describe carefully the procedure for sampling concrete to make concrete cubes, and the curing and crushing of cubes. Discuss the possible causes of a very high cube result. Explain how such a result would affect the standard deviation of a set of cube results.

3.14 An ultrasonic pulse takes $33.3\,\mu s$ to travel through a 100 m cube of density $2400\,kg/m^3$. Find the dynamic E value for the concrete, assuming Poisson's ratio $= 0.2$. At what frequency would a 500 mm beam made of the same concrete at the same time resonate if clamped at its midpoint? A 100 mm cube made from the same mix failed at a load of 300 kN. If the static E value is 0.8 times the dynamic value, calculate the strain at failure of the cube.

3.15 Define the terms 'characteristic strength' and 'standard deviation'. A concrete mix was designed to give a characteristic strength of $25\,N/mm^2$ at 28 days with an anticipated standard deviation of $4.0\,N/mm^2$, 2 per cent failures permitted. The first fifty cube results were as follows, in N/mm^2:

36.3	41.2	36.1	38.9	39.1	36.7	42.0	43.9	41.6	37.8
39.9	40.8	42.0	40.3	38.1	36.2	44.0	40.5	38.6	43.4
44.3	40.7	37.5	37.5	36.1	48.9	43.6	40.2	38.6	37.8
29.7	36.1	34.5	37.9	31.3	47.5	43.6	41.6	46.1	36.0
34.4	39.7	45.8	43.4	43.7	38.6	32.5	47.5	46.0	41.4

Assuming that a change in cement content of $5\,kg/m^3$ produces a change in mean strength of $0.8\,N/mm^2$, suggest how the cement content of the above mix could be altered.

3.16 Explain the meaning and limitations of the term 'coefficient of variation' in relation to variation of concrete strength. A concrete mix is to have a characteristic strength of $25\,N/mm^2$ with 5 per cent failures permitted. If the coefficient of variation is assumed to be 15 per cent, calculate the target mean strength.

3.17 Give reasons why lightweight aggregate concrete is becoming increasingly widely used. State two ways in which design or production techniques differ from those of dense concretes and indicate typical applications of lightweight concretes.

3.18 Produce batch quantities for $1\,m^3$ of dry lean concrete to the following specification:

Mean compression strength at 28 days: $15\,N/mm^2$

Cement Ordinary Portland, apparent relative density 3.15

Aggregate Apparent relative density 2.6; fine aggregate to be 40 per cent of total aggregate; aggregate absorption 1.5 per cent

Free
moisture
content 4.5 per cent by weight of dry materials

Calculate, also, the theoretical dry density of this concrete mix.

3.19 Discuss the connections between:

(a) moisture movement and creep

(b) drying shrinkage and carbonation shrinkage in concrete.

References

1. F. M. Lea, *The Chemistry of Cements and Concrete*. Arnold, 1970.

2. A. M. Neville, *Properties of Concrete*. Pitman; third edition, 1981.

3. T. D. Robson, 'The Characteristics and Applications of Mixtures of Portland and High Alumina Cements', *Chemistry and Industry*, 1952.
4. *Road Note 4 – Design of Concrete Mixes*, Road Research Laboratory, HMSO, 1950..
5. *Manual of Concrete Practice 1978, Part 1, Materials and properties of concrete construction practice and inspection of pavements and slabs.* American Concrete Institute.
6. *Design of Normal Concrete Mixes.* Department of the Environment, HMSO 1975.
7. *Hot Weather Concreting.* Cement and Concrete Association Advisory Note 10, 1966.
8. A. Pink, 'Winter Concreting', *Cement and Concrete Association Technical Advisory Series*, 1978.
9. D. C. Spooner, 'Discrepancies in Concrete Cube Testing', *Cement and Concrete Association Paper pp/25*, 1968.
10. 'The Performance of Existing Testing Machines', *Concrete Society Working Party Report. PCS 62*, 1971.
11. J. Kolek, 'An Appreciation of the Schmidt Rebound Hammer', *Magazine of Concrete Reseach*, Vol. 10, No. 28, 1958.
12. 'Introduction to Statistical Methods for Quality Control', *Cement and Concrete Association Advisory Note No. 8*, 1965.
13. *Authorization Scheme for Ready Mixed Concrete.* British Ready Mixed Concrete Association, 1972.
14. H. C. Erntroy and B. W. Shacklock, *Design of High Strength Concrete Mixes.* Cement and Concrete Association, 1954.
15. L. S. Blake, 'Lean Mix Concrete Bases'. *The Surveyor*, No. 117, 1958.
16. *Specification for Roads and Bridge Works.* Department of Transport HMSO 1976.
17. A. Short and W. Kinniburgh, *Lightweight Concrete.* Applied Science Publishers, 1978.
18. 'Admixtures for Concrete', *Technical Report TRCSI*, Concrete Society, 1967.
19. *Principles of Modern Building.* Vol. 1, HMSO 1959.
20. D. F. Orchard. *Concrete Technology*, Vols. 1 & 2. Applied Science Publishers Ltd, 1979.
21. M. R. Rixom (Ed). *Concrete Admixtures: Use and Applications.* Construction Press (Cement and Concrete Association), 1977.
22. L. J. Murdock and K. M. Brook. *Concrete Materials and Practice.* Arnold, 1979.

Relevant British Standards

Comments

BS 12:	1978 *Portland cement (ordinary and rapid hardening).*
BS 146:	1973 *Portland blastfurnace cement.*
BS 915:	1972 *High alumina cement.*
BS 1370:	1979 *Low heat Portland cement.*
BS 4027:	1980 *Sulphate resisting Portland cement.*
BS 4246:	1974 *Low heat Portland blastfurnace cement.*
BS 4248:	1972, 1974 *Super sulphated cement.*
BS 5224:	1976 *Specification for masonry cement.*

Aggregates

BS 812: *Methods for sampling and testing of mineral aggregates sands and fillers.*

BS 877: Part 2 1973 (1977) *Foamed or expanded blastfurnace slag lightweight aggregate for concrete.*

BS 882 & 1201: 1973 *Aggregates from natural sources for concrete (including granolithic).*

BS 1047 1974 (1977) *Specification for air cooled blastfurnace slag coarse aggregate for concrete.*

BS 1165: 1966 (1977) *Clinker aggregate for concrete.*

BS 3681: 1973 *Methods of sampling and testing of lightweight aggregates for concrete.*

BS 3797: 1976 *Lightweight aggregates for concrete.*

Concrete

BS 473 & 550: 1971, 1980 *Concrete roofing tiles and fittings.*

BS 1881: Parts 1–6 *Methods of testing concrete.*

BS 2028 & 1364: 1968 *Precast concrete blocks.*

BS 3148: 1980 *Tests for water for making concrete.*

BS 3892: 1965 *Pulverised fuel ash for use in concrete.*

BS 4408: Parts 1–5 *Recommendations for non-destructive methods of test for concrete.*

BS 5075: Part 1 1974 *Accelerating admixtures, retarding admixtures and water-reducing admixtures.*

BS 5328: 1981 *Methods of specifying concrete including ready-mixed concrete.*

BS CP 110: 1972 *The structural use of concrete.*

Chapter 4

Metals

Metals display a considerable number of properties not found in any other major group of materials, for example, high tensile and compressive strength as well as the ability to deform plastically without damage; surface oxidation in the atmosphere; and good heat and electrical conduction properties. The latter properties are easily explained by reference to the nature of the metallic bond but other properties require a more detailed examination of metal structure if they are to be understood.

Metallic crystals

Crystals have been defined as very large, regular arrays of atoms conforming to a given pattern and the basic repeat unit is known as the unit cell. Virtually all pure elements, when in solid form, pack in a crystalline manner and metals are no exception. Unit cells of metals are also quite simple, since the metallic bond is non-directional in character. It results in close packing of metallic ions such that attraction due to bonding is balanced by ion-ion repulsion. Corresponding to any one metal ion is an equilibrium distance at which neighbouring ions will try to position themselves.

The shape of unit cell produced may be predicted easily by studies of close packing of spheres. The maximum number of spheres that can be made to touch a single sphere of equal size is twelve and this can be obtained in two ways, the sphere in each case being surrounded by a hexagon of spheres with all spheres in the same plane (Fig. 4.1(a)). The other six occur in two groups of three above and below this hexagon, fitting in the spaces between those in the original hexagon. In one case, however, the upper triplet is directly above the lower triplet and, in the other case, each upper sphere is above a gap in the lower triplet (see Fig. 4.1(b) and (c)) respectively. The former is known as a hexagonal close-packed lattice (HCP) and the latter as a face-centred cubic lattice (FCC). In the latter, the corners of the face-centred cube have been shaded (Fig. 4.1(d)), in case it is difficult to see the relationship between the hexagonal structure and the cubic unit cell. These unit cells are more commonly represented as in Fig. 4.2. Also included is the body-centred cubic (BCC) unit cell in which the atoms of some

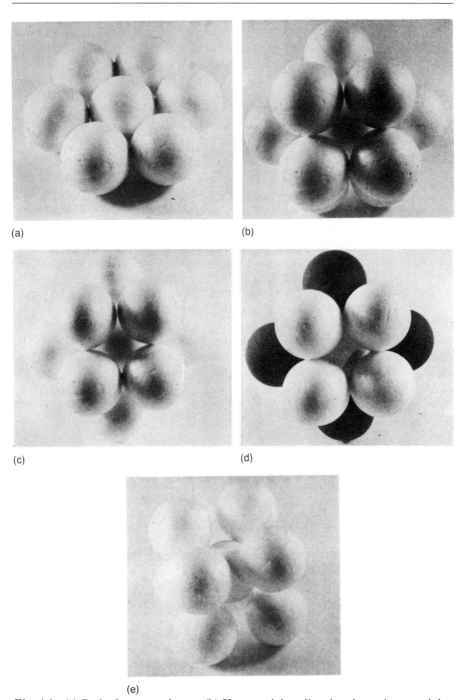

Fig. 4.1 (a) Basic hexagon shape; (b) Upper triplet directly above lower triplet; (c) Upper triplet above gaps in lower triplet; (d) As (c), but coloured to show face-centred cubic structure; (e) The body-centred cubic lattice

Table 4.1 Crystalline form of some common metals

Crystalline structure FCC	HCP	BCC
Aluminium	Zinc	Iron (below 910 °C)
Nickel	Magnesium	Niobium
Copper	Titanium	Molybdenum
Lead		Vanadium
Iron (910–1390 °C)		Chromium
		Tungsten

metals (for example, iron at room temperature) pack. This structure is less close-packed, each atom having eight near neighbours. The reason for this is that iron at room temperature has a degree of co-valency in its bonding, with the BBC structure in this case of lower energy than either of the above forms and, therefore, more stable, owing to the partially directional quality of bonds which results. The FCC and HCP structures are also of different energy and it is normal for metal atoms to pack in one or other form in given conditions. Table 4.1 shows the classification of some common metals.

The deformation properties of pure metals in particular groups are similar and they depend on the symmetry of atoms within the crystals. If a crystal could be observed under the microscope, planes of atoms would be immediately apparent, rather like lines of plants in a mechanically planted array, only in three dimensions. The mechanical properties depend on the population and spacing of these planes and they are influenced by certain imperfections which occur in virtually all metallic crystals.

Slip planes in metal crystals

It has already been explained in Chapter 1 that plastic distortion in metals takes place as a result of shear or slip in crystal planes, the bonds between ions continuously breaking and re-forming as distortion occurs. The ability of metals

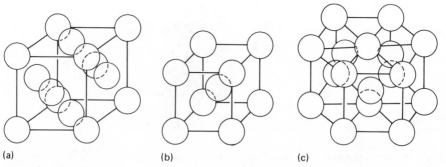

(a) (b) (c)

Fig. 4.2 Metallic crystals: (a) Face-centred cubic; (b) Body-centred cubic; (c) Hexagonal close-packed

to withstand plastic flow without damage is largely due to the non-directional character of the metallic bond, combined with the fact that, in a pure metal, all ions are of identical size.

Crystal slip does not take place haphazardly: it occurs in certain planes between which the metallic bond is more easily broken. These planes are normally the most densely packed planes in the crystal, since such planes are more widely separated than any others and the bonding between atoms in adjacent planes is, therefore, weaker. A further requirement for crystal slip is that atoms involved should move in such a direction that interatomic spacings remain as large as possible in order to minimise ion-ion repulsion. This results in slip taking place only in specific directions, which are also close-packed directions (Fig. 4.3).

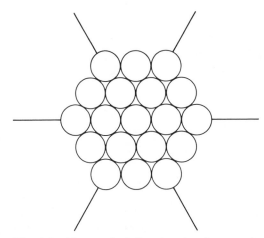

Fig. 4.3 Close-packed directions in a hexagonal array. These are the directions of slip in face-centred cubic and hexagonal close-packed crystals

It will be realised that, in real materials, the applied shear stress would not, in general, be in the exact orientation of any one slip plane or direction. Hence, the more non-parallel, densely-packed planes a crystal contains and the more close-packed directions within each plane, the more likely slip would be to occur under a given stress. Hence, there are three factors affecting the ability of a crystal to flow under stress:

(a) the closeness of packing of crystal planes. The HCP and FCC structures each contain the hexagonal array and, hence, would be most ductile from this point of view
(b) the number of non-parallel close-packed planes in the crystal
(c) the number of close-packed directions in each close-packed plane

The product of the numbers in (b) and (c) is called the number of slip systems for that crystal. Inspection of an FCC crystal, for example, would reveal four non-parallel sets of hexagonal planes. Figure 4.2(a) has been drawn in such a way as to illustrate one such set of planes. There are three close-packed directions in each plane (the three non-parallel sides of each hexagon) and, therefore, $4 \times 3 = 12$ slip systems. The FCC metals (Table 4.1) are widely used on account of their ductility, though this results in yield stresses which are relatively low compared to metals of other crystal groups.

There is only one set of hexagonal planes in the HCP structure (Fig. 4.2(c)) and, again, three slip directions, as in the FCC crystal, giving three slip systems. Hence, HCP metals are generally less ductile with higher yield stresses than FCC metals.

The BCC group is rather more complicated. There are six densely-packed planes and these join diagonally opposite edges of the unit cell (Fig. 4.2(b)). In each plane, there are two close-packed directions (body diagonals), giving 12 slip systems. There are, however, other planes of lower-density packing along which slip can take place, each set including the close-packed body diagonal direction. In fact, there are 48 slip systems in total. BCC metals are, nevertheless, generally less ductile than FCC metals because of the lower density packing within slip planes which, therefore, slip less easily.

Imperfections in crystals

The crystals in all bulk metals contain imperfections in their structure. Some of these, such as impurities remaining after extraction from the ore, are normally unwanted but difficult to remove. Other 'impurities' may be included intentionally to modify the properties of the metal, as in alloying. Imperfections may be classified as point imperfections, line imperfections and surface imperfections, and the presence of each has an important influence on the properties of the bulk metal. The diagrams which are used to represent imperfections are drawn using simple cubic arrays for simplicity. It should be appreciated that, although they serve the purpose of illustrating imperfections, they are not, in general, actual slip planes, since they are not densely packed and, indeed, the FCC and HCP crystal types do not contain such simple cubic planes.

Point imperfections

1. Vacancy　A lattice site is unoccupied. This defect arises if the speed at which the crystal is grown is too high for perfect packing to take place. Slower-cooled metals contain fewer vacancies. There is a tendency for atoms to move towards the gap as if the vacancy were causing a vacuum at that point and this is illustrated in Fig. 4.4 by distortion of the lattice lines.

2. Substitutional impurities　These may occur if a foreign material is present in the metal. Provided the atoms are of similar size (for example, zinc and copper, the atomic diameters of which are in the ratio 1:1.04), the impurity ions may fit into lattice sites of the host element. If the ionic diameters are quite different,

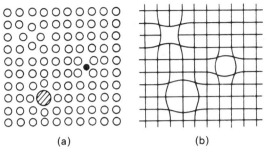

| (a) | (b) |

Fig. 4.4 Point imperfections: (a) Representation of a vacancy, a large substitutional impurity and an interstitial impurity; (b) The lattice lines which indicate the stresses resulting from the imperfections in (a). Where lattice lines are close together, there are compression zones. Where they are further apart, there are tensile zones

then the impurity material cannot 'dissolve' in the parent metal in this way. Metals of the same crystal classification dissolve more readily in one another. Copper and nickel, for example, which are both FCC, dissolve in any ratio in one another. Substitutional impurities form the basis of most types of alloy production.

3. Interstitial impurities If foreign atoms which are much smaller than the host ions are present, they may occupy space between lattice sites, causing distortion of the lattice. Carbon in iron, forming steel, is an example of this type of impurity. There will be a limit to the amount of such 'impurities' which can be 'dissolved' in the metal. In the case of iron at room temperature, this limit is less than 0.01 per cent by weight of carbon, since its presence causes considerable distortion of the BCC iron lattice.

Line imperfections (dislocations)
Although these are already present in large numbers in unstressed metals, their nature may be understood by considering the effect of stresses on a metal block consisting of a large, perfect crystal (Fig. 4.5).

If the block is fixed at the base (Fig. 4.5(a)), the application of force in the position and direction shown would cause a distortion of the lattice such that, in the most heavily stressed areas of the crystal, upper atoms will tend to occupy positions almost over atoms adjacent to those they were previously above. On increasing the stress, the crystal will finally slip along a slip plane by one atom spacing, producing a 'screw dislocation' as in Fig. 4.5(b). Screw dislocations are represented by the symbol ⌒ or ⌒, since they may have a clockwise or anti-clockwise sense. Note that, apart from the distortion of the lattice, it is perfect all round the dislocation which extends as a line through the crystal: hence, the term 'line imperfection'. If the stress is maintained, a further plane of atoms slips and the dislocation moves at right angles to the stress direction until finally the entire upper half of the crystal has moved one atom spacing to the left (Fig. 4.5(d)).

157

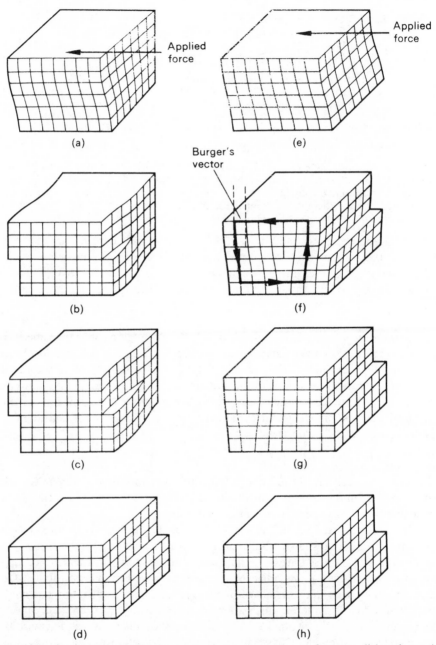

Fig. 4.5 (a) to (d) Crystal slip by production and movement of a screw dislocation; (e) to (h) Crystal slip by production and movement of an edge dislocation

If the stress is applied centrally to the block, then the distortion would be as in Fig. 4.5(e). The dislocation would, in this case, be an extra plane of atoms in the upper part of the crystal, in a plane at right angles to the stress direction, known as an 'edge dislocation' and represented thus: ⊥ (Fig. 4.5(f)). The dislocation will move parallel to the stress direction until the entire upper half of the crystal has slipped one atom spacing.

Note that the slipped crystal finishes up with a perfect lattice of slightly different shape as a result of each kind of dislocation movement. This process may continue further by repeated dislocation formation and movement, causing eventual failure of the crystal, unless the dislocations are obstructed in some way.

Burger's vector This is obtained by counting equal numbers of lattice spacings around the dislocation. For example, if, for the edge dislocation in Fig. 4.5(f), five spacings are travelled, downwards, to the right, upwards and then to the left, a gap is found to remain and this is the Burger's vector of the dislocation. This is equal to the distance which the crystal will slip as a result of the dislocation movement and, since a larger distance will require more energy, dislocations tend to operate in planes which are close packed, these planes having smaller values of Burger's vector.

The effect of dislocations The importance of dislocations is due to the fact that they allow the slip process to take place in small steps, in lines of atoms, instead of whole planes, so that the deformation occurs at a stress much lower than that which would be required to cause the upper part of the block to slip bodily by simultaneous disruption of all bonds in the slip plane. The situation is analogous to moving a carpet by forming a 'ruck' in it: only one part moves at a time although, eventually, the whole carpet moves. The movement of caterpillars is similar. Dislocations act as a 'low gear', producing the same net effect as slip of complete planes but at much lower stresses. Although the example of stressing a crystal, given above, was used to explain the origin of dislocations, these defects are, in fact, present in large numbers in unstressed materials, due to imperfect crystal formation during cooling. They may also occur in closed loops in the metal, the dislocations in places then being partially edge and partially screw dislocations. When materials are stressed, plastic flow takes place by movement and multiplication of dislocations already present, rather than by creation of dislocations as above. Figure 4.6 shows, for example, the effect of shear stress on a crystal containing an edge dislocation. In this case, the extra plane and the associated dislocation move to the right. This is because the plane to the right of the extra plane is distorted and the extra plane eventually joins to the lower half of this distorted plane, leaving the upper half as the new 'extra' plane. Since the dislocation was already present, this effect occurs at much lower stresses than the plastic flow illustrated in Fig. 4.5.

Surface imperfections
These arise due to the fact that, on cooling from liquid, metal crystals begin to form on a multitude of nuclei simultaneously, rather than by gradual growth of

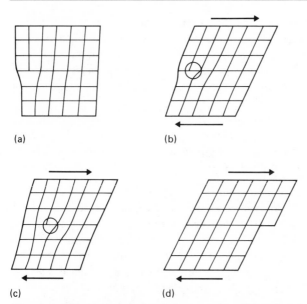

Fig. 4.6 Plastic flow assisted by an edge dislocation (points of instability circled): (a) Zero stress; (b) Elastic deformation under shear stress (unstable area circled); (c) Extra plane having moved one spacing (new unstable area circled); (d) Dislocation moved to edge of crystal

single crystals. The crystals grow to a point where they meet and then, since orientations of different crystals will be different, there will be narrow bands of semi-ordered structure known as grain boundaries (Fig. 4.7). The size of crystal formed depends on the cooling rate of the metal: if cooling is slow, as in annealed metals, crystals tend to be large, as they form fewer nuclei and have more time to form. Rapid cooling reduces crystal size and very rapid cooling (for example, quenching) may completely prevent crystal formation.

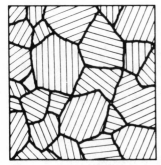

Fig. 4.7 Grain boundaries in metals. The straight lines represent atomic planes

Deformation of metals

The following general effects occur when load is applied. On first stressing the metal beyond its elastic limit, crystal planes will begin to slip by movement of dislocations already present. If the metal crystals are large and the metal is pure (for example, wrought iron), considerable distortion will be possible without weakening, although the material will gradually harden as dislocations arrive at grain boundaries, where they must stop. (Adjacent crystals, having different orientations, cannot normally allow continued movement.) Hence, dislocations will tend to pile up behind one another if they are of the same type (Fig. 4.8(a)). This process is known as work-hardening. It is a disadvantage in many manufacturing processes, since it is accompanied by decreased ductility, resulting in increased power consumption in shaping processes, greater wear on machinery and increased likelihood of damage to the component being made. Heating of the component at an intermediate stage in the shaping process (annealing) allows crystals to redistribute themselves so that softening occurs and the original properties of the metal will be restored. Some metals, notably lead, recrystallise at room temperature and, therefore, do not work-harden (see Table 4.2). They have, in consequence, excellent forming properties. Conversely, those metals which work-harden can be 'cold-worked' to improve yield stress. Metals such as steel and copper are often used in work-hardened form. To some degree, dislocations may, on movement, cancel one another: for example, if an extra plane of atom in upper layers of the metal travelling one way encounters a similar plane in lower layers travelling in the opposite direction, the two dislocations will cancel (Fig. 4.8(b), (c)). If the upper plane were one spacing above the lower, a vacancy would be formed (Fig. 4.8(d)).

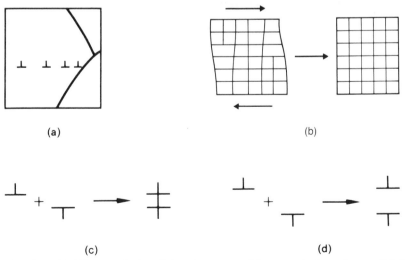

(a)   (b)

(c)   (d)

Fig. 4.8 (a) Pile-up of edge dislocations caused by a grain boundary; (b) Annihilation of dislocations by plastic flow; (c) Simple representation of the situation in (b); (d) Combination of dislocations to form a vacancy

Table 4.2 Approximate recrystallisation temperatures of some common metals

Metal	Recrystallisation temp. (°C)
Iron	400–500
Copper	100–200
Aluminium	150–250
Lead	Below room temp.
Zinc	Below room temp.
Tin	Below room temp.

The behaviour of dislocations may be changed considerably by reduction of temperature. In BCC crystals, in particular, dislocations move less easily, so that, on stressing below a certain temperature, stress concentrations arise around dislocations but plastic flow does not occur. This may lead to cracks if the energy needed to propagate microcracks is less than that needed to yield the crystal and, in such cases, failure within the crystal may occur. Failures of this type which occur suddenly and without plastic flow are called brittle fractures. Since yield is associated with shear stresses, brittle fracture can sometimes occur when applied stresses are such that there is no shear component – biaxial tensile stress is an example. When this type of stress is present, great care is necessary to avoid brittle failure.

Grain size can affect a number of properties. For example, in smaller crystals (finer grain structure), there is less scope for dislocation movement, so that yield stress is increased. It might be expected that the poor bonding at grain boundaries would cause premature failure at these positions but, fortunately, grain-boundary failure stresses are normally considerably greater than yield stresses of ordinary bulk metals at normal temperatures, so that grain-boundary failure without yielding is not a common phenomenon. Failure at grain boundaries may, nevertheless, play a significant role in overall failure, especially at high temperatures when grain boundaries are quite weak. This does not, however, imply that high-temperature fracture would be brittle, since plastic flow in the crystal occurs more easily at higher temperatures and flow may also be possible in boundaries before failure if the temperature is high enough. Hence, the amount of plastic flow before fracture generally increases as temperature rises.

If metals contain 'impurities', these will, in general, tend to make it harder, since they interact with dislocations, blocking their paths. For example, an interstitial impurity at the end of an extra plane of atoms will cause the dislocation to 'lock' at this point (Fig. 4.9(a)). If the foreign metal is present to a degree above its solubility, it may form separate compounds at grain boundaries. It is for this reason that carbon is included in steel: it has a strengthening and hardening effect on iron. Another means of strengthening metals is by substitutional impurities. For example, two substitutional atoms slightly larger than the host

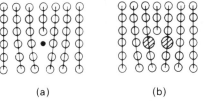

(a)   (b)

Fig. 4.9   Relief of the tensile stress at the end of an edge dislocation by: (a) An interstitial impurity atom;   (b) Two substitutional impurity atoms

atoms, just below a dislocation plane, would cause the dislocation to stop, unless a higher stress were applied (Fig. 4.9(b)).

Where dislocations are locked at each end of the line, it is possible, on continued increase of stress, for the centre part of it to move further, bowing out, and, eventually, completely enclosing the original obstructions, giving rise to a new dislocation (Fig. 4.10). This is known as a Frank Read source. There are several other ways also in which dislocations can overcome obstructions.

Alloys

An alloy consists of a metal mixed intimately with one or more metals (or, in some cases, non-metals) of a different type. The other metal may be dispersed in the first, possibly in the form of a 'solid solution', though metals do not have to be soluble in one another to form alloys. For one metal to 'dissolve' in another, the atoms of the former must be accepted into the lattice of the other and this may be possible in two ways, interstitially or substitutionally. In each case, the solubility of the foreign material will depend on its size: in the former, atoms should be small, while in the latter, they should be within about 15 per cent of the size of those of the host material. Certain valency requirements must also be satisfied. Substitutional alloys are the most common. There is a very large range of these and many metals used in the construction industry today are alloyed in this way to some degree. If atomic diameters are very similar, then solubility may be complete so that, on cooling any proportion of two metals in liquid form, a single

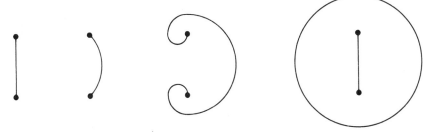

Fig. 4.10   Stages in the distortion by stress of a locked dislocation to form a new dislocation

163

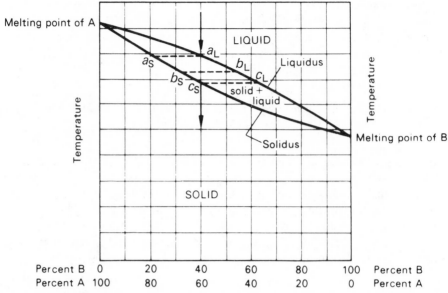

Fig. 4.11 Equilibrium diagram for two metals A and B which are completely soluble in one another

crystalline material is obtained. This is not to say that the two metals are evenly mixed in all crystals in the solid. A property of all alloys, whether or not solubility is complete, is that different crystals have different proportions of the constituent metals, unless, after formation, the structure has been able to diffuse to a uniform composition.

The basic principle of alloy formation can be considered by reference to temperature-composition diagrams. Consider two metals A and B which are completely soluble in one another, having melting points as shown in Fig. 4.11. On cooling a mixture, for example, of composition 60:40, A:B (indicated by the vertical line), solid will first begin to form at the temperature represented by points a and it will be of composition corresponding to point a_s. As the temperature falls to a value corresponding to points b, solid with b_s per cent of A exists so that the remaining liquid will be richer in metal B and will, in fact, be of composition corresponding to point b_L. (The lower and upper lines are on this account known as the solidus and liquidus lines respectively. At any given composition, the alloy cannot be all solid above the solidus line and it cannot be all liquid below the liquidus line at that composition.) Eventually, on reaching points c, the average composition of the solid will be denoted by c_s and, since this is that of the original liquid, the metal must now be completely solid. Between temperatures corresponding to a and c, solid and liquid exist together in equilibrium, hence, alloys show a plastic stage on cooling. This property in itself has been most useful, with application, for instance, in wiping joints using lead pipes. The resultant solid is known as a single-phase solid, since all crystals are of one type though with varying composition, the core of each crystal being rich in metal A and the outer parts rich in metal B. In fact, if thermal energy were sufficient, diffusion of each metal would take place from richer to leaner areas, ultimately causing even distribution.

Alloys in which the two metals are completely soluble do exist, for example, copper and nickel, but their mechanical properties are very similar to those of the pure metals and there may not always be much advantage in using them in alloy form.

Most commonly used alloys consist of metals which are only partially soluble in one another, for example, zinc and copper, producing brass. When copper contains up to 36 per cent zinc, an FCC crystalline form known as 'alpha' brass results, as in pure copper. Between 36 and 46 per cent zinc, a second type of crystal appears, known as 'beta' brass, which is of BCC structure. Finally, above 46 per cent zinc, a complex phase known as 'gamma' brass is produced.

The simplest general form of temperature composition diagrams for metals which are partially soluble in one another is shown in Fig. 4.12. The material (phase) produced when B dissolves in A is known as alpha phase and when A dissolves in B as beta phase. Note that these solubilities, denoted by the sloping lines at the left and right of the figure at the base, increase with temperature, as do all solubilities. The liquidus line this time reaches a minimum value at a point known as the eutectic point, signifying that the melting point of two-phase metal alloys is, for most proportions of its constituent metals, lower than the melting

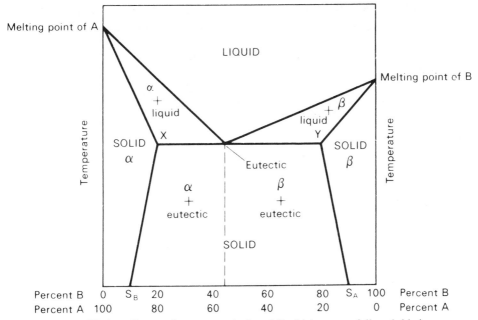

Fig. 4.12 Equilibrium diagram for two metals A and B which are partially soluble in one another

165

points of each of the pure metals. The products which result on cooling a mixture of these metals are as follows (see Fig. 4.12):

1. Percentage of B below the percentage solubility s_B at room temperature. The alloy will begin to solidify at the temperature where the vertical composition line intersects the liquidus and finish solidifying where this line intersects the solidus. The properties of the resultant product will be similar to those of pure metal A.

    A similar argument applies to percentages of A below the solubility limit s_A dissolved in B.

2. Percentage of B below the high-temperature solubility level X but above the room temperature level. The alloy will solidify as in (1) except that, when the temperature occurs at which the alpha phase becomes saturated, pure metal B containing some of A (i.e. beta phase) must begin to separate. If cooling is slow, the beta phase will form in grain boundaries but if cooling is rapid, the metal will be trapped, producing quite different properties in the alloy.

3. If the percentage of metal B is higher than that in (2) but below the eutectic composition, the liquid will commence to solidify, producing alpha-phase material at the point given by the intersection of the composition line with the liquidus, as before. Solidification will continue until the temperature has fallen to the solidus line, the remaining liquid at this temperature having eutectic composition. However, because, owing to the limited solubility of each metal in the other, formation of a single phase of this composition is not possible, the solid which solidifies must contain proportions of alpha (B in A) and beta (A in B) phases at their respective solubility limits X and Y. Hence, the resulting alloy contains some alpha crystals and some of the alpha + beta mixture. As the alpha + beta mixture cools, argument (2) applies, owing to the decreasing solubilities. A similar argument applies if the composition of the liquid is between the eutectic value and that corresponding to point Y.

The nature of the alpha + beta mixture (eutectic) is such that the alloys containing it are much less ductile than pure phases. Alloys containing some eutectic may, therefore, be cast rather than cold-worked. Cast iron is a typical example.

Mechanical properties of metals

These may be described under the headings of tensile strength; creep; impact strength; fatigue; and hardness.

Tensile strength

The elastic nature of deformation of materials has been described in Chapter 1 and this is obviously of prime importance, since nearly all metal components are designed to undergo elastic movement only. But to estimate factors of safety, it is essential to know at what point elastic movement changes into plastic flow. Also, since plastic movement during manufacture is responsible for considerable modification of metal properties, an understanding of both the elastic and plastic portions of stress-strain curves is of advantage. Although most components in service may be under compressive or shear stresses as well as tensile stresses, tensile tests are the standard way of assessing strength and this is perhaps appropriate since, for example, steel for reinforcement is principally under tension, as is the lower flange in a simply-supported beam.

Tensile tests are carried out by loading uniformly to destruction either bars or wires (as in the case of reinforcement or prestressing wire) or carefully cut strips of the metal component.

The exact nature and significance of stress-strain relationships produced by tensile testing depends on the nature and formation process of the metal and the differences are best understood by consideration of the behaviour of some simplified structures.

If a single perfect crystal were stressed, the yield-point stress would, in the absence of dislocations, be very high. The stress would be dependent, however, on the orientation of the applied stress with respect to that of close-packed planes – it could vary quite widely, especially in a HCP crystal in which there is only one set of close-packed planes. Once dislocations have formed and yielding has occurred, further plastic flow would take place with no further stress increase – in fact, depending on test-machine characteristics, a yield point drop may be obtained since dislocations, once formed, travel easily in the absence of interference from impurities or other obstructions. Hence, in this case, the yield stress would be equal to the ultimate stress (Fig. 4.13).

If the metal were polycrystalline but each crystal were perfect, the yield stress would correspond to an average value, taking into account the random orientation of grains. There may, again, be a yield-point drop, as newly-formed dislocations travel easily through crystals but, unlike the single crystal, dislocations cannot now proceed unhindered from one grain to the next (assuming recrystallisation does not occur) and so there is a further progressive rise of stress with strain as

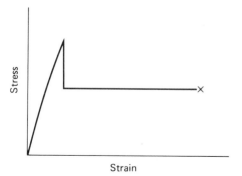

Fig. 4.13 Stress/strain diagram for a single, perfect crystal. The yield point would depend on the crystal orientation

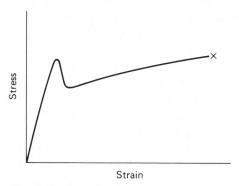

Fig. 4.14   Stress/strain diagram for a polycrystalline metal (perfect crystals)

work-hardening occurs (Fig. 4.14). It should be emphasised that, since the dislocation-free crystals are never obtained in practice in bulk metals, these stress-strain relationships do not occur in practice: they have been described in order that the effects of the various crystal defects be understood.

When stress is applied to a polycrystalline metal containing dislocations, yielding occurs much earlier, since there is now no need to generate dislocations, the sole requirement being to cause the existing ones to move. In most metals, the presence of dislocations, together with other impurities and associated internal stresses, often causes plastic flow at very low stresses. In such metals, there is no clearly defined yield point, since the stress at which individual dislocations begin to move depends on their position. Stress-strain graphs of the form shown in Fig. 4.15 result and this is exhibited by most non-ferrous metals. Working stresses in such metals are normally based on '0.2 per cent proof stress'. To

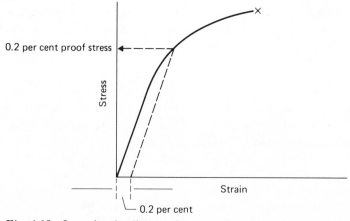

Fig. 4.15   Stress/strain diagram for a metal which does not have a well-defined yield point. Instead of yield stress, a stress is used corresponding to 0.2 per cent plastic strain and known as the 0.2 per cent proof stress

obtain this stress, a line is drawn on the stress-strain graph, parallel to the curve at the origin but commencing at 0.2 per cent strain (Fig. 4.15). The stress at which this intersects the curve is the stress required. The addition of substitutional impurities to give single-phase alloys does not fundamentally alter this behaviour, although yield stress may be increased, due to the resulting distortions within crystal planes.

The case is quite different when interstitial impurities are present, as in ferrous metals. The dislocations in the crystals then tend to gather congregations ('atmospheres') of interstitial impurities around them, as in Fig. 4.9(a). Light elements, such as carbon and nitrogen, dissolve in this way. On stressing the material, these atmospheres restrain the movement of dislocations, causing an artifically high yield point. As a consequence, when the yield point is reached and the dislocations move clear of the impurities, they become more mobile and the stress in the metal suddenly drops. An alternative possible cause could be the creation of new dislocations just before yielding which then multiply rapidly, moving more slowly as they multiply, assuming the strain rate to be constant. This multiplication of dislocations on yielding allows straining to continue at a reduced stress. The form of a stress-strain curve is, therefore, as in Fig. 4.16.

The reduction in stress is known as a yield point drop (point A). It cannot occur in substitutional alloys because the larger substitutional impurities have much lower mobility than interstitial impurities and cannot move to dislocation sites. On removal of load at point X, the dotted line is followed as the stress reduces, being retraced on reloading so that the material is now effectively stronger than originally, in the sense that its yield point is now higher. Note, also, there will be no yield-point drop on retesting. On the other hand, if the metal is left for some days, the interstitial atoms will diffuse back to dislocation sites so that, on loading, a yield-point drop again occurs. This process is known as strain aging and the metal becomes effectively stronger by the action of dislocation pinning. The yield-point drop may be restored quite quickly by heating the metal to about 200 °C or higher.

(Where a yield-point drop occurs, design codes are normally based on the lower yield stress, since the upper point is difficult to measure and varies from specimen to specimen.)

Figure 4.16 is, in fact, typical of the form of the stress-strain curve for mild steel. In addition to the above features, the following points are worthy of note:

1. There is normally a slight deviation from Hooke's law (i.e. stress proportional to strain) before the elastic limit is reached – point B.
2. As strains increase, the metal will become thinner, so that the true stress in the metal is actually higher than that obtained by calculations based on the original cross-sectional area.
3. From point C onwards, deformation continues at a single point on the bar only, since, due to a stress concentration at this point, perhaps caused by a slight dent in the bar, plastic movement is sufficient to cause a local reduction in cross-sectional area known as 'necking'. The apparent stress-strain curve

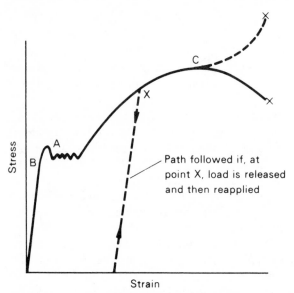

Fig. 4.16 Stress/strain diagram for mild steel

appears to have a negative gradient from this point but, in fact, the true stress in the necked region is still increasing (dotted line).

4. Since failure occurs after significant plastic flow, it is normally referred to as 'ductile'. After extensive plastic deformation, there is a tendency for small voids ('inclusions') to form in grains, possibly started where second-phase particles separate from the matrix. These grow and, on the principles of Griffith's theory, concentrate the stress in remaining parts of the crystal. The crystal subsequently fails in tension (cleavage), forming a fracture surface in the most heavily stressed central region. The external annulus fails finally in shear at 45° to the tensile axis, leading to a 'cup and cone' fracture.

It should be noted that, when considerable work-hardening is carried out as, for example, in cold-drawn prestressing wire or cold-worked steel reinforcing bars, the strain-aging effect mentioned above is small compared to the hardening effect obtained by dislocation interaction. Hence, yielding of these materials is similar to that of non-ferrous metals, as in Fig. 4.15, and proof stresses are again employed.

Creep

This is defined as time-dependent strain which occurs when a steady stress is maintained. The phenomenon has been described in concrete but, although the same effect occurs in metals, the cause is quite different.

Creep in metals can be satisfactorily explained by reference to the dislocations they contain. All dislocations have a certain amount of thermal energy and this

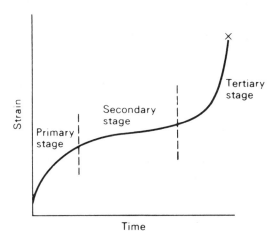

Fig. 4.17 Stages in the fracture of a metal, due to creep

will fluctuate, according to statistical laws, from place to place in the metal and with time. If occasions arise when a dislocation, previously locked by other dislocations or defects, has sufficient thermal energy, then it will, when the metal is under stress, tend to climb over the obstacle and thereby allow some plastic movement in the metal. A typical strain-time diagram for a metal undergoing creep is shown in Fig. 4.17. During the first stage, known as primary creep, strain increases rapidly from the initial instantaneous value, the rate falling off as dislocations become trapped. During the secondary stage, diffusion of atoms leads to a gradual increase of strain as dislocations interact and annihilate one another. The process is known as 'recovery'. Finally, in the third stage, necking occurs, with eventual failure. It is clear that increasing stress and increasing temperature will both contribute to creep strain so that the scale of the time axis will depend on the stress, temperature and metal used: it may vary between minutes and years. Reducing the temperature or the stress may reduce the creep rate to the extent that the secondary and/or tertiary stages of Fig. 4.17 are not reached. It would seem likely, also, that some creep could occur even at low temperatures, since even then there would be some statistical probability of dislocation movement. Although creep does occur at low temperatures, significant strains do not normally occur at temperatures below about 40 per cent of the melting point temperature of the metal in K. Lead, for example, has a melting point of 327 °C = 600 K. Room temperature (20 °C) equals 293 K and this is 49 per cent of 600 K, so that lead would be expected to creep at normal temperatures. This fact is well known and adequate restraint of lead components, which are stressed due to their weight, is essential in order to avoid distortion with time. The melting point of iron is, on the other hand, 1539 °C, so that creep would not be expected in ferrous metals at normal temperatures. A related phenomenon does, however, occur in cold-worked ferrous metals on stressing. The distortion of the crystals on cold-working leads to stresses in steels which tend to reduce by dislocation movement when a component is stressed in service.

This is known as 'relaxation' and allowances must be made, for example, for the loss of prestress that occurs in prestressed concrete, particularly when the working stress is near the characteristic strength of the material. Relaxation does not, however, lead to ultimate failure of the component, even under high stress, and it can be removed by initially stressing the wire beyond its in-service stress. If a metal is at a temperature at which creep is likely, its performance will be improved with increase of grain size (and, therefore, reduction in the number of grain boundaries), since grain boundaries at such temperatures tend to be receptive to dislocations, thus permitting plastic flow. Work-hardening increases creep-resistance, provided recrystallisation does not occur. In lead, for example, a small amount of cold-working is beneficial but extensive cold-working would initiate recrystallisation and, therefore, the improvement in creep-resistance would be lost. Creep-resistance can be improved by alloying, although metals which dissolve readily in the parent metal are not, unfortunately, very effective in pinning dislocations at high operating temperatures. Various methods of producing precipitates or dispersions of alloying elements have been developed where high-temperature creep-resistance is required.

Impact strength

Impact testing measures the toughness of metals, that is, their ability to absorb energy quickly. There are many possible causes of shock loading in buildings – even the slamming of a door may produce considerable impact stresses. When a structure is subject, for example, to the use of heavy loading equipment, failure may occur due to the shock of impacts on it. Some idea of impact strength can be gathered from the area under the stress-strain graph obtained from a tensile test, since this is related to the energy absorbed during the test. Brittle metals exhibit very little strain before failure, so that the area is small, while annealed pure metals may undergo very large strains before failure. However, the object of impact testing is to determine performance under rapid or shock loading and stress-strain curves tend to change in form under such conditions so that their use is limited.

The energy absorbed by impact of a metal, in practice, is measured by means of a small notched specimen of the metal. The impact is produced by a pendulum and the energy absorbed by the specimen is proportional to the difference in heights of the pendulum when at rest before and after impact, a further indication of brittleness being given by the proportion of the cross section of the specimen which has failed in a brittle manner. Figure 4.18 shows the load test, although, more recently, the Charpy test has been commonly used, in which the notched specimen is supported as a beam, with the notch at the centre, and impacted from behind. The energy absorbed is affected by the following factors:

1. The temperature. The impact strength of metals depends on the degree to which plastic flow can take place in the small interval of time between initial impact and fracture. If the yield point of the metal is increased, as occurs on cooling, thermal energy of dislocations is reduced and, therefore, plastic

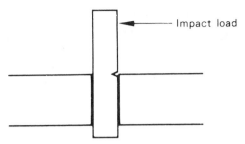

Fig. 4.18 One form of impact-testing apparatus

flow will be more difficult. As a result, the energy absorbed during impact will decrease. In the case of some metals, notably BCC structures such as ferrous metals, the impact strength may drop very rapidly with temperature (Fig. 4.19). This may be attributed to the fact that, on cooling, a temperature is reached at which the yield point stress exceeds the fracture strength, so that virtually no plastic movement occurs. This transition is known as the ductile-brittle transition and, for low-carbon steels, it takes place between 0 and $-50°$C, dependent on the type of impact (see 4, p. 174). The ductile-brittle transition is more gradual for higher-carbon steels but note that impact strength of medium/high-carbon steels is quite sensitive to temperature changes at normal temperatures. The effect of lowering temperature on HCP metals such as titanium and zinc is similar to BCC metals but, in the case of FCC metals, such as aluminium, copper and lead, there is no such transition and ductile behaviour is exhibited even at very low temperatures.

2. The geometry of the notch at which failure occurs. A smaller radius at the root of the notch produces a larger stress at this point, so that cracks which

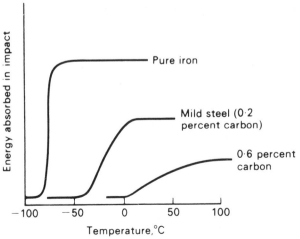

Fig. 4.19 The nature of the ductile-brittle transition for steels of different carbon content

originate here form more quickly. The impact strength of metals in service depends, similarly, on surface defects and stress concentrations in them. The ductile-brittle transition temperature is also raised by any stress-concentrating mechanism.

3. Grain size. Coarser grains correspond to reduced yield stresses and might, therefore, be expected to increase resistance to impact failure. A more important effect, however, is that slip planes are longer in coarse-grained crystals, so that there is a greater tendency for dislocations to form clusters, giving rise to stress concentrations and, subsequently, cracks. Grain boundaries, in addition, tend to stop any cracks from being transmitted. Hence, by grain refining, as occurs in normalising or by addition of some alloying metals (such as niobium or manganese in steel), impact strength may be increased.

4. The straining rate caused by the impact. The more suddenly the impact occurs, the less time will be available for absorption of energy by yielding. It is known that yield stresses tend to be higher when loading is more rapid, because dislocations take a finite time to move in order to cause yielding. Hence, a very severe impact may cause metals that are normally ductile to behave in a brittle manner. Again, this effect is particularly marked in BCC metals, due to dislocation pinning and, in HCP metals, due to their inherent low ductility.

Fatigue

This is defined as a reduction in strength caused by continued variations in loading. The phenomenon came to light as a result of aircraft crashes caused by fatigue in wing structures, because of continued vibration and load reversal. It is also quite possible for fatigue to occur in bridges where, because of traffic movement, stresses are continually fluctuating.

Fatigue damage normally starts at a fault in the metal, such as a weld fault, sharp concave corner or void. Each of these causes a local concentration of stress, resulting in yielding at that point.

Over a period of time work-hardening occurs, reducing the ability of the metal to flow under stress and, eventually, leading to the formation of micro-cracks. These further concentrate the stress and, therefore, propagate until the stress in the remaining material is sufficient to cause failure. There is, very often, virtually no visible distortion before failure and the presence of fatigue cracking can usually be ascertained only by close inspection or non-destructive testing techniques. In situations where stress reversals are encountered, great care may, therefore, be necessary to avoid catastrophic failures.

Fatigue performance of metals may be investigated by rotation of a bar supported in bearings at both ends and loaded at its centre point. As the bar rotates about its own axis, the load causes fluctuation of the bending moment. Alternatively, in the case of larger components, for example, steel beams, a fluctuating load may be applied to the mid-point of a simply-supported span.

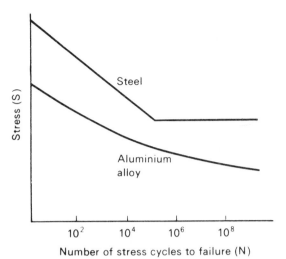

Fig. 4.20 S-N curves for steel and an aluminium alloy

The number of stress reversals N to cause fracture at a given stress S is measured and results are plotted in the form of an S-N curve (Fig. 4.20).

Curves are of two types. Metals in which strain aging occurs show a certain stress below which fatigue does not occur. This is because, for example, in the case of steel, the carbon 'atmospheres' prevent dislocation movement. The stress is, in the case of mild steel, about 0.4 times the ultimate tensile strength (known as the endurance ratio). In metals which do not exhibit strain aging (for example, aluminium), failure may occur at very low stresses on continued stress reversal.

Fatigue strengths increase with tensile strength or decrease of temperature, and decrease in the presence of impurities, surface defects and corrosive environments. Tensile stresses tend to cause cracks to propagate so that they result in lower fatigue strengths than compressive stresses. If a compressive stress can be imparted to the surface as, for example, by carburising or nitriding, fatigue strength will thus be increased. Refining grain structure also increases fatigue resistance, since, as mentioned under 'Impact strength', smaller grains tend to reduce stress concentrations and grain boundaries are able to inhibit the spread of micro-cracks.

Hardness

The hardness, as such, of metals for constructional purposes is not normally an important criterion. Hardness testing, however, has been used for quality-control purposes during the manufacture of, for example, rolled steel joists, since local deformation of metal is involved and it is possible for a given metal to correlate hardness and yield strength. 'Brinell' hardness is measured by pressing a hardened steel ball into the surface of the metal under a load appropriate to the softness of the metal. In the case of steel, the load is normally about 30 kN with a 10 mm diameter ball. The diameter of the dent is measured microscopically and the Brinell hardness is then equal to:

$$\frac{\text{load}}{\text{surface area of the indentation}}$$

In some metals, hardness may be limited to a maximum value, since it is indicative of a brittle structure. For example, BS 4622 for grey cast iron pipes includes the use of the hardness test for this purpose.

Metallic corrosion

This may be described under the headings oxidation, electrolytic corrosion and acidic corrosion.

Oxidation

Although the metallic bond has shown itself to be such that metals often have considerable strength and toughness in a mechanical sense, almost all metals are intrinsically unstable in an oxygen-containing atmosphere at normal temperatures. This is due to the fact that it is not possible for a crystal lattice to be perfect at the surface of the metal grains. Therefore, the metal atoms at the surface tend to be highly reactive and, in the case of most metals, combine very quickly with oxygen to form a more stable arrangement. Oxygen molecules in the atmosphere split into atoms, each of which contains six electrons in its outer shell, thus requiring two electrons to make a stable octet. These electrons are supplied by atoms at the surface of the metal so that ionic bonding occurs and a metallic oxide is formed (Fig. 4.21). The precise behaviour of a particular metal with its oxide

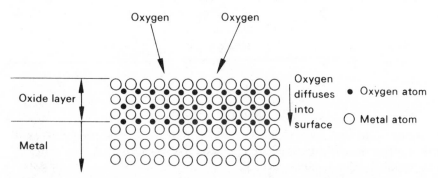

Fig. 4.21 The combination of oxygen with the surface film of a metal to form an oxide layer. In this case, the oxide lattice is coherent with the metallic lattice and the oxide coating is, therefore, tenacious and impermeable

coating depends on a number of factors, as follows:

1. The relative stability of the metal and its oxide. This varies from metal to metal – gold is, in fact, more stable than its oxide in normal conditions, although a surface layer of oxygen atoms does exist to satisfy the bonding requirements of surface atoms. Other metals, such as silver and copper, have a relatively small heat of formation with respect to their oxides, that is, the energy release when the oxides are formed is small so that the oxides are not extremely stable and the metals are corrosion-resistant in clean atmospheres. Increasing oxygen pressure always increases stability of oxides in the same way that an increase of humidity in the atmosphere increases the tendency for water to exist in liquid form.

2. The physical properties of the oxide layer. In order for the oxidation process to continue, oxygen must have access to metallic ions below the surface of the existing oxide layer. The rate at which this can happen depends on the permeability of the oxide coating to metallic ions and/or oxygen ions. In the case of some metals, notably those the atoms of which have only one or two electrons in their outer shell, the metallic ion is smaller than that of the metal from which it was formed. Thus, shrinkage of the metal occurs on oxidation, resulting in stresses in the oxide film and, possibly, cracking. The film will, therefore, be porous and will allow further oxygen to penetrate it so that oxidation continues. Such behaviour is shown by, for example, magnesium, the oxidation rate of which, with respect to time, is linear, that is, the film thickness is proportional to time.

    In other metals, ionic sizes may be comparable to, or larger than, pure metal atoms so that the oxide film is impervious and, possibly, in compression. Iron and copper are examples of this and since, in this case, ions must diffuse through the oxide coating, oxidation rates will decrease as the film thickness increases, though oxidation will never cease completely. This may be expressed in the form:

    $$\frac{dx}{dt} = \frac{k}{x} \quad \text{where } x = \text{film thickness}, t = \text{time and } k = \text{a constant}.$$

    $$x^2 = kt + C \quad (C = 0 \text{ if } x = 0 \text{ when } t = 0)$$

    or $x = \sqrt{kt}$

    The equation represents a parabolic relationship between film thickness and time.

    In some cases, the oxide itself may be very tightly bound to the metal or it may be so stable that it will not permit diffusion of ions or electrons through it to allow further oxidation. In this case, the growth rate of the film will decrease exponentially and, after a time, oxidation will cease. Zinc, chromium, lead and aluminium exhibit this behaviour, each having wide use in building as a result. Aluminium goods are often artificially oxidised (anodised) after manufacture to give a uniform protective coating. The above arguments apply to dry non-polluted oxygen-containing atmospheres. Pollutants or dampness may give rise to other reactions, accelerating corrosion.

3. Temperature. As with any chemical reaction, oxidation proceeds by 'chance encounters' of oxygen and metallic ions and, since temperature increases thermal energy and diffusion rates of ions, it will inevitably increase oxidation rates. Hence, for example, metals obeying the exponential law at room temperature may obey the parabolic law at higher temperatures. Oxide layers formed at room temperature are, in general, too thin to be visible but films produced at higher temperatures become visible initially by interfering with reflected light, as occurs when steel is 'tempered'. Steel ingots, before hot-rolling may form considerable thicknesses of 'mill scale', a grey coating, in quite short times and most metals in the earth's crust exist in the form of oxides ('ores'), which is indicative of high temperatures at some stage in their history.

4. The effect of alloying elements. Alloying elements are often added to metals in order to produce a protective film on their surfaces. Restrictions are, however, placed on the use of alloying elements, since they may also alter the mechanical properties of the parent metal. For example, aluminium, when alloyed with iron, forms an effective oxide coating but affects its forming properties. Hence, use in percentages required for protection is confined to treatments applied to the finished article. Perhaps the most important alloying elements for iron are chromium and nickel. Chromium forms a protective oxide layer while nickel has the effect of preserving the austenitic state (see 'Stainless steel'). Alloying elements added for other reasons may, by oxidation, affect the properties of the parent metal. Carbon in steel, for example, oxidises more quickly than iron and is lost as a gas, so that the surfaces of carbon-steel components tend to soften on aging.

Electrolytic and acidic corrosion

These are caused in the first instance by the tendency for metals to dissolve (ionise) in aqueous solutions. If the surface of a metal becomes moist, metallic ions enter the water, leaving behind a negative charge on the remaining solid metal.

$$M \rightleftharpoons M^{(n+)} + n(e^-) \quad \text{n equals the valency}$$

metal   metal ion   electron(s) − (remain on metal)

The arrow shown indicates that the reaction may proceed in either direction. This reaction may, theoretically, take place to some degree in any solid material in an attempt to balance the concentration of ions in the solid and adjacent liquid but, in the case of metals, it is particularly important due to the effect of the negative potential which builds up on the remaining metal with respect to the solution. Metallic ions continue to form until the electrons which are left behind have set up a sufficient negative voltage to oppose further release of positive ions. Even then, the equilibrium should be regarded as dynamic rather than static, that is,

Table 4.3 Standard electrode
potentials of pure metals

Metal	Electrode potential (volts)
Magnesium	−2.4
Aluminium	−1.7
Zinc	−0.76
Chromium	−0.65
Iron (ferrous)	−0.44
Nickel	−0.23
Tin	−0.14
Lead	−0.12
Hydrogen (reference)	0.00
Copper (cupric)	+0.34
Silver	+0.80
Gold	+1.4

Note that the most reactive metals are
the alkali and alkaline earth metals
which hold their electrons most loosely

ionisation still occurs but is balanced by the opposite process – deposition or
'plating out' of metal.

The magnitude of the negative voltage which arises depends on the type of
metal, the temperature and other factors. In practice, there is the problem of
measurement of this potential, since the other 'reference' electrode which must be
used for measuring the difference in voltage between the metal and the solution
will itself produce an electrode potential, so that a relative reading only is
obtained. The problem is overcome by use of a standard 'hydrogen' electrode.
Table 4.3 gives the standard electrode potentials of some common metals in
solutions of their ions, with respect to the hydrogen reference electrode. Metals
which are more reactive than the hydrogen electrode produce negative voltages,
while those that are less reactive produce positive voltages. The former are known
as anodic metals and the latter as cathodic or noble metals. Electrode potentials
are also affected by the state of the surface of the metal. Imperfections in the
surface, such as grain boundaries or points of intersection of dislocation lines with
the surface, will result in weaker bonding of atoms, easier dissolution and higher
effective electrode potentials at these points. It should be emphasised that all
metals have some tendency to dissolve, including those below hydrogen in the
table.

So far, although the basic mechanism of ionisation and electrode potentials has
been explained, the causes of continued corrosion, which occurs when ionisation
proceeds with little or no hindrance over long periods of time, is not yet apparent.
In the above examples, corrosion stops when the electrode potential is reached.
Corrosion can only continue if the actual potential of the metal changes for some
reason, so that more metal must dissolve in attempting to restore its original

179

value, that is, the electrons which are the cause of the potential must somehow 'drain away' from the metal. This electron-consuming reaction may occur in two ways:

In the presence of acids: acidic corrosion

Acids contain free hydrogen ions which, on reaction with electrons, produce hydrogen gas:

$$2H^+ \quad + 2e^- \quad \longrightarrow \quad H_2 \uparrow$$

in solution   from metal   gas

The supply of electrons required for this reaction is obtainable from metals which are above hydrogen in the table of electrode potentials. Hence, these metals dissolve in many acids. The more concentrated the acid is, the more rapidly will a metal corrode, since such acids contain greater concentrations of hydrogen ions. Metals below hydrogen in the table do not corrode in normal acids because hydrogen itself, which may be regarded as a 'metal', tends to ionise to a greater degree than these metals. Therefore, hydrogen, rather than the metal, will remain in ion form. The corrosion of the 'noble' metals requires an oxidising as well as an acidic effect. This is, however, provided by certain concentrated acids or mixtures of acids.

If the metal is joined to a different metal which gives rise to a lower negative potential: electrolytic corrosion

Consider, for example, strips of copper and zinc immersed in the same solution and joined by an electrical conductor (Fig. 4.22). The zinc would normally reach a voltage of -0.76 V on the hydrogen scale and the copper, $+0.34$ V. Therefore, on joining them, there must be a potential difference of 1.1 V between the zinc and copper. Electrons will flow through the wire from the zinc to the copper (corresponding to a flow of conventional current in the opposite direction) and the zinc will continue to dissolve, in an attempt to replace them, since the process will cause a reduction in its negative electric potential. The copper, on the other hand,

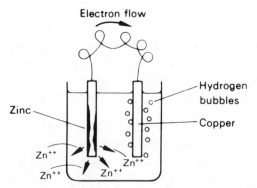

Fig. 4.22 Electrolytic corrosion resulting from zinc and copper rods immersed in an aqueous solution while in electrical contact

will donate electrons to positive ions in solution in an attempt to maintain its former voltage of $+0.34\,V$. If the solution contains hydrogen ions, they will collect electrons from the copper, forming hydrogen gas:

$$2H^+ \qquad + 2e^- \qquad \longrightarrow H_2 \uparrow$$

in solution   from copper   gas

The zinc ions which dissolve will form a zinc salt by combination with negative ions in solution. If, for example, the solution contained sulphate ions, then zinc sulphate would form.

The corroding metal (in this case, the zinc) is known as the anode and the protected metal (in this case, the copper) as the cathode. Electron flow is always from the anode to the cathode. Note that the above arrangement is the principle of the Daniell cell, in which the electromotive force of 1.1 V is used for the supply of small quantities of electric power. As with the Daniell cell, however, the electrolytic action does not proceed unhindered until the zinc is destroyed. Many other corrosion reactions are similarly slowed down, due to the resistance to ion movement in the solution. This may be caused, for example, by formation of insoluble films on the anode. Aluminium, for this reason, normally behaves *cathodically* with respect to zinc and chromium is corrosion-resistant in the same way. Alternatively, hydrogen gas bubbles evolved at the cathode may tend to form a 'third electrode' and also resist the flow of further positive ions to the cathode. This is known as polarisation.

Alternative causes of electrolytic corrosion   There are a number of instances where commonly used combinations of different metals in building or constructional engineering result in electrolytic corrosion: examples are given in Table 4.4. Just as important, however, and less obvious, are instances in which electrolytic corrosion cells may form within a single metal in the presence of moisture. Table 4.5 gives a number of possible causes. The effect of grains and electrolyte concentration in causing corrosion will be readily appreciated, as these both cause changes of electrode potential but the effects of oxygen and stresses require some amplification, as both occur commonly and steps must be taken to prevent consequent deterioration of metals.

The role of oxygen in electrolytic corrosion

Oxygen plays a part in many corrosion processes but the case of steel is particularly important and, therefore, by way of example, the effects of oxygen on steel are discussed. If steel is immersed in fairly pure water, there is only a very slight chemical reaction: rusting of steel is chiefly electrolytic, the anodes and the cathodes being different parts of the same piece of steel. The anodes may be stressed regions, for example, the head of a nail, or grain boundaries. Although the electrode potential of steel varies slightly from place to place on this basis, corrosion of the metal in pure water is very slow. Ions form at anodes:

$$Fe \quad \longrightarrow Fe^{++} \qquad + 2e^-$$

metal   ferrous ion   electrons remain
        in solution   on metal

Table 4.4 Some common situations in which electrolytic corrosion occurs

Situation	Metal which corrodes	Remedy
Galvanised water cistern or cylinder with copper pipes; traces of copper deposited due to water flow	Galvanised film corrodes electrolytically at point of contact with the copper particles. Film is destroyed, then steel corrodes similarly	Use a sacrificial anode in cistern. Otherwise use a plastic cistern or copper cylinder
Brass plumbing fittings in certain types of water	Zinc-dezincification	Use low zinc content brass or gunmetal fittings
Copper ballcock soldered to brass arm	Corrosion of solder occurs in the damp atmosphere resulting in fracture of joint	Use plastic ball on ballcock
Copper flashing secured by steel nails	Steel corrodes rapidly	Use copper tacks for securing copper sheeting
Iron or steel railings set in stone plinth using lead	Steel corrodes near the base	Ensure that steel is effectively protected by paint
Steel radiators with copper pipes	Steel radiators corrode	Corrosion can be reduced by means of inhibitors

In the water:

$$H_2O \longrightarrow H^+ + OH^-$$

At the cathode:

$$2H^+ + 2e^- \longrightarrow H_2 \uparrow$$

from the water   electrons from cathodes   gas

and in the water:

$$Fe^{++} + 2(OH)^- \longrightarrow Fe(OH)_2 \downarrow$$

ferrous hydroxide precipitate (green)

Since water is only slightly ionised, the reaction is very slow and a steel nail immersed in boiled or distilled water may not show any visible corrosion product for some time.

Steel corrodes quite rapidly in ordinary water, however, and this is due to the presence of oxygen which reacts with electrons from cathodes to form the hydroxyl ions required by the above equation, to cause rusting:

$$2H_2O + O_2 + 4e^- \longrightarrow 4(OH)^-$$

from cathode   hydroxyl ions

Iron exhibits two valencies – of two and three – and 'rust' is, in fact, ferric hydroxide, $Fe(OH)_3$, obtained when ferrous hydroxide is further oxidised by air,

Table 4.5 Situations in which electrolytic corrosion of a single metal may occur

Cause	Anode	Examples	Remedy
Grain structure of metals	Grain boundary	Any steel component subject to dampness	Keep steel dry
Variations in concentration of electrolyte	Low concentration areas	All types of soil	Cathodic protection
Differential aeration of a metal surface	Oxygen-remote area	Improperly protected underground steel pipes	Cathodic protection
Dirt or scale	Dirty area (oxygen remote)	Exposure of some types of stainless steel to atmospheric dirt	Use more resistant quality or keep the surface clean
Stressed areas	Most heavily stressed region	Steel rivets	Protect from dampness

although the product will be black – anhydrous magnetite, Fe_3O_4 – if the air supply is limited, as in many closed heating circuits. (It follows that changing the water in central heating circuits will, initially, increase the corrosion rate, since a new supply of oxygen is injected with fresh water.) Corrosion products form in solution rather than at anodes or cathodes and the exact position depends on the diffusion rates of the positive and negative ions. In the case of steel, Fe^{++} ions are smaller and, therefore, more mobile than $(OH)^-$ ions, so that they meet near the cathode. Hence, unlike atmospheric corrosion, the corrosion product is incapable of protecting the metal, since it does not form on the corroding part, the anode.

A further common feature of corroded steel is pitting. This occurs because ferric oxide (mill scale) itself behaves cathodically with respect to iron which may be exposed by a scratch in the oxide coating, so that the steel continues to corrode, causing cavities, while rust builds up on cathodes until it covers the entire surface (Fig. 4.23). Another factor contributing to pitting is the fact that the anode, being normally much smaller in area than the cathode, corrodes

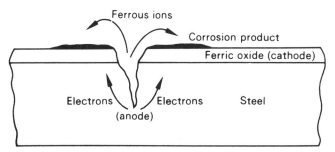

Ferrous ions

Corrosion product

Ferric oxide (cathode)

Electrons   Electrons   Steel

(anode)

Fig. 4.23 Pitting of steel originating from a crack in the oxide coating

183

at a faster rate (even so, the total loss of weight caused by pitting will be less than that caused by uniform corrosion of the surface under similar conditions, since the small anodic area acts as a 'bottle neck' in the corrosion process).

Steel corrosion may also occur by 'differential aeration', that is, when different parts of the same piece of metal are exposed in different degrees to oxygen. Oxygenated areas tend to form cathodes due to the production of hydroxyl ions, as explained above. Steel posts, for example, tend to corrode just below ground level, the corrosion cell consisting of an anode just below the ground where the oxygen level is relatively low and a cathode just above the ground where the oxygen level is higher. Underground steel pipes are sometimes seriously corroded by the action of bacteria in anaerobic (that is, oxygen-free) soils such as clays, which contain sulphates and organic matter. The bacteria cause the sulphates to react with and remove the hydrogen which would normally prevent corrosion by causing polarisation at cathodes.

The effect of pH values

Yet another factor affecting corrosion of metals is the pH value of the mixture with which they are in contact. Just as a reaction involving electrons such as $Fe \rightarrow Fe^{++} + 2e^-$ depends on the e.m.f. of the metal with respect to solution, so a reaction such as $Fe^{++} + 2(OH)^- \rightarrow Fe(OH)_2$ will be dependent on pH, since it is affected by the balance of hydroxyl ions in solution. The equation $2H_2O + O_2 + 4e^- \rightarrow 4(OH)^-$ will be affected both by the electrode potential of the metal and the pH of the solution. Diagrams relating the relative stability of different states of a metal to their electric potential and the pH of the solution are known as Pourbaix diagrams. A simplified form of that for ion is shown in Fig. 4.24.

The boundary lines between Fe and Fe^{++} ions and between Fe^{++} and Fe^{+++} ions is horizontal since, as explained above, electrons only are involved in the

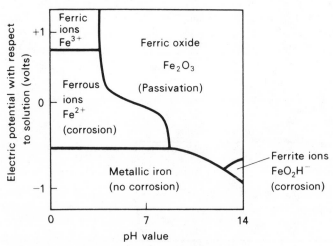

Fig. 4.24 Pourbaix diagram for iron/water

change: pH has no effect. Note, however, that at higher pH values – that is, alkaline environments – ferric oxide, Fe_2O_3, is, within a range of voltages, more stable than the metal and forms a protective coating on it. This process is known as passivation and it prevents electrolytic corrosion.

The passivating effect of alkaline environments in steel is, of course, responsible for the protection of steel in reinforced concrete and is the basis of some types of corrosion inhibitor for boiler systems. The effects of alkaline and acidic environments on steel are also well illustrated by the fact that a bricklayer's trowel, left uncleaned, will not corrode for some time, whereas a plasterer's float, if left in this way, will develop a layer of rust in a few hours, due to the acidic solution resulting from gypsum plasters. Corrosion of steel, similarly, is greatly accelerated if saline solutions are present, as in sea water or in concrete containing chlorides.

Although Pourbaix diagrams are extremely useful in showing how metals react to varying conditions, they should not be taken as a final indication of their corrosion properties, since factors already mentioned, such as polarisation, the nature of the corrosion product, impurities in the metal and water, and movement of the latter also play a part.

Stress corrosion cracking
Some alloys, when under a tensile stress and in corrosive conditions simultaneously, have exhibited cracking, leading to sudden failure. This may occur in certain environments well below the yield point of the metal and may have disastrous consequences where considerable loads or pressures are sustained.

Stress corrosion may be caused either because a tensile stress at a point assists dissolution of metal, effectively altering its electrode potential, or simply due to corrosion of parts of a metal which would otherwise prevent spreading of a crack. The latter occurs in grain boundaries which would normally bond grains effectively together but which, in corrosive environments, become anodic (Table 4.5), producing hairline cracks.

Stress corrosion may be regarded, in some cases, as an extension of pitting, as occurs in steel. As a pit becomes deeper, the stress at the root becomes higher, causing increased corrosion at this point, so that a crack propagates through the metal. This type of cracking has led to explosions of riveted boilers. Seepage of treated boiler water past rivets, and subsequent evaporation, leads to concentration of alkali around them (the alkali is used in water treatments for passivation of the metal). As the Pourbaix diagram indicates (Fig. 4.24), large concentrations of alkali which produce high pH values may lead to local corrosion of the steel rivets, causing pitting and eventual failure as above. Riveted connections are particularly vulnerable to this type of attack, since some are inevitably stressed more than others, but stress corrosion may also occur in welded connections, which are more common today, if the process results in residual stresses in the metal. Chloride solutions increase the severity of such corrosion, although its incidence can be avoided by annealing after welding.

Alloy corrosion

Some alloys tend to exhibit corrosion due to electrochemical differences between the grain boundaries and the grains themselves, particularly if grain boundaries contain a different phase, as in the case of annealed steels. In certain stainless steels, in particular, chromium carbide forms at grain boundaries when it is heated, as in welding, so that, in certain environments, electrolytic corrosion will occur with chromium carbide as cathodes and neighbouring chromium depleted areas as cathodes. This leads to cracking and eventual fracture under stress. High-strength aluminium alloys are similarly affected.

Protection of metals against corrosion

Wherever possible, the choice of metal for a given situation should be such that electrolytic corrosion does not arise, since effective protection methods involve, firstly, the initial cost of treatment and, in many cases, the subsequent cost of maintenance. In damp atmospheres, metals which form impervious corrosion films are most suitable and the use of different metals in contact in these situations should, if possible, be avoided. In particular, small anode areas will corrode rapidly when in contact with large cathodes, for example, copper sheet fixed with steel nails. Extra care is necessary in polluted atmospheres or corrosive environments which will accelerate corrosion. A number of metals are very prone to certain types of chemical in solution: these are described under the headings of individual metals. The task of protection of metals in corrosive situations may be tackled from several standpoints: a metal may be protected by coating with an impervious coating, by reversal of the corrosion reaction making it into a cathode (cathodic protection), by passivation or by means of inhibitors.

Protection by impervious coating

This is a very common method of protection of metals, since it is cheap and, in many cases, the only feasible method, for example, protection of structural steels, though some types of paint possess an inhibitive property in addition to their waterproofing qualities. The provision of a waterproof coating on metals depends on a number of factors relating to the paint and its application. The most important are outlined below:

1. Crevices, as formed by joints where metal components touch, tend to trap moisture by capillarity. Evaporation is, in any case, slower, due to reduced air circulation and the latter will itself tend to create anodes in crevices, as explained above. Furthermore, the corrosion product will tend to trap moisture and, in the case of riveted connections, cause stresses due to the volume increase which accompanies corrosion. These stresses will increase the corrosion rate and accelerate failure. Particular attention should, therefore, be paid to restricted spaces and they should not be painted when damp. Protection may be achieved by insertion of a protective paste, for example, red lead for steel.

2. The film must be unbroken for effective protection, unless it is an inhibitive film. For example, although structural steel is often protected by a prefabrication primer, this will be damaged during fabrication and should be made good afterwards. Otherwise, corrosion will occur by differential aeration at discontinuities in the protective coating.

3. The surface of the metal must be suitably prepared. For example, mill scale should be removed from steel before priming, since it has a different co-efficient of thermal movement from steel and will tend to flake off in time. In factory processes, scale is normally removed by acids, as in pickling or phosphating. These methods are, however, not suitable for site application: shot- or grit-blasting is more effective. Wire-brushing achieves little if substantial thicknesses of rust are present.

4. Since no paint is perfectly waterproof, the protection afforded depends on the thickness of the film. Sharp edges often protrude through a single coat of paint, due to its surface-tension effect, so that, if such edges cannot be rounded off before painting, extra coats of paint should be applied at these points. Thixotropic versions of paints have the advantage that greater thickness can be obtained. For the same reason, polyvinyl chloride (PVC) coatings, factory applied, give excellent protection, provided they are not punctured, and are now commonly used for protecting a wide variety of components. A number of metals are often applied to steel to give impermeable coatings. Examples are tin, lead, nickel and aluminium. The latter is especially useful for structural steel, since it can be sprayed in situ after erection.

Cathodic protection

If the electric potential of a metal in aqueous solution can be maintained at its equilibrium value, then corrosion will not take place since, as explained, the metal only ionises in order to try to establish this potential. If the electric potential is held by some means at a value more negative than the electrode potential, then the metal will behave cathodically and, although hydrogen may be generated from solution by the excess electrons in the metal, corrosion cannot occur. This is known as cathodic protection and is illustrated by the lower part of the Pourbaix diagram in Fig. 4.24. It would be misleading to suggest that the exact value of the standard electrode potential of the metal must be maintained for full protection. If, for example, in the case of steel pipes in hard waters, a protective 'scale' of a magnesium or calcium salt forms, protection will be achieved at a voltage which would, in normal conditions, cause the steel to behave anodically. If, on the other hand, the concentration of ions in solution is reduced as, for example, when there is flowing water, there will be a constant diffusion of ions away from the metal and corrosion will occur, even though it is held at its normal electrode potential. The corrosion rate is, in all cases, proportional to the difference between the *actual* potential of the metal and its *effective* electrode potential, under the given conditions.

In order to protect a metal from corrosion, electric current must be so supplied to it that the draining away of electrons from it is counterbalanced. Conventional current will, therefore, be *away* from the metal to be protected. This current may be provided by means of a second cell, either in the form of another more anodic metal, known as a sacrificial anode, or by a direct current source connected into the corrosion cell.

Sacrificial anodes

The use of these in protection of steel is very widespread. To be effective, metals used must be higher in the electrochemical series than iron. It might be considered that protection would automatically be achieved with any such metal but this is not the case since, initially, the corroding metal will be some margin below its standard electrode potential and the sacrificial anode must be of sufficiently negative potential to increase the negative potential of the corroding metal by this margin. The impressed e.m.f. required depends on the resistance of the solution: if it is low, then a metal near to iron in the table will be satisfactory, for example, zinc. High-resistance solutions will require a metal higher in the series, such as magnesium, if the steel is to be fully protected. The situation is exemplified in Fig. 4.25.

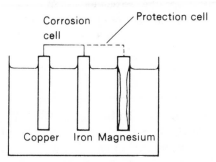

Fig. 4.25 Cathodic protection using a sacrificial anode. The protection cell must be sufficiently active to restore iron to its standard electrode potential in spite of the influence of the copper

The metal which was formerly corroding now behaves as a cathode with respect to the sacrificial anode, which must, therefore, be near to the protected metal. Large areas of steel will need a number of sacrificial anodes, so positioned that all parts are maintained at the requisite negative voltage with respect to solution. The ideal form of sacrificial anode is, therefore, a uniform and continuous coating, zinc being most commonly used for the purpose, since it behaves anodically to steel but has reasonable durability in normal atmospheres. The following coatings offer protection to steel in this way:

Hot-dip galvanising Steel is prepared by degreasing, pickling and flux application, the latter ensuring metal-to-metal contact between steel and zinc. The component is then dipped in molten zinc at a temperature of about 450 °C. Initially zinc/iron alloys form on the surface of the steel but these are covered, on continued immersion, by a layer of pure zinc. Coatings in the region of 100 μm are produced and these may provide full protection for up to 10 years. Thicker coatings can be provided but these are more likely to crack. Coatings may be painted at a later stage to give very long service.

Zinc spraying This is not chemically bonded to the steel, so the prepared surface is roughened to give mechanical grip. Molten zinc is atomised and projected at the steel surface, forming a slightly rough layer, which is porous initially, becoming impervious when the zinc reacts with moisture. The method can be used on large fabricated structures and thicknesses of over 200 μm of zinc can be obtained, giving excellent durability.

Electroplating This produces an even zinc coating of about 30 μm thickness, the process being limited to articles which are small enough to fit into the bath. The process is also used to plate wire or sheet, since the coating has good flexibility.

Sherardizing Prepared articles are tumbled in fine zinc dust just below its melting point – at about 380 °C. A good bond forms, the zinc having a thickness of about 30 μm which, in the case of nuts and bolts, for example, does not impair the action of the thread. Durability is clearly less than that obtained from greater thicknesses.

Zinc-dust paints These comprise finely divided zinc particles in either an organic or an inorganic drying medium. The degree of sacrificial protection depends on the electrical conductivity of the hardened film and, generally, requires a large proportion of metallic zinc. These coatings are often used as prefabrication primers, though adequate surface preparation such as grit-blasting is essential to provide a clean, slightly rough surface to grip the paint.

Impressed current method
Protection of underground steel pipes has, in the past, been successfully achieved by this method. By connection of the negative terminal of a direct current source to the steel, the positive terminal being connected to a further electrode in the soil, electrons are supplied to the steel, maintaining it at a sufficiently negative voltage to avoid corrosion (Fig. 4.26). As with sacrificial anodes, the supply of electrons at any one part of the pipe depends on a completed cell being formed at that point, with the dc source. Hence, due to soil resistance, electrodes must be positioned at intervals along the pipe, the actual interval depending on the resistance of the soil. The current consumed will also depend on the soil resistance, being higher in more corrosive conditions. The other electrode will be at a positive potential and will, therefore, corrode unless made of a noble metal. Steel electrodes, for example, will require replacement, whereas more expensive platinum or carbon electrodes would be corrosion-resistant. Impressed currents

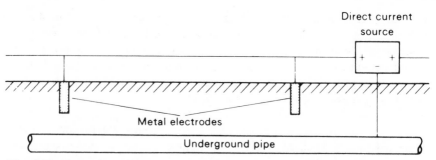

Fig. 4.26 Protection of an underground steel pipe by the impressed current method

used for protection of underground steel pipes may adversely affect neighbouring buried metals. Also, direct currents in populated areas may interfere with the pipes themselves: such currents were at one time produced by electric-railway power supplies. Alternating currents are now more common but even these may adversely affect some buried metals, such as aluminium, the oxide of which has a rectifying action. Neither the above impressed current nor the sacrificial anode method is intended to obviate the need for painting of underground pipes. Complete protection by these methods alone would be very costly. They are merely intended to supplement the protection given by traditional waterproof coatings, such as bitumen, which may not be 100 per cent effective due to, for example, incomplete coverage or damage during laying of the pipe.

Passivation and use of inhibitors

Passivation is based on Pourbaix diagrams. If the pH value of the environment in which the metal is to be used, and the potential of the metal, are such that it is covered by a stable, impervious corrosion film, then corrosion will cease. For example, steel in an alkaline environment is passivated, though aggressive ions, such as those of chlorine, will destroy the protective film, allowing corrosion to continue. Hence, steel in reinforced or prestressed concrete is protected, though the use of calcium chloride in such concretes is not recommended. By charging positively, steel can be passivated even in acidic environments (Fig. 4.24), since ferric oxide is formed. The method relies, however, on careful control of the applied voltage, which depends, in turn, on the concentration of the acid concerned. The method is used for the protection of steel storage vessels. It is known as anodic protection.

Inhibition (anodic-cathodic) Inhibitors are added to corrosive media to resist corrosion of metals immersed in them. They may retard either the anodic or cathodic reactions of a system. For example, if steel anodes can be coated with a layer of ferric oxide, Fe_2O_3, corrosion will not be possible. This requires an oxidising agent, for example, sodium chromate, and a slightly alkaline environment, to ensure that the ferric oxide is stable. Sodium chromate will work in a de-aerated solution but other inhibitors, such as sodium carbonate or sodium silicate, require an external supply of oxygen. Hence, these inhibitors would not be effective in, for example, boiler circuits where oxygen contents are low. The above might seem contradictory to earlier statements about the accelerating effect of oxygen on corrosion. The accelerating effect is still theoretically present but, in this case, the oxygen in combined form with the metal produces a situation in which corrosion cannot occur, in spite of the fact that the oxygen in solution behaves as a depolariser. The Pourbaix diagram for iron shows that oxide coatings are not stable at low pH values so that other methods must, in these cases, be used.

An example of inhibition by the interference of salts with cathodic products occurs in hard natural water. Calcium carbonate and magnesium hydroxide, which form a scale on the metal, prevent the penetration of oxygen to act as a depolariser. Unfortunately, such scales tend to accumulate, increasing the frictional resistance of pipes and adversely affecting their heat-conduction properties. Other inhibitors, such as polyphosphates, retard cathodic and anodic reactions, though, as in the case of all inhibitors, the presence of aggressive ions such a nitrates, sulphates and chlorides, tends to reduce their efficiency. Soft waters, which often contain carbon dioxide dissolved to form carbonic acid, may be improved by addition of alkalis such as sodium carbonate (washing soda), which will precipitate calcium carbonate from solution. Excess use of alkalis is, however, not recommended: it can lead to localised corrosion cells.

Ferrous metals

The element iron is second only to aluminium in abundance: it is relatively easily extracted from its ore and can be modified by alloying to form a vast number of products with widely different properties. These facts account for the dominant role played by this metal in many aspects of construction.

Production of iron

Iron, like many metals, occurs in the form of an ore, generally iron oxide, together with earthy material, such as silica and alumina. The first stage in the production of iron involves the blast furnace, in which the iron oxide is reduced to iron by carbon monoxide produced from ignition of coal and limestone, combustible gases providing the necessary heat. The impurities and calcium oxide from the limestone collect as a slag on top of the liquid iron, which is run off. The iron itself is run into moulds forming 'pigs' which contain between 2 and 4 per cent carbon and quantities of silicon, sulphur, phosphorus and manganese.

Products based on iron

The impurities listed above have a marked effect on the microstructure of iron and, by modification of pig iron to differing degrees, materials are produced having, apparently, quite different properties.

Iron is allotropic – it exists in several different crystal forms. Up to a temperature of 910 °C, iron is body-centred cubic (BCC) and dissolves very little carbon – less than 0.01 per cent at room temperature, increasing to 0.04 per cent at 700 °C. (This relatively low solubility in a crystal structure, which is not as closely packed as FCC structures, is due to the fact that the FCC crystal nevertheless supplies the largest interstitial sites – the centre of each cube.) The resulting product, called alpha iron or ferrite, is soft, ductile and readily cold-worked. At 910 °C, the BCC crystal structure changes to FCC and this lattice can accommodate up to 1.7 per cent carbon by weight interstitially, (or 9 carbon atoms per 100 iron atoms), the material being known as gamma iron or austenite. In fact, a further change occurs in pure iron at approximately 1390 °C before melting, in which the crystal structure reverts to BCC. Pure iron melts at 1537 °C. Liquid iron can dissolve substantial quantities of carbon, since it is non-crystalline, but a eutectic point occurs at a temperature of 1130 °C, with a carbon composition of 4.3 per cent.

The various forms of iron-carbon alloy are based on the above phases and their properties depend greatly on the quantity of carbon in the original molten metal. They are considered in order of increasing carbon content.

Wrought iron (BS 51)
This is the purest form of iron, containing about 0.02 per cent carbon, which is almost completely dissolved interstitially in the iron lattice. The metal is tough and ductile with a yield point of about 210 N/mm^2 and a tensile strength of about 350 N/mm^2. It is produced from pig iron by melting in a reverberatory furnace, in which impurities are oxidised into slag. As the iron becomes purer, its melting point rises and it, therefore, becomes 'pasty'. Balls of iron are withdrawn, and the slag, which is more fluid than the iron, is forced out by steam hammering. The iron is then rolled into bars or the process repeated to obtain greater purity.

Wrought iron was formerly used for structural members subject to tensile stresses (compression members being made from cast iron). Steel has, of course, replaced these materials in such situations, though wrought iron is still used for ornamental ironwork, chains and hooks, since it has admirable working properties, and great toughness and corrosion-resistance. More general use of the metal has, however, given way to steel, since the latter is much cheaper to produce.

Steel

Steel may be defined as an alloy of iron and carbon, in which the carbon is fully dissolved in the high-temperature FCC gamma iron form. Steels may, therefore, contain up to 1.7 per cent carbon. Austenitic steel, as it is known, is, at this high temperature, soft, ductile and suitable for forging and rolling – commonly referred to as 'hot-working'. Heavy steel sections are, therefore, invariably heated to temperatures over 910 °C for forming purposes. It will be clear that, on cooling, carbon must be rejected from the crystals as they revert to the BCC form. Pure carbon does not, however, form on cooling but rather iron carbide, Fe_3C, which contains 6.67 per cent carbon and is known as 'cementite'. Cementite has a different crystal structure from ferrite, with properties more like a ceramic than a metal, since the high percentage of carbon atoms (6.67 per cent by weight corresponds to 25 per cent numerically) increases strength and prevents plastic deformation. The form in which the cementite is produced depends on the carbon content of the steel and the formation of the various compounds is best understood by reference to iron-carbon equilibrium diagrams. Figure 4.27 shows

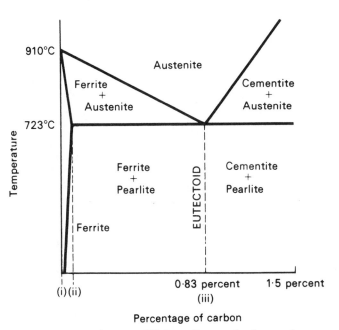

Fig. 4.27   Part of the equilibrium diagram for iron-carbon compounds

the portion of the iron-carbon equilibrium diagram which is concerned with the various types of steel formation. When austenitic steel cools slowly, so that alpha iron is produced, the resulting steel must contain suitably balanced proportions of ferrite and cementite, and the mechanism of changes is rather similar to that by which a two-phase alloy solidifies from a liquid mixture.

1. If the carbon content corresponds to the area to the left of line (i), pure ferrite is formed, ferrite crystals growing gradually from the former austenite crystals, as the temperature is decreased from 910 °C, until a completely new crystal structure is produced (Fig. 4.28(a)).
2. If the carbon content corresponds to the area between lines (i) and (ii), ferrite crystals form initially, as above, but since the solubility of carbon decreases with reducing temperature, cementite crystals must begin to form, occupying a small space in grain boundaries.

193

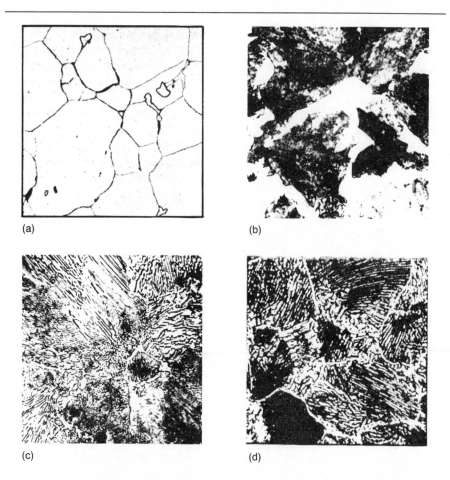

(a) (b)

(c) (d)

Fig. 4.28 Photographs of polished, etched sections of steel with differing carbon content: (a) Carbon content almost zero. Grain boundaries are clearly visible; (b) 0.5 per cent carbon. Ferrite grains are light and pearlite grains dark; (c) 0.83 per cent carbon, eutectoid steel. In this case, the ferrite/cementite layers are clearly visible; (d) Hypo-eutectoid steel. Cementite appears as light-coloured layers around the pearlite grain boundaries

3. If the carbon content corresponds to the area between lines (ii) and (iii), ferrite grains begin to form at 910 °C, carbon being rejected into the remaining austenite. The austenite composition follows the upper critical line, while that of the ferrite follows the lower critical line. Figure 4.29 follows stages in the ferrite crystal growth. At 723 °C, the austenite contains 0.83 per cent carbon and cannot cool further without changing its crystal structure. At this point, known as the eutectoid (as distinct from *eutectic*, which would be used for a liquid/solid equilibrium diagram), an intimately mixed combination of ferrite and cementite will form, this combination being known as 'pearlite' since, under the microscope, polished and etched specimens have a pearly appearance. Steels containing a carbon content in

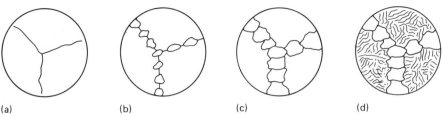

Fig. 4.29 Stages in the cooling of a hypo-eutectoid steel: (a) Over 910 °C austenite grains; (b) 850 °C ferrite grains begin to grow at boundaries; (c) 800 °C ferrite grains continue to grow; (d) 723 °C remaining austenite changes in pearlite

this range are known as 'hypo-eutectoid steels' and consist of a mixture of ferrite crystals grown at the higher temperature and pearlite crystals formed at 723 °C. Steels with a carbon content at the lower end of this range, for example, 0.1 per cent carbon, would comprise mainly ferrite. In Fig. 4.28(b), which shows a section of steel with a 0.5 per cent carbon content, there is a slight preponderence of pearlite (the darker material).

4. If a steel containing 0.83 per cent carbon is cooled, no crystal change occurs until the temperature of 723 °C is reached and then a transformation to pure pearlite occurs, resulting in a microscopic structure, as shown in Fig. 4.28(c).

5. When austenite of carbon content above 0.83 per cent (hyper-eutectoid) is cooled, cementite begins to separate from austenite grains at a temperature indicated by the upper critical line of Fig. 4.27, the carbon content of remaining austenite being reduced progressively until, at 723 °C, the eutectoid composition of 0.83 per cent is reached. Since cementite contains 6.67 per cent carbon and it is rare for steels to contain much over 1 per cent carbon, these cementite layers are usually quite thin. At 723 °C, the austenite changes into pearlite, as previously described. Figure 28(d) shows a steel of carbon content approximately 1.2 per cent, the cementite layers being visible around pearlite grains. Figure 4.30 shows the stages in the process.

The above transformations will only take place as stated if cooling is very slow, allowing diffusion of carbon from within the austenite crystals to form ferrite and cementite products.

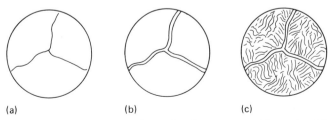

Fig. 4.30 Stages in cooling of a hyper-eutectoid steel: (a) Over 900 °C austenite grains; (b) 800 °C cementite layers forming at grain boundaries; (c) 723 °C remaining austenite changes to pearlite

195

The properties of ferrite are similar to those of pure iron, while cementite is intensely hard but brittle. Pearlite, a mixture of these two in the proportions 88 per cent ferrite and 12 per cent cementite, is, as would be expected, intermediate in properties. The material is much harder than ferrite but less hard than cementite, plastic deformation being possible along the ferrite layers. Pearlite is stronger than ferrite but weaker than cementite.

Steels may be divided in respect of carbon content into:

Low-carbon steels, containing up to 0.15 per cent carbon
Mild steels, containing 0.15 to 0.25 per cent carbon
Medium-carbon steels, containing 0.2 to 0.5 per cent carbon
High-carbon steels, containing 0.5 to 1.4 per cent carbon

It will be appreciated that the major factor affecting the properties of steels is their carbon content. The situation is represented in Fig. 4.31, which shows how elongation at failure, ultimate tensile strength and Brinell hardness of annealed steels depend on their carbon content. Low-carbon steels exhibit excellent forming properties, are easily welded and have moderate strength. These 'mild' steels are most widely used in the construction industry. The tensile strength of medium-carbon steels is higher than that of mild steel and, equally important, such steels benefit to a greater extent from the heat-treatment processes described later. Impact resistance, weldability and ductility are, however, adversely affected. High-carbon steels, which include the eutectoid composition, are highly susceptible to heat treatment and may be hardened to a very high degree. Ap-

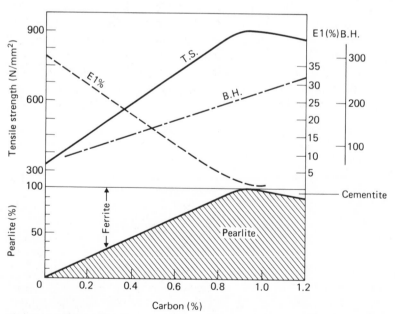

Fig. 4.31 Effect of carbon content on tensile strength, elongation and Brinell hardness of annealed steel (From Ref. 7)

plications are, however, limited by the very low elongation at failure of such steels.

There are many factors other than carbon content which affect the properties of steels and a number of these are now considered:

(a) The method of forming the metal

The basic grain structure of a steel depends on the history of the product while in the austenitic state. Within the austenitic range of temperatures, thermal energy is high and the crystals tend to grow continuously, smaller crystals merging into larger ones, so that products maintained in the austenitic state for sometime tend to have a coarse-grain structure, leading to an unsatisfactory structure at lower temperatures. A fine-grain structure, generally, is preferable, since it results in increased yield strength, toughness and ease of heat treatment. There are, of course, practical limitations to the size of grain which can be obtained. Ingots allowed to cool in air will tend to have a finer-grain structure in external layers than internal layers which cool more slowly. Hot rolling breaks down the grains, destroying the grain structure of the original ingot and resulting in a more even size distribution. Recrystallisation takes place continuously during hot-rolling. Cold-rolling distorts or breaks down the grains and leaves the structure in a stressed, though harder and stronger, state, since cold-rolling is carried out at a temperature which is too low to allow recrystallisation to occur. Larger steel components, for example, steel joists, would require too much energy to be produced in cold-rolling, hence, they are hot-rolled. Smaller products, for example, wire, can be cold-worked or 'drawn', however, and this process results in smaller grain size and higher strength.

(b) The cooling rate

Treatment by heat may produce a change of phase, crystal redistribution or passage of a constituent into, or out of, solid solution. The phase diagram given in Fig. 4.27 only applies to steels cooled so slowly that carbon is able to diffuse from austenite grains to form equilibrium products. When the cooling rate is faster than this, diffusion to equilibrium states cannot complete and a frozen condition of non-equilibrium is obtained. In order of decreasing rapidity, the main processes are: quenching (cooling by immersion in water, oil or iced brine), normalising (controlled cooling in still air) and annealing, in which, by slow cooling, steel is brought more or less to equilibrium conditions.

Quenching/tempering Quenching of a medium- or high-carbon steel completely prevents diffusion of carbon atoms so that they are held in an unstable condition in a body-centred tetragonal lattice (Fig. 4.32(a)). Quenching in iced brine or water is particularly drastic, since very high heat removal rates are obtained by vaporisation of water at the metal surface. In some cases, distortion or cracking of the article may result. The resultant material, which is called 'martensite', is intensely hard and brittle, and internal stresses are so high that further heat treatment is invariably carried out to improve toughness. The process is known as

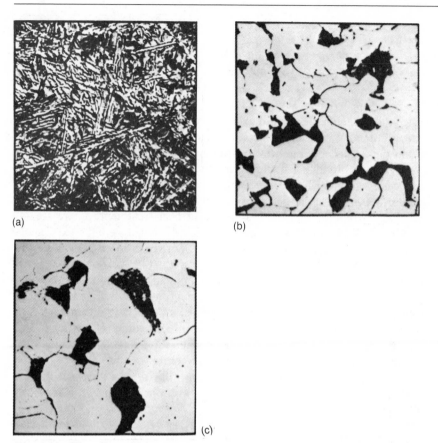

Fig. 4.32 The effect of heat treatment on a 0.13 per cent carbon steel: (a) Martensite, obtained by quenching; (b) Fine-grain structure, obtaind by normalising; (c) Coarse-grain structure, obtained by annealing

'tempering' and involves heating to a temperature which is sufficient to allow some diffusion of carbon to form small cementite crystals. Temperatures of about 200 to 400 °C are normally used: higher temperatures cause greater loss of tensile strength and hardness but increased toughness, as increased quantities of carbon are rejected and ferrite begins to form. This structure is known as a sorbitic structure. The degree of tempering is often measured by the temper colour resulting from the oxide layer, as explained under 'Oxidation'. Colours change from straw (at approximately 230 °C), to brown, then purple and finally blue (at approximately 300 °C).

Normalising This involves heating the steel to a temperature slightly above the upper critical line and 'soaking' for a time to allow small austenite grains to form. This is followed by cooling in air, resulting in a fine ferrite-pearlite grain structure in hypo-eutectoid steels (Fig. 4.32(b)). Such steels are slightly harder and stronger than annealed steels, though heavy sections cannot be normalised so easily because cooling rates will be correspondingly lower.

Annealing This relieves internal stresses resulting from cold-working, forging or welding, and may serve to refine an excessively coarse-grain structure. It involves heating the steel as in normalising so that austenite grains form. The essential part of annealing is that cooling is very slow – often carried out in the furnace so that equilibrium products form, as given in Fig. 4.27. Such steels will exhibit higher ductility and are easier to machine, though they have lower yield strength than normalised steels. It is quite possible to over-heat during annealing, leading to austenite grains of excessive size such that, on cooling, ferrite crystals form *within* austenite grains as well as at boundaries (Widmanstätten structure), leading to weakness and brittleness. Conversely, in under-annealing, austenite may only partially form, some areas remaining unrefined – this may occur, for example, near to welds. Figure 4.32(c) shows a section of an annealed steel.

In a further type of annealing, known as 'sub-critical annealing', the steel is heated to about 600 °C, which is sufficient to allow regrowth of ferrite grains distorted by cold-working. Sub-critical annealing may be carried out several times during extensive cold-working of steel products.

(c) The effect of alloying elements

Steels may be classified as 'plain carbon steels' or 'alloy steels', according to the quantities of alloying elements they contain, though even plain carbon steels often contain small quantities of other elements which have significant effects on their properties. The most common elements found in plain carbon steels are:

1. Sulphur and phosphorus. These both increase the brittleness of steels, so that very small percentages only are allowable (for example, 0.05 per cent).
2. Manganese. This may be used for deoxidation purposes, in which case, it would be removed as a slag, but mild steels still benefit from its presence since it 'dissolves' in ferrite and refines the grain structure, increasing strength and hardness. High-yield steels normally contain more manganese than mild steel, which usually contains about 0.5 per cent.
3. Silicon. This has an effect similar to that of manganese, only to a lesser degree.
4. Niobium. This element forms a carbide within the ferrite lattice, refining the grain structure and increasing the yield strength of steels. It also tends to increase the temperature of the 'ductile-brittle' transition but the problem may be overcome by normalising, if high impact strengh is required.

(d) The degree of deoxidation of the steel

Iron oxide forms on the surface of molten steel very quickly, due to its high temperature, and then combines with carbon in the steel, forming iron and carbon-monoxide gas. The gas dissolves in the steel but tends to form bubbles on cooling, as its solubility decreases. To avoid porosity in the ingots, therefore, the evolution of gas must be controlled. The addition of manganese, silicon or aluminium prevents gas formation, a slag being formed instead. A steel in which no gas forms is known as a 'killed' steel. Shrinkage in these ingots produces, however, a waste area at the top, so that killed steels are more expensive than the forms described below.

Semi-killed steels contain a proportion of gas which compensates for shrinkage and permits more efficient use of ingots. They are also known as 'balanced steels'.

Rimming steels (non-deoxidised) contain large quantities of gas in the form of blow-holes. Although this might seem unsatisfactory, rimming steels have the advantage that the surface layers are usually very pure, since the gases sweep away impurities from the ingot surface, hence, these steels are suitable for drawing and pressing. Working of the metal closes and welds the blow-holes, provided they are deep-seated, so that they do not adversely affect mechanical properties.

Steel for structural uses

Steel for structural uses may be divided into hot- or cold-rolled steel sections for structural steelwork, on the one hand, and bars or wire for reinforced and prestressed concrete, on the other. Each material is covered by relevant British Standards, which form the bases of codes of practice.

Weldable structural steels (BS 4360)

Since welding has largely replaced riveting in both shop and site fabrication of steelwork, the above British Standard forms the basis of hot-rolled structural steel sections. The standard describes four grades of steel which are equally suitable for welded, riveted or bolted connections. The grades are designated 40, 43, 50 and 55, corresponding to minimum ultimate tensile strengths of 400, 430, 500 and 550 N/mm^2, respectively as measured in accordance with BS 18: 'Methods of tensile testing of metals'. Each grade of steel contains sub-divisions corresponding to steels of different yield stress and impact requirements. Steels should be in the 'semi-killed' deoxidation condition, unless used in thin sections, to minimise risk of blow-holes. Table 4.6 indicates maximum carbon content and minimum yield stress, ductility and impact strength of examples of steel sections, other than hollow sections, up to 16 mm thick and over 63 mm thick. Note the following:

1. Carbon content generally decreases from subdivision A to E, corresponding to increased impact resistance of the latter. In each case, impact strength is indicated by the energy absorbed by standard notched specimens at a given temperature. Steels with higher impact strength will absorb more energy at a given temperature (or equal energy at a lower temperature). Subdivision E steels, particularly high-grade types, are likely to be normalised.
2. Hot-rolling of thicker sections tends to be completed at relatively high temperatures – for example, 1100 °C. Hence, the austenitic and, ultimately, the ferritic grain structure, are coarser than those of thinner sections, resulting in lower yield stresses.

Table 4.6 Some properties of weldable structural steels for sections other than hollow sections BS 4360: Part II

Grade	Max. Carbon content (Ladle analysis)	Typical minimum yield stresses (N/mm²)		Minimum elongation on gauge length of 200 mm	Charpy V-notch impact test		
		Up to 16 mm thick	Over 63 mm thick		Temp (°C)	Min. average energy (J)	Max. thickness (mm)
40A	0.22	—	—	22	—	—	—
40B	0.20	240	210	22	Room temp.	27	50
40C	0.18	240	210	22	0	27	50
40D	0.18	240	210	22	−15	27	50
40E	0.16	255	225	22	$\begin{cases} -20 \\ -30 \end{cases}$	34 27	50 50
43A1	0.25	—	—	20	—	—	—
43A	0.25	255	225	20	—	—	—
43B	0.22	255	225	20	Room temp.	27	50
43C	0.18	255	225	20	0	27	50
43D	0.18	255	225	20	−15	27	50
43E	0.16	270	240	20	$\begin{cases} -20 \\ -30 \end{cases}$	34 27	50 50
50A	0.23	—	—	18	—	—	—
50B	0.20	355	325	18	—	—	—
50C	0.20	355	325	18	0	27	40
50D	0.18	355	By agreement	18	−10	27	40
55C	0.22	450	—	17	0	27	19
55E	0.22	450	—	17	$\begin{cases} -20 \\ -30 \\ -40 \end{cases}$	47 41 27	63

3. Yield strengths increase as tensile strengths (represented by grade designation) increase. Grade 43 A, for example, is the normally used 'mild steel' for general structural purposes, while grades 50 B and C correspond to 'high-yield steel' without and with impact-strength requirements, respectively. Note that high-yield steel does not necessarily contain more carbon than mild steel. The manganese content of high-yield steel is, however, normally higher than that of mild steel, typical figures being 0.8 and 0.5 per cent, respectively (BS 4360 requires a maximum of 1.5 per cent for most steels to ensure weldability). Alternatively, higher strengths may be obtained by additions of the metal niobium or by normalising, both of which refine the grain structure of the steel.

4. Ductility of steels decreases as their strengths increase. This factor is measured by the elongation of steel samples during tensile testing, ductile samples showing greater elongation.

BS 4360 gives similar requirements for plates, round and square bars, and hollow sections, together with diagrams showing the positions from which samples should be cut for tensile and impact tests and bending tests. The standard also specifies a maximum 'equivalent carbon content', which is important for welding and takes into account the presence of alloying elements such as manganese, chromium and copper.

Requirements relating to quality, width, length, flatness and weight tolerances are given.

Hot-rolled sections (BS 4: Part 1; BS 4848: Parts 2, 4, 5)
The latter British Standard, of which only Part 2 (Hollow sections), Part 4 (Equal and unequal angles) and Part 5 (Bulb flats) are at present complete, contain co-ordinated metric sizes, while BS 4 deals with remaining sections. These may be in the form of universal beams, columns and bearing piles, joists, T bars and channels, and are normally manufactured from weldable structural steels, as described above. The standards give dimensions and tolerances for respective sections. For example, mass per unit length tolerances are -4 per cent on minimum mass/unit length for hollow sections and typically $\pm 2\frac{1}{2}$ per cent on specified mass/unit length for joists, T bars, channels, angles and bulb flats. Tolerances under the specified depth of joists and channels are of considerable importance, since extreme fibre stresses and deflections increase greatly for a small decrease in overall depth of sections. Table 4.7 shows required tolerances for the depth of joists and channels. Hot-rolled sections have a very wide application in all aspects of structural engineering and building for loadbearing purposes.

Cold-rolled steel sections (BS 2994)
These are produced by cold-rolling from steel strip. The specifications for material are described in BS 1449: Part 1, which covers carbon steel plate, sheet and strip, in both hot- and cold-rolled conditions. BS 1449 gives a code relating to the deoxidation condition, the type of rolling, the degree of temper and the grade of material, the designation of the material depending on whether the specific requirements are based on formability, strength, temper or suitability for heat-treatment. The standard also gives requirements relating to composition, mechanical properties and tolerances. BS 2994 gives sizes in common production, together with dimensions and tolerances.

Use of structural steel (BS 449)

The stability of any metal component in a given situation depends on the magnitude of the load, the types of stresses it induces and, also, on the properties of the component. The properties of steel have been outlined by the British Standards mentioned above and BS 449 shows how, by consideration of loading types and arrangements, members of suitable dimensions can be selected.

Table 4.7 Dimensional tolerances on specified depth for
hot-rolled joists and channels (BS 4)

Nominal depth		Maximum permissible variation from specified depth	
Over (mm)	Up to and including (mm)	Over (mm)	Under (mm)
—	305	3.2	0.8
305	381	4.0	1.6
381	432	4.8	1.6

BS 449 gives certain requirements relating to impact strength of welded elements manufactured from BS 4360 steels during erection or in the completed structure, since brittle failure may occur at joints if impact strength is low. The impact energy requirements of BS 4360 apply to certain thicknesses only (see Table 4.6) and, since impact strengths of thicker sections which have a coarser grain structure are less, BS 449 specifies a separate impact strength for such welded sections, when in tension, of at least 27 joules by the Charpy V-notch test at 0 °C. The standard also requires that steel to be used in cold climates should have an impact strength of not less than 27 joules at the lowest ambient temperature likely to be encountered. This may require one of the C, D or E types of steel from BS 4360. Again, if a member is of critical importance, subject to high restraint or shock loading, a steel with high impact-resistance should be specified.

In the section on design and details of construction, BS 449 specifies that the thickness of steel used for external constructions exposed to weather should not be less than 8 mm, or 6 mm for unexposed steel (with the exception of webs or packings). Sealed tubes or sections may be of 4 mm minimum thickness in exposed situations or 3 mm in unexposed situations, since corrosion in these cases can only occur from the external face. The above figures need not be adhered to if special measures are taken to protect steel from corrosion. Design methods for members in bending, compression and tension are given.

The allowable tensile or compressive stress due to bending depends on the grade of steel and the thickness and, possibly, the type of section. Table 4.8 shows typical maximum allowable stresses. These may be compared with the minimum yield-point stresses from BS 4360 given in Table 4.6. The compressive stresses allowed in Table 4.8 are reduced in cases of long, slender beams to ensure satisfactory performance. In some cases, other criteria may be involved in selection of suitable sections, for example, deflection.

All BS 4848 sections are available in Grades 43 and 50 steels, though the majority of rolled steel sections are grade 43 – 'mild steel' – since it is more economical for manufacturer and supplier alike to concentrate on larger quantities

Table 4.8 Maximum permissible stresses for steel members
in bending (BS 449)

Form	Grade	Thickness	Maximum allowable tensile or compressive stress (N/mm^2)
Rolled I	43	All	165
beams	50	Up to and incl. 65 mm	230
		Over 65 mm	Ys/1.52
	55	Up to and incl. 40 mm	280
		Over 40 mm	260
Plate girders	43	Up to and incl. 40 mm	155
		Over 40 mm	140
	50	Up to and incl. 65 mm	215
		Over 65 mm	Ys/1.63
	55	Up to and incl. 40 mm	265
		Over 40 mm	245

Value of Ys to be agreed with manufacturer and not greater
than $350 N/mm^2$. There are, of course, requirements for
bearing and shear stresses in sections; the tensile and compressive stresses are given for comparison (a) with yield stresses in
steel and (b) with other metals or materials

of a particular grade of steel. In some cases, however, high-yield – grade
50 – steel may be more economical, generally, where higher stresses are encountered; where a required section falls in a 'gap' in standard sizes of grade 43 steel;
and, particularly, for fabrication of plate girders which may be used for large
spans as in bridges. (There is, in fact, a separate British Standard for the structural
use of steel in bridges, BS 153.) More recently, higher grades of steel have
become available, for example, à grade 77 weldable steel which has low carbon
content (0.08 to 0.17 per cent) but significant quantities of manganese, molybdenum, silicon and titanium. Quenching and tempering the fully killed steel results
in a fine-grained material of minimum yield point $700 N/mm^2$. This material has
been used for hollow sections of thickness up to 10 mm and outside measurements up to 150 mm (round or square). Its use is, on account of its high cost,
restricted to crane jibs and similar situations where a high strength/weight ratio is
essential.

The use of cold-rolled steel sections in building is covered by Addendum No. 1
to BS 449. The metal thickness is, of course, lower than in hot-rolled sections so
that, although light in weight and economical, additional factors such as local
weakness or torsional stiffness, must be considered in design. Hence, although

cold-forming tends to increase yield strengths, particularly at corners, permissible stresses are, in general, slightly lower than in hot-rolled sections. These sections are widely used for channels, angles and lintels where low or medium loadbearing capacity is required.

Steel for reinforcement of concrete

Reinforcement may be used for the following reasons:

1. To take the tensile stresses in concrete beams or slabs.
2. To withstand shear stresses in beams which are greatest near the supports. These give rise to complementary tensile stresses in such regions which require the use of additional reinforcement – either in the form of stirrups or bent-up bars at the end of simply-supported beams.
3. To carry a proportion of the compressive stress and to withstand tensile stresses which may arise due to eccentric loading, as in columns.
4. Reinforcement may be used near the surface of mass concrete structures to control cracking by drying or carbonation shrinkage.
5. In some cases, secondary reinforcement is used to prevent spalling of concrete surfaces due to fire.

The bond between concrete and steel

When reinforced concrete is loaded so that the reinforcement is under a tensile stress, some strain in the concrete must occur before the steel provides the necessary restraint and, therefore, cracking in tensile regions may occur. If there were no stress transfer between the steel and concrete, the steel would clearly be of no use at all in restraining the latter and, if a steel reinforcing bar were fixed only at its ends, a single large crack would almost certainly appear at the point of maximum tensile stress. For example, the mid-point of a simply-supported beam under a uniformly distributed load would crack if the beam were reinforced in this way. If the steel is bonded to the concrete, stress transfer would occur at all points along the length of tension members and, if cracks occurred, they would be in the form of a large number of very small cracks. Such cracks are more acceptable, since they are less likely to allow penetration of air and moisture which would corrode the steel. The precise nature of the bond between steel and concrete is not fully understood but its strength depends on the following factors:

(a) The area of contact between the steel and the concrete. This may be increased by use of larger numbers of smaller-diameter bars, which would have a higher surface area for a given sectional area. In the case of higher stresses in the steel, bars having hooked ends may be used, since these provide more effective anchorage than straight bars. Attention must still be given to local bond, however, if the formation of wide cracks is to be avoided.

(b) The strength of the concrete. Bond strength increases with the crushing strength of the concrete, though the relationship is not linear.

(c) The nature of the steel surface. The presence of a thin layer of rust increases the bond characteristics of plain round bars, though excessive rust, resulting

Table 4.9 Properties of steels for reinforcing concrete

Designation	Size (mm)	Minimum characteristic Strength (N/mm^2)	Maximum carbon (per cent)	Minimum elongation at failure on $5.65 \sqrt{S_0}$. (per cent)	Minimum bending radius in diameters
Hot rolled steel Grade 250 (plain round) BS 4449	All	250 (425 max.)	0.25	22	2D
Hot rolled steel Grade 460/425 (deformed high yield) BS 4449	6–16	460	0.4	12	3D
	>16	425	0.4	14	3D
Cold worked steel BS 4461	6–16	460	0.25	12	3D
	>16	425	0.25	14	3D
Hard drawn mild steel wire BS 4482	5–12	485	0.25	—	—

Note Characteristic strengths of hot-rolled bars are based on yield strength with 5 per cent failures. In the case of cold worked bars or drawn wire, they are based on 0.2 per cent proof stress with 5 per cent failures. The value of S_0, used to determine gauge length for elongation measurements, is equal to the original cross sectional area of the test piece.

in a reduced cross-sectional area would be clearly unacceptable. Deformed bars have greater bond strength but this is *reduced* by the presence of rust. Mechanical impact, or handling as when fixing a reinforcement, should normally reduce rust to acceptable levels. Wire brushing is useless. The presence of oils on bars severely reduces the bond.

It is unfortunate that high-strength bars for reinforcement do not have a significantly greater modulus of elasticity than mild steel bars, so that strains will be greater at the larger stresses which are permissible. In these cases, therefore, deformed bars are used to provide the increase in bond strength necessary. Table 4.9 shows selected properties of the most commonly used reinforcing steels.

In addition to the above requirements, the British Standards specify chemical composition, impurities, ultimate tensile strength and rebend test requirements. Hard-drawn steel wire is commonly used for fabric reinforcement and precast products, such as pipes. The welded intersections in fabric reinforcement give good bond with the concrete, especially if the wire is indented and, in many types of slab construction, this results in lower fixing costs than when bars are employed. There is, as yet, no classification in British Standards for the local bond strengths obtained from plain, twisted or ribbed bars, though BS CP 110 allows them to be used in the approximate stress ratios 1 : 1.25 : 1.5. Design may be based on a local bond stress in tension of between 1.7 and 2.7 N/m^2 for plain bars, depending on the concrete strength. BS CP 110 specifies separate values for anchorage bond strengths.

Reinforcing bars manufactured in the UK can be quite easily identified visually.

Grade 250 hot-rolled steel bars (BS 4449) are normally of plain round section but may also have ridges or corners parallel to the longitudinal axis of the bar. They may be preferred where rebending is necessary, for links and stirrups, or where unusually complex bending schedules are required.

Grade 460/425 hot-rolled steel bars (BS 4449) are of round section with straight ribs and ridges (Type 2, deformed bars). Both types of hot-rolled bar will normally have a grey mill-scale covering, unless weathered.

Cold-worked steel bars (BS 4461) may be either of twisted square section (Type 1 deformed) or of twisted ribbed circular section (Type 2 deformed). The mill scale on such bars will have been removed by the cold-working process.

High-yield steel reinforcing bars are generally preferred to mild steel bars on economic grounds and they are also rather more tolerant of rough handling on site, since greater strains can be accommodated without yielding. The choice between different types of high-yield steel will normally be according to local availability and cost.

Bars with yield stresses of 500 N/mm^2 are available, though there is no British Standard specification for these at present and, when used, particular attention may need to be given to avoiding excessive deflections and cracking of concrete under service stresses.

Steels for prestressed concrete

The chief difference between prestressing and reinforcing steels is that plastic deformation of prestressing steels is not required. In consequence, carbon or alloy contents can be increased, giving much higher working stresses. These are, however, linked to another equally important attribute of prestressing steels, that of extensibility. Since elastic moduli of prestressing steels are either similar to, or slightly lower than, those of reinforcing steels, working stresses correspond to much greater strains. Values in the region of 5000×10^{-6} are typical, with the result that prestress losses due to shrinkage, creep and other causes do not seriously reduce the operating stress in the steel (though they must be allowed for).

Prestressing steels can be broadly categorised into high-tensile steel wire (either plain or in the form of strand) and alloy-steel bars.

The use of carbon steel in wire form has the attraction that, by a combination of heat-treatment and cold-drawing, very high tensile strengths can be achieved. In a typical process, high-carbon steel is quenched from the austenitic state into a lead bath at about 500 °C. This gives a very finely divided network of cementite particles in a ferrite matrix, which imparts sufficient ductility to permit extensive cold-drawing. Depending on the load-carrying capacity required, wires, which may have diameters of up to 7 mm, may be used individually or in stranded form. The latter comprise 7 or 19 wires spun in helical form as hexagonal sections about a straight core. (The hexagonal sections are the same as those which form the basis of the HCP and FCC crystal structures: Fig. 4.1.) An advantage of wire and strand is that they can be coiled in long lengths for storage, thereby obviating the need to form joints in tendons for large structures.

Wire and strand are available in the 'as drawn' or 'as spun' conditions, respectively, though these forms have the drawback of not paying-out straight after coiling and undergoing relaxation (plastic distortion) at stresses over approximately 50 per cent of characteristic strength. Products are, therefore, normally either heat-treated at about 350 °C to overcome the problem of paying-out straight, or subjected to a similar process while under stress, the latter leading to low-relaxation wire or strand. Two slightly different grades of wire are available in most sizes, while 7-wire strand may be in the form of 'standard', 'super' (having higher tensile strength) or 'drawn' (having been passed through a die and heat-treated before coiling). Selected properties of available sizes of wire and 7-wire strand are given in Table 4.10, together with details of 19-wire strand which is available 'as spun' in sizes 25.4 mm, 28.6 mm and 31.8 mm and, as 'treated', in size 18 mm.

In some cases and, particularly, in pretensioned prestressed concrete, bonding with the concrete is essential. For this purpose, indented or crimped wires may be employed. Full bonding with the concrete using plain or indented wires requires a transmission length of 100 diameters according to BS CP 110, while the transmission length for strand is, in terms of the diameter, much smaller, typically 200 mm for 9.3 mm diameter strand. The gradual decrease of prestress towards the end of pretensioned lintels, for example, is not normally a problem, since bending stresses are lower at these positions.

Alloy-steel bars rely on significant quantities of alloying elements, such as manganese, rather than high carbon content or drawing, to produce high strength. Bars are available either smooth or with ribs, according to bonding requirements. Joints and anchorages are provided by means of threads which are rolled on to avoid the loss of strength associated with a cut thread. Two grades are available – 'hot-rolled' or 'processed' – the latter involving cold-working and possibly, in addition, tempering. Selected properties of hot-rolled bars are indicated in Table 4.10.

Site heating, welding and cutting of studies

Reference to Table 4.2 shows that, if heated to temperatures above about 450 °C, steels are likely to change in properties, by recrystallisation, annealing or even chemically, in order of increasing temperature. Welding of mild steel does not pose problems since the metal welds easily and is not likely to be severely affected

Table 4.10 Properties of steels for prestressing concrete

Material	Example of sizes available (mm)	Specified characteristic load (kN)	Equivalent stress (N/mm²)	Minimum elongation on gauge length stated	Relaxation at 70 per cent of characteristic stress for 1000 hours		Carbon content (per cent)
					Normal	Low	
High-tensile steel wire BS 5896	4	21.0 ⎱ 22.3 ⎰	1670 ⎱ 1770 ⎰	3.5 per cent on g.l. 200 mm (max. load)	8	2.5	—
	7	60.4 ⎱ 64.3 ⎰	1570 ⎱ 1590 ⎰				
7-wire strand (standard) BS 5896	9.3	92	1770	3.5 per cent on g.l. ≯500 mm (max. load)	8	2.5	—
	15.2	232	1670				
19-wire strand BS 4757				3.5 per cent on g.l. ≯600 mm (max. load)			0.6–0.9
As spun	25.4	659	1558		9	—	
As spun	31.8	979	1483		9	—	
Treated	18	370	1762		7	2.5	
High-tensile alloy steel bars BS 4486 (hot-rolled)	20	325 ⎱ 1300 ⎰	1030	6 per cent on g.l. $5.65\sqrt{S_0}$. (on fracture)	3.5	—	—
	40						

Note Characteristic strengths are based on breaking load with 5 per cent failures, though minimum proof stress values are also specified.

by the process. There is, however, much skill involved in the welding process, and brittleness and cracking will result if the weld is of poor quality. At high temperatures, grain boundaries tend to accommodate stresses due to shrinkage and, therefore, a fine-grained weld structure is preferable. This is obtained by avoiding overheating, which would also damage surrounding parent metal. Welding of high-yield steel presents greater problems and preheating of the heat-affected zone may be necessary to avoid metallurgical changes during the welding process. Cold-worked steels will recrystallise on welding so that yield strength will be reduced. In all cases, particular care is needed when members are in tension. Prestressing steels are not normally welded – this should not be necessary and, in any case, their high carbon/alloy content makes welding difficult.

If heat is required to assist in bending reinforcement, this should be in the form of steam only.

Cutting is best carried out by a high-speed abrasive wheel, which avoids heating of the steel, though an oxyacetylene flame will produce a cutting rather than a melting action if an excess of oxygen is used (the oxygen causes rapid oxidation of steel in the flame and, since iron oxide melts at a lower temperature than steel, the oxide is dispersed by the flame). The ends of bars or wire are not normally under stress but, in post-tensioned prestressing systems, it is particularly important that a tendon is not overheated at its anchorage.

Fire-resistance of steel

It is unfortunate that the electronic properties of metals which give rise to their formability also result in high thermal conductivity and decrease of strength at only moderate temperatures. The high conductivity of metals results in rapid transfer of heat to metal structures in case of fire, unless in some way protected, so that collapse of steel structures may occur very rapidly in serious fires. Although, on heating to a temperature of about 250 °C, the yield strength of hot-rolled steels increases, continued heating to about 550 °C weakens the steel to the point where, based on normal factors of safety, yield is likely to occur. However, even before this has occurred, considerable distortion of the structure by expansion of the softening material may take place. For example, a 10 m beam heated to 400 °C will expand by approximately 50 mm. It is clear, therefore, that steel structures must be protected, as far as possible, from fire and this is usually achieved by cladding, either in concrete or, better, lightweight insulating materials such as asbestos, vermiculite, lightweight concrete and lightweight plasters. Cold-drawn steels for reinforcing or prestressing concrete will be seriously affected at relatively low temperatures, for example, 450 °C, though a considerable degree of protection is afforded by the concrete itself.

Future developments in structural steels

With prices of raw materials rising continuously, the advantages of steels which can be used at higher stresses are self-evident, though it will also be evident that high yield strength was traditionally obtained at the expense of some other important properties, such as notch ductility or weldability. In addition, when steel sections are reduced in thickness, problems of, for example, excessive deflection or greater vulnerability to corrosion may arise.

Much research has been carried out into obtaining steels having higher service stresses while retaining satisfactory toughness and weldability, and it is found that the most promising steels are those of low alloy content containing as little as 0.03 per cent carbon, together with low sulphur and oxygen content for good formability. High yield strength is obtained by producing a very fine dispersion of ferrite grains. This involves careful processing of steels containing the micro-alloying elements aluminium, niobium, vanadium or titanium, the processing involving controlled rolling at progressively lower temperatures. Optimum properties depend on the reduction of section per pass and on the time between passes. Applications of such techniques are likely to include tubular assemblies in constructional engineering and perhaps, ultimately, ordinary structural steel sections, where increased manufacturing costs will be offset by reductions in the mass of steel required for a section of given strength. At the present time, however, mild and high-yield steels remain the most economical method of producing conventional structures, the more sophisticated high-strength steels being reserved for situations such as large-span structures where very high strength/weight ratio is required.

Alloy steels

These contain substantial proportions of alloying elements. They may be included for the following reasons:

(a) To increase strength and hardness. For a given cooling rate, the BCC elements tungsten, molybdenum and vanadium enhance these properties.

(b) To increase hardening properties. It is very difficult to harden effectively large steel sections by quenching, since, although martensite will be produced on surface layers, the bulk of the metal will tend to form pearlite. In any case, quenching is drastic and results in a distorted, brittle structure. By incorporating alloying elements in steels, they can be made to produce martensite without quenching, so that the material will harden uniformly throughout its section. Elements having this effect manganese, molybdenum and chromium.

(c) To increase corrosion resistance. Aluminium, copper and chromium have this effect. Structural steels and sheet containing 0.2 per cent copper are available: these form a protective brown oxide layer on exposure. They could have application in buildings, allowing the steel frame to be situated externally, perhaps as an architectural feature and with less danger of damage by fire. Most important, at present, however, are stainless steels which are based on the effect of chromium (see below).

(d) To preserve the austenitic state. Metals such as manganese and nickel, which are FCC, tend to preserve the austenitic structure of steel down to temperatures as low as room temperature. For example, a 13 per cent manganese steel is used on the teeth of mechanical shovels to resist the severe abrasion encountered. Impact or abrasion changes the surface layers of the austenite structure into martensite, which resists wear and damage.

(e) To produce special properties. Steels containing 36 per cent nickel, for example, have a very low thermal movement (approximately $2 \times 10^{-6}/°C$ at normal temperatures, compared to $11.6 \times 10^{-6}/°C$ for ordinary steel). They are known as 'invar' steels and are used in surveyors' tapes and similar applications.

A very large number of alloy steels can be produced by the incorporation of alloying elements as above, though these are mainly used in mechanical engineering applications. In addition, surface hardening may be used, for example, flame-hardening in which, by heating of the surface of a metal component and then quenching immediately, martensitic surface layers are produced on a tough, resilient core. A similar effect may be obtained by nitriding or carburising, which involve heating components in nitrogen- or carbon-rich atmospheres which combine with surface layers, giving a hardening effect.

Stainless steels
Owing to their corrosion resistance, these are the most widely used alloy steels in the construction industry. Resistance to corrosion is achieved by incorporation of chromium in steel. On immersion in water or dilute acids which contain oxygen, an impervious chromium-oxide film is formed and any faults in the coating are quickly repaired. Chromium in quantities up to 27 per cent of the steel may be used, 18 per cent being a common figure. Best results are obtained with a single-phase metal, since two phases (for example, ferrite and pearlite in ordinary steel) will tend to corrode electrolytically with one another. The addition of nickel preserves the austenitic state and, for this reason, up to 10 per cent nickel is included in the austenitic steels. The most common types of stainless steel are 18–8 (percentages of chromium and nickel, respectively) and 18–10–3 (the last figure indicating 3 per cent molybdenum). The second type is more expensive but has greater corrosion resistance and is more suitable for external use, for example, in cladding or internally where cleaning is not practicable and, therefore, differential aeration is a possibility. Caution is necessary when welding austenitic stainless steels, since, at the high temperature involved, chromium carbide forms at grain boundaries which may cause corrosion of chromium-depleted regions nearby. This problem may be avoided if steels of very low carbon content are used or if the steel is stabilised with niobium or titanium, which reduce the tendency for chromium to migrate.

Ferritic stainless steels also exist and, though they are cheaper than austenitic stainless steel, due to their low nickel content, they have relatively poor corrosion resistance, especially if welded, hence, they are used internally. They have low carbon content and, therefore, good formability: applications include balustrades, lift fittings and pressed steel sinks.

A harder steel is obtained by quenching from about 1000 °C producing martensitic stainless steel if significant carbon is present. However, although used for cutting implements, such as knives, corrosion-resistance and formability are not as good as for austenitic steels. The impact strengths of ferritic and martensitic stainless steels are poor, especially at low temperatures, since they exhibit a ductile-brittle transition.

Since stainless steels depend for their protection on a chromium-oxide coating, resistance to corrosion will be reduced in oxygen-remote situations or where there is differential aeration, as, for example, in underground pipes. The effect will be exaggerated in the presence of chlorides or sulphates. The 18–10–3 grade is most resistant to such conditions but longest life will, in general, be obtained where oxygen has ready access to all parts of the surface, in order that the passivating oxide film can re-form if, for any reason, it is disrupted. The presence of nickel enhances corrosion resistance in less oxidising acids, such as hydrochloric and sulphuric acids.

Use of stainless steel   Stainless steel is manufactured mainly in the form of steel plate, sheet and strip (BS 1449: Part 2) or light-gauge tubing (BS 4127). The material is now used for a wide variety of pressed fittings, internally and externally, for example, cladding of window sections, toilet and kitchen furniture, flue pipes and roof coverings. Stainless steel tubing for domestic purposes is comparable in price with copper and prices fluctuate less than those of the latter. Although work-hardening makes bending more difficult, stainless steel tubes have much greater bursting pressures than copper, so that when compression fittings are used, freezing of the tube will tend to cause sliding at the joints rather than bursting of the tubes. This obviates the need for pipe replacement, though it may result in the emission of a full bore of water on complete failure of a joint. When soldering tubing, the use of chloride-based fluxes is not recommended, since they cause corrosion of the tubing, especially if jointing is completed some time before the system is brought into use or flushed out. Special fluxes, such as those based on phosphoric acid, should be used.

Cast iron

Carbon dissolves to the extent of 1.7 per cent in austenite and cast iron may be conveniently defined as a carbon/iron alloy containing carbon in excess of this percentage. It will be recalled that the compound cementite contains 6.67 per cent carbon, so that cast irons containing up to this percentage of carbon might be expected to exist in the form of gamma iron plus cementite above 723 °C and pearlite plus cementite below 723 °C. This may be the case but carbon in the form of graphite may also occur in the metal due to decomposition of cementite, resulting in much reduced strength if the graphite is present in flake form. There are several forms of cast iron, depending on the condition of the carbon in the metal, but they are all eminently castable (hence the name) and, as a result of their high carbon content, have a melting point as low as 1130 °C – much lower than that of steel. In fact, the solid/liquid portion of the iron-carbon equilibrium diagram is of eutectic form, 1130 °C being the eutectic temperature obtained with 4.3 per cent carbon. The chief forms of cast iron are given below.

Grey cast iron (BS 1452)

This contains silicon which tends to cause the breakdown of cementite into iron and carbon. Hence, the metal is graphitic and, therefore, not as strong as other forms, having a tensile strength of about 200 N/mm². The presence of flakes of graphite also gives rise to stress concentrations and brittleness, fractured surfaces having a grey colour. However, in the thicknesses cast, corrosion is not normally a problem and grey cast iron has been extensively used for boiler castings, radiators, pipes, baths and gutters. Its use for external rainwater systems is diminishing, as a result of developments in plastics, but it remains the only material for the purpose, other than lead, which has been proved to have first-class durability over the course of many years. BS 1452 described various grades of grey cast iron in the form of pipes and fittings, cast either in sand moulds or centrifugally. The latter process produces a stronger, harder product.

Spheroidal graphite cast iron (BS 2789, BS 4772)

In this type of iron, the flake graphite in the molten iron is made to crystallise into spheres by addition of magnesium and ferrosilicon. Hence, the stress concentrations are removed and a more ductile material is produced. By annealing after casting, the pearlite can be made to decompose, resulting in a ferritic structure with graphite nodules, giving even greater ductility but lower strength. BS 4772 describes ductile iron pipes containing carbon in the spheroidal state, which are widely used in underground applications. Casting methods are as for grey cast pipes but tensile strengths are much improved, being not less than 420 N/mm².

White cast iron (BS 4844)

This contains carbon in the form of cementite and may be produced by rapid cooling of small castings or by the effect of sulphur, both of which tend to stabilise cementite. White cast iron is intensely hard and brittle and is so named because fractured surfaces are white. Where greater toughness is required, castings can be rendered malleable by heat-treatment which causes decomposition of cementite and formation of a ferritic structure.

Non-ferrous metals

The most important non-ferrous metals in construction are aluminium, lead, copper and zinc, together with associated alloys. Table 4.11 summarises principal properties of these metals in the commercially pure state.

Table 4.11 Properties of chief non-ferrous metals (commercially pure). Metals listed in order of increasing ultimate tensile strength, together with iron for comparison

Metal	Relative density	Melting point °C	Elastic modulus kN/mm^2	Ultimate tensile strength (N/mm^2)	Coeff. of thermal expansion $\times 10^{-6}$ per °C
Lead	11.3	327	16.2	18	29.5
Zinc	7.1	419	90	37	up to 40
Aluminium	2.7	659	70.5	45	24.0
Copper	8.7	1083	130	210	16.7
[Iron	7.8	1537	210	540	11.6]

Aluminium

It is seldom appreciated that aluminium, in the form of Al_2O_3, is the most common metallic element in the earth's crust, being present, for example, in most types of rock and clay. It is unfortunate that extraction of aluminium is expensive and is not normally economical in the case of rocks and clays. Bauxite, $Al_2O_3.2H_2O$, is the chief mineral used for extraction of aluminium. Extraction of the metal is not possible by means of reducing agents, such as carbon, used for steel: an electrolytic method is used, after conversion of the bauxite to aluminium hydroxide. Hence, aluminium is expensive, owing to the cost of extraction rather than to any lack of abundance.

The widespread use of a reactive metal such as aluminium stems directly from the fact that a coherent, impervious oxide film forms on the surface of the metal immediately on exposure to air. The oxide coating conducts positive aluminium ions but not electrons (hence, its action as a rectifier), so that, once a certain thickness is reached, the resistance of the corrosion film will prevent further corrosion. If increased protection to corrosion is required, anodising may be carried out. This involves immersion of aluminium in chromic, oxalic or sulphuric acid solutions and inducing corrosion electrolytically, using a direct current source of about 50 V, with the aluminium as the anode and a steel cathode. The oxide film forms as in normal corrosion but in a more uniform and greater thickness, due to the increased voltage. The films obtained using some acids are initially porous so that dyes can be used, producing a coloured finish and the surface then sealed. Film thickness may vary between 35 μm, suitable for aggressive environments, and 1 μm, which must be painted. Aluminium oxide films are very vulnerable in the presence of certain ions, notably OH^- ions, as occur in caustic environments. For example, anodised aluminium is corroded by fresh or damp cement paste with production of hydrogen, hence, it should not be used in contact with damp concrete: indeed, the same reaction is used for generation of hydrogen during production of 'aerated' concretes. BS 1615 describes a number of tests relating to physical and chemical properties of anodic coatings on aluminium. The unprotected metal also corrodes in the presence of

215

metals such as copper or iron, especially if chloride ions are present. Coatings of bitumen will be effective in such circumstances. Hence, in general, aluminium should not be allowed to come into contact with damp brickwork, plaster, timber or soil. Paints containing copper, mercury, lead or graphite may be harmful and should be avoided: resin-based primers containing chromates and iron oxide may be used. Magnesium oxychloride, as used in flooring, should not be in contact with aluminium as it will also cause corrosion.

Pure aluminium, though not of high strength, is very suitable for weathering and foils. A common use is, for example, as a lining for plasterboard, since it has low emissivity and very high vapour resistivity. A further useful property of aluminium is its high electrical conductivity. This property, combined with its light weight, makes it preferable to copper for transmission wires, in spite of the higher electrical conductivity of the latter. Most aluminium, however, is manufactured in alloy form.

Aluminium alloys (BS 1470–1475; 1490)

There is a very wide range of alloys which may have enhanced strength or corrosion resistance. Alloys containing magnesium are, like the pure metal, corrosion-resistant and, since magnesium is of similar atomic size to aluminium (they are adjacent in the periodic table), it will dissolve to a limit of about 5 per cent in aluminium at room temperature. The single-phase alloy so formed, therefore, has considerable ductility which, combined with its corrosion-resistance, makes it suitable for pressed components of moderate strength, for example, corrugated roofing, or where superior corrosion-resistance is essential. However, since pure magnesium alloys are single-phase, they do not benefit from heat-treatment. Incorporation of combinations of copper, magnesium, silicon, manganese and chromium produces alloys which can be welded and extruded and yet have 0.2 per cent proof stresses up to $435 \, N/mm^2$ on heat-treatment (cf grade 43 A steel, minimum yield stress $225–255 \, N/mm^2$). The extrudability of such alloys makes them ideal for relatively complex extruded sections, such as complete window frames.

The presence of silicon or copper in aluminium increases its strength by the process of precipitation or age-hardening. At high temperatures, these elements dissolve to the extent of several per cent in aluminium. However, on cooling, the solubility decreases so that metal crystals tend to precipitate at grain boundaries. If aluminium is cooled quickly by quenching, there will be insufficient time for precipitation and a super-saturated (solid) solution of silicon or copper in aluminium is obtained. The 'impurities' will then, over a period of 4 to 5 days, diffuse within the aluminium lattice to form clusters which oppose dislocation movement, strengthening and hardening the metal. By heating to between 100 °C and 200 °C for 2h to 20h, the diffusion process leads to even higher strength. These processes are known respectively as solution and precipitation treatments. Alloys containing copper should be protected if used externally. Protection may be in the form of sprayed pure aluminium, or, for aluminium-alloy sheets, pure aluminium cladding.

Table 4.12 Properties and uses of some aluminium products

Alloy	Essential alloying elements (per cent maximum)				Typical minimum 0.2 per cent proof stress	Application
	Mn	Si	Mg	Cu	(N/mm^2)	
SIB-H4	0.05	0.3	—	0.05	—	Flashings, weatherings, can be hand formed
	(Al content 99.5 per cent min.)					
NS3-H4	1.5	0.6	0.1	0.1	—	Roofing, general applications, good durability
HE9-TF	0.1	0.7	0.9	0.1	160	Extrusions for window frames
HE30-TF	1.0	1.3	1.2	0.1	255	Structural sections

A large range of alloys exists, described in BSS 1470 to 1475, and a complete explanation of the letter code is not possible here, but Table 4.12 shows the codes, proof strengths and applications of some alloy products used in building. The prefix 'N' refers to metals which do not benefit from heat-treatment, though strength and ductility still depend on the degree of cold-working applied, 'O' being annealed and 'H1' to 'H8' indicating the degree of strain-hardening. The prefix 'H' denotes a heat-treatable alloy. 'S' stands for sheet and 'E' for extrusions. The number in each code relates to the alloy composition. The letters 'TF' imply that the alloy has been solution heat-treated and precipitation-treated. Aluminium is also available in cast form, denoted 'LM', which is used in components such as door handles and ornamental work, (BS 1490).

Structural use of aluminium
The chief advantage of aluminium lies in its low density compared to that of steel: densities are in the approximate ratio 3:1, steel:aluminium. Some of this advantage is, of course, lost, owing to the reduced stiffness of the latter but, even so, an aluminium structure is not likely to be more than half the weight of its equivalent in steel. A further advantage is that in mild, unpolluted atmospheres, aluminium may be left unpainted. The embrittlement which occurs in steels on cooling is also absent in aluminium owing to the FCC structure, although, at temperatures above 150 °C, loss of strength is rapid and aluminium alloys melt at about 600 °C. Temperature movement of aluminium is almost double that of steel, though its modulus of elasticity is only one-third; therefore, although allowances for expansion are necessary, temperature stresses in a restrained member will be only about two-thirds of those in a similarly restrained steel member. The low elastic modulus of aluminium is a disadvantage with respect to lateral stability in compression members: this should be carefully checked during design.

Aluminium-alloy sections for structural use are normally extruded rather than rolled, since the former is the more versaile. A large number of sections is available so that, provided care is taken to select the best section for a given purpose, there is some compensation for the extra cost of aluminium compared to steel, which is only available in standard sections. Design codes are, therefore, inevitably different from those of steel and this is, perhaps, one of the reasons why the structural use of aluminium is not more widespread.

Welding of aluminium has, in the past, presented problems, partly due to the oxide film which must, of course, be removed before joining components. This may be achieved by electric arc-welding in an inert gas, such as argon, which excludes oxygen. Porosity in welds also reduces strength and 'joint efficiency' factors are used when designing welded connections. Alloys, if welded in the 'TF' condition, will revert to the 'TB' conditon (that is, solution-treated only), though the original properties can be restored by heat-treatment. Tempered metals, for example, NS lB-H4, will revert to the annealed 'O' condition in welded zones.

Lead

The excellent durability and ease of working of lead are responsible for the former widespread use of the metal in weatherings, flashings and pipes. Its use in these situations is now declining, since the material is expensive and the lower ductility of other metals is no disadvantage for components which are formed by machine. Lead occurs naturally in the form of galena (lead sulphide), which is imported from the USA, Australia or Canada. The metal is extracted by conversion of lead sulphide to lead oxide, which is then reduced by carbon to the metal.

Lead is the densest common metal, having a relative density of 11.3. It also has a low melting point, equal to $327\,°C$ and high thermal movement – $29.5 \times 10^{-6}/\,°C$. The strength of the metal is low, ultimate strengths ranging from about $20\,N/mm^2$ for impure leads to $11\,N/mm^2$ for very pure lead.

On exposure to the atmosphere, lead forms a protective coating of lead carbonate which is innocuous and does not stain adjacent brickwork or stonework. Although lead is by no means the most reactive of metals used in building, it may undergo electrolytic corrosion with metals such as copper if, in damp conditions, the metals touch. However, corrosion will only be serious where relatively large areas are in contact and lead coverings may be secured by copper nails, due to the small area of the latter and protection afforded by the corrosion product (galvanised or steel nails are not suitable for use with lead, since they may corrode rapidly as a result of the relatively reactive nature of zinc or steel and the small anodic area provided by the nails). Lead is also attacked by some types of organic acid – notably acetic acid, which forms the basis of vinegar – and is not highly suitable for domestic waste systems in soft-water areas. Moisture which has been in contact with peat, oak or teak and, to some extent, pitch pine, may also have a corrosive effect. Lead components are best protected by bitumen-impregnated tape in such situations.

Uses of lead

Lead pipes (BS 602 and 1085)   As would be expected with a metal fairly near its melting point, lead creeps, above a certain stress. BS 602 and 1085 recommend minimum pipe thicknesses for water service and distributing pipes. BS 602 describes pure lead pipes while BS 1085 relates to silver-copper lead which contains 0.003 to 0.005 per cent of silver and copper. Such material has greater tensile strength, fatigue-resistance and creep-resistance, so that it can be used with slightly reduced wall thicknesses for a given water pressure. A further type, which contains 0.05 to 1 per cent tellurium and 0.06 per cent copper, is amenable to work-hardening and has greater tensile strength and fatigue-resistance than ordinary lead.

Waste pipes and gas pipes which are not subject to hydrostatic pressure are normally thinner than water-service pipes. The working properties of lead pipes depend on the grain size distribution, the grains being visible if a section of pipe is polished and etched. The above British Standards give qualitative requirements for the size and uniformity of grain structure in lead pipes, to obtain a suitable balance between creep-resistance (improved by coarse-grain structure) and impact strength, to resist pressure 'surges' (improved by fine-grain structure) caused, for example, by water hammer.

Extruded lead pipes and meter connections for gas supplies are still widely used because of their corrosion-resistance and ductility, though their use for water-service pipes is decreasing due to cost, competition from plastics and the possibility of contamination of water. Pure or soft waters tend to dissolve lead, since they contain carbon dioxide which combines with the metal to form a soluble form of lead carbonate. In hard water containing calcium carbonate, a lead carbonate film forms on pipes, preventing dissolution of the metal. Local authorities normally restrict the lead content of mains water to 0.1 parts per million and soft water may require treatment to keep lead contamination to this limit.

Owing to their flexibility, water-filled lead pipes will withstand freezing several times, though, on the same account, the infill around underground lead pipes may, over a period of time, cause leaks due to abrasion. Lumps of brick or concrete should not be used in infill materials.

Lead sheet and strip (BS 1178)   Lead sheeting for roofing purposes has, to some extent, been replaced by other materials but, even so, there are many modern examples of lead roofing, cladding and fascias which combine great durability with aesthetically pleasing effect, particularly in 'prestige' building. When used in such large areas, joints must be provided to allow for thermal expansion. The maximum dimension in any direction should not exceed 3 m, sheet normally being used in strips about 1 m wide. BS 1178 gives code numbers from 3 to 8, corresponding to thicknesses between 1.25 and 3.55 mm, together with a colour code. Thicker sheets should be used where dressing is required or if mechanical damage is likely, for example, due to foot traffic. The admirable working properties of lead sheet are, in part, due to the fact that, at room temperature, lead is above its recrystallisation temperature, hence, it does not work-harden. These properties are further enhanced by the ease with which joints can be made by 'lead-burning'. Provided surfaces to be joined are cleaned and a reducing flame is used, no flux is necessary for this process, which uses ordinary lead as the filler metal.

Lead strip is still widely used for damp-proof courses, since it has unsurpassed damp-proofing qualities. It should be protected from contamination by cement mortar by coating both sides with a bituminous paint. Lead-cored bituminous felts overcome this problem. A further aesthetic use is in leaded-light windows.

Lead solders (BS 219) (Soft solders)   These normally consist of a proportion of tin and lead, possibly with a small percentage of antimony. Tin-lead alloys produce the type of phase diagram shown in Fig. 4.12, the melting points being:

327 °C – pure lead.
232 °C – pure tin.
183 °C – eutectic composition consisting of 37 per cent lead and 63 per cent tin.

When a low melting point is required, as for spigot-type joints on lead pipes, the eutectic composition (tinman's solder) may be used, though this solder is expensive, due to its high tin content. Solders for general uses are about 60:40; lead:tin, combining relative cheapness with a reasonably low melting point. Solders for wiping joints in lead pipes are about 70:30; lead:tin, in order to give a long plastic stage.

Copper

The element occurs naturally in the form of ores containing copper, iron and sulphur. Since the metal is almost indestructible, a good deal is also recovered as scrap and reprocessed. Some impurities are removed by flotation, and then by oxidation in a converter. The metal is then refined either by furnace or electrolytically, according to use, the latter producing the purest metal.

Copper is the noblest of metals commonly used in building – it behaves as a cathode to the others, with the exception of stainless steel, hence, it will be protected by almost any metal it touches, at the expense of the other metal. It forms an attractive green patina of the basic sulphate on exposure to a damp atmosphere, though, unless attention is given to detailing, washings from it may stain adjacent materials. Copper is resistant to most common acids and to sea water (but see below under 'Copper tube').

The tensile strength of copper depends on its purity, about $200 \, \text{N/mm}^2$ for the pure metal. Its main applications result from either its ductility or its very high electrical and thermal conductivity, the latter being $385 \, \text{W/m} \, °\text{C}$ (pure metal), the highest of any building material. Pure copper has a melting point of 1083 °C, so that creep is not a problem at normal temperatures.

Uses

Copper tube (BS 2871)   Copper is the most commonly used material for central heating and domestic water tubing, owing to its lightness and admirable working properties. In the hard-drawn form, it can be used with wall thicknesses as low as 0.5 mm and is, therefore, cheap, though tube in this form will fracture if bending is attempted: fittings must be used where bends are required. This type of tube is covered by BS 2871: Part I, Table Z. The same standard also specifies Table X tube, which is slightly thicker and not work-hardened to the same degree, so that bends can be obtained. Table Y tube is available in half-hard or annealed forms, which have thicker walls and may be used for forming tighter bends than Table X tube, or for underground service pipes. Copper tubing for water supplies has generally very high corrosion resistance, though it has been known to undergo corrosion in some acidic waters, such as those obtained from peaty catchment areas or containing carbonic acid (although, unlike ferrous metals or lead, pitting is only slight). Such water should be treated with sufficient lime to neutralise acidity without causing pipe scaling. Dirt or impurities in pipes may cause electrolytic corrosion, so that cleanliness during installation is essential, especially in soft-water areas. It is advisable to protect copper tubes chased into gypsum plasters with a coating of bitumen, particularly if damp conditions are prevalent. No protection should be necessary when buried in ordinary soils.

Copper tube is also used in waste and soil systems, pipes over 50 mm diameter normally being bronze-welded or silver-soldered. Copper fittings may be used with copper tubing, capillary end-feed or solder ring-type fittings producing cheap, unobtrusive joints. They are also used with stainless steel tube in the absence, at present, of any similar product made in stainless steel.

Copper sheeting (BS 2870)   This is used for a variety of purposes in building, in damp-proof courses, for weatherings and flashings, and as a roofing or cladding material. A number of forms are available, work-hardened to various degrees. Annealed copper is essential for roofing, since manipulation is necessary but, where sheet is to some degree self-supporting, a half-hardened temper should be used. Copper sheeting should be fixed with copper nails, since other metals would be prone to rapid electrolytic corrosion. Welding is most easily carried out on deoxidised copper which contains a small percentage of phosphorous: the small amount of cuprous oxide which occurs in non-deoxidised ('tough pitch') sheet tends to react with hydrogen in the flux or gas, causing unsoundness due to steam formation. The presence of arsenic in copper increases its strength at 200 °C and above, and also improves corrosion resistance. Copper may be alloyed so that it benefits from solution treatment and precipitation-hardening where higher-strength sheet is required.

Copper alloys

Brasses   Zinc has an atomic radius similar to that of copper and dissolves to form a single phase FCC alloy in contents up to 36 per cent. The brasses obtained are

221

known as alpha brasses: they are ductile and have high tensile strength, particularly, if the zinc content approaches the solubility limit or if work-hardened. Since, during the process of work-hardening, most distortion takes place at grain boundaries, these may corrode electrolytically with the grain body, leading to 'season cracking', unless stresses are relieved by annealing. Alpha brasses are used for pressing (such as in door furniture), stamping or drawing.

Alpha-beta brasses contain 36 to 46 per cent zinc, the beta phase (BCC) increasing as percentages approach the upper figure. They are less ductile than alpha brasses but are suitable for high-temperature extrusion, rolling or casting. They are used in window sections, often having a bronze colour due to incorporation of a small percentage of manganese. Alpha-beta brasses are used for plumbing fittings, screws and general brassmongery.

Beta brasses contain more than 46 per cent zinc, though brasses containing more than 50 per cent zinc are not used. These brasses have melting points lower than 900 °C, compared to 1083 °C for pure copper, and are used for brazing.

Copper and copper-alloy tube fittings (BS 864: Part II) These are classified as capillary fittings, non-manipulative fittings (type A), which use compression rings and manipulative fittings (type B), in which the tube at or near the end is formed into a flange which is compressed on to the fitting. Copper capillary fittings are described under uses of copper, though capillary fittings are also obtainable in brass. Joints are, perhaps, more conveniently made using compression fittings, though they are rather more obtrusive. 'Pull out' of type A fittings is more likely than in type B fittings and, for this reason, their use is not permitted underground. If, on the other hand, type B fittings are to be used with stainless-steel tube, the latter should be cut with a fine-toothed saw rather than a tube cutter to avoid work-hardening of the ends and possible splitting as a result.

Dezincification of brass Brass is an alloy of zinc, which is at the reactive end of the electrochemical series, and copper, which is at the noble end. It is not surprising, therefore, that, under certain conditions, the zinc may corrode electrolytically with the copper. This will possibly result in blockage of hot-water fittings by the corrosion product; leakage; or even breakage. The brasses worst affected by dezincification are those with relatively high zinc content, for example, duplex (alpha-beta) brasses, containing about 40 per cent zinc, which are suitable for hot-stamping of plumbing fittings. In theory, any brass containing 15 per cent or more of zinc may corrode in this way but attack in alpha brasses may be prevented by incorporation of small quantities of arsenic. BS 2871 describes such brasses.

The severity of dezincification depends on the properties of the water, attack being most likely when the pH value is over 8 (that is, alkaline) and chlorides are present. The presence of temporary hardness tends to reduce attack. The reaction rate increases with temperature so that hot-water fittings are most commonly affected. Where such conditions are encountered, an alternative material should be used, such as copper, gunmetal (a bronze containing about 2 per cent zinc) or a protected alpha brass. Note, however, that, since oxygen is involved in the corrosion process, brass fittings in recirculatory systems, such as central-heating circuits, are largely immune from dezincification.

Bronze This is an alloy of copper and tin. Most bronzes have a tin content slightly over its solubility limit of about 6 per cent, so that they are generally harder and stronger than brasses. They have great durability, so that they are used for sculpture and ornamental work, and in place of brass where corrosion-resistance is essential.

Zinc

The element occurs in the form of zinc sulphide (zinc blende), extraction being carried out by concentration of the ore using a flotation process, conversion to zinc oxide and then reduction, using carbon, to the metal.

The metal has a low melting point (419 °C) and high thermal movement – up to $40 \times 10^{-6}/$ °C in sheet form, the actual value depending on the direction of rolling, since the HCP crystal structure is non-isotropic.

The tensile strength of pure zinc is low but it may be increased by hot-working or alloying, though the ductility of zinc is, owing to its HCP structure, less than that of copper, lead and aluminium. Cold weather or severe working may make it necessary to warm the metal. It is, however, self-annealing since, at room temperature, it is above its recrystallisation temperature.

Many uses of zinc are based on the fact that it forms a coherent protective coating of zinc oxide or zinc carbonate on exposure to the atmosphere, though polluted or marine atmospheres increase the corrosion rate. Nevertheless, zinc is claimed to have good durability in most environments and rolled zinc sheeting has been used for roofing, weatherings and rainwater goods. Adequate allowance for thermal movement must be made by means of joints in large areas of metal and better durability is obtained when the slope is sufficient for foreign material to be washed off. The metal forms an impervious corrosion product when in contact with cement but will be corroded by the acids which occur in timbers such as western red cedar or oak. Creep will occur above certain stresses, though resistance can be improved by alloying with metals such as titanium and copper.

The most important use of zinc results from its position in the electrochemical series (Table 4.3). A coating of the metal will protect any metal below it in the series, even if scratched, though durability of the product naturally depends on the thickness of zinc and the aggressiveness of the environment. However, zinc or zinc coatings should not be allowed to contact copper or other more noble metals, which would greatly accelerate corrosion. As well as in the processes described under 'electrolytic corrosion', zinc is often used in zinc chromate form in anti-corrosive paints, though such paints, being porous, should be regarded as primers.

The low melting point of zinc is advantageous in the above applications but particularly so for die-casting in which, when alloyed with aluminium and magnesium, a wide variety of hardware components and fittings is produced. The metal is also used in paint pigments, such as zinc oxide and lithopone.

Problems

4.1 Examine Table 4.1 and give three properties of metals which appear to be characteristic of their crystalline groups.
4.2 Discuss, with examples, the roles played by point, line and surface imperfections on the deformation properties of metals.
4.3 Explain what is meant by a metal grain. Discuss the effects of grain size on the properties of metals and describe procedures by which it may be controlled.
4.4 The results of a tensile-strength test on a 12 mm diameter mild steel specimen are given in Table 4.13 below.

Table 4.13 Results of tensile-strength test on mild steel specimen, 12 mm diam

Load	Extension	Load	Extension	Load	Extension
0	0.00	33.4	2.0	50.9	10.0
26.9	0.10	37.0	3.0	52.9	12.0
27.4	0.30	39.8	4.0	54.3	14.0
26.7	0.60	44.3	6.0	53.7	16.0
29.1	1.0	48.0	8.0	50.7	17.0

Loading in kN
Extension in mm, read from an extensometer with a 100 mm gauge length. (MIOB pt.1 1975)

    (a) (i) Using these results, draw the load extension curve, indicating on it the limit of proportionality, the upper yield point and the maximum load.
       (ii) Obtain values of the modulus of elasticity and ultimate strength of this specimen.
    (b) Discuss what would be the effect on the specimen of
       (i) maintaining a constant load of 20 kN for a long period at elevated temperatures
       (ii) rapidly alternating the load between 8 and 18 kN for an extended period of time.

4.5 Indicate five ways in which alloying may affect the properties of a metal. Give an application of each in the construction industry.
4.6 Give two illustrations of the application of Griffith's theory to the failure of metals.
4.7 Explain briefly the conditions in which corrosion of steel is likely to occur. Describe three possible methods of protection, giving situations in which each is used.
4.8 Calculate the factors of safety based on minimum yield-point stresses for grades 43C, 50C and 55C of steels in the form of I beams (Table 4.6) less than 16 mm thick, taking the maximum permissible stresses as given in Table 4.8.
4.9 Compare the requirements for reinforcing and prestressing steels with respect to:
    (a) strength
    (b) geometric properties of bars and wires

(c) ductility

(d) weldability

and explain how these are governed by the composition and manufacturing processes.

4.10 Write an account on stainless steels, giving properties and uses of the various grades.

4.11 Contrast the properties of aluminium alloys and steel under the headings:

(a) general mechanical properties

(b) protection, durability

(c) high-temperature performance

(d) low-temperature performance.

4.12 Compare the properties of lead and copper, and contrast their uses in:

(a) roofing

(b) water-service pipes.

References

1. A. H. Cotrell, *Introduction to Metallurgy*. Arnold, 1968.
2. J. B. Moss, *Properties of Engineering Materials*. Butterworths, 1972.
3. F. W. Bailey, *Fundamentals of Engineering Metallurgy*. Cassell, 1961.
4. U. R. Evans, *The Corrosion and Oxidation of Metals*. Arnold, 1961.
5. J. C. Scully, *Fundamentals of Corrosion*. Pergamon, 1966.
6. L. P. Bowen, *Structural Design in Aluminium*. Hutchinson, 1966.
7. E. C. Rollason, *Metallurgy for Engineers*, 4th edition. Arnold, 1973.
8. R. M. E. Diamant, *The Prevention of Corrosion*. Business Books Ltd., 1971.
9. *Design Engineering Handbook; Metals*. Product Journals Ltd., 1968.
10. H. J. Sharp (Ed.), *Engineering Materials*. Heywood, 1966.
Additional information may be obtained from Metal Development Associations. See also Bibliography.

Relevant British Standards

BS 4: Part 1: 1972. *Hot rolled steel sections.*
BS 18: *Methods of tensile testing of metals.*
BS 153: Parts 1–4: 1972. *Steel girder bridges.*
BS 219: 1977. *Soft solders.*
BS 449: Part II: 1969. *Use of structural steel in building.*
BS 449: Part 2: 1969 Addendum No. 1 1975. *The use of cold formed steel sections in building.*
BS 602 & 1085: 1970. *Lead and alloy pipes for other than chemical purposes.*
BS 864: Part 2: 1971. *Capillary and compression fittings of copper and copper alloy.*
BS 1178: 1969. *Milled lead sheet and strip for building purposes.*
BS 1449: *Steel plate, sheet and strip.*
BS 1452: 1977. *Grey iron castings.*
BS 1470–1475; 1972. *Wrought aluminium and aluminium alloy products.*
BS 1490: 1970. *Aluminium and aluminium alloy ingots and castings.*
BS 1615: 1972. *Anodic oxidation coatings on aluminium.*
BS 2789: 1973. *Iron castings with spheroidal or nodular graphite.*

BS 2870: 1980. *Rolled copper and copper alloys; sheet strip and foil.*
BS 2871: 1971. *Copper and copper alloys. Tubes.*
BS 2994: 1976. *Cold rolled steel sections.*
BS 4127 Pt. 2; 1972. *Light gauge stainless steel tubes.*
BS 4360: 1979. *Weldable structural steels.*
BS 4449: 1978. *Hot rolled steel bars for the reinforcement of concrete.*
BS 4461: 1978. *Cold worked steel bars for the reinforcement of concrete.*
BS 4482: 1969. *Hard drawn mild steel wire for the reinforcement of concrete.*
BS 4483: 1969. *Steel fabric for the reinforcement of concrete.*
BS 4486: 1980. *High tensile alloy steel bars for prestressed concrete.*
BS 4622: 1970. *Grey cast iron pipes.*
BS 4757: 1971. *Nineteen wire steel strand for prestressed concrete.*
BS 4772: 1971. *Ductile iron pipes and fittings.*
BS 4848: Parts 2, 4 and 5. *Hot rolled structural steel sections.*
BS 5896: 1980. *Specification for high tensile steel wire strand for the prestressing of concrete.*

Chapter 5

Organic materials

The term 'organic' traditionally refers to materials which are derived from living tissues, for example, timber, leather and cotton or wool. More recently, the term has come to be used for a wider range of materials which, in common with the above, have properties dependent to a large degree on the presence of carbon in their structure. Plastics, paints, adhesives, mastics and bitumens fall into this larger group.

Plastics materials

The backbone of each of these materials is normally the carbon atom, which has two s and two p electrons in its outer shell. These electrons become 'hybridised' (see Ch. 1) and, with a valency of four, carbon is very largely co-valent in character – it seeks to gain a stable octet of electrons by sharing with those of other atoms. Elements which often combine with carbon in this way are hydrogen, chlorine and fluorine (valency 1), oxygen (valency 2) and nitrogen (valency 3). There are a great many substances which have a relatively simple arrangement of carbon and other atoms. The paraffin series is an example:

$$
\begin{array}{cc}
\text{H} & \text{H} \quad \text{H} \\
| & | \quad | \\
\text{H—C—H} & \text{H—C—C—H} \qquad \text{etc.} \\
| & | \quad | \\
\text{H} & \text{H} \quad \text{H}
\end{array}
$$

methane CH_4 ethane C_2H_6

In the paraffins, each carbon atom shares *one* of its electrons with another atom.

It is also possible for carbon atoms to share two or even three electrons with one another. For example:

$$
\begin{array}{cc}
\text{H} \qquad \text{H} \\
\quad \text{C}=\text{C} \qquad\qquad \text{H—C}\equiv\text{C—H} \\
\text{H} \qquad \text{H}
\end{array}
$$

ethylene C_2H_4 acetylene C_2H_2

Such compounds are said to be *unsaturated* because double and triple bonds are often quite easily broken to form single bonds with other atoms or molecules.

227

Many organic substances have a relatively simple molecular structure and, therefore, a small molecular weight. They usually exist, however, in gaseous or liquid form, resulting from the short-range bonding that they contain. In order to produce solids, the molecular size of these simple units must be increased. The process is known as polymerisation and, by it, many small molecules (monomers) can be linked to form large molecules – polymers. In order to produce a suitable degree of rigidity, polymers may need to have very large molecular weights – often over 100 000. There are two principal ways of polymerising materials and the resulting products tend to have characteristic properties.

Addition polymerisation

In this process, monomer molecules containing C=C double bonds can be made to combine by means of initiator substances, such as benzoyl peroxide. The polymerisation of ethylene will be taken by way of example. The initiator first dissociates into unstable free radicals:

$$I—I \rightleftharpoons I- + I-$$

Initiator   2 free radicals
molecule

A free radical can now combine with an ethylene molecule:

$$I- \ + \ \underset{H}{\overset{H}{\diagup}}C=C\underset{H}{\overset{H}{\diagdown}} \longrightarrow I-\underset{H}{\overset{H}{C}}-\underset{H}{\overset{H}{C}}-$$

The product again contains a free radical, causing it to combine with another ethylene molecule:

$$I-\underset{H}{\overset{H}{C}}-\underset{H}{\overset{H}{C}}- \ + \ \underset{H}{\overset{H}{\diagup}}C=C\underset{H}{\overset{H}{\diagdown}} \longrightarrow I-\underset{H}{\overset{H}{C}}-\underset{H}{\overset{H}{C}}-\underset{H}{\overset{H}{C}}-\underset{H}{\overset{H}{C}}-$$

This is the *propagation* stage of polymerisation. It will continue until, as ethylene molecules become used up, two growing chains combine or the free radical at the end of a chain combines with a free radical formed by an initiator molecule. By this process, ethylene is converted into polyethylene (normally called polythene), having the formula:

$[—CH_2—CH_2—]_n$

where n is a large number.

At each end of such a chain, there would be an initiator fragment:

$$-\underset{H}{\overset{H}{C}}-\underset{H}{\overset{H}{C}}-I$$

It is found, in practice, that there are often many more end groups than a simple chain structure would suggest and this is caused by branching during polymerisation:

$$
\begin{array}{ccccc}
H & H & H & H & H \\
| & | & | & | & | \\
-C-&C-&C-&C-&C- \\
| & | & | & | & | \\
H & H & & H & H \\
& & | & & \\
& H-&C-&H & \\
& & | & & \\
& H-&C-&H & \\
& & | & & \\
& & H & &
\end{array}
$$

Such branches may be formed when, for example, a growing molecule collides with a section of a completed molecular chain and transfers its free radical, the growing molecule, therefore, becoming 'dead' instead. Branches will affect the properties of the polymer, as explained later.

In a further type of addition, polymerisation, monomer molecules of different types may combine, for example butadiene and styrene:

Butadiene

Styrene

Repeat distance

Double bonds are opened in both the butadiene and styrene molecules, though one double bond remains in each repeat unit. A chain structure is again produced

229

but, since two different monomers are involved, the polymer is described as a 'co-polymer'. Where double bonds are present in the polymer, they can, in some circumstances, form links between chains leading to a more rigid 'cross-linked' structure. Substances such as butadiene, in which there are two positions where additions can occur, are described as 'bi-functional'.

Condensation or step polymerisation

In this type of reaction, a small molecule, often water, may be produced as a by-product. For example, polyesters are produced when a dihydroxy alcohol reacts with a dicarboxylic acid (the *di* prefixes imply two alcohol (—OH) and acid (—COOH) groups in the respective compounds):

$$\underset{\text{Dicarboxylic acid}}{\text{HO}-\overset{\overset{\text{O}}{\|}}{\text{C}}-\text{R}_1-\overset{\overset{\text{O}}{\|}}{\text{C}}-\text{OH}} \;+\; \underset{\text{Dihydroxy alcohol}}{\text{HO}-\text{R}_2-\text{OH}} \longrightarrow$$

$$\underset{\text{Ester}}{\text{HO}-\overset{\overset{\text{O}}{\|}}{\text{C}}-\text{R}_1-\overset{\overset{\text{O}}{\|}}{\text{C}}-\text{O}-\text{R}_2-\text{OH}} \;+\; \text{H}_2\text{O}$$

where R_1 and R_2 are hydrocarbon groups.

The reaction can be repeated, producing a long-chain molecule which is the basis of polyester fibres. Alternatively, however, polyfunctional acids and alcohols can be used, these having three or more reactive groups. In such cases, a three-dimensional molecular network is formed by the condensation process – one way of producing rigid polyesters. The term 'step polymerisation' is sometimes preferred to 'condensation polymerisation', since polymerisation occurs by multiplication of ester molecules rather than addition of ester monomers singly. In some cases, also, there may not be a small molecule produced from the reaction.

Structure of thermoplastics materials

When polymers retain a chain structure, there being no primary bonds between the chains, the material is described as 'thermoplastic'. Thermoplastics usually exist in the solid state at room temperature, due to the effect of van der Waals' forces between chains but, on heating, softening soon occurs, as thermal energy overcomes these weak bonding forces. Such polymers are, therefore, easily moulded by heating, although, unless by drawing, the chains are orientated in the direction of stress, thermoplastics usually have limited strength. The strength of individual thermoplastics depends on the extent of bonding between chains, which depends, in turn, on the polarity of the polymer molecule. Polyethylene is, for example, non-polar, since bonds are entirely co-valent and chains are bonded only weakly but by, for example, replacing one hydrogen atom by a chlorine atom, forming polyvinyl chloride $(-CH_2-CH.Cl-)_n$, interchain forces are increased, producing a stiffer polymer. This effect is obtained because chlorine is electronegative and inclined to form polar bonds, thereby leading to dipoles at regular points in the polymer chain. Thermoplastics are generally produced by addition polymerisation.

Structure of thermosetting materials

These are usually much more rigid than thermoplastics on account of the extended three-dimensional primary bonding which they contain. Unlike thermoplastics, they are not softened by heat but, rather, they decompose if heated sufficiently. As explained above, thermosets are most likely to be obtained by polymerisation of polyfunctional monomers, although it is also possible to produce them by crosslinking of thermoplastics.

Crystallisation of polymers

The polymers most likely to crystallise are those having a molecular structure comprising simple regular chains. Linear polyethylene with its simpler hydrocarbon back-bone has, for example, a strong tendency to crystallise. However, even polyethylene does not exhibit 100 per cent crystallisation, since the long chains must be folded back on each other and there will always be some chain entanglement, causing amorphous regions. Crystal growth in polymers is initiated by nuclei, as in other materials and, on account of the chain structure of linear polymers, folded chains grow radially from the nucleus to give 'spherulites' (Fig. 5.1). The size of the spherulites and, hence, the properties of the polymer can be controlled by varying the number of impurity nuclei in the melt material.

Branched polyethylene will show a lower degree of crystallisation, as will polymers the molecular chain of which is not regular, such as polyvinyl chloride.

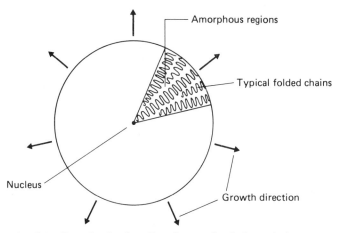

Fig. 5.1 Growth of spherulites from polyethylene chains

In many thermoplastic polymers, the extent of crystallinity is, therefore, small and properties are characteristic of amorphous materials; for example, many thermoplastics are transparent to light. Crystallinity in thermosetting polymers is generally negligible, the extensive three-dimensional framework being rather similar to that of ordinary glass.

Physical state of polymers

The physical form which a polymer takes depends in a complex way on a number of factors, of which the most important are its molecular weight, its degree of crystallinity and the temperature. In the case of polymers of low molecular weight, the situation is relatively simple, polymers behaving as either amorphous (glassy) or crystalline solids; or, on heating, viscous liquids. In the solid state, molecular energy is purely vibrational while in the liquid state a translational component is possible. As molecular weight is increased, an intermediate stage is introduced in which molecular chains are entangled, as in solids, but flexibility resulting from bond rotation is possible. Since the bond directions in tetravalent carbon are well defined, adjacent hydrogen atoms in, for example, a single hydrocarbon chain are staggered in order to minimise repulsion of hydrogen atoms (Fig. 5.2). Bond rotation involves the approach of hydrogen atoms and it

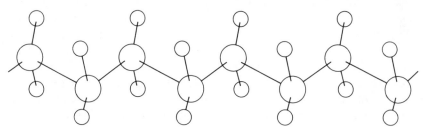

Fig. 5.2   Alternating of bond directions in polyethylene chain so as to minimise repulsion between hydrogen atoms

will, therefore, not be possible, except where thermal energy is sufficient to overcome the temporary repulsion associated with it. When, on heating, bond rotation becomes possible, it provides an intermediate state – the 'rubbery' state between the brittle solid and viscous liquid states of a polymer of high molecular weight. The temperature range over which this state is exhibited increases with molecular size and it is found that there is, in addition, a diffuse transition zone between rubber and liquid, due to the fact that there is a statistical distribution of molecular and crystal sizes in the material – some molecules effectively 'melt' before others (Fig. 5.3). The essential characteristics of a rubber are low elastic modulus combined with great extensibility under tensile stress, which results from straightening of the former random zig-zag chains. In the case of crystalline polymers, there is a further intermediate flexible state between rigid solid and

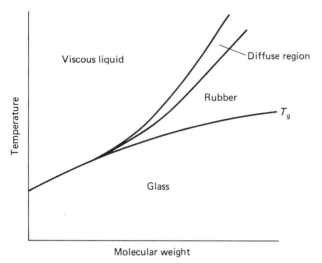

Fig. 5.3 Physical states of amorphous polymers

rubber, on account of the extra rigidity produced by crystalline regions, (Fig. 5.4), the rubbery state being obtained when, on heating, crystallites melt. The temperature at which bond rotation becomes possible is known as the 'glass transition' temperature, Tg, while the approximate temperature at which the rubber changes to liquid is described as the 'flow temperature'. The term 'melting point', Tm, is generally used in relation to crystallites only. Both Tg and Tm depend on molecular weight of the polymer. Table 5.1 shows typical values for

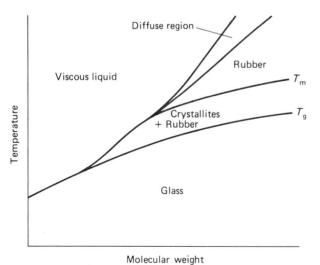

Fig. 5.4 Physical states of crystalline polymers

Table 5.1 Glass transition temperatures (*Tg*) for common
thermoplastics, together with melting point
temperatures (*Tm*) for crystalline forms[*]

Polymer	State	Tg (°C)	Tm (°C)
Polyethylene			
linear (H.D.)	95% cryst.	−120	143
branched (L.D.)	60% cryst.	−120	115
Polypropylene	60%	− 27; 0	165
Nylon 66	cryst.	57	265
PTFE	95% cryst.	−120	327
PVC	Amorph.	80	—
Polystyrene	Amorph.	80–100	—
Polymethylmethacrylate	Amorph.	80–100	—
Polycarbonate	Amorph.	150	
ABS	Amorph.	71–112	—

[*] The latter are generally slightly higher than softening point temperatures, as measured by the Vicat test. *Tg* values of amorphous
polymers are similar to Vicat softening temperatures.

the common thermoplastics. Note that crystalline melting points are only given
for those polymers which crystallise to a significant extent.

Modes of use of polymers

These fall into three general areas:
1. Crystalline polymers may be employed over a wide temperature range, since
   they have considerable rigidity both above and below their glass transition
   temperature, there being only a small change of stiffness during the transition.
   Above their *Tg*, such polymers are more likely to be leathery, while below
   their *Tg* they are more likely to be brittle.
2. Amorphous polymers are rubbery when above their *Tg* and are, therefore,
   used as elastomers in this state.
3. Amorphous polymers are inclined to be hard though rather brittle below their
   Tg. Many such polymers are utilised in this state.
   While the above are generalised properties, it should be appreciated that the
behaviour of individual polymers depends on their molecular structure, size and,
in many cases, the rate of cooling, since, as in metals, this affects the degree of
crystallisation and the size of crystallites, if formed. It is also possible to reduce
the *Tg* of thermoplastic polymers by use of solvents which interfere with
attraction between molecular chains – especially in polar molecules such as
polyvinyl chloride. The science of 'molecular engineering' in polymers is still
advancing rapidly and it is possible that some of the less satisfactory properties
of polymers, such as low rigidity and softening temperature may be improved,
resulting in new applications.

Thermoplastic materials

Polyethylene (polythene) $[-CH_2-CH_2-]_n$

Polyethylene has the simplest chemical structure of any polymer and is also one of the cheapest and most widely-used plastics. The plastic is manufactured in two basic forms involving either high- or low-pressure processes. The high-pressure process, which was first to be developed, gives a branched polymer which, therefore, has a low relative density (0.92) and fairly low softening point (90 °C). The more recent low-pressure process produces a polymer of higher crystallinity, having a higher relative density (0.96) and softening point (120 to 130 °C). This is produced using ionic catalysts instead of free radical catalysts.

The absence of polarity in the polymer results in great chemical stability: polyethylene does not dissolve in any solvent at room temperature. It is also unaffected by acids or alkalis. A further consequence of non-polarity is electrical insulation – polyethylene has extremely good insulating properties. One property resulting from the relatively weak intermolecular bond is, however, high thermal movement – the coefficient of linear expansion is approximately $120 \times 10^{-6}/°C$. The polymer is well above its Tg ($-120 °C$) at ordinary temperatures and is, therefore, tough, even in cold weather. It undergoes embrittlement, however, on exposure to ultra-violet light, due to cross-linking. This can be substantially reduced by incorporation of carbon black. Permeability to gases is relatively high, caused by diffusion of molecules from one void to another, assisted by bond rotation. Permeability of the high-density variety is, however, only 20 per cent that of low-density polyethylene.

The chief use of low-density polyethylene is for sheeting for damp-proof courses and membranes for vapour barriers and temporary shelters, although, on account of its crystallinity, transparency is not as good as that of, for example, clear PVC sheeting unless very thin films are used. Further uses include tubes, down-pipes and cisterns, though the polymer is not suited to hot-water services. Carbon black should be incorporated for external purposes. Polyethylene products have excellent resistance to impact, unless embrittlement occurs. One disadvantage of the non-polar structure is, however, that surfaces have a very low surface tension, having a rather greasy touch and are not, therefore, amenable to painting or to joining by adhesives. Mechanical roughening assists in providing a bond, while fusion welding is the most common way of forming joints. Epoxy resins may be used if the surface is oxidised by means of concentrated acid. In situations where higher strength or stiffness is required, high-density polythene is preferred. A further application of polyethylene is in insulation of co-axial cables.

Polypropylene $[-CH_2-CH.CH_3-]_n$

This has a structure very similar to polyethylene, apart from the extra methyl group. In most commercial forms, the chain structure is stereo-regular and 'isotactic' – that is, the configurations of all carbon atoms attached to the methyl groups are the same. In a simplified planar projection this may be represented:

$$\begin{array}{ccccc} H & CH_3 & H & CH_3 & H \\ | & | & | & | & | \\ -C- & C- & C- & C- & C- \\ | & | & | & | & | \\ H & H & H & H & H \end{array}$$

The polymer crystallises in a helical form with three methyl groups in each rotation, giving rise to a fairly high softening point (150 °C). This, together with higher stiffness than that of polyethylene, forms the basis of most uses of polypropylene. The polymer is used for rigid units, such as manhole mouldings and waste systems, and may be a possibility for hot-water pipes and cylinders. Polypropylene is an example of a polymer which undergoes several transitions on cooling, caused by changes in different modes of movement in the molecular chain. The dominant change occurs at 0 °C and it leads to brittleness in the polymer at low service temperatures. Impact-resistance can be improved by block co-polymerisation with small amounts of ethylene. Polypropylene is also more susceptible to oxidation and ultra-violet rays than polyethylene – it must be stabilised for external use. A further use of the polymer is in fibre reinforcement and general-purpose string, since, on drawing, it produces a fibre of fairly high strength and flexibility. Polypropylene has a particularly low relative density (0.90).

Polyvinyl chloride (PVC) $[-CH_2-CH.Cl-]_n$

In this polymer, every fourth hydrogen atom is replaced by a chlorine atom, the arrangement being partly syndiotactic:

$$\begin{array}{cccccc} Cl & H & H & H & Cl & H \\ | & | & | & | & | & | \\ -C- & C- & C- & C- & C- & C- \\ | & | & | & | & | & | \\ H & H & Cl & H & H & H \end{array}$$

There is not, however, sufficient stereo-regularity in the distribution of the chain atoms to enable crystallisation to occur, hence, the polymer is amorphous and is obtainable in clear sheet form. The unplasticised polymer has considerable strength and rigidity below its Tg of approximately 80 °C (more commonly referred to as 'softening point temperature'). A major use of PVC is, however, based on the plasticised form: plasticisers, such as esters, interfere with inter-chain attraction and, hence, reduce the softening temperature of the polymer. The main use of PVC in the construction industry is in unplasticised form. Rainwater goods are now very commonly manufactured from this material, since it is easily extruded or moulded to the desired shape. It is important, however, to give adequate support to gutters and long pipes and to allow room for expansion – the expansion coefficient is approximately $60 \times 10^{-6}/°C$. Expansion joints normally take the form of rubber gaskets in gutters and 'O' rings in pipes. When rigid joints are acceptable, they are easily and cheaply made by solvent welding, there being, unlike polyethylene, a number of solvents which will dissolve PVC. The two units are joined by a collar and the joint is made by solution and resolidification of surface layers in contact. PVC waste systems are common, although, where the effluent is at a high temperature, such as in the case of automatic washing machines, a polymer having a higher softening point would be recommended. A more recent use of PVC is in extruded window frames, often incorporating double glazing. The PVC is coloured by pigments and a surface requiring no maintenance is thereby obtained. Ordinary PVC is unstable in the presence of heat and ultra-violet light, so that stabilisers must be used in such applications. These are normally based on lead, though compounds based on the metals cadmium and barium produce better colour stability. Clear, unplasticised PVC is often used in rooflights and corrugated roofing, though light transmission and impact-resistance invariably deteriorate with time. Low-temperature brittleness is especially a problem with unplasticised PVC. It can be improved by incorporation of elastomers such as nitrile rubber. Stabilised, plasticised PVC is widely used in floor coverings and in electrical insulation.

Polyvinyl fluoride (PVF) $[—CH_2—CH.F]_n$

This polymer has a similar structure to PVC, except that, since the fluorine atom is smaller than the chlorine atom, it has a much greater tendency to crystallise. PVF combines high temperature-resistance and toughness at low temperatures with very good weather-resistance. It is used as coating material for wood and metal, being much more durable than paint films.

Polytetrafluoroethylene (PTFE) $[—CF_2—CF_2—]_n$

This has some of the characteristics of polyethylene, being a crystalline linear polymer. However, since fluorine atoms are larger than carbon atoms, they are arranged in a spiral formation about the zig-zag carbon backbone. There is close interlocking between chains, leading to a polymer with a high melting point, $327\,°C$, in spite of the fact that bonding between the chains is not strong. Since the polymer is non-polar, there are no solvents at ordinary temperatures and PTFE has a very low coefficient of friction – less than that of wet ice upon wet ice. This property forms the basis of most applications – the polymer is used to line pipes which carry solid materials, for sliding bridge bearings and as a non-stick coating on cooking utensils. It is also available in tape form for sealing threaded joints in water or gas pipes. PTFE has excellent resistance to weathering and to moisture, though it is degraded by ultra-violet light.

Styrene-based polymers

Styrene consists of a simple combination of ethylene and benzene in which the double-bond structure of the former is retained. This is responsible for the ease with which it polymerises. The chief polymers based on styrene are polystyrene and acrylonitrile butadiene styrene, which are both thermoplastic.

Polystyrene This polymer has a chain structure similar to polyethylene, except that it is atactic, that is, there is no regular configuration of the carbon atoms containing the benzene rings in the chain. The polymer does not, therefore, crystallise but forms an amorphous thermoplastic with a softening point (Tg) of 80 to 100 °C. The polymer degrades at high temperatures and has a characteristic odour on burning. It is quite rigid, though brittle at ordinary temperatures, is attacked by a number of solvents and has poor weathering resistance.

Many applications are based on its cheapness and rigidity: these include containers and lining materials for refrigerators. A large amount of the polymer is produced in the form of expanded polystyrene, which has one of the lowest thermal conductivities obtainable – approximately 0.033 W/m °C. The polymer in the form of small beads is heated so that great expansion occurs. The beads are then softened by steam and pressurised so that they stick together. Expanded polystyrene is widely used as an insulating material for general household purposes, in rolls for application to wall surfaces, in floor and roof insulation, as a preformed cavity infill and for ceiling tiles. The plastic burns readily, however, and may, therefore, constitute a fire hazard. Expanded polystyrene may, in sufficient thicknesses, have vapour-resistant qualities but it is not as effective as vapour barrier of foil or polyethylene. Further important applications of the foam include use as a preformed insulant for cavity walls and as a void-former in structural concrete.

Acrylonitrile butadiene styrene (ABS) ABS polymers are two-phase systems comprising co-polymers of styrene – acrylonitrile and the rubber, butadiene styrene. A variety of materials can be obtained and these are characterised by good impact strength, temperature-resistance and solvent-resistance. They are more expensive than common plastics but have, nevertheless, found application in window fasteners, rainwater goods and moulded articles, such as telephones. They have a higher softening point than PVC and are, therefore, more suitable for domestic waste systems. They cannot, however, be solvent-welded in the same way. They are also used in gas piping.

Acrylic plastics
These are based on acrylic acid, $CH_2\!=\!CH.COOH$ (note the ethylene group). The commonest polymer is polymethyl methacrylate:

$$\left[-CH_2-\overset{\displaystyle CH_3}{\underset{\displaystyle COOCH_3}{\overset{|}{\underset{|}{C}}}}- \right]_n$$

The methyl and ester groups are not interchangeable and, since the polymer is atactic, it must, therefore, also be amorphous, the polar groups producing a rigid solid with a Tg of 80 to 100 °C. It is commonly known as 'Perspex', a clear, hard sheet material. Methyl methacrylate polymerises readily by application of heat, so that acrylic sheet is formed simply by pouring a partly polymerised syrup into a mould and then warming it. Very good surface finishes can be obtained with good weathering properties. The plastic is used for the diffusion of light, as in illuminated ceilings and signs. Baths are now made out of the polymer, which is cheaper and easier to install than the traditional material, cast iron, though of inferior durability and stability. Scratches may be polished out but the plastic is susceptible to burns and to some organic solvents. Some types of paint include acrylic resins.

Nylons

The chemical name for this polymer is 'polyamide' and it may be obtained by polymerisation of amino acids or lactams, or by reaction of diamines with dicarboxylic acid.

Amino acids have the formula NH_2R COOH, where R is a hydrocarbon radical, the corresponding polymer being $[-NHRCO-]_n$ – Note than an 'H' is removed from one end of the repeat unit and an 'OH' from the other: the acid polymerises by a condensation reaction.

Lactams have the form:

$$R \underset{CO}{\overset{NH}{<}}$$

and polymerise when the ring is opened. Nylons obtained from amino acids or lactams are characterised by a single number representing the number of carbon atoms in the repeat unit. For example, caprolactam contains 6 carbon atoms and polymerises to nylon 6:

$$\left[-\underset{O}{\overset{|}{C}}-(CH_2)_5-\underset{H}{\overset{|}{N}}- \right]_n$$

When hexamethylene diamine:

$$\underset{H}{\overset{H}{>}}N-(CH_2)_6-N\underset{H}{\overset{H}{<}}$$

is reacted with adipic acid:

$$H-O-\underset{O}{\overset{|}{C}}-(CH_2)_4-\underset{O}{\overset{|}{C}}-O-H$$

nylon 66 is produced by a condensation reaction in which a hydrogen atom is taken from each end of the hexamethylene diamine to combine with a hydroxyl group from each end of the adipic acid, forming water. The chemical formula for this nylon is, therefore:

$$\left[-\underset{\underset{H}{|}}{N}-(CH_2)_6-\underset{\underset{H}{|}}{N}-\underset{\underset{O}{\|}}{C}-(CH_2)_4-\underset{\underset{O}{\|}}{C}- \right]_n$$

Nylons are linear polymers and, therefore, thermoplastic and, since the polar NHCO groups are regularly spaced, the polymers crystallise, the strong inter-chain attraction resulting in high melting points. Nylon 6 has, for example, a melting point of 225 °C, while Nylon 66 has a melting point of 265 °C. Nylons are also characterised by high strength, flexibility, toughness, abrasion resistance and solvent resistance. They tend to become brittle in sunlight, however, unless they are stabilised or carbon black is added. Products may be moulded, extruded or drawn. Moulded articles, which are normally manufactured from Nylon 66 include catches, latches and rollers: extruded products include central-heating tube, drawn products and nylon ropes. The ease of cutting of nylon central-heating tubes makes installation very simple, though thermal movement should be allowed for and sharp objects could cause damage in service.

Polycarbonates
These are obtained by reactions of polyhydroxy compounds with carbonic acid derivatives. The polymer has excellent transparency and is tough and rigid up to temperatures of over 100 °C. Weathering resistance is good and sheets of the polymer are used as a glazing material of high impact-resistance.

Elastomers

The rubbery state has already been briefly described as a state intermediate between solid and liquid, in which bond rotation of carbon-carbon bonds in the linear polymer backbone is possible. Since zig-zag arrangements are statistically more likely than straight polymer chains, elastomers exist as randomly entangled (amorphous) chains of this type. On stretching such a polymer, chains tend to become straighter, causing bond rotation within them and, hence, slight resist-ance to stretching. Elastomers must have the ability to recover fully when stress is removed and this is achieved either by slight cross-linking (vulcanisation) of chains to prevent their becoming permanently re-orientated or, alternatively, ensuring that the molecular size is large enough to produce sufficient chain entanglement. It is an advantage if, on stretching fully, some degree of crystallisation occurs, since this increases resistance to further stretching at this stage. Many elastomers exhibit this property as strains reach their maximum value (in the region of 500 per cent) and molecular chains tend to become closer and straighter. Elasticity is, of course, only exhibited over a limited temperature range. On cooling below their Tg, elastomers become brittle, while on heating, softening and, ultimately, melting occurs. Some elastomers, such as natural rubber, styrene-butadiene rubber (SBR) and nitrile rubbers contain double bonds and are, therefore, susceptible to oxidative degradation, due to the action of heat and light in the presence of oxygen or ozone. Degradation takes the form of chain cleavage leading to tackiness and, ultimately, embrittlement. Such rubbers must be protected by antioxidants. It is also possible to increase the abrasion- and tear-resistance of elastomers. For this purpose, finely-divided reinforcing agents, such as carbon black are used – these form secondary bonds with the elastomer molecules. Elastomers which include carbon black will, of course, be dark in colour.

The elastic moduli of elastomers lie generally in the range 7 to $17\,N/mm^2$ at 300 to 400 per cent elongation – roughly 1 per cent of the elastic moduli of corresponding polymers when below their Tg.

Natural rubber and synthetic polyisoprene

Natural rubber is obtained from latex in trees in tropical regions, including parts of Africa and South America, and Malaysia, the most important species being 'Hevea braziliensis'. Chemically, natural rubber consists chiefly of Cis 1.4 polyisoprene:

$$\begin{array}{cccc}
CH_3 & & CH_3 & \\
| & & | & \\
C{=}CH & & C{=}CH & \\
/ & \backslash & / & \backslash \\
{-}CH_2 & CH_2{-}CH_2 & CH_2{-} &
\end{array}$$

The polymer adopts an entangled helical conformation which may be stiffened by vulcanising with sulphur and other ingredients. Sulphur atoms link adjacent polymer chains by the influence of double bonds. When less than 5 per cent sulphur is used, natural rubber has great flexibility but, when more than 30 per cent is used, a highly rigid structure, known as ebonite, results. The cross-links also help avoid crystallinity in the unstretched state, while still permitting crystallisation on stretching fully. Natural rubber is often reinforced with carbon black and must be protected from oxidation. The material is relatively cheap and has very good elasticity and dynamic properties. It is used widely for bearings of all types, for example, bridge and machine bearings. In some cases, whole buildings have been supported on rubber bearings to stop vibration transmission, for example, from underground trains. Latex silicone compositions have been injected into masonry for damp-proofing purposes. Natural rubber is also used in the tyres of large earth-moving vehicles, since less heat is generated during the severe flexing which such tyres undergo.

Styrene-butadiene rubbers SBR (Buna S rubbers)

The term 'Buna S' relates to the fact that polymerisation of butadiene was formerly initiated by sodium Na, styrene being used to form a co-polymer. These are cheaper than natural rubber, though tear-resistance and resistance to oxidation are poor, unless treated. They have only a slight tendency to crystallise on stretching, though abrasion-resistance is good. SBR rubbers are used widely for general purposes.

Butadiene acrylonitrile rubbers (NBR Buna N or Nitrile rubbers)
These are similar to SBR rubbers but have better resistance to oils and hydrocarbon solvents. They are widely used in contact adhesives, gaskets and seals.

Butyl rubber
This is a co-polymer of isobutylene and isoprene and has good sunlight and oxidation-resistance, due to the smaller number of double bonds present. The elastomer is also impermeable to gases and resistant to acids and oils. It is used in mastics and sealants, and land-fill site liners.

Polychloroprene ('Neoprene')
This has very good all-round chemical stability and, since it crystallises on stretching, it combines high extensibility with high strength. It is used in contact adhesives and sealing strips and for glazing and 'O' rings.

Silicone rubbers
Silicone, like carbon, has a valency of four, though polymers with a pure silicon backbone are unstable. Instead, the siloxane link forms the basis of polymers:

$$-\overset{\displaystyle |}{\underset{\displaystyle |}{Si}}-O-\overset{\displaystyle |}{\underset{\displaystyle |}{Si}}-$$

Silicone elastomers are normally polydimethyl siloxanes, often reinforced with silica. Cross-linking in certain forms (room-temperature vulcanising, RTV, types) can be activated by atmospheric moisture. Resistance to extremes of temperature is good and they are widely used in caulking compounds. Note that polydimethyl siloxanes are non-polar and, therefore, have very low surface tension and good water-repellent properties.

Polysulphides (Thiokol)
These contain at least four sulphides per monomer molecule, two of which form part of the polymer backbone. They have very good all-round chemical stability and are widely used in mastics and sealants.

Thermosetting materials

Phenolic resins
Phenol formaldehyde was one of the earliest synthetic resins to be produced, given the name Bakelite. The chemical formula of phenol is C_6H_5OH, which, on

reaction with formaldehyde, gives methylol derivatives:

$$\text{HOCH}_2-\underset{\underset{\displaystyle \text{CH}_2\text{OH}}{|}}{\overset{\overset{\displaystyle \text{OH}}{|}}{\underset{\underset{\displaystyle \text{C}}{\overset{\displaystyle \text{C}}{|}}}{\text{C}}}}\quad\overset{\displaystyle \text{C}}{\underset{\displaystyle \text{C}}{}}-\text{CH}_2\text{OH}$$

These can be linked by condensation reactions involving the methylol groups:

$$-\text{CH}_2\text{O}\boxed{\text{H}+\text{HO}}\text{H}_2\text{C}-\longrightarrow -\text{CH}_2\text{OH}_2\text{C}-\ +\ \text{H}_2\text{O}$$

Extensive bonding gives a hard, brittle, heat-resistant polymer. Being thermosetting, extrusion cannot be carried out: products are manufactured from resins of low molecular weight which are normally ground to a powder, compounded with a filler, hardener and other ingredients, and moulded by heat, which causes cross-linking. The manufacturing process produces a dark colour, normally brown or black. Widest use of phenolic resins has been electrical goods, such as switches and plugs, though use for such components has decreased and laminates now form the largest market for the resin. Such laminates are formed from phenolic resin-impregnated paper and have a sufficient degree of flexibility for use in protective coverings to working surfaces and wall boards, while retaining a hard surface. The laminates themselves are brown and resemble mica but usually have a coloured plastic coating. Phenolic resins are widely used as wood adhesives.

Amino resins
These are resins based on the amino group or amide group. The most important are urea and melamine formaldehydes:

Melamine   Urea

Each amino group reacts with formaldehyde, by addition, to form methylol compounds:

$$-\text{NH}_2+\text{HCOH}\longrightarrow -\text{HNCH}_2\text{OH}$$

These compounds are then polymerised by condensation to form rigid polymers.

Urea-formaldehyde resins are similar in properties to phenol-formaldehyde resins, except that they are clear – hence, a wider range of colours is obtainable. They are also more moisture-resistant and have greater impact strength. They are used in electrical fittings, for rigid moulded articles, such as toilet seats, and in adhesives. In expanded form, urea formaldehyde is, on account of its low cost, used widely as a cavity-wall infill material, though, since substantial quantities of water are involved, surfaces must be porous to allow drying out.

Melamine-formaldehyde resins have extremely good resistance to water, heat and chemicals, and can be coloured. They are widely used as surfacing coatings for decorative laminates based on phenolic resins and in adhesives.

Polyester resins
The production of linear polyesters used in fibres has already been described. Polyester moulding resins are based on mixtures of unsaturated and saturated dicarboxylic acids, the former providing sites for cross-linking, while the latter help reduce brittleness. Styrene is commonly used as the cross-linking agent – its own double bond opening during the process. This has the advantage that water is not given off during curing. Moulding resins are polymerised until they form viscous liquids and then an inhibitor is added to prevent further polymerisation. On adding the 'hardener' – usually an initiator such as an organic peroxide – the resin hardens at a rate dependent on temperature. Fully cured resins are hard and tough, and are commonly used with glass fibre, which bonds well and gives good impact and strength properties. When used in adhesives, polyester resins have been shown to have greater fire resistance than the other commonly used adhesives – epoxy resins – especially if a limestone filler is employed. Polyester resins have also been used in resin cements (see Ch. 6).

Epoxide (epoxy) resins
The chemical components of these resins are complex, involving phenolic and other groups. The epoxide group is, however, the most important. It contains oxygen in the form:

$$
\begin{array}{c}
\text{O} \\
/ \;\; \backslash \\
\text{R---CH---CH}_2
\end{array}
$$

The phenolic compounds are used to produce, by condensation, a linear polymer with epoxide groups at each end. Curing is then obtained by cross-linking through opening of the epoxide ring. A wide range of cross-linking agents (hardeners) can be used, the main groups being amines and acid anhydrides: the mechanism may involve coupling or condensation. Epoxy resins are characterised by low-curing shrinkage, good chemical resistance, particularly to alkalis, and good adhesive properties, though they are more expensive than polyester resins. Resins are prepared in the form of partly-polymerised liquids, which polymerise more fully on curing. They have been used in flooring compositions, paints, adhesives and for glass-reinforced composites.

Polyurethanes (see also, 'Paints')

These are formed as a product of isocyanates and polyesters or polyhydroxy materials. It is not possible to classify polyurethanes as thermoplastic or thermosetting, since many different forms exist, some with chain-like molecules and, therefore, thermoplastic; others heavily cross-linked and, therefore, thermosetting. Polyurethanes are often used in foamed form, for example, in cavity filling for domestic dwellings and in a more flexible form for spraying on pipes for thermal-insulation purposes. In each case, they bond well to the background. Most polyurethane is foamed, using carbon dioxide, which eventually diffuses outwards from cells, being replaced by air. Polyurethanes may be used up to temperatures of about 120 °C, depending on grade – an advantage over polystyrene foams. They are also less flammable, though, in common with polystyrenes, more flexible types dissolve in some organic solvents and acids.

Flexible polyester and polyether foams come under the general heading of polyurethanes, being used for upholstery, sponges and cushions. Other polyurethanes are used for resilient gaskets in clay pipes and in surface coatings.

Plastics in fire

Since virtually all plastics are organic in nature, they decompose readily in fire and, consequently, many of them constitute a hazard, possibly for the following reasons:

1. They may emit toxic gases – usually carbon monoxide.
2. They often contribute to the development of fires by flaming and/or heat emission.
3. They may emit dense smoke, thereby making escape more difficult.
4. Melting of sheet materials may vent the fire, increasing the rate of spread.

The fire hazard associated with plastics depends, in a complex way, on the type of plastic and its mode of use. The reader is referred to BS 476, which deals with a number of criteria used in the overall assessment of properties of materials in fires, and to BS 2782 and BS 4735, which relate to fire properties of specific plastics types. It is found that many plastics perform badly in several of the above respects – for example, polyethylene, polypropylene, polystyrene, acrylic resins, ABS, polyurethane, GRP and rubber, which all burn readily. Acrylic resins are an additional hazard because their flash-over temperature is only 290 °C. Some plastics which do not burn readily, nevertheless produce dense smoke in fire – for example, polyvinyl chloride, which also produces hydrogen chloride gas. Polystyrene and GRP produce dense smoke, while polyurethane produces hydrogen cyanide gas on combustion. The greatest fire hazard is, in general, caused by plastics in foamed or sheet form, since oxygen is much more readily available in this state. Serious disasters have been caused, for example, by combustion of vertical acrylic sheeting, due to the extremely rapid spread of flame in this situation, and by polyurethane foams in cushions, due to rapid combustion and the toxic fumes emitted. Expanded polystyrene ceiling tiles are not recommended in areas where there is a fire risk, since they melt easily and may feed the fire, especially if the adhesive is used in 'dabs' rather than as a continuous film. Fire-retardent grades of these polymers, as well as GRP, polypropylene and polystyrene, are available but have not in the past been widely used on account of increased cost. Many thermoplastic adhesives contain flammable solvents, constituting a considerable hazard during use and until solvent evaporation is complete. In some cases, plastics may help retard the development of fire, for example, collapse of PVC downpipes may prevent their transmitting fire vertically. Collapse of thermoplastic roof lights could reduce the build-up of heat in an enclosure, hence, delaying 'flash-over'. However, such collapse might also vent the fire and, therefore, increase local rates of burning or, in the case of external fire, the spread from a neighbouring building.

Bitumens and related products

Although these are not plastic in the normal sense of the word, they are in many ways similar and may be conveniently described here. Bitumens are essentially hydrocarbons and their derivatives but they include elements such as sulphur, oxygen and nitrogen. At room temperature, the material may have a consistency varying between that of a hard, brittle solid and a thick, viscous liquid. The liquid form can be regarded as a two-phase material containing solid compounds of high molecular weight, dispersed colloidally in a fluid phase of lower molecular weight, the solid fraction consisting of an amorphous network of linear hexagonal aliphatic hydrocarbon chains of fairly low length. Involved in the definition of bitumens is the requirement that they dissolve in carbon disulphide.

Bitumens occur naturally in the form of asphalt, for example, Trinidad Lake asphalt, and in certain rocks, and have been used successfully over many centuries in a wide variety of applications. They are now more commonly produced synthetically, either by distillation or by 'air-blowing' of oil, the bitumen being left as a residue after the evaporation of volatile fractions. The properties of the final bitumen depend on the composition of the crude oil, the type of production process and the temperature to which it is heated. Bitumens may be of the 'straight-run' type, which have high viscosity and will need to be heated to become workable, or the 'cut-back' variety, which have lower viscosity, due to the addition of fluxing oils such as kerosene or creosote.

Bituminous materials have the chemical stability characteristic of the paraffin family of materials, being resistant to acids and alkalis. There is, however, some degree of unsaturation in them so that oxygen from the atmosphere tends to cause cross-linking by oxidation and subsequent embrittlement, particularly when exposed to ultra-violet light. Resistance may be increased by using surface coatings of already oxidised bitumen in the case of roofing felts and protecting from the sunlight wherever possible with light-reflecting mineral aggregates, such as limestone. Note that many oils from which bitumens are derived will seriously soften or erode bituminous asphalts.

Bitumens are examples of visco-elastic materials – they are able to flow plastically under gradually-applied stresses but may undergo brittle fracture if subjected to sudden stress. Hence, there are two prerequisites for successful use: first, that these materials are not subjected to significant sustained stress which would cause creep; and second, that sudden movements should be avoided. The precise extent of each of these effects depends, in practice, on the viscosity of the bitumen (measured by penetration values), the temperature and the presence of fibres or stabilising materials, such as aggregates. 'Blown' bitumens are, in general, less temperature-susceptible than distilled bitumens.

Tars are related to bitumens, these being mainly of aromatic composition and derived from the condensate obtained from the distillation of coal during the production of smokeless fuels. The crude tar or pitch is fluxed back with oils to give required properties. Applications of tars are often based on their low viscosity at high temperatures, such that they can be sprayed – surface dressings for roads are an example. Tars also resist softening by fuel oils better than bitumens, though they are generally more temperature-susceptible than the latter.

The following applications are based on the flexibility and water-proofing qualities of bitumens.

Roofing felts (BS 747)
These contain blends of bitumens incorporated in mineral fibres, such as asbestos or glass, or organic fibres, such as wood pulp. Felts incorporating organic fibres are suitable for lower layers of built-up roofing, or in flat roofs where a bitumen covering is to be applied. Types to which an oxidised bitumen coating has been applied during manufacture are, in all cases, more satisfactory than unsurfaced saturated grades. A granular mineral surfacing, when applied, increases protection from the sun, allowing use as the external surfacing material on sloping roofs. Reinforced grades are available where felts have to be self-supporting, for example, under tiling.

Other types of felt include sheathing felts containing long fibres which are, therefore, dimensionally stable, being used under asphalt roofing and flooring; and asbestos and glass-fibre felts, which are more durable than organic fibre felts. Flat roofs and built-up felt roofs, in particular, have given widespread problems in the past, these largely being associated with moisture penetration. The critical requirements of a built-up felt roof are: first, that falls should be sufficient to avoid ponding of water which would eventually penetrate; and secondly, that successive layers are effectively bonded to one another without air or moisture pockets. The latter requires that roof coverings be built up in dry weather, there also being some skill in obtaining continuous bonding at all parts of the felt. Hot-applied bitumen generally gives better results than cut-back varieties.

Bituminous mixtures
The most important bituminous mixtures in building are asphalts – these consist of bitumens with inert mineral material which increases their rigidity, stability

and abrasion resistance. The mineral may already be present in naturally occurring bitumen – for example, lake asphalt – or it may be added, in which case, it is usually graded, crushed limestone (BSS 988, 1076, 1097, 1451). Asphalts which are essentially solid and impermeable at room temperature, but which soften on heating, are known as 'mastic asphalts'. The limestone aggregate is of maximum size, 2.36 mm, graded down to 150 μm. Important uses include roofing, tanking and flooring. Roofing or tanking grades are normally softer than flooring grades, the former requiring flexibility while the latter require hardness and abrasion resistance. Although bitumens are acid-resistant, limestone is susceptible to acids, hence, siliceous fillers and aggregates should be used in such conditions. Asphalts are also widely used as road-surfacing materials, combining a smooth riding surface with excellent skid-resistance and impermeability to moisture. For this purpose, some small degree of oxidation is advantageous, since it results in weathering so that the coarse aggregate remains exposed. Lake asphalt and pitch-bitumen are valued because they oxidise in this way. Lake asphalt also has lower solubility in certain solvents than synthetic bitumens. (Since bitumens have a tendency to soften when in prolonged contact with oil, bituminous surfacings subject to heavy contamination, such as near bus stops, often deteriorate in this way.) Asphalts for roads must be carefully blended mixtures of binder, filler, and fine and coarse aggregates, in order to combine flexibility and strength in all weather conditions. Most bitumens used in road construction are of the straight-run type and these are heated before placing. Cut-back bitumens are, however, useful for such applications as repair work and footway surfaces, since they can be placed without heat. Provided excessive thicknesses are avoided, the fluxing oil evaporates fairly quickly, causing stiffening. Macadams are a further form of bituminous mixture widely used in civil engineering: they have, in general, a coarser particle grading than asphalts. Whereas asphalts rely on a stiff mortar for rigidity, macadams rely on particle interlock. Hence, asphalts contain a higher proportion of mortar, distances between aggregate particles being greater.

Further uses of bitumens include damp-proof courses, paints, adhesives and thermoplastic flooring tiles. The latter also contain inert fillers, resins and asbestos fibres (BS 2592).

Bituminous emulsions
Emulsions comprise small particles of bitumen dispersed in water by means of an emulsifying agent. Emulsifying agents may be anionic or cationic. The former are negatively charged and, since they are soluble in bitumen, impart a negative charge to the surfaces of particles, causing them to repel one another, thus stabilising the emulsion. Stearates are examples of anionic emulsifiers, the aqueous phase being alkaline in this case. Cationic emulsifiers operate on a similar basis except that they impart positive charges to the surfaces of the bitumen particles, the aqueous phase being acidic. Cetyl trimethyl-ammonium bromide is an example. The speed of 'break' of emulsions can be controlled and it also depends on temperature. Cationic emulsions generally break faster than anionic

emulsions, possibly because many solid materials are thought to be charged negatively, thus having a slight neutralising effect. Anionic emulsions are usually cheaper, however.

Bitumen emulsions are widely used for damp-proofing purposes, such as the provision of damp-proof membranes on concrete floors. On breaking, by evaporation of water, the film changes from dark brown to black in colour. Anionic emulsions are normally used for this purpose. Bitumen emulsions are also used extensively in road construction, for example, as a tack-coat during resurfacing, good adhesion being obtained to damp surfaces. Further applications include use as a curing membrane for lean concrete road-bases and as an adhesive for porous materials.

Sealing compounds

There is an enormous range of materials available for sealing purposes in construction, representing the widely-differing requirements of individual situations. When assessing the suitability of a sealant for a particular situation, consideration should be given to the following:

1. The size of the gap to be filled
2. The movement of the gap to be filled
3. The surface nature of the materials to be joined
4. The degree of resilience/abrasion-resistance required
5. The amount of maintenance envisaged
6. The degree of exposure to environment or chemicals
7. The lifetime required
8. The methods of application available
9. The temperature range in service

Materials will be considered under the headings: Brittle materials, Putties, Mastics and Elastomeric sealants.

Brittle materials
Mortars based on cement, gypsum, lime and other materials should only be used in situations where movement is minimal or where small cracks are no disadvantage, for example, pointing of brickwork and stonework. Common applications of these materials in situations where they are not likely to give long life are in roofing flaunchings and for fixing wc pans to the soil pipe. In each case, cracking of mortar or jointing material is likely, due to stresses imposed by relative movement. Ductility of these mortars can be improved by addition of emulsified resins such as polyvinyl acetate.

Putties
These are used primarily for glazing and are designed to act as a bedding material, as well as a filler and sealant. Linseed oil putties comprise processed vegetable oils and whiting (ground chalk). A hard skin forms by oxidation within 4 to 8 weeks,

depending on temperature. In timber frames, stiffening is assisted by loss of oil into the wood. In metal casement windows, this is not possible, so that putties are employed of a slightly stiffer consistency and containing accelerators such as gold size. The use of metal casement putty may also be preferred in timber-framed windows where, as a result of the use of preservatives or primers, the wood has less ability to absorb oil.

Putties will shrink and ultimately crack unless excessive oxidation is prevented by painting, after the original hardening period. Excessive hardening also impairs the sealing and bonding properties of the putty. The shelf life of putties is limited because the linseed oil tends to separate and hardening in the container occurs, unless oxygen is excluded.

Mastics

These may be regarded as of a basically non-hardening nature, although films may be formed. The mastics must be sufficiently viscous to resist sagging in the thicknesses required but sufficiently ductile to flow plastically when joint movement occurs. Mastics may be based on vegetable oils, synthetic polymers or bitumens.

Bitumens or bitumen/rubber blends are widely used for joint sealing in civil-engineering applications, such as roads and bridges. They are normally used in horizontal joints, being liquefied by heating and then poured into the joint. Stiffening occurs on cooling and quite large joints can be sealed in this way, giving long life, provided adhesion to the joint surfaces is not lost. Brittleness may cause sealant failure at low temperatures. Bituminous mastics are relatively cheap.

Oil-based mastics comprise vegetable oils and resins blended to give suitable oxidation characteristics, together with fibres and fillers. They form a skin within a few days, though hardening continues over a period of years, and life is not normally longer than 10 years, due to the cracking that ensues. Oil-based mastics have poor resistance to abrasion. They are, however, relatively cheap. Impregnated tapes are also available, particularly suitable for joining sheet materials, as in roofing. For best durability, such tapes should have a protective aluminium covering.

In addition to oil-based mastics, compounds based on acrylic and butyl polymers are available, these becoming semi-elastomeric as a result of solvent evaporation. This process may result in shrinkage of larger thickness but these mastics are somewhat superior in terms of abrasion-resistance and durability to oil-based mastics. They are intermediate in cost between oil-based and elastomeric types.

Elastomeric sealants

These have the advantage of being much more resilient than mastics, together with the ability to withstand greater joint movement (in the region of 20 per cent). Anticipated life is also longer – about 25 years in the case of polysulphide sealants.

This type is most effective in the two-pack form, though curing can, as with silicone sealants, be achieved by means of atmospheric moisture. One- and two-part polyurethane sealants are also available. Elastomeric sealants are considerably more expensive than the above types but, nevertheless, find wide application, especially in modern glazing systems.

Although elastomeric sealants bond well to metals, brick, glass and many plastics, it is important to pay attention to joint design. The maximum sealant depth is usually about 15 mm and only the sides of the joint should be bonded, since elastomers do not change in volume when stressed: tensile stresses cause waisting and compressive stresses, barrelling. The joint width must be adequate to absorb all movements, with joint depth usually equal to about half the joint width. Fillers such as expanded polyethylene should be used for deep joints and polyethylene film should be used to prevent bonding of the sealant to the filler (Fig. 5.5).

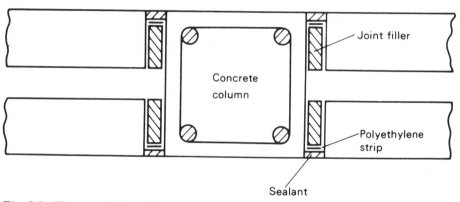

Fig. 5.5   The use of joint filler and sealant between concrete column and brickwork panels

With all types of sealant, adequate preparation is essential – surfaces should be clean and dry. They may need sealing, if friable, or priming, if bonding characteristics are poor.

Tests for sealants

There are many respects in which a sealant may prove to be unsatisfactory, the complexity of the problem being reflected by the variety of tests detailed in BS 3712: Parts 1–3 (Methods of testing building sealants). The tests measure homogeneity, relative density, extrudability, penetration, slump, seepage, staining, shrinkage, alkali-resistance, shelf life, paintability, application time, change in consistency, skinning properties, tack-free time and adhesion of fresh material to mature sealant. Selected tests can be applied, as required, to particular sealants and, in addition, there are BS specifications for silicone-based building sealants (BS 5889) and two-part polysulphide-based sealants (BS 4254). It must be emphasised that these tests are essentially laboratory tests of a standardised nature and that in-situ performance will depend additionally on the detailing of the joint, the quality and cleanliness of surfaces to be joined, the standard of workmanship during application, the extent of joint movement and the influence of the environment. Such performance can only be accurately determined from long-term experience of use.

Adhesives and adhesion

The advent of synthetic resins has completely revolutionised the field of adhesives and they are quite rapidly finding use in situations where, previously, there would have been no chance of success. Resins can be used, for example, in loadbearing situations, where moisture, heat or chemical pollution is likely, and where there is little in the way of a physical key. It must be emphasised that two surfaces cannot be joined without the establishment of bonds between them. In more traditional types of glue and cement, there is little bonding between the adhesive and the surface. The material depends for its action on penetration of the surface so that, on setting such that chemical bonding within the adhesive is established, the portions of set material beneath the material surface interlock (rather than bond) with surface layers, resulting in tensile strength (Fig. 5.6). Such adhesives are

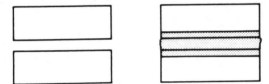

Fig. 5.6 The traditional method of bonding absorbent materials. The 'adhesive' penetrates the surfaces and, on hardening, forms a mechanical key. There is little true adhesion. Examples include inorganic cements and plasters

really cohesive instead of adhesive. Hence, non-porous surfaces, such as glass or metals, were very difficult to stick together and the advent of plastic materials has led to requirements for joining these also. Many resins now produced are, however, in the true sense of the word, adhesive – they stick to the surface by bonding with it, whether or not it is porous. The exact nature of the bond depends on the adhesive and the surface to be bonded and, though the bonding mechanism in most cases is not fully understood, it is true to say that the existence of primary bonds is not a prerequisite for successful adhesion: van der Waals' bonds will result in satisfactory properties, provided a sufficient number is established. The bonding properties of materials can be predicted from a knowledge of their surface energies. Surface energy may be defined as the energy required to form unit area of new surface. It is always positive, due to surface tension effects in solids and liquids. It is well-known, for example, that two drops of the same liquid on contact will merge to form a larger drop, since, in so doing, the total surface area of liquid will be reduced, resulting in a more stable

252

Fig. 5.7 Surface energy in liquids. On touching, two globules coalesce, forming a single larger globule of surface area less than the original total surface area

arrangement (Fig. 5.7). Solid objects behave similarly, though the effect is less obvious. Adhesion between a solid and liquid may be obtained either if the solid is *soluble* in the liquid, in which case the surface solid material migrates into the liquid forming a mixture or alloy (Fig. 5.8); or, if one '*wets*' the other, in which case adhesion will occur at the interface (Fig. 5.9(a)).

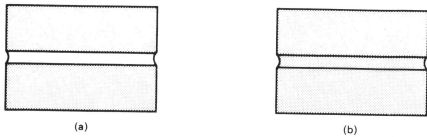

(a)   (b)

Fig. 5.8 Joining of surfaces by solvent welding: (a) Immediately after application of solvent; (b) Some time later. The solid dissolves and diffuses into the solvent until the solvent itself solidifies. The layer of solvent should be thin

(a)   (b)

Fig. 5.9 Adhesion of a liquid to a solid: (a) If the surface tension of the solid is higher than that of the liquid, the liquid wets the surface; (b) If the surface tension of the solid is lower than that of the liquid, the liquid does not wet the surface. The same effect occurs if there is a thin coating on the solid of a material of low surface tension; for example, grease

The solubility of one material in another depends on the molecular structure of each and, in particular, the *polarity* of molecular groups, that is, the charge eccentricities of the molecular bonds. A term which summarises polarity is 'solubility factor', which may be used for organic materials and solvents to predict the type of solvent required for, say, solvent-welding, or to safeguard against use of plastics in contact with certain organic liquids. To be soluble in a certain solvent, the polymer should have a similar solubility parameter. Table 5.2 shows typical values for some common polymers and solvents. Hence, chloroform may be used for solvent-welding PVC or polystyrene; phenol will dissolve nylon. (There are exceptions where, for example, due to crystallinity, polymers are

Table 5.2 Solubility parameters of some common polymers and solvents. Polymers usually dissolve in a solvent of approximately equal solubility parameter

Polymer	Approximate solubility parameter
PTFE	6
Polyethylene	8
Polypropylene	8
Polyisoprene	8
Polystryrene	9
Polymethyl methacrylate	9
PVC	9
Amino resins	10
Expoxy resins	10
Phenolic resins	11
Nylon	13
Solvent	
Carbon tetrachloride	8.6
Benzene	9.2
Chloroform	9.3
Acetone	10.0
Phenol	14.5
Water	23.4

insoluble in solvents of similar solubility parameter. Polyethylene is, for this reason, insoluble in any organic solvent at room temperature.) This type of solubility should not be confused with, for example, the dissolution of metals in acids: the latter type of reaction is normally irreversible and due to chemical attack. Unlike the above example, the product is entirely different, having a new molecular structure. Since solution of organic polymers is principally due to separation of molecular chains, heavily cross-linked polymers will not dissolve, though swelling may occur if such a material is subjected to potentially active solvents, that is, solvents which would dissolve less heavily cross-linked varieties of the polymer.

Closely related to the solubility parameter of polymers are their surface-tension values and this is to be expected, since both derive from molecular properties. Polyethylene, for example, has a much lower surface tension than more polar polymers. The requirement for wetting (and, hence, adhesion) of a liquid to a solid is that the liquid has a surface tension less than that of the solid, since, if it is greater, the liquid would be cohesive, tending to form globules on the solid surface (Fig. 5.9(b)). Surface tensions of solid materials are roughly in the order of solubility parameters, with inorganic materials having much higher values. Hence, water wets inorganic materials and epoxy resins will adhere to them, as well as to some thermosetting plastics. On the other hand, many of the polymers with low surface tension are water-repellent and cannot be joined by epoxy resins. Surface treatment of polyethylene is required, for example, if epoxy resins are to adhere to it. The surface tension of the material must be increased and this can be achieved by oxidation – by an oxidising acid, for instance. It is important when joining materials with epoxy-type resins that the surfaces be completely clean, since even a very thin coating of grease or similar material may reduce considerably the effective surface tension of the surface, impairing the bond. Appropriate solvents should be used for this purpose. Similar arguments apply to solvent-welding.

There are, of course, cases in which water-repellent properties are advantageous. If, for example, the surface tension of stonework could be reduced, it would become water-repellent and, therefore, more resistant to the effect of moisture. This can be easily achieved using silicone resins, which have an extremely low surface tension. Release agents for concrete work on a similar principle. If, on the other hand, wetting is required, this can be achieved by *reduction* of the surface tension of the liquid, as is obtained by adding surface-acting, substances such as soap, to water. Some workability acids for concrete work on this principle – the water is able to wet particles more effectively, decreasing interparticle friction.

Types of adhesive

It is not easy to classify adhesives according to use, since many varieties are multi-purpose in their application. Hence, they are here divided into natural adhesives (glues), and thermosetting and thermoplastic synthetic adhesives, though the first four to be described are used mainly for timber products. In this context, durability is of extreme importance and BSS 1203 and 1204 give four classifications as to the suitability of timber glues for various situations. They are as follows:

WBP stands for weather- and boil-proof types.
BR indicates boil-resistant types that fail on prolonged exposure to weather.
MR refers to moisture-resistant but not boil-resistant adhesives.
'Int' adhesives are resistant to cold water but, unlike the above, are not required to be resistant to micro-organisms.

A further general point which should be considered when selecting an adhesive is the mechanism of curing or hardening. While most of the adhesives described below are truly adhesive (that is, they bond to the receiving surface), the curing processes of some still require an absorptive surface – to allow removal of water or solvent, for example. Such adhesives would not be effective if used to join *two* non-absorbent surfaces.

Animal glues (BS 745)
These have been used for centuries in carpentry and joinery, and are obtained from the skin or bone of cattle and sheep. The major constituents of animal glues

255

are proteins – large molecules occurring in gelatinous form, softening to form a viscous liquid at temperatures above about 40 °C and gelling to form to solid at lower temperatures. Animal glues are normally sold in powder form, and are melted in warm water to give a solution of suitable viscosity. Cooling of the liquid after application results in rapid gelling, producing some strength, and drying finally produces a tough and rigid product. Note that the removal of water from the glue during curing is essential: wood assists in this process, due to absorption. Glued joints in wood should be as strong as the wood, though damp conditions will, of course, reduce strength and animal glues are not suitable for external use unless adequately protected from moisture (BS 1204, 'Int' rating). The glue will harden gradually in the pot but can be softened by reheating with water.

Casein glues (BS 1444)
Casein glues are of rather similar structure to animal glues, though they are derived as a precipitate from skimmed milk by the action of acids. Glues are obtained in powder form which also contains an alkaline solvent, necessary to dissolve the glue on addition of water. Mixing is carried out cold and setting is partly by evaporation or absorption of water and partly by a natural gelling process. The latter reaction results in a limited pot life of glues, once mixed – usually about 6 hours. Some degree of water-resistance can be obtained by incorporation of formaldehyde but use is normally confined to dry situations ('Int' rating).

Thermosetting adhesives

Urea formaldehyde
This is one of the commonest adhesives used in joinery for general purposes, producing a strong rigid joint if the glue-line is thin. To make the adhesive, formaldehyde and urea in aqueous solution are allowed to react together to a certain stage and the reaction is then 'stopped' while the resin is still liquid. These resins would then be of two-pack form, since a hardener is required to initiate the final stage of the hardening process. Alternatively, the water may be evaporated, giving a powder which has a longer shelf life than the liquid forms. On addition of water, the original properties are restored and setting commences on adding the hardener. Some varieties contain both the resin and hardener in powdered form, mixed together so that water only need be added. Urea-formaldehyde adhesives have little natural 'tack', so that they are best suited to joining porous materials, such as wood or cork. Pressure is essential to hold surfaces together during curing.

One problem occur with this and other resins is crazing, which tends to occur with large volumes of adhesive as might be used when gaps of, say, 1 mm, have to be filled. Crazing is caused by shrinkage occur during the condensation reaction. It can be reduced by fillers which are used in gap-filling glues. If restricted pot life is a problem, joints can be made by the separate application method in which the resin is applied to one surface and the hardener to the other, so that setting does not commence until the joint is made. In this way, strong bonds can be obtained as quickly as 10 minutes after making the joint, though there is still time to position the components accurately, unlike 'contact' adhesives. Urea-formaldehyde adhesives are used for fabrication of flush doors, laminated timber and decorative laminates. Hardening of glue-lines will occur at room temperature but it may be accelerated by hot presses, strip heating or, most recently, radio-frequency heating, which may enable curing times as low as a few seconds to be used. Although urea-formaldehyde has good water-resistance at normal temperatures, very hot water or prolonged wetting breaks the resin down – it has the MR rating. Hence, laminates, for example, around kitchen sinks should be bonded by a more resistant adhesive. Further important uses of urea-formaldehyde resins are for particle board and plasterboard partitioning.

Melamine-formaldehyde resin adhesives
These are usually in powder form and are mixed with water to give a colourless resin. They set on heating to 100 °C and give good weather resistance (BR rating), though they are more expensive than urea-formaldehyde adhesives.

Phenol formaldehyde
These are available as liquids which polymerise on heating to temperatures over 100 °C and are used for assembly of plywood sheets. The resin is applied, the sheets formed and compressed and the laminates then subjected to a hot press, which causes hardening in a period of about 5 minutes. Film varieties have also been used: these bond the surfaces on warming. Cold-curing phenolic adhesives are also available. These are insoluble in water and set by addition of strong acids so that the glue is acidic, having pH values as low as 1. They have been used for assembly gluing of wood, though the setting reaction is exothermic and too much hardener tends to reduce pot life, on account of the accelerating effect of heat on the curing rate.

Phenolic adhesives are hard but brittle, so that fracture in wood joints is possible, especially if thick glue-lines exist. Moisture resistance is excellent: they have the WBP rating of BS 1204. Correct mixing, application and curing are important, so that they are best suited to factory use.

Resorcinol formaldehydes
These are related to phenol-formaldehyde adhesives but, unlike the latter, will cold-cure under neutral conditions by addition of formaldehyde. Adhesives consist of a water-soluble liquid resin obtained by mixing resorcinol with a quantity of formaldehyde which is insufficient to cause cross-linking. The 'hardener' is, or contains, formaldehyde, which completes the process. Curing can be carried out cold or accelerated by moderate heat.

Resorcinol adhesives are important in laminated timber, since they have very good durability in extremes of weather (WBP rating), though, since timber may not stand up to such conditions unprotected, preservatives should be used: most preservatives do not affect the bond obtained. These adhesives are also useful for joining wood products and laminates to brick, concrete and asbestos backgrounds, and are tolerant of a certain amount of moisture. Grades containing fillers should be used when bonding to uneven substrates. In common with phenolic adhesives, resorcinol types are strong but brittle.

Epoxy resins
These are a most important development, since, with the exception of some thermoplastics, they form a good bond with almost any material. This is considered to be due, at least in part, to the low shrinkage of these resins on curing, so that surface shear stresses do not arise. A further contribution to adhesion is probably due to the presence of hydroxyl groups in the polymer. There are many different curing agents and, as these become built into the final cross-linked molecule, one particular curing agent will probably be best suited to the particular physical and chemical properties of each situation. With certain hardeners, the use of the correct quantity is important, although the polyamide hardener for two-part general household purposes is chosen partly because, in this case, the effect is minimised. Greatest bond strength with this hardener is obtained by high curing temperatures – 100 °C or over.

An alternative to the two-part method is to produce limited reaction between resin and hardener during manufacture and then to stop the reaction, which results in a one-part adhesive that can be hardened by heating. Such resins are used as film adhesives.

Epoxy resins can also be modified by combining with other polymers, which may, for example, improve flexibility or impact strength, though usually at the expense of tensile strength. Polysulphide and vinyl polymers can be used for this purpose. Epoxy resins have, in general, excellent mechanical strength and creep resistance, and are resistant to weather, acids, alkalis and most hydrocarbons. They are now widely employed for structural joints between many types of material, including glass, metal, thermosetting plastics and concrete. Although the adhesive is expensive, applications are likely to increase as the construction team becomes more fully aware of the advantages of glued joints.

Alkyl cyanoacrylate adhesives
These have the advantage of polymerising very rapidly when spread in thin films, the reaction being catalysed by water which, in the very small quantities required, is present on most surfaces. The adhesives are, however, expensive, so that uses are confined to bonding of small objects having surfaces which closely conform to one another.

Polyurethane adhesives
Though not widely used, these have a useful property not possessed by the other adhesives, that they will join unvulcanised rubber to metal. Water-resistance properties are intermediate between those of urea and phenolic adhesives.

Thermoplastic adhesives

The setting action of these may occur as a result of cooling, solvent evaporation or by emulsion coalescence. Hence, the term 'curing', implying chemical changes, is not always appropriate. As is characteristic of thermoplastics themselves, adhesives so based are more flexible but weaker and more prone to creep than thermosetting adhesives, so that they are not normally used for 'structural' purposes.

Polyvinyl acetate (PVA)

This is probably the most important thermoplastic adhesive in building, chief applications being as a wood adhesive for internal use and as a bonding agent for concrete. The polymer is obtained from acetylene and acetic acid and is most commonly used in emulsion form. The monomer liquid is emulsified in water, forming very small droplets which are then polymerised by the action of heat and a catalyst. The adhesive sets when the solid particles, on evaporation or absorption of the moisture, cohere to form a tough film which is no longer water-soluble. The chief advantage of PVA adhesives is that they are water-miscible and do not require the use of a hardener, though one of the materials to be joined must be absorbent. Thin glue-lines with absorbent materials set quickly, though gap-filling properties are less satisfactory. Properties of joints are characteristic of thermoplastic adhesives – they have better impact resistance than thermosetting adhesives but prolonged stress will cause creep and ultimate failure.

A further common use of PVA emulsions is as a bonding agent between new and old concrete. The resin may be diluted and applied to the substrate or added to the new mix, in which case it enables thinner sections and screeds to be applied with reduced danger of cracking. PVA emulsions are often used to seal surfaces such as plaster before tiling and as an internal ceramic tile adhesive, in which case, gap-filling properties would be imparted by incorporation of fillers.

Polystyrene adhesives

These normally operate on the solution principle, containing some dissolved polystyrene also. Polystyrene, PVC and polymethyl methacrylate can be joined in this way, though the solvents are highly flammable.

Bituminous adhesives

These form good bonds with a number of materials, are moisture-resistant and flexible. Natural or synthetic rubber and solvents may be included to give the desired combination of elasticity and strength. Adhesives are obtainable in the following forms:

Water-based emulsions   These form an effective bond between porous materials in situations where long-term tensile stresses are not present. They are also used for laying wood-block flooring and PVC or thermoplastic tiles.

Solvent types Used in laying linoleum, and for PVC and thermoplastic tiles, though tests should be carried out to ensure that staining does not occur. Both solvent and emulsion types rely on some degree of absorbency in the substrate to allow absorption/evaporation of the water or solvent.

Hot-applied varieties These are used for wood-block flooring and in built-up felt roofing. Application temperatures are in the region of 150 to 200 °C.

Rubber-based adhesives

Many rubber-based adhesives rely on a very high degree of tackiness, which results in good adhesion to most surfaces, including, in some cases, thermoplastics such as polyethylene. Rubbers may also possess the property of auto-adhesion, in which two films bond immediately on touching. The origin of such behaviour is complex but it depends on the ability of molecules in the two films to diffuse and interlock when the surfaces are pressed together. This depends, in turn, on the viscosity of the adhesive.

The most important rubber-based adhesives in the construction industry are 'contact' adhesives – the adhesive is applied to both surfaces and, after solvent evaporation, the surfaces are carefully brought together, giving immediate auto-adhesion. If one of the surfaces is porous, they can be brought together immediately, the solvent dispersing subsequently by diffusion. Neoprene is widely used in contact adhesives.

Latex-modified cements are used for bonding ceramic tiles to a variety of backgrounds, including metal.

When bonding materials such as polyethylene in which adhesion is, in the absence of any polarity, due solely to dispersion forces, the cohesive strength of the adhesive must be kept low in order to distribute stresses as evenly as possible at the interface. Flexible polyisobutane, of carefully chosen molecular weight distribution, can be used to give a reasonable bond between polyethylene sheets in this way.

Paints

Paints are surface coatings generally suitable for site use, marketed in liquid form. They may be used for one or more of the following purposes:

1. To protect the underlying surface by exclusion of the atmosphere, moisture, chemicals, fungi and insects
2. To provide a decorative, easily-maintained surface
3. To provide light- or heat- reflecting properties
4. To give special effects, for example, inhibitive paints for protection of metals; electrically-conductive paints as a source of heat; condensation-resistant paints

Externally, (1) and (2) will be of greatest importance: internally, (2) and (3) are more important.

Painting constitutes a small fraction of the initial cost of a building and a much higher proportion of the maintenance cost. It is, on this basis, advisable to pay careful attention to the subject at construction stage. Furthermore, there are a number of situations in which restoration is both difficult and expensive once the original surface coating has failed and weathering has affected the substrate, for example, clear coatings on timber. In these situations, particular care is necessary.

Paints consist essentially of a vehicle and pigment, the former being responsible for setting, gloss and impermeability, while the latter is responsible for opacity, colour and, to some extent, strength. Other materials, such as driers, solvents and extenders, may also be added. Once applied, the coating must harden within a few hours. The hardening process may be due to one of the following:

(a) Polymerisation by chemical reaction with a hardener or by oxygen (or, in some cases, moisture) in the air
(b) Coalescence of an emulsion
(c) Evaporation of a solvent

Categories (a) and (b) may be referred to as convertible coatings, since, on hardening, coatings cannot easily be restored to their earlier liquid state. Note, however, that there are no new primary bonds produced when emulsions in category (b) coalesce. Type (c) is non-convertible, since the liquid state can be restored simply by adding a suitable solvent. The most important paints in the first category are oil-based paints.

Oil-based paints

These were traditionally based on linseed oil (obtained from flax seeds) or tung oil (obtained from soya beans) and, although satisfactory properties can be obtained by refining these oils, they are now usually modified by alkyd resins. Some understanding of the drying action of oils used in paints can be gained from an examination of the organic acids which form their basis. Vegetable oils, such as linseed oil, consist of combinations of triglycerides of fatty acids. Glycerol has the formula:

$$CH_2-OH$$
$$|$$
$$CH\ -OH$$
$$|$$
$$CH_2-OH$$

while fatty acids have a variety of formulae, each containing the —COOH (acid) radical, for example, stearic acid, $CH_3(CH_2)_{16}COOH$ (no double bonds) and oleic acid, $CH_3(CH_2)_7CH=CH(CH_2)_7COOH$, one double bond. On reaction, these form products of the type:

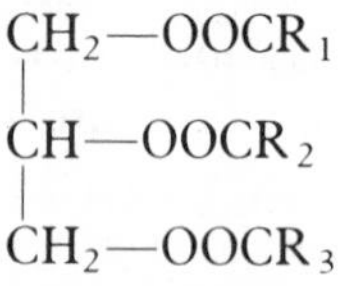

$$CH_2-OOCR_1$$
$$CH-OOCR_2$$
$$CH_2-OOCR_3$$

where R_1, R_2 and R_3 are the hydrocarbon sections of the acids. Water is also produced, the OH coming from the glycerol and H atoms from the acid radicals.

Quite large molecules may result from this process and the oil may be made to polymerise if double bonds in the hydrocarbon sections give rise to cross-linking. For example, the chain $-CH_2-CH=CH-CH_2-$ combines with a similar chain by means of oxygen. The oxygen may become directly involved (Fig. 5.10 (a)) or may simply initiate C—C bonds (Fig. 5.10 (b)). These linkages may

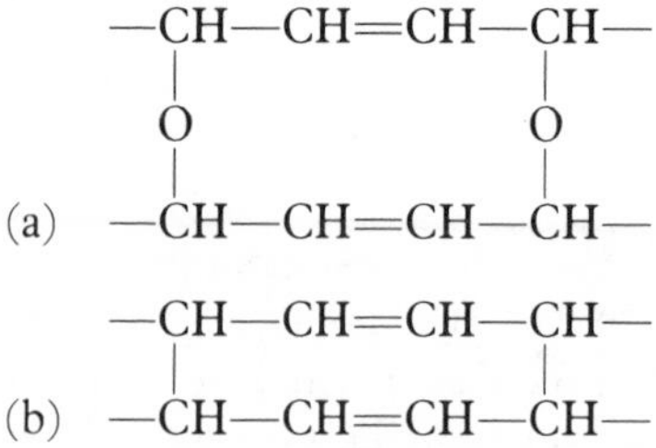

```
        —CH—CH=CH—CH—
          |             |
          O             O
          |             |
(a)     —CH—CH=CH—CH—

        —CH—CH=CH—CH—
          |             |
(b)     —CH—CH=CH—CH—
```

Fig. 5.10 Cross-linking of molecular chains in a drying oil by means of oxygen: (a) oxygen directly involved in link; (b) oxygen not directly involved in link

occur between any neighbouring hydrocarbon chains, so that oxygen from the atmosphere causes gradual cross-linking of molecules until a solid film is produced. The strength and stiffness of the solid depends on the number of unsaturated groups in the original glyceride and, hence, on the acid type present. Stearic acid, for example, is saturated, therefore it would not form a drying oil. Acids containing a smaller number of unsaturated groups would result in oils which produce soft films, more suitable for mastics, while acids containing a large number of unsaturated groups might produce hard, brittle films. Certain metallic compounds based on lead, cobalt and manganese can be incorporated in the oils, accelerating curing. These are referred to as 'driers'. They are characterised by having more than one valency value, so that they can effectively 'carry' oxygen into the molecular network to assist in polymerisation. Boiled linseed oil, which has hardening properties superior to those of ordinary linseed oil, contains metal compounds incorporated by heating.

Once hardened, oil-based paints behave as thermosetting plastics, being resistant to solution in the oils from which they are formed. Such paints form films in the can unless a protective coating of, say, white spirit is applied.

Alkyd resins

These are a form of polyester resin and play an important part in modern oil paints. They are produced by mixing a polyhydric alcohol with phthalic anhydride (so-called because it is derived from phthalic acid by extraction of a water molecule). Figure 5.11 shows the reaction with a difunction alcohol containing a drying-oil residue. A long-chain molecule is formed with a number of unsaturated groups in the drying-oil residue. These dry by the action of oxygen, as in oil-based paints. Gloss retention, durability and colour retention properties of alkyd-modified drying oils are much better than those of pure alkyd or pure oil and, since the polymers are more polar, they are stronger and more adherent to the substrate than pure oils. Vehicles containing a high proportion of oil are known as 'long-oil' vehicles and these are tough, flexible and suitable for external use. Medium- and short-oil types are more suitable for internal use.

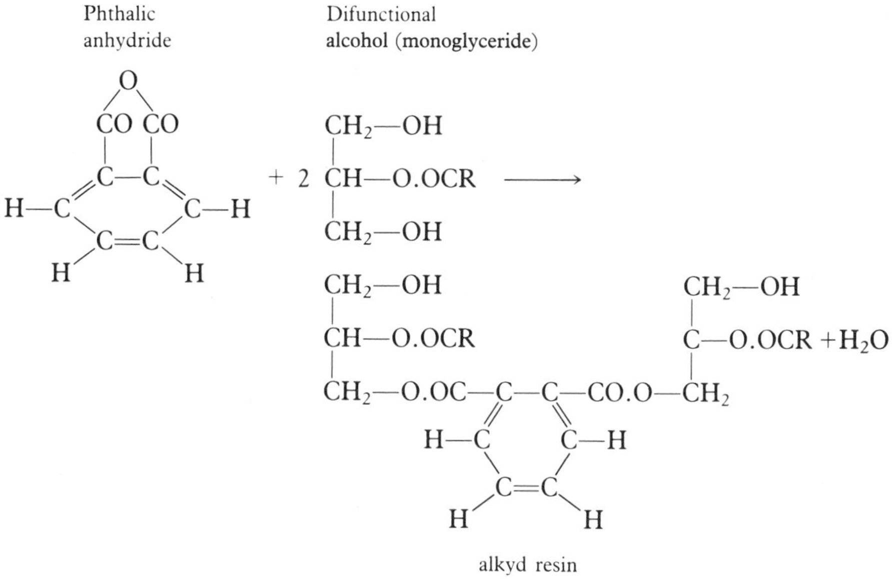

Fig. 5.11 Formation of a linear alkyd resin by reaction between phthalic anhydride and a difunctional alcohol. If a trifunctional alcohol were used, a rigid cross-linked structure would be obtained

Polyurethane paints

These are available in a variety of forms. The hardest films are obtained from two-pack versions of the resin. The resin itself is a polyester, as are the alkyd resins, though produced by a different process, involving a dibasic acid:

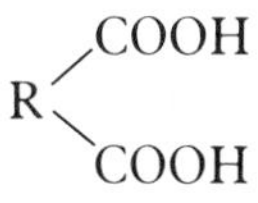

$$R\begin{cases} COOH \\ COOH \end{cases}$$

a diol:

$$R\begin{matrix} \diagup OH \\ \diagdown OH \end{matrix}$$

and a polyol, for example:

$$R\begin{matrix} \diagup OH \\ - OH \\ \diagdown OH \end{matrix}$$

The resulting ester has several OH groups which are reacted with isocyanates (containing NCO groups ($-N{=}C{=}O$)). A typical reaction is

$$HO-R_1-OH + 2[OCN-R_2-NCO] \longrightarrow$$

$$OCN-R_2-\underset{\underset{H}{|}}{N}-\underset{\underset{O}{\|}}{C}-O-R_1-O-\underset{\underset{O}{\|}}{C}-\underset{\underset{H}{|}}{N}-R_2-NCO$$

↑⎯⎯⎯ urethane ⎯⎯⎯↑
links

The isocynates cause polymerisation by linking the hydroxyl groups belonging to esters.

When an excess of isocynate is used, the polymers terminate in $-NCO$ groups, which can result in cross-linking, due to moisture in the atmosphere. This process also gives rise to carbon-dioxide gas and is used in the formation of expanded polyurethane.

Two-pack polyurethane resins may be used, polymerisation occurring if there is an excess of $-OH$ groups in one pack and of $-NCO$ groups in the other. The two-pack varieties produce extremely good film properties, though tolulene-diisocynate vapour can be dangerous if inhaled. Also, temperature tends to affect the curing rate and two-pack paints which require accurate mixing are, themselves, a disadvantage for general site use. Various types are available: hardest resins may be used on furniture, while more flexible grades are required for external use or flooring. Note that curing of two-pack polyurethanes is not dependent on the atmosphere.

Air-drying polyurethane paints and varnishes
These are commonly used in building for a wide variety of purposes. They are really modified drying oils. For example, by means of glycerol, hydroxyl groups are introduced into an air-drying oil, producing a monoglyceride.

$$2\begin{matrix} CH_2-OH \\ | \\ CH-OH \\ | \\ CH_2-OH \end{matrix} + \begin{matrix} CH_2-COOR \\ | \\ CH-COOR \\ | \\ CH_2-COOR \end{matrix} \longrightarrow 3\begin{matrix} CH_2-OH \\ | \\ CH-COOR \\ | \\ CH_2-OH \end{matrix}$$

oil   monoglyceride

The addition of a polyisocynate to the monoglyceride will cause some polymerisation by action on hydroxyl groups, as previously. The polyurethane 'oil' will then dry, by the effect of oxygen on unsaturated bonds, the film having similar properties to two-pack varieties, though not normally as hard or tough. In varnishes, in particular, some polyurethane coatings may not withstand the thermal and moisture movements which occur when applied to wood. South-facing aspects exaggerate the problem.

Moist-curing polyurethane varnishes
These are sometimes claimed to react with water in damp timber, forming an impervious film. Although the polymerisation process involves moisture, quantities required are only small, approximately 1 per cent by weight of the paint. Hence, they will not 'dry' wet timber. Paints of this variety cannot be produced, since pigments normally contain sufficient moisture to cause them to set in the can.

Saponification of oil-based paints and varnishes

It has been explained that oil-based paints are glycerides of organic acids, that is, they are formed from glycerol. If an alkali, such as calcium hydroxide, contacts such an oil-based film, there is a tendency to revert to glycerol with the production of the corresponding salt.

oil-based film	metallic hydroxide		glycerol		metallic salts
CH_2—$COOR_1$			CH_2—OH		$MCOOR_1$
CH —$COOR_2$	$+$	$3MOH$ $\longrightarrow$	CH —OH	$+$	$MCOOR_2$
CH_2—$COOR_3$			CH_2—OH		$MCOOR_3$

This leads to the breakdown of films and formation of a scum. Hence, oil-containing paints (including polyurethanes) should not be used on alkaline substrates, such as Portland cements. Alkali-resistant primers, such as PVA emulsion paints, should first be applied.

Emulsion paints

These are now very widely used in interior decorating. Examples are polyvinyl acetate (PVA) emulsions, which are suitable for application to new cement or plaster. The molecules are very large but are dispersed in water by colloids to give particles of approximately 1 μm in size. Hence, these paints have the advantage of being water-miscible, although, on drying out, coalescence of polymer particles occurs, resulting in a coherent film with moderate resistance to water (Fig. 5.12). The film is, however, not continuous, so that the substrate can, if necessary, dry out through the film. Acrylic emulsions for painting of timber have now been produced, including a form which results in a gloss finish.

265

 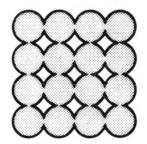

Fig. 5.12   Coalescence of an emulsion to form a coherent but non-continuous film

Solvent-based paints

From some points of view, non-convertible coatings are an advantage, since such paints do not form films in the can and subsequent coats bond into one another. On the other hand, the hardened films are much less tolerant of certain organic solvents than convertible types. Examples of solvent-based paints are cellulose and bituminous paints.

Cellulose paints

The cellulose constituent is the form of nitro-cellulose dissolved in a solvent such as acetone. Plasticisers are added to give elasticity and synthetic resins to give a gloss, since pure cellulose gives little gloss.

Drying usually occurs rapidly but well-ventilated areas are essential and the paint is highly flammable. Cellulose paints are most suited to spray application (though retarded varieties for brushing are available). These properties, together with the fact that the paints give off a penetrating odour, tend to restrict the use of cellulose paints to factory application. In these conditions, high-quality finishes can be obtained and the resulting coat has good resistance to fungal attack and to chemicals, including alkalis.

Bituminous paints

These are intended primarily for protection of metals used externally and have poor gloss-retention properties. Thick coats give good protection, though the solvents used sometimes cause lifting, if applied over oil-based paints, or bleeding, in subsequently-applied oil-based coats. Sunlight softens the paint, though resistance can be improved by use of aluminium in the final coat. Chlorinated-rubber paints have similar properties: uses are often based on their resistance to alkalis.

Pigments

The chief object of these is to impart opacity and colour to the paint. In white paints, pigments are used without need for dyes, titanium dioxide being one of the most important. This pigment occurs in two forms, anatase and rutile, the latter having greater resistance to 'chalking' – gradual wearing away of paint, due to binder destruction. 'Coloured' pigments are now frequently obtained by use of organic dyes, though these are not as durable as more traditional inorganic pigments. Extenders, such as calcium carbonate, known as whiting, are added to reduce the cost of the paint and obtain the desired flow properties.

Painting specific materials

Ferrous metals

Steel forms the largest bulk of metals used in building and is one of the most difficult to maintain. Paint systems normally consist of primers, undercoats and finishing coats. Primers are designed to grip the substrate, to provide some protection (possibly by inhibition) to the steel and to act as a suitable base for subsequent coats. Inhibitive primers include red lead (lead oxide), zinc dust, zinc chromate and zinc phosphate. Of these, red lead, though toxic, is often still preferred because it is fairly tolerant of poorly-prepared surfaces and is amenable to application in thick coats. Metallic lead primers, though non-inhibitive, are fairly tolerant of poor surfaces and may be easier-flowing and quicker-drying than red lead. They also have superior chemical resistance. On account of their toxicity, lead-based primers are not recommended for use in domestic situations. Where a decorative finish is required, alkyd or aluminium paints may be used. Red oxide (micaceous iron oxide) is a moderately effective primer and is used both in undercoats and finishing coats.

Generally, the wetter the situation and the more aggressive the climate or atmosphere, the more coats should be given. In extreme situations or where extended life without maintenance is required, protection is only likely to be achieved by impregnated wrappings; bituminous or coal tar coatings; thick, factory-formed films; or prior treatment, such as galvanising.

Non-ferrous metals

Zinc and aluminium are the non-ferrous metals most likely to require surface coatings and each provides a poor key for paint, unless surface treatment is first carried out. Zinc, in particular, reacts with most oil-based paints, forming soluble salts which reduce adhesion. Zinc should be degreased with white spirit, followed by roughening of unweathered surfaces with emery paper or etching treatment. Primers containing phosphoric acid are available for this: they often also contain an inhibitor, such as zinc chromate. Other suitable primers contain calcium plumbate, zinc dust or zinc oxide. For aluminium, etching is again an advantage, followed by zinc chromate or red oxide primers. Lead-based primers are not suitable.

Wood

Preliminary treatment includes stopping holes and treatment of knots with shellac. A primer is essential to penetrate and yet block the pore structure. Undercoats are not normally satisfactory here, since they often do not penetrate the wood and may flake off later. Lead-based primers have been replaced by newer types such as aluminium (BS 4756) and acrylic emulsion primers (BS 5082), the latter being more tolerant of a rather high moisture content than alkyd types. Undercoats are used to obtain the desired colour, contributing to the film thickness and, therefore, protection, though the gloss coat provides the bulk of the protection. Alkyds and polyurethanes form the basis of most paints, though newer types, such as acrylic emulsions, are now available for external use. These may be slightly porous but it may be questioned whether an absolutely vapour-proof surface coating on wood is required externally, on account of the tendency for moisture to diffuse *outwards* through the building. Modern practice in relation to vapour barriers is to install them as near to the interior side as possible, with *moisture* barriers only externally to allow any vapour in the walls to escape. Hence, some small degree of porosity in an external paint film might not be a disadvantage.

Plastics

Most plastics in common use do not require painting, and paint coats, once applied, cannot be removed by normal techniques. Paints, on the other hand, will reduce the rate of degradation of plastics such as polyethylene. Adherence is poor unless the surface is first roughened to give a mechanical key.

Rheology of paints and related materials

It is well known that the behaviour of solids under stress is described by the use of stress/strain diagrams and, at least at low stress values, a given stress defines a given strain for a particular material. The relationship is clearly different for liquids, since, in the absence of long-range order, the application of stress will cause immediate relative motion within the body of liquid: there is no elastic stage. The equivalent of a stress/strain diagram for liquids would, therefore, be a graph relating shear stress to strain rate and this relationship will depend on the nature of short-range bonding, practically observed as the viscosity of the liquid. For many liquids, usually of low molecular weight, a straight-line graph would be obtained, at least for low shear stresses (Fig. 5.13). Such liquids are described as Newtonian. A typical consequence of this relationship between shear stress and

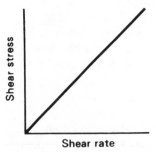

Fig. 5.13 Newtonian liquid. Shear rate proportional to shear stress

shear strain in that the velocity of a liquid in a pipe varies parabolically from the maximum value (at the centre) to zero (at the walls), assuming flow is non-turbulent.

As the molecular weight of a liquid is increased, viscosity increases, though interaction between molecular chains alters the relationship between shear stress and shear strain. At small stresses, some such liquids shear at a lower rate than would be expected, while others have the characteristics of a solid, supporting a small shear stress without continuous movement (Figs. 5.14 and 5.15). Such behaviour is non-Newtonian. The form of Fig. 5.14 is obeyed by paints, in which

Fig. 5.14 Non-Newtonian, shear rate lower than would be expected at low shear stresses

large molecules tend to become tangled together. Small shear stresses are insufficient to cause alignment, while larger stresses achieve this, resulting in decreased viscosity. The viscosity of paints must be carefully controlled by regulation of molecular chain size, since a paint must be sufficiently liquid to brush or spray and yet sufficiently viscous to resist sagging or curtaining on vertical surfaces after application. It is found that these properties are best achieved when there is a grading of molecular weights in a way similar to that by which aggregates for concrete are graded.

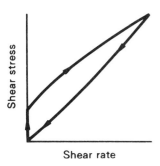

Fig. 5.15 Non-Newtonian, semi-solid properties are displayed at low shear stresses. Such liquids are thixotropic, the degree of thixotropy being proportional to the area enclosed by the increasing and decreasing shear stress cycle

Some types of paint exhibit colloidal properties and obey the form of Fig. 5.15. This is caused by van der Waals' bonds and can be useful, since the gel structure of the paint breaks down under shear stresses due to brushing and re-forms afterwards, improving the stability of the fresh film. Such paints, known as *thixotropic*, are attractive to the amateur, since they are tolerant of poor application technique and to the professional, since they allow thicker coats to be applied, where required. The area enclosed by the complete stress/strain-rate curve of Fig. 5.15 indicates the degree of thixotropy.

Timber

Although one of the earliest materials to be used in building, timber is by no means out-dated and still plays a major part in general building, particularly in domestic dwellings and furniture. Advances in the field of adhesives have increased enormously the potential of the material and better methods of testing, combined with increased understanding of timber properties, have enabled timber to be used at quite high stress levels. At the same time, the material can be worked with simple hand tools, is resistant to many types of chemical and atmospheric pollution and can be finished to give aesthetically pleasing effects. This section does not attempt to deal exhaustively with all the properties and applications of the wide range of varieties that exists. Instead, the fundamental properties and applications will be described. The reader is referred to specialist works for further information.

The physical and chemical structure of timber

Wood is a naturally-occurring fibrous composite, the fibres being of cellulose and occupying about two-thirds of the bulk and the matrix, lignin, which binds the fibres together. Bonding parallel to the grain is, therefore, primary in nature and, hence, very powerful so that, on stressing in this direction, failure usually occurs by shear between the cells formed from the cellulose fibres. Bonding across the grain is, on the other hand, of secondary nature so that tensile strength, radially or tangentially, is much reduced. From some points of view – for example, working – this is an advantage but from others it is a disadvantage. For instance, it is responsible for many of the defects arising from moisture-content changes. Cellulose contains hydrophilic hydroxyl groups and is, therefore, able to absorb substantial quantities of water – atmospheres of 100 per cent humidity result in a moisture content of about 30 per cent by dry weight and immersion in water may result in 200 per cent absorption. Volume changes result, illustrated, for example, by the swelling of cellulose wallpaper adhesives on adding water. Drying shrinkage in timber is, however, highly directional, being between 4 and 10 per cent tangentially, about two-thirds of this radially and negligible (about 0.1 per cent) longitudinally.

The relative values of these figures are easy to appreciate from the structure of the wood; longitudinally, there is great strength, due to the cellulose fibres; tangentially, timber is relatively free to shrink; while radially, the lower movement may be caused by cells in these directions known as rays (Fig. 5.16). Rays grow radially and, as their separation increases, new rays form between them, the process repeating indefinitely. Note also the spring and summer wood layers, and the outer 'sapwood' which carries the food.

Timber may be divided into softwoods (obtained from coniferous trees) and hardwoods (obtained from broad-leaved species). The latter are usually, but not always, harder, denser, stronger and more stable, though more difficult to machine, than softwoods. They contain a higher proportion of cellulose than the latter. The active part of the tree is the cambium layer from which material is formed to carry out four major functions – protection, mechanical support, food conduction and food storage. In spring, the cambium cells divide to form new cambium cells, together with new wood internally and bark externally, the bark providing protection from external agencies. In softwoods, support and food conduction requirements are fulfilled by a single-cell type, tracheids, having

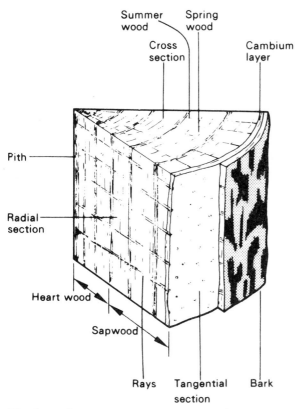

Fig. 5.16 Cross section, and radial and tangential sections, through a 5-year-old softwood log

271

fairly thick walls, especially in summer wood, which provides most mechanical support. In hardwoods, support is provided by dense, long, thin cells called 'fibres', while food conduction is carried out by wide, thin-walled cells called 'vessels'. Some hardwoods, such as oak, are 'ring-porous,' having a predominance of vessels in spring wood and a predominance of fibres in summer wood. All support and conduction cells are aligned vertically in the trunk. Food storage in both softwoods and hardwoods is provided by tissues known as 'parenchyma', which may be present horizontally, in rays or vertically, distributed between other cells. The rays in hardwoods are usually much more clearly visible than in softwoods: in some types of oak, in particular, the ray structure is more pronounced than the growth rings, giving oak its attractive figuring.

Conversion

Conversion is the process by which logs are cut up before seasoning. The actual method of cutting individual logs must be a compromise between that which results in most economical use of timber and that which results in the most desirable timber properties. An understanding of the effect of conversion methods on properties requires an examination of the effect of seasoning on the geometry and mechanical performance of timber.

Seasoning

'Green' timber contains large quantities of moisture, typical average figures for softwoods being 130 per cent (sapwood) and 60 per cent (heartwood), based on dry weight. On conversion, timber begins to dry out, reaching an equilibrium moisture content dependent on the type of timber, the ambient temperature and the humidity, in a time which depends on the above parameters and on the size of timber. Typical average values for the equilibrium moisture content of timber at 20 °C are, at 60 per cent relative humidity, 13 per cent; and at 90 per cent, 20 per cent. Substantial shrinkage of timber does not begin until the moisture content falls to fibre saturation value, about 27 per cent. Below this, shrinkage and moisture content have an approximately linear relationship. Higher temperatures result in lower moisture content: for example, at 30 °C, the above figures would be reduced by about 10 per cent of their previous value. Timber near to radiators or under-floor heating may reach a moisture content as low as 8 per cent. Seasoning may be carried out for the following purposes:

1. To reduce moisture content to a level below that required for fungal attack (about 20 per cent)
2. To obtain, with as little distortion as possible, the moisture content appropriate to the conditions of use of the timber. Ideally, timber should not be used at a moisture content more than 5 per cent different from that which it will finally assume. Otherwise, further movement is likely, with corresponding deformation. Timber for flooring should, for example, be supplied at lower moisture content than carcasing timber, for which a figure of 20 per cent is acceptable

3. Some preservatives and adhesives require a fairly low moisture content before application

It is most important that seasoning be so carried out that the moisture content of timber is reduced progressively. If, for example, drying out is too rapid, surface layers will tend to shrink first, causing splitting or stretching. Splitting, in itself, is undesirable and stretching may mean that, when the inner sections finally shrink, they are restrained by the now deformed outer layers, so that inner layers crack. Large or dense timbers are particularly prone to this, since internal wood takes some time to dry out. Hence, drying schedules must take account of timber type, size, original moisture content and use. Air-seasoning normally avoids these problems but takes some months to complete and does not reduce the moisture content below about 20 per cent, so that faster methods such as kilns are more commonly used, water diffusing through the timber much faster at higher temperatures, since it has lower viscosity. In kiln-seasoning, the timber is carefully stacked so as to permit air circulation and then heated, the humidity being maintained at a high level by means of steam jets until the timber reaches a uniform temperature. The initial temperature of the timber depends on its type and section but would normally be in the region of 60 °C for softwood and 40 °C for hardwood. As the moisture content reduces, the temperature is raised up to 30 °C above the initial values, the humidity subsequently falling. Kiln-seasoning takes about one week per 25 mm thickness for softwoods and about two weeks per 25 mm thickness for hardwoods, though precise times depend on the wood type and application. Most imported timber in the UK is seasoned before shipping. Once seasoned, it is, of course, essential to preserve its low moisture content, otherwise at least part of the benefit will be lost.

The effect of seasoning on various timber sections is shown in Fig. 5.17. Since tangential shrinkage is greater than radial shrinkage and outer layers tend to

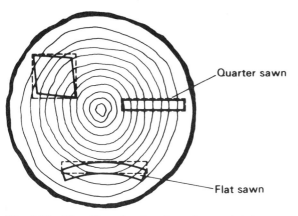

Fig. 5.17   The effect of grain orientation on shrinkage properties of timber. The cheapest way of conversion of timber is to make parallel cuts through the log, known as through-and-through cutting. Most of the resulting timber will then be flat-sawn rather than quarter-sawn

shrink more than inner layers, growth rings usually straighten on seasoning, producing, for example, cupping in boards. This is often unacceptable, as in flooring, where attempts to straighten the cupped boards would cause splitting. If cupping cannot be prevented, it is often better to relate this to the mode of use of the section: for example, skirting boards are better machined as in Fig. 5.18(b) rather than Fig. 5.18(a). Wherever possible, timber should be sawn parallel to the longitudinal grain: if growth rings intersect the longitudinal surface, bowing, springing and twisting may occur and strength and wearing properties are adversely affected (Fig. 5.19). Quarter-sawn boards are preferable generally to flat-sawn, though the latter produce a more attractive figure if appearance is important. The ends of timbers also often contain fissures (shakes and checks), due to stresses imposed when end shrinkage is restrained by the body of the

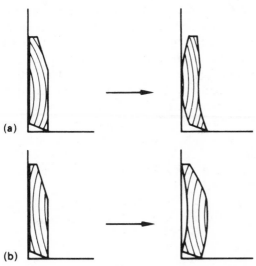

Fig. 5.18 Methods of machining skirting boards: (a) Board on drying cups away from wall at edges; (b) Board on drying cups away from wall at centre, which is preferable

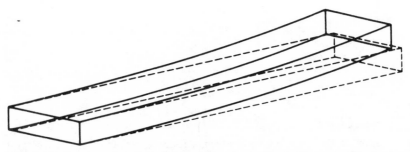

Fig. 5.19 Bowing of timber due to intersection of growth rings with the longitudinal surface. The effect also occurs when seasoned flat-sawn timber is machined to size. In this case, it is due to shrinkage stresses in the timber

timber. Ideally, it might be considered better to season timber before conversion in order to avoid these dimensional changes after machining but this is normally impracticable, since the large bulks of timber would take long periods to season, would be difficult to stack and would give rise to large shrinkage fissures.

There are, of course, many practical difficulties associated with control of the moisture content of timber in building but the following general rules should be adhered to as far as possible:

1. Do not store timber on site longer than is absolutely necessary
2. Specify moisture content for internal timber, particularly flooring and doors. On specification of certain types of door, additional precautions may be necessary. Panels in panelled doors may split on drying if assembled and glued at high moisture content. Veneered doors should be of the same veneer each side to avoid bowing by differential shrinkage or movement
3. Store all timber under cover. Units such as doors should be kept in a heated store if possible and not installed until the building is weather-proof, reasonably dry and, if possible, heated in winter
4. The occupier should not apply severe heating during early stages of occupation

Mechanical properties of timber

Since timber is a non-isotropic material, its strength properties are heavily dependent on the orientation of stress in relation to the grain direction. To describe fully the mechanical properties of timber, a number of different tests must, therefore, be applied. Standard tests are normally carried out on perfect ('clear') specimens of timber in order to give a maximum strength for each type of species. In bulk timber, this strength must be modified by factors depending on the stress situation, section size and the presence of imperfections, when calculating allowable stresses. Clear specimens are normally small – typically, of 20 mm square section – in order that adequate numbers of clear specimens be obtainable from smaller trees. BS 373 describes methods of testing small, clear specimens of timber.

In contrast to ceramics, the tensile strength of timber is much higher than its compressive strength when measured parallel to the grain, since compression causes buckling of the fibres. The tensile strength of most softwoods is, for example, in the region of $100 \, \text{N/mm}^2$ (tested dry) while compressive strength is about $40 \, \text{N/mm}^2$. Failure in tension is mainly due to shear failure between fibres or cells – the tensile strength of individual tracheids may be several times the figure given above.

Bending stresses are very commonly applied to timber in service and, as would be expected, flexural strength, as measured by the modulus of rupture, is intermediate between tensile and compressive strength, values for dry softwoods, being typically, in the region of $80 \, \text{N/mm}^2$. In simple bending, the upper compression layers buckle, causing the neutral axis to move downwards during the test so that, ultimately, the lower part of the specimen fails in tension. The modulus of rupture is normally quoted, on the assumption that simple bending theory applies: if allowance were made for movement of the neutral axis, the magnitude of the modulus of rupture would be similar to the strength measured in pure tension.

The shear strength of timber parallel to the grain is low – about $11 \, \text{N/mm}^2$ for dry softwoods – though this is not a common problem, since shear stresses in beams of normally used sections and spans are much smaller than bending stresses.

Hardness of timber is another important property, since it affects indentation and wear of flooring. BS 373 describes a test which measures the load required to press a steel ball of $11.3 \, \text{mm}$ diameter into timber to a depth equal to its radius. Typical dry softwoods give loads of approximately $3 \, \text{kN}$, while hardwoods, such as oak, may give twice this load.

In addition to the above properties, others such as cleavage strength, impact bending strength and modulus of elasticity may be measured as required. Some hardwoods will give results up to twice those for softwoods, depending on the wood type and the test carried out. The hardwood greenheart performs particularly well in all the tests.

Factors affecting strength

There are a great many factors affecting the strength of bulk timber and the nature of the material is such that widely-differing results can be obtained from differing specimens of the same species. Hence, the factors to be given are only one aspect of variations: in order to make the best use of sound timber and, at the same time, identify samples of low strength, current practice depends on carrying out simple tests on each piece of timber used.

Density

Despite the fact that the solid density of the fibrous component of wood is approximately $1500 \, \text{kg/m}^3$, the density of dry bulk timber is rarely over $1000 \, \text{kg/m}^3$, softwoods having densities in the region of $500 \, \text{kg/m}^3$, while hardwoods have densities averaging about $700 \, \text{kg/m}^3$. These densities give an indication of the air-void content which, as with ceramic materials, can be correlated with strength. Timber strength is, however, much less sensitive to air voids than that of concrete, an approximately linear relationship existing between compressive strength and the relative density of air-dry timber. As a rough guide, the compressive strength of clear timber can be taken to be 100 times its relative density – for example, a softwood having a relative density of 0.5 would have a compressive strength of about $50 \, \text{N/mm}^2$.

Rate of growth

When softwoods grow rapidly, the proportion of spring wood tends to increase and, since this is of relatively low density, strength is adversely affected. Rate of growth is, therefore, a factor which is considered in visual stress grading. The situation is much less simple in hardwoods, summer wood also growing faster, in general, when conditions are suited to rapid growth.

Moisture content

The strength of timber rises approximately linearly as moisture content decreases from fibre saturation and may increase threefold when the oven-dry state is reached. At a more common moisture content in the region of 15 per cent, the strength would be approximately 40 per cent higher than in the saturated state, depending on the type of wood. The mechanism of the strength increase is rather similar to that of shrinkage in concrete, the contraction resulting in decreased inter-fibre spacings and, therefore, stronger bonding between fibres.

Slope of grain

Significant deviation of the fibre direction from the longitudinal axis of timber may result from inaccurate sawing but is more commonly due to irregular growth of the tree. The tensile strength of timber drops rapidly as the slope of grain increases and tensile strength perpendicular to grain direction is very small, typically 3 N/mm^2. As would be expected, the effect on compressive strength is much less marked and that in bending is, therefore, intermediate – a $10°$ slope of grain producing a bending-strength fall of about 20 per cent.

Knots

Knots correspond to branches of the tree and result in severe distortion of growth rings in the trunk. There are two basic types – live knots, which correspond to branches which are living at the time of felling, and dead knots corresponding to dead branches and often found lower down on the trunk. Both types reduce strength but dead knots cause a larger strength reduction because, in these, the cambium layer is discontinuous and the knots tend to contract, often falling out of thin sections, such as boards. The effects of knots depends on their position in the section, being generally more serious in tensile areas than compression areas. The effect in bending is much more severe when knots are near to one edge of the timber. The difficulty of visually assessing the weakening effect of knots is one of the disadvantages of visual stress-grading of timber.

Stress grading of structural timber

The attractive properties of timber for structural purposes are high specific strength, ease of construction and finishing, aesthetically pleasing appearance and durability. These are offset to some extent by the variability of timber properties which require careful grading, combined with a statistical approach to obtain the best safe performance. Indeed, The Building Regulations now require stress-graded timber for structural applications, so that a significant proportion of timber is graded before use. There are two methods of grading; visual and mechanical.

Visual stress grading (*BS CP 112; BS 4987*)

A grade is ascribed to each piece of timber by measuring the size of knots and fissures, slope of grain and, in the case of softwoods, the spacing of growth rings. Grades are designated, using BSCP 112, by comparison with perfect ('basic') timber of the same species. The grades 75, 65, 50 and 40 are given accordingly. The stress-grading requirements for timber to be used in laminated beams are slightly different from those for other forms of structural timbers, since some types of defect will have different effects on the overall structure. BS CP 112, for example, does not give growth-ring requirements, although it is clear that no wane can be permitted for 'architectural' grades. Allowable maximum knot sizes are also rather less. Laminating grades LA, LB and LC are designated. In BS 4987, the grades 75, 65, 50 and 40 are replaced by two visual grades – 'General structural', GS, and 'Special structural', SS. These are judged to be approximately similar to grades 35 and 50 respectively, though the method of measurement of knots is rather different, being based on a 'Knot Area Ratio' KAR method (Fig. 5.20). As before, the timber beam sections are divided into centre half, and upper and lower quarters, but the area of knot in each cross-section is assessed instead of the surface dimensions only. Hence, a knot area ratio is established, the permissible value being reduced if the upper or lower quarters have more than half of their area occupied by knots.

Grading in this way may appear to be a time-consuming process but experienced labour can classify rapidly most timber specimens. Typical (long-term) stress values for a 'green' basic grade (perfect) softwood, such as pitch pine, are approximately $15\,\text{N/mm}^2$ in flexure or tension, $11\,\text{N/mm}^2$ in compression and $1.7\,\text{N/mm}^2$ in shear (parallel to grain). The term 'green' implies a moisture content of over 18 per cent. Moduli of elasticity are usually in the range 5 to $15\,\text{kN/mm}^2$. As might be expected of a material in which secondary bonds play

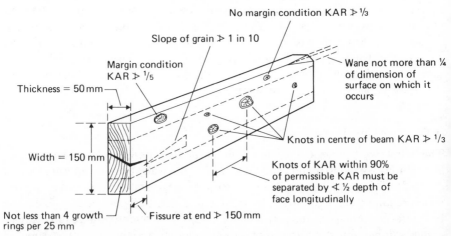

Fig. 5.20 Some aspects of the visual stress grading requirements of BS 4987 for Special Structural grade. There are further requirements relating to other types of fissure, distortion and abnormal defects.

an important part, the long-term strength of timber is considerably below its short-term strength. Reductions of 40 per cent or more are necessary on short-term test results for components which will be under sustained loads, quite apart from factors of safety introduced to take account of statistical variations and decay hazards.

Mechanical stress grading
A computer-controlled machine has been developed for this purpose, based on the good correlation which has been observed between the modulus of rupture and modulus of elasticity of timber. The regression equation:

Modulus of rupture $(N/mm^2) = 0.00413E + 7.6$

where E is the modulus of elasticity in N/mm^2, has been obtained from numerous tests. The method involves passing timber sections through rollers which apply a standard load, according to the section size, and then automatically measuring the deflection which depends, of course, on E. Any bowing in the timber is automatically allowed for. The process is repeated on each 150 mm length of the timber and the grade is automatically recorded by means of sprayed dyes. A long mark is sprayed at the end of each length, corresponding to the lowest grade for that length.

A visual check is carried out to ensure that grade requirements are met for wane, rot, fissures, insect attack and distortion. The mechanical method has the advantages that, unlike visual grading, the effect of density on strength and stiffness is automatically considered and the effect of knots is much more accurately assessed. The BS CP 112 machine grades are M75 and M50 and the BS 4987 grades are MSS and MGS, the M in all cases standing for 'Machine'. These grades, given in terms of decreasing strength and elastic modulus, are M75, MSS, M50 and MGS, MSS being only slightly better than M50. It is likely, in the long term, that mechanised grading will largely supersede visual grading on account of its speed and accuracy.

Decay of timber

Wood is inherently a highly durable material, the cellulose/lignin composite being unaffected by normal atmospheric conditions. Deterioration of wood results from enzyme action in the cellulose fibres, this being associated with living organisms, in the form of either fungi or insects. In each case, the cellulose reverts to glucose, which is used as food by the organism.

Fungal attack
Fungi grow from spores which are present in the air and which lie dormant in timber until conditions are suitable for growth. All fungi require a moisture content of at least 20 per cent to grow, since moisture is essential to permit the diffusion of enzymes into the wood to cause the break-down process and to permit

diffusion of the glucose back into the fungus after break-down. Fungi are rendered dormant by freezing temperatures and may be killed by high temperatures – perhaps over 40 °C. Temperatures within dwellings are normally ideal for growth. There are two major wood-rotting fungi – dry rot or 'serpula lacrymans', (formerly referred to as 'merulius lacrymans') and wet rot or 'coniophora puteana' (formerly referred to as 'coniophora cerebella).

Dry rot, the most serious form of attack, is so named because it leaves the wood in a dry, friable condition, usually characterised by breaking of the wood into small cubes. The fungus is propagated by spores which germinate, sending out branching strands, 'hyphae', spreading the attack and forming cotton-wool like patches, called mycelium. Hyphae may be able to draw moisture from adjoining damp materials such as brickwork and plaster which may also become infected. Finally, fleshy, fruiting bodies, the 'sporophore', are formed and these bear the red spores which propagate the fungus. Timber has little strength once attack has reached this advanced stage. Vulnerable situations include:

1. Roof members, if the roof is not fully waterproof, or near eaves.
2. Floor joists bearing on to solid walls.
3. Floor members in contact with concrete or when inadequately ventilated.

Remedial measures involve cutting away and burning all affected timber, including timber within 600 mm of visibly affected areas, which may contain hyphae. Timber should be replaced with suitably protected new timber. Existing unaffected timber should also be treated and, most important, the fault eradicated. It is often very difficult to eliminate dry rot which has grown into walls. Special types of plaster are, however, available to resist growth and further attack. The composition of these is usually complex, including zinc oxychloride, boric acid and ammonium chloride, with whiting (calcium carbonate) and sand as fillers. Problems of this type can be avoided in the first place by careful attention to roofing and flooring details, and ventilation. It is, in general, poor practice to allow timber to contact brick or concrete without some impervious separating membrane, particularly in solid walls or foundation concrete. Careful maintenance of roofing and guttering should avoid problems in roofing timbers. In timber-framed buildings, it is wise to treat all timber with preservative before construction and the use of an effective vapour barrier near to the internal side of the construction is essential. This prevents diffusion of water vapour from inside the building, where its pressure is often higher, into the structure where, on cooling, it could result in condensation. A *moisture barrier* should be provided externally to prevent rain penetration and yet allow small quantities of moisture in the structure to evaporate. In timber-framed flat roofs, it is unwise to enclose timber between an internal vapour barrier and the impervious bitumen coating unless adequate ventilation is ensured.

Wet rot thrives in wetter conditions than dry rot, the optimum moisture content being approximately 50 per cent. The obvious visible signs are softness and friability of timber, often beneath a relatively sound surface layer. In some cases, such as in window frames where wet rot is common, the first signs are often

Table 5.3 Some types of insect attack on seasoned timber

Beetle	Life cycle	Visual signs	Timber attacked
Common furniture (*Anobium punctatum*)	3–5 years Emergence, May–Aug.	Beetles 5 mm long, granular dust, $\frac{1}{2}$ mm diam. flight holes.	Sapwood of untreated hardwoods or softwoods.
House longhorn (*Hylotupes bajulus*)	3–11 years	A few large holes up to 10 mm, surface swelling, beetles 10–20 mm in length.	Sapwoods of softwoods (Surrey).
Death watch (*Xestobium rufovillosum*)	4–10 years. Emergence, March–June.	Large bun-shaped pellets, ticking during mating period, May–June.	Mainly hardwoods, especially if old or decayed.
Powder post beetle (*Lyctus* species)	1–2 years Emergence, June–Aug.	10 mm exit holes, fine dust.	Sapwood of wide-pored hardwoods, partly or recently seasoned.

undulation of the paint film rather than cracking. White mycellium may also be visible but fruiting bodies are uncommon. This form of rot is more easy to eradicate than dry rot: only visibly affected timber need be removed and eradication of the fault causing the dampness should cure the problem. Wet rot is, nevertheless, quite widespread in situations where faults lead to prolonged high moisture content.

Insect attack

There are a number of insects that attack newly-felled timber. However, seasoning usually eradicates these, so that the chief interest of the builder will be in insect attack in timber in use and, particularly, structural timber. Table 5.3 shows some common types of attack. Sapwood is most prone to attack, since the cells contain food and are of an open structure, though the latter also results in much better penetration of preservative into sapwood than heartwood. Affected timber is best removed, burned and replaced by adequately protected new timber. Brush treatment of existing unaffected timber may not eradicate the problem. The use of a pressure spray in flight holes will destroy most active beetles or larvae.

Preservatives for timber

Although some varieties of timber (for example, oak and cedar) are naturally very durable even when unprotected, most building timbers require protection unless kept dry, and future repair or replacements can be very difficult and expensive if fungal or insect attack gains a positive hold. The National House Building

Council now requires effective preservative treatment after machining of structural or externally-used timber. Timber should be protected in any situation in which the moisture content is likely to exceed about 20 per cent, where inspection or maintenance are not practicable or in areas where specific forms of attack, such as insect attack, are common. Preservatives should be toxic to fungi and insects, chemically stable, able to penetrate timber and non-aggressive to surrounding materials, particularly metals. There is a very wide range on the market, though basic properties are as given below.

Tar-oil preservatives
Creosotes are probably the best-known examples (BS 144). These are only suitable for external use, since they give rise to a noticeable colour and smell, and render timber unsuitable for painting. They are, however, cheap and can be applied on timber at a fairly high moisture content. They tend to creep into porous adjacent materials such as cement renderings and plaster.

Water-based preservatives (BS 3452, 3453, 4072)
These consist of salts based on metals, such as sodium, magnesium, zinc and copper, and also arsenic and boron. Copper-chrome-arsenate is a common example (BS 4072). They are very tolerant of moisture in the timber, are odourless, non-flammable, non-creeping and do not stain timber, which may be painted on drying out. However, swelling occurs on treatment, which may be a disadvantage in some situations. Drying out may take some time and corrosion of metals in contact with treated timber may occur during this period. Although some types combine chemically to some degree with the wood, these preservatives are not generally suitable for external use, since there is a tendency to leach out. They are, however, relatively cheap and are widely used for the preservation of joinery and structural timber used in construction.

Organic-solvent preservatives
Typical examples are chloronaphthalenes, metallic naphthenates and pentachlorophenol (BS 5707). Penetration is excellent provided timber is fairly dry, hence, they are often preferred where only brush or spray application is feasible. They are non-creeping, non-staining and quite suitable for brush application: they do not corrode metal and may be painted over later. Some of the solvents are, however, flammable, so that fire risk is increased until timber has dried out. On account of the organic solvents used in them, they are generally more expensive than the other types. They are widely used in joinery after fabrication, in renovation work and for in-situ treatment in buildings.

Application methods
These are described in order of decreasing effectiveness. Pressure methods give greatest penetration. In the 'full cell' method, the timber is first evacuated so that preservative is drawn into the cells, this being effective but rather wasteful. The empty-cell method involves first pressurising the timber then injecting the

preservative at greater pressure and, finally, releasing the pressure, causing cells to eject excess preservative. In the hot-and-cold-tank treatment, the timber is heated to about 85 °C in the preservative, drawing in more preservative on cooling. The effectiveness depends on the duration of steeping. Dipping usually implies that the timber is submerged for a few minutes only. Brushing and spraying are possible in situ but are not as effective as the above methods. Repeated application will, to some extent, improve protection. A rather different approach – 'Timborising' – has been used in which newly-felled green timber is dipped into a boron compound, diffusion then taking place over a period of time, so that protection to the body of timber is obtained. This type of treatment and the pressure method are the only ones which give adequate penetration of preservative. Incising – the cutting of fine slots to a depth of about 20 mm – may be necessary for adequate penetration of low-permeability timbers, such as Douglas fir.

Timber and wood products

Recent years have seen an enormous increase in the variety of products, mainly on account of advances in mechanised techniques and the introduction of synthetic-resin binders. As a result, wastage of timber is minimised and many products are quite cheap. The following are important in building, properties of each being controlled by British Standard Specifications.

Fibre building boards (BS 1142)

These are produced by pulverising of wood down to individual fibres and then compressing them to form large sheets. Small percentages of adhesive – usually phenolic – may be used to act as a binder though fibres have inherent adhesive properties and are, to some degree, self-binding. Several different types of product are obtained, according to the degree of compression of the fibres. BS 1142 classifies fibre building boards as hardboard, medium board and softboard, according to density.

Hardboards have a density of over $800 \, \text{kg/m}^3$, being fully compressed and normally having one smooth side, the other side having a mesh texture. Thicknesses are in the range 3.2 to 6.4 mm and flexural strengths are quite high, over $45 \, \text{N/mm}^2$. Standard hardboards are susceptible to moisture and should be conditioned by application of water to the mesh side before use. This ensures that, in conditions of service, the sheets are under tensile rather than compressive stress. Prolonged dampness will cause irreversible swelling and strength loss in standard hardboards. These boards, nevertheless, find wide application in dry situations, being used in internal flush doors, built-in units, partitions and in flooring beneath sheet or tile coverings. Tempered hardboard, having a density over $960 \, \text{kg/m}^3$, may be used in damp situations, finding application in roofing soffits and external claddings.

Medium boards have densities in the range 350 to $800 \, \text{kg/m}^3$, being subdivided into high and low density sub-groups. These may have a variety of finishes, and are used in partitions and wall linings in thicknesses of 6 to 12 mm. They can also be used as an intermediate sound-absorbent layer on concrete or timber floors.

Insulation boards have lowest density, below $350\,kg/m^3$, with a thermal conductivity in the region of $0.05\,W/m^2\,°C$. They, therefore, contribute considerably to thermal insulation when used as ceilings, sarking and sheathing. The latter would normally be bitumen-impregnated to improve moisture resistance. Standard thicknesses are 13, 19 and 25.4 mm. Various finishes are available when used for wall and ceiling linings, and they can be treated similarly to plasterboard, either used 'dry' or given a skim coat of plaster. Alternatively, they may be papered direct, provided a hardboard primer is first applied. A further use of insulating boards is to accommodate irregularities in sub-floors, though a further covering such as hardboard would, of course, be necessary to provide mechanical protection. All boards, especially the lower-density varieties, are susceptible to fire, though surface spread of flame can be reduced by the use of fire retardents.

Particle boards (chipboards) to BS 5669

These consist of small particles or splinters of wood, bonded together with synthetic resins, the resin normally occupying about 8 per cent by weight of the dry board. Fibres are usually randomly orientated, parallel to the plane of the board, and the wood chips are graded, with coarser chips at the centre of the board. The strength and moisture resistance of chipboards depends greatly on the type of adhesive used. Those based on urea formaldehyde lose about 60 per cent of their strength and increase in thickness by about 10 per cent on wetting. Recovery does not occur on drying, hence, such chipboards must be kept dry during use. Melamine-formaldehyde/urea-formaldehyde mixtures or phenol formaldehyde adhesives give much lower strength reduction and expansion on wetting and show recovery on drying. BS 5669 classifies chipboards as:

Type I   – Standard
Type II   – Flooring
Type III – Improved moisture resistance

Chipboard is now very widely used in flooring, although Type II is recommended, the 20 mm thickness having a flexural strength of at least $17\,N/mm^2$ compared to $12.5\,N/mm^2$ for Type I chipboard. Where there is the possibility of dampness Type II/III should be used, which combines the properties of both types. In addition to the problems of strength loss and swelling of non-moisture-resistant types, damp chipboard is vulnerable to fungal attack. Adequate support must be given to chipboard, since creep appears to be greater than in solid timber. Other uses include sarking and roof decking, although the above comments concerning moisture still apply. The material may also be used for shuttering for concrete provided the surface is sealed before use. Chipboard is not as easy to fix with nails as solid timber and should be predrilled before screwing. Edges are subject to damage by impact or abrasion during handling. Chipboard, nevertheless, offers significant economic advantages over solid timber boarding in respect of both materials and fixing for the applications given above.

Plywood (BS 1455)
Plywood consists of glued wood panels comprising outer and inner sheets, the grains in adjacent sheets being at right angles. An odd number of plies is normally used, since this enables symmetrical distribution of plies about the centre sheet. Hence, if the moisture content changes, equal and opposite bending effects occur, due to differential movement of symmetrically opposed sheets. As a result, plywood can be used in situations with variable moisture content with minimum distortion. Sheets behave more isotropically in the plane of the sheet than solid timber and, although flexural strength is not as high as in a solid timber sheet loaded parallel to the grain, it is much greater than a solid timber loaded across the grain. Sheets can also be much larger than would be available in solid timber. The flexural strength and stability of plywood increase with the number of plies. Also, since the glue-lines restrain surface cracking due to the stresses imposed by moisture changes, there is a limit to the thickness of surface plies that can be used. In order to achieve greatest flexural strength, the face grain should be parallel to the span, especially if a small number of plies is used.

The working properties of plywood are similar to those of ordinary timber, though it can be nailed or screwed without risk of splitting, since there are no cleavage planes. Impact strengths are much better than those of ordinary timber, for the same reason. Performance standards for plywood tend to be rather complicated, since they are often those of the country from which they are imported, but colour codes are now quite commonly used, as they are for other timber products.

When used decoratively, the surface veneers are usually of hardwood. BS 1455 gives three grades – grade 1 indicating knot- and defect-free veneers, jointed at the centre, if at all. Where painting is anticipated, grade 2 veneers are suitable. These, though flat, may be jointed and contain sound knots, fine splits or repairs in the form of smooth inserts. Grade 3 plywoods are used when appearance is unimportant. The above requirements may be applied to either or both faces. Most plywoods have a characteristic figure in surface veneers resulting from the method of producing them, which involves rotary cutting from the log.

Plywoods are also very widely used for cladding, as formwork for concrete and for structural purposes.

Blockboard (BS 3444)
This consists of strips of wood, between 7 and 25 mm wide, glued together and sandwiched between veneers. The grain of the veneers is at right angles to that of the strips. When long sheets are required, the strips normally run parallel to length and, in addition to the veneers already described, further veneers are included with outer sheets having grain parallel to the long axis. These boards are

285

generally suitable for internal purposes only. Blockboards are widely used in furniture, for interior doors and for shelving.

Laminboard (BS 3444)

This is similar to blockboard, except that the strips are less than 7 mm in width. As a result, strength and stability are improved. Both laminboard and blockboard are broadly referred to as 'plywoods'.

Jointing methods for timber

Traditionally, nails, wood screws and bolts have been used, the strength of joints so obtained increasing in that order. In the case of wood screws, undersized holes are necessary to minimise danger of splitting and, if joints are subject to bending, hardened types will give a stronger joint than mild steel. Bolts (and to some extent, screws) enable transfer of load by friction between wood components, although, on account of the low compressive strength of timber, load-spreading washers are essential. More recently, gusset plates have been introduced, highly suited to quantity production of roof trusses, provided timbers are of consistent thickness at joints. Galvanising is essential for long life. The strongest joints are obtained by the use of timber connectors. These either have teeth to grip both pieces of timber or incorporate rings which fit into pre-cut grooves. Bolting of timbers together then gives great shear strength. Adhesives are, of course, also important: these are described under that heading.

Laminated timber (BS 4169)

This form of construction is by no means new, though it is only recently, with the advent of high-strength adhesives, that its full potential has been realised. The high strength/weight ratio of timber and the ease with which virtually any shape can be produced are the chief reasons behind the success of laminated timber. In fact, the material is highly competitive with steel where larger spans under moderate load are required, as in roofing. Spans of over 100 m have been obtained.

Timber may be laminated vertically (that is, in the plane of bending) or horizontally (at right angles to the plane of bending), see Fig. 5.21. The former have been shown to give higher strength, though application is limited to beams of constant section. Horizontal laminations have the advantages that weaker grades of timber can be located at the centre of beams where stresses are likely to be lower. The allowable stresses in horizontally-laminated timber are, in general, slightly lower than those in solid, perfect timber, so that the chief advantage is gained when the finished laminate is much larger than could be produced from a single piece. Strength increases with the number of laminations for a member of a given section, though costs also increase and wastage of timber in planing is such that there is little point in using a large number of very thin laminates.

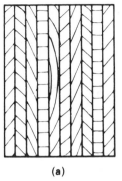
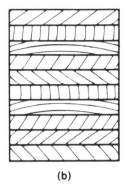

(a)　　　　　　　　　　　　　　　　　**(b)**

Fig. 5.21 Sections through a laminated timber beam: (a) Vertically laminated; (b) Horizontally laminated

Thicknesses in the region of 20 mm are usually satisfactory, though smaller values may be necessary when tight bends are required. Joints are normally required to be spaced by at least 24 times the laminate thickness: finger joints are now considered to be most satisfactory. If beams or arches taper, best performance is obtained by tapering internal rather than external members. Units are coated with glue and then pressed together so that excess glue is expelled. Radio-frequency treatment enables curing to be carried out very rapidly.

Other forms of timber construction

Developing parallel to space frames in steel construction have been three-dimensional roof structures in timber, with essentially similar properties, allowing large spans to be used on account of their low weight and high rigidity. Alternatively, rigidity can be achieved from the shape of the roof itself, as in hyperbolic paraboloid types.

One of the most important timber products in modern building construction is plywood. If laminates are fixed on to a simple timber frame, they impart great rigidity and strength, in fact, carrying the bulk of the load. This is known as 'stressed-skin construction' and is widely used in the fabrication of beams ('box beams'), in roofing and for the frames of complete structures, such as houses, and even multi-storey blocks of flats. Although such structures have been extremely successful, it is important to allow for the likelihood of higher movement, especially during and immediately after construction, compared to other materials. If construction is carried out in wet weather, considerable shrinkage will result and this should be allowed to occur before finishes are applied. Finishes should also be capable of a certain degree of movement if unsightly cracking is to be avoided. Completely 'dry' finishes are in this respect better than more traditional finishes. Sound insulation between timber-framed dwellings and flats might be considered a problem but, by careful design, detailing and construction involving floating floors, structurally independent composite party walls and insulating materials, the grade 1 sound-insulation standard can be achieved.

Thermal properties and fire-resistance of timber

The thermal conductivity of timber is low, varying from approximately 0.12 W/m °C for softwood to 0.16 W/m °C for some hardwoods. As a result, heat losses through the material are small (though this has, in the past, caused pattern-staining in otherwise uninsulated roof structures) and timber resists the formation of condensation better then metals. The same property is responsible for the relatively good performance of timber in serious fire. 'Burning' of wood occurs due to ignition of flammable gases, which are given off when the temperature of the material exceeds about 300 °C. On burning, charcoal is produced which, though of little strength, is valuable in reducing heat flow to underlying wood. Charcoal itself, however, burns at a temperature over 500 °C so that, in a severe fire, charring and, hence, strength reduction, take place at an approximately linear rate, generally considered to be 0.64 mm/minute for flat surfaces of softwoods and medium-density hardwoods. When the fire encroaches from all sides of a member, as for example, in columns, the rate may be slightly higher. The design stresses of BS CP 112 allow a substantial margin – approximately 2.25 – between design and failure, so that the durability of a beam in fire is often quite large, being the time taken for charring to reach the stage at which, on account of the decreasing cross-sectional area, failure stresses are reached. It is found that laminated beams, which are usually bonded with the WBP adhesives phenol or resorcinol formaldehydes, have fire-resistance similar to that of solid timber of the same dimensions. Metal connectors, on the other hand, greatly accelerate destruction and are a potential hazard in roof structures unless protected. Plywood box beams are also less fire-resistant than laminated or solid timber, since the thickness of wood is usually smaller. Although timber floors might also be considered unsatisfactory, the normal first-floor construction in houses has usually quite good fire-resistance, largely due to its enclosed nature and the underlying plaster ceiling. In this respect, however, plywood is better than tongue-and-groove boards, which are better than flush boards, since a large number of joints or gaps increases ventilation. In timber-framed buildings, satisfactory fire-resistance can be achieved by use of plasterboard on walls and ceilings, though firestops are also necessary in wall structures containing large vertical cavities.

A number of fire-retardant preparations are available. Some types impregnate the timber, increasing the proportion of charcoal and decreasing combustible gases in a fire. This treatment is carried out on seasoned timber cut to its final size. Typical chemicals include aqueous solutions of monammonium phosphate, borax and ammonium chloride, and preservatives are often included. Alternatively, intumescent paints, varnishes or pastes may be used. These form protective films under the action of fire, preventing access of oxygen. Fire retardants are valuable in reducing surface spread of flame in cladding materials and partitions.

Class 1 performance under BS 476, Part 7 can be obtained (Class 3, untreated). Charring rates are, however, not greatly reduced and the best protection against structural failure is the provision of extra (sacrificial) timber to protect underlying material.

Problems

5.1 Compare and explain the reasons for differences/similarities in the properties of polyethylene and polypropylene at various temperatures.

5.2 Classify as thermoplastic/thermosetting and write notes on:
polyvinyl chloride
phenol-formaldehyde polymers
polyvinyl acetate
polymethyl methacrylate.

5.3 What are the problems/advantages in the use of plastics for hot-water services? Indicate suitable plastics and precautions that would be necessary in design and installation.

5.4 Discuss the likely future of plastics materials in building under the headings:
(a) structural
(b) services
(c) finishes.

5.5 Describe the chief mechanisms by which adhesives bond to materials. Indicate the limitations of each and give illustrations.

5.6 Suggest the requirements of adhesives which would be used to join:
(a) glass to glass for stained glass windows
(b) phenolic-based laminated to particle board
(c) decorative panelling to brickwork background
(d) new to old concrete
(e) two lengths of PVC.

5.7 By what possible mechanisms can paint harden? Give examples and advantages or disadvantages of each type of paint.

5.8 What considerations dictate the flexibility of sealant required for a given situation? Give illustrations and, in the case of elastomeric sealants, indicate any other requirements necessary for a satisfactory joint.

5.9 Give the chief reasons for seasoning timber and explain why installed timber should be of moisture content approximately equal to its final equilibrium value. In what situations is this particularly important? What steps should be taken to ensure that such timber satisfies this condition?

5.10 Explain why the properties of timber, such as moisture movement and strength, are directional. How are these properties affected in:
(a) fibre building boards
(b) chipboard
(c) plywood.

5.11 Compare timber and steel in respect of:
(a) strength/weight ratio
(b) durability

(c) fire-resistance

(d) aesthetics.

Hence, suggest in what situations they are likely to be used for structural purposes.

5.12 A timber beam of section 200 mm × 300 mm is exposed to fire on its soffit and faces. If charring occurs at a rate of 0.64 mm/minute and the beam was initially under its design load with a factor of safety of 2.25, predict whether or not a fire-resistance of 1 hour will be obtained.

References

1. J. A. Brydson, *Plastics Materials*. Iliffe, 1970
2. P. Reboul and R. G. Bruce Mitchell. *Plastics in the Building Industry*. Newnes, 1968
3. R. Houwink and G. Salomon, *Adhesion and Adhesives*. Elsevier, 1965
4. P. M. Fisk, *Advanced Paint Chemistry*. Leonard Books, 1961
5. P. M. Fisk, *The Physical Chemistry of Paints*. Leonard Books, 1963
6. *Introduction to Paint Technology*. Oil and Colour Chemists' Association
7. H. E. Desch, *Timber, its structure and Properties*. Macmillan, 1968
8. E. Levin, *Wood in Building*. The Architectural Press, 1971
9. C. R. Coggins, *Decay of Timber in Buildings*. Rentokil Ltd, 1980

Relevant British Standards

BS 144: 1973. *Coal tar creosote for the preservation of timber.*

BS 373: 1957. *Testing small, clear specimens of timber.*

BS 476: Parts 3–8. *Fire tests on building materials and structures.*

BS 745: 1969. *Animal glue for wood.*

BS 747: 1977 *Specification for roofing felts.*

BS 988, 1076 1097 1451: 1973. *Mastic asphalt for building (limestone aggregate).*

BS 1142: Parts 1–3. *Fibre building boards.*

BS 1203: 1979 *Specification for synthetic resin adhesives (phenolic and aminoplastic for plywood).*

BS 1204: *Synthetic resin adhesives (phenolic and aminoplastic for wood).* Part 1: 1979 *Gap-filling adhesives.* Part 2: 1979 *Close contact adhesives.*

BS 1282: 1975. *Guide to the choice, use and application of wood preservatives.*

BS 1444: 1970. *Cold setting casein adhesive powders for wood.*

BS 1455: 1972. *Plywood manufactured from tropical hardwoods.*

BS 2592: 1973. *Thermoplastic flooring tiles.*

BS 2782: Parts 1–10. *Methods of testing plastics.*

BS 3444: 1972. *Blockboard and laminboard.*

BS 3452: 1962. *Copper/chrome water-borne wood preservatives and their application.*

BS 3453: 1962 (1979) *Fluoride/arsenate/chromate/dinitrophenol water-borne wood preservatives and their application.*

BS 3712: Parts 1–3. *Methods of test for building sealants.*

BS 4072: 1974 *Wood preservation by means of water-borne copper/chrome/arsenic compositions.*

BS 4169: 1970 *Glued-laminated timber structural members.*

BS 4254: 1967 *Two-part polysulphide-based sealants for the building industry.*
BS 4735: 1974. *Assessment of horizontal burning characteristics of cellular plastics and rubbers when subject to a small flame.*
BS 4756: 1971. *Ready-mixed aluminium priming paints for woodwork.*
BS 4978: 1973 *Timber grades for structural use.*
BS 5082: 1974 *Water-thinned priming paints for wood.*
BS 5669: 1979 *Specification for wood chipboard and methods of test for particle board.*
BS 5707: Parts 1–3. *Solutions of wood preservatives in organic solvents.*
BS 5889: 1980. *Specification for silicone based building sealants.*
BS CP 112: Parts 2 & 3. *The structural use of timber.*

Chapter 6

Fibre-reinforced materials

Introduction

This chapter is devoted to fibrous composites developed relatively recently and, in addition, a brief description of resin cements is given.

The materials discussed to this point are divided into three main groups, the properties of which may be summarised under the following headings.

Ceramics
On a volume basis, these are the cheapest materials. They have high compressive strength and are very rigid. They can be formed, using cements, into large structures of complex shape. They are, however, brittle and exhibit low tensile strength on account of microscopic cracks which are usually present in them. Hence they cannot withstand, unassisted, large tensile, flexural or impact loads. Chemically, they are relatively stable. They have low thermal movement but, since many ceramics are porous, they are subject to moisture movement and moisture-associated deterioration.

Metals
The higher-strength metals have the highest modulus of elasticity and tensile strength of any commonly-used building material, though they also have high density. They are, at present, a most important structural material, being the only group which will withstand satisfactorily high tensile stresses. They are also formable, though heavy sections or castings require high manufacturing temperatures, while lighter sections, such as sheet or strip, can often be worked at ordinary temperatures – these properties result in widespread uses for pressed or craftsman-formed components. Metals are generally the most prone of the three groups to atmospheric attack. They are costly.

Organic materials
Plastics, the chief synthetic organic materials, are characterised by low modulus of elasticity, variable ductility and moderate tensile properties. They soften at relatively low temperatures but are resistant to many chemicals and to attack by moisture. They are extremely versatile and, within the general limits given above,

292

can be modified to suit specific requirements. On a cost basis, they are becoming increasingly competitive with other materials.

The shortcomings, as well as the chief attributes of the three major groups, are evident. Regarding chemical or atmospheric instability, it has been possible by means of a study of the nature of degradation or attack, to select materials according to the situation required, or to modify or protect them if the environment is potentially harmful. As regards mechanical properties, there are perhaps three major problem areas which restrict the use of certain materials:

1. The low tensile strength of most ceramics
2. The brittleness of most ceramics
3. The low elastic modulus of those plastics which are sufficiently ductile to be viable for structural uses

Although research is continually taking place into ways of improving metals, it may be said that the above problems have given rise to the most urgent investigations, with the result that a number of new materials have been developed which are certain, in the future, to find increasing application in construction.

It would appear that ceramics and plastics could be regarded as opposite groups of materials, in the sense that one is rigid and brittle, while the other is ductile and tough. Two chief methods of overcoming the disadvantages of ceramics have been undertaken – fibre reinforcement and the incorporation of resinous materials. The former technique is by no means new: lime plasters were traditionally reinforced with horse-hair, while the use of reinforcement in concrete is fundamental to its use in almost all situations. Fibre reinforcement may also be used, in certain cases, to overcome the problem of the low elastic modulus of plastics. The principles of the use of fibres are discussed first, followed by types of available fibre and typical applications.

Principles of fibre reinforcement

These are elucidated by a consideration of the effect of incorporation of fibres upon the three properties listed above, that is, tensile strength, impact strength and elastic modulus. In each case, it is borne in mind the type of material to which, in practice, the technique might be applied. The following notation is used:

Symbols f and E stand for stress and elastic modulus, respectively. There are two suffixes for each symbol: in the first, f stands for fibre, m for matrix and c for composite. In the second, t stands for tension, c for compression and s for sheer. The symbol V denotes volume fraction (one suffix only). Hence, for example:

E_{ct} denotes elastic modulus of composite in tension

V_f denotes volume fraction of fibres.

Tensile strength

There are two quite distinct mechanisms by which incorporation of fibres could improve the tensile strength of materials such as concrete. The first involves the fibres themselves carrying a substantial proportion of the stress, such that the matrix remains within its tensile stress capacity while the composite carries a relatively high stress. The second produces a similar effect to that in conventional reinforced concrete, though on a smaller scale, that is, the fibres do not prevent cracking but they enable relatively high tensile stresses to be carried by control of cracking in the matrix, crack interfaces being held together by the fibres. These two techniques are considered in turn:

(a) Increasing pre-cracked strength
This requires that fibre and matrix be rigidly bonded, there being no relative movement between them. The stress carried by the composite can only exceed that carried by the matrix if the fibres have greater stiffness than the matrix, so that, for a given strain, the fibres are more highly stressed than the latter.

If fibres are parallel to the direction of stress, the tensile stress in the composite f_{ct} is given by the expression:

$$f_{ct} = f_{ft} \cdot V_f + f_{mt}(1 - V_f) \tag{6.1}$$

The stress in the fibres f_{ft} will be $f_{mt} \cdot (E_{ft}/E_{ct})$, hence, to maximise composite strength, the ratio E_{ft}/E_{ct}, together with the value of V_f, needs to be as large as possible.

This mechanism is not very suitable for increasing the pre-cracked strength of normally mixed concrete, since it is difficult to incorporate large-volume fractions of fibres in conventional mixing. Some increase in strength may, however, be obtainable.

Take, for example,

$f_{mt} = 3\,\text{N/mm}^2$ (tensile strength of concrete)
$E_{mt} = 30\,\text{kN/mm}^2$
$E_{ft} = 210\,\text{kN/mm}^2$ (steel fibres)
$V_{ft} = 0.02$ (conventional mixing).

The stress in the steel fibres is:

$$f_{ft} = f_{mt} \cdot \frac{E_{ft}}{E_{ct}} = 3 \times \frac{210}{30} = 21\,\text{N/mm}^2$$

hence, the tensile strength of the composite is:

$f_{ct} = 21 \times 0.02 + 3 \times 0.98$
$= 3.36\,\text{N/mm}^2$.

Such an increase would not normally justify the expense of adding fibres and the steel fibres in this situation are also under-utilised – they carry a maximum stress of $21\,\text{N/mm}^2$, which is very much lower than their yield stress (the order of

$1000\,\text{N/mm}^2$). The f_{ct} value given above is also a maximum, since smaller increases would be obtained if fibres were not fully aligned with the stress or if there were bond failure between fibre and matrix. It will be appreciated that the applications of this method of pre-cracked strength improvement are limited.

(b) Increasing post-cracked strength
This may be illustrated by considering a simplified arrangement of a single long fibre embedded in a cylinder of matrix (Fig. 6.1) Load/strain diagrams are used rather than stress/strain diagrams, since, unlike stresses:

Load in composite = Load in matrix + Load in fibres.

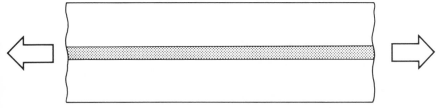

Fig. 6.1 Single continuous fibre in a brittle matrix. Load is applied to the fibre and matrix

Fibre and matrix, separately, might have load/strain curves as shown in Figs. 6.2(a) and (b), respectively. The gradient of a load/strain diagram will be dependent on the area of cross-section of the specimen. Supposing, for example, matrix and fibre are to be of similar stiffness, the ratio of the gradients in Figs. 6.2(a) and (b) would be in the ratio of their cross-sectional areas. The former graph is steeper than the latter, since fibres normally form a small volume fraction and do not usually contribute the major part of stiffness. Figure 6.2(b) indicates much larger strains in the fibre before failure than occur in the matrix. On

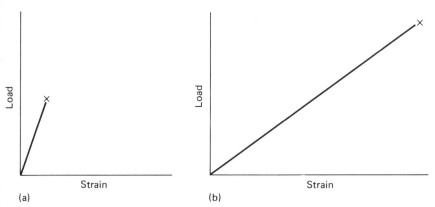

Fig. 6.2 (a) Load/strain relationship for the matrix part of the composite shown in Fig. 6.1; (b) Load/strain relationship for the fibre part of the composite shown in Fig. 6.1

295

combining the fibre and the matrix, the load/strain curve would change as follows:

The initial gradient of the curve would be equal to the sum of the individual gradients (Fig. 6.3), since, at a given strain, each part would carry loads as before and the total load would be the sum of these. It will be supposed, initially, that E values are equal, so that there will be no shear force on the fibre/matrix interface. At the same strain as previously, the ceramic will crack. The form of the remainder of the stress/strain curve will depend on the extent and type of bonding between fibre and matrix.

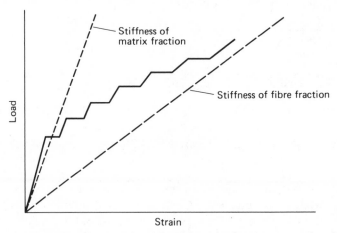

Fig. 6.3 Possible load/strain relationship for the composite shown in Fig. 6.1. The initial gradient is equal to the sum of the gradients in Fig. 6.2(a) and (b)

If there were no bonding, then the matrix would pull off the fibre – hence, the fibre would be of no use unless the fibre were itself attached to the testing machine and this, in practice, is unlikely.

If the fibre were bonded to the matrix then, when the first crack forms, there would be a slight, sudden extension as the fibre at the point of cracking takes all the load. Figure 6.4 shows the stresses/forces likely to result in the fibre around the cracked area. The surface shear stress in the exposed region is zero (Fig. 6.4(b)) and, assuming a degree of 'pull-out' has occurred, would increase to some roughly constant value caused by friction in the slipped regions each side of the crack. At the first point, where the fibre matrix bond remains intact, the shear stress would rise to a maximum value, subsequently falling off to zero towards the fibre ends. The tensile load in the fibre (Fig. 6.4(c)) is obtained by integrating the surface shear stress with respect to fibre surface area, moving towards the crack. This load is clearly a maximum at the crack and equal to the former tensile load of the composite. The tensile load in the matrix is, at any point, equal to the difference between total load and fibre load (Fig. 6.4(d)).

The remainder of the stress/strain diagram can now be considered (Fig. 6.3). The first crack corresponds to a short horizontal line representing the instan-

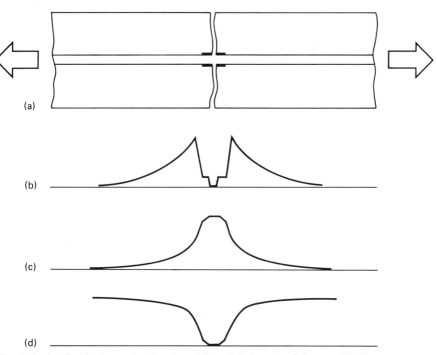

Fig. 6.4 (a) Cracked matrix showing debonded length of fibre; (b) Shear stress on fibre; (c) Tensile load in fibre; (d) Tensile load in matrix

taneous increase of strain which occurs as the fibre stretches to carry the total load at the point of cracking. Assuming that the first crack occurred at the weakest point in the matrix, the load can now be increased until the next weakest part cracks, giving a further step. The process then repeats until there is a regular pattern of cracks, each crack reducing the tensile stress in the matrix at that position to a value below its tensile strength. If the matrix became useless due to extended cracking, the gradient of the load/strain diagram would approach a value corresponding to the stiffness of the fibre component, assuming the fibre was effectively anchored at its ends. In practice, however, the matrix should support some proportion of the load, due to shear/friction with the fibres, so that the line of Fig. 6.3 corresponding to fibre stiffness would represent the minimum gradient possible. The detailed load/strain relationship will depend on a number of parameters relating to the fibre and matrix as follows (it is assumed, for the moment, that a single continuous fibre is employed and that changes in properties described below can be achieved independently).

(i) Volume fraction of fibre. A high volume fraction gives greater post-cracking load and smaller crack width, since the fibre would extend less in order to carry the additional load caused by cracking. The gradient of the last part of the load/strain diagram would also rise.

(ii) Elastic modulus of fibre. A high E value would have an effect similar to using a high fibre volume fraction (although, in practice, it would increase the probability of fibre pull-out).

(iii) Bond between fibre and matrix. A high bond strength would again reduce crack widths, thereby causing more frequent cracking: hence, the steps of Fig. 6.3 would become smaller but more numerous.

(iv) Strength variation within matrix. If the matrix material were completely uniform, all parts of the matrix would reach their failure stress at the same time and this would cause a more sudden change of gradient on first cracking. In practice, however, there are natural strength variations in the matrix material, weak points cracking first. The rate of change of slope of the load/strain diagram on cracking should, therefore, give an indication of the extent of local variations in the matrix material (or of alternative causes of stress variation in different parts of the matrix).

(v) Fibre strength. Increasing the strength of continuous fibres will increase the length of the final part of load/strain graph, thereby increasing ductility prior to failure (assuming bond failure does not occur). The fibre strength required, in practice, will depend on the post-cracking characteristics required as well as on the volume fraction and bonding properties with the particular matrix used.

Consideration must finally be given to fibres of finite length and to the effect of randomly orientated fibres.

The possibility of 'pull-out' clearly increases as fibres become shorter. Consider a fibre of length l and diameter d, subject to a surface shear stress f_{fs}, which, for simplicity, is supposed to be uniform, along half its length. The fibre is best utilised if its length is sufficient to enable the shear force to develop a stress equal to the tensile strength of the fibre f_{ft}. Hence, if the fibre has diameter d:

$$f_{fs} \cdot \pi d \frac{l}{2} = \pi \frac{d^2}{4} \cdot f_{ft}$$

$$\text{or} \quad l = \frac{d f_{ft}}{2 f_{fs}}$$

$$\text{or} \quad \frac{l}{d} = \frac{f_{ft}}{2 f_{fs}} \tag{6.2}$$

The ratio l/d is known as the *aspect ratio* and it is simply related to the ratio of fibre tensile strength to fibre bond strength. A great deal of fibre technology hinges on this simple equation; if a fibre has a high tensile strength – for example, steel – then either a high bond strength would be required to avoid pull-out well before f_{ft} is reached or fibres of high aspect ratios would be required. Steel fibres have, in fact, a failure (yield) stress in the region of $1000 \, \text{N/mm}^2$, whereas the effective bonding strength to concrete is only about $3 \, \text{N/mm}^2$. Efficient use of such fibres in concrete, therefore, requires aspect ratios of at least $160 - 40 \, \text{mm}$ fibres would require a diameter of approximately $0.25 \, \text{mm}$, which may tend to cause buckling of fibres during mixing. If a certain minimum fibre diameter is considered practicable, then a minimum fibre length, known as the critical fibre length, is required to ensure that the full tensile capacity of the fibre can be utilised. The problem of bond becomes greater as fibres become stronger – carbon fibres have strengths of over $2000 \, \text{N/mm}^2$ – so that very high bond strength or very thin fibres are necessary to utilise this strength.

From the point of view of the composite, short fibres produce an additional problem, since across any one crack there will be a substantial proportion of fibres embedded to a length less than $l/2$ on one side and more than $l/2$ on the other side. The former ends would, therefore, tend to pull out, even if the aspect ratio were theoretically adequate. A reduction in failure load to about half that obtained with long fibres will be obtained in this way when the aspect ratio is just sufficient, as defined above. The reduction is greater when shorter fibres are used or if fibres are not aligned with the stress. For this reason, either aspect ratios higher than that given by the above equation would be necessary, or a higher volume fraction of fibres to compensate for pull-out of a proportion of them.

As regards fibre orientation, fibres will work most efficiently when aligned parallel to the stress direction. There are often difficulties in achieving this, however, and there are also instances where random fibre orientation is necessary to provide post-cracking strength in more than one direction. Experiments have shown that, where fibres are only orientated in a plane, their efficiency in any one direction in the plane is approximately one-third of that of fibres which are fully aligned in that direction. Where fibres are randomly orientated in three dimensions, this factor falls to about one-sixth, the material then behaving isotropically.

A simple expression for post-cracked strength is the first part of the earlier expressed for pre-cracked strength.

$$f_{ct} = f_{ft} \cdot v_f \tag{6.3}$$

This applies to long fibres which are fully aligned with the stress. Values of f_{ct} will be reduced, as explained above, when short and/or randomly arranged fibres are employed. A further requirement emerging from this equation is that there will be a 'critical' volume fraction of fibres required if the fibres alone are to carry the load supported by both fibre and matrix before cracking.

Flexural behaviour

It is shown in Chapter 3 that, although failure in flexure in ceramics is initiated by tensile failure of extreme 'fibres', flexural stresses calculated from application of simple bending theory to failure loads are substantially in excess of direct tension test reults. This is explained as being, at least, partly due to upward movement of the neutral axis during testing. The principle applies in the post-cracking behaviour of flexural specimens and it is found, in addition, that the distribution of stress in the enlarged tensile region is much more uniform than the stress distribution in an uncracked specimen. Figure 6.5 shows a simplified stress

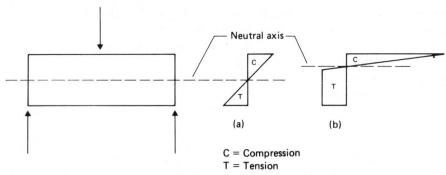

C = Compression
T = Tension

Fig. 6.5 Possible stress distributions in rectangular section beam due to bending: (a) Assumed distribution in calculating modulus of rupture; (b) Simplified representation of stress distribution in fibrous composite at failure. For a given tensile failure stress, distribution (b) gives a much increased failure load

distribution across a cracked beam compared to the distribution used in ordinary bending theory. The tensile region is found to occupy about three-quarters of the beam section. The result of these effects is that, unless the compressive strength of the composite is unusually low, (say, less than five times the tensile strength), the critical fibre volume fraction is reduced compared to direct tension, and the post-cracked flexural strength, as calculated using bending theory, is considerably greater than the strength given by equation 6.3. The maximum increase is three times for movement of the neutral axis to the upper surface of the beam but, in practice, increases of about twice are more usual. Flexural strength will, in common with tensile strength, be reduced when short or randomly arranged fibres are employed.

Elastic modulus

Elastic modulus must also be considered in the pre and post-cracked conditions and, in each case, formulae similar to those employed for tensile strength can be used.

The value corresponding to the pre-cracked state is, for example, given by:

$$E_{ct} = E_{ft}V_f + E_{mt}(1 - V_f) \qquad (6.4)$$

for long fibres orientated parallel to the stress (compare with equation 6.1). The elastic modulus corresponding to multiple cracking is given by

$$E_{ct} = E_{ft}V_f \qquad (6.5)$$

for the same situation and this is similar to equation 6.3.

The contribution of fibres to stiffness represented by $E_{ft}V_f$ in each of the above equations will, of course, be reduced when there is a degree of randomness in orientation. Reduction factors similar to those given above should be applied to the fibre to give the elastic modulus in such cases. The value of E_{ct} in equation 6.5 would also be reduced progressively by fibre pull-out, if it occurs. Fibre pull-out would be unlikely in the uncracked state, except, perhaps, in the case of a flexible matrix such as a resin, so that, in most cases, equation 6.4 would not need to be so modified.

Impact strength

The energy absorbed by a unit during a destructive test is proportional to the area under its stress/strain diagram and, although energy absorption characteristics may alter when sudden impact occurs, it is found, in general, that stress/strain diagrams give a good indication of resistance to impact generally. The area under diagrams of the form of Fig. 6.3 will be largely dependent on the degree of post-cracking ductility. This can be increased by use of long fibres having relatively low bond strength and high failure strain. Polypropylene in cement satisfies these requirements and produces excellent impact resistance, while asbestos fibres in cement bond well and have low failure strains, resulting in poor impact resistance. Figure 6.6 shows corresponding typical stress/strain graphs for each. It is unfortunate that requirements for high impact strength often result in low tensile strength, so that it may be difficult to obtain both at the same time: a composite comprising, for example, a mixture of polypropylene and asbestos fibres might help in this respect.

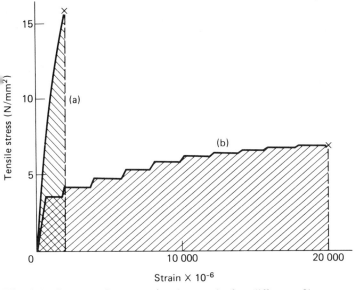

Fig. 6.6 Areas under stress/strain graph for different fibre types in cement matrix: (a) Rigid, strongly bonded fibres such as asbestos; (b) Soft, weaker bonded fibres such as polypropylene

Types and properties of fibres

The three basic groups of materials each make contributions to the range of fibres which exists for reinforcement of materials. In the 'ceramic' group there are glass and asbestos fibres; in the 'metallic' group, steel fibres; and in the 'organic' group, carbon and polypropylene fibres. Properties are summarised in Table 6.1.

Ceramic fibres

The inherent weakness in tension of bulk ceramics has already been linked to the presence of flaws which, according to Griffith's theory, result in greatly amplified internal stresses. It is known that the size of these flaws reduces greatly as the physical size of ceramic units decreases – this is presumably related to reductions in stress differentials caused, for example, by temperature gradients during manufacture. Fibres may, therefore, be, in some cases, 100 times stronger than their bulk equivalents and this, combined with much smaller bending radii associated with small diameters, gives fibres a degree of flexibility which is quite unattainable with bulk equivalents.

Glass fibres

Glass fibres are manufactured by drawing filaments from the base of platinum crucibles (bushings) containing molten glass. Each bushing contains several hundred holes and the filaments so formed are collected to form strands and then wound onto a drum. Individual filament diameters depend on glass properties, hole size and drawing speed, though they are usually about 10μm. A 'size' such as polyvinyl acetate is used to bind filaments together and protect them from damage during fabrication at a later stage (these fibres should not be confused with glass fibres for thermal-insulation purposes, which are much coarser and produced by a different process). The strands, which are normally of approximately elliptical section, typically 0.6 mm by 0.08 mm, may be formed into continuous lengths called roving, woven into cloth or chopped to form matting. Cloth consists of continuous fibres and, therefore, results in much greater composite strength than chopped-strand matting (fibre length, approximately 40 mm).

It is unfortunate that ordinary borosilicate or 'E' glass is attacked by alkalis contained in Portland cements. A special alkali-resistant fibre has now been developed for use with such cements; it contains a fairly large proportion of zirconium oxide ZrO_2 and is marketed under the trade name 'Cem-Fil'.

Asbestos fibres

Since they occur naturally, their use is, perhaps, more traditional than that of other fibre types. Strength values vary greatly, increasing in the order amosite, chrysotile, crocidolite, though the latter, 'blue asbestos', is no longer in current use, due to the health hazard involved. The strength of crocidolite lies in the range 200 to 4000 N/mm², though some small reduction may occur with age. Chrysotile, which is commonly used commercially, has strength in the range 200

Table 6.1 Typical properties of some common fibres in order of decreasing elastic modulus

Fibre type	Relative density	Modulus of elasticity (kN/mm^2)	Ultimate tensile strength (N/mm^2)	Specific modulus of elasticity (kN/mm^2)	Specific tensile strength (N/mm^2)	Strain at failure (per cent)
Carbon high modulus	1.9	420	2100	221	1105	0.5
Carbon low modulus	1.9	240	2400	126	1260	1
Steel (low-carbon)	7.8	200	1100	26	141	Necks
Asbestos (chrysotile)	2.6	160	200–2000	62	385 (Av.)	2
'E' glass	2.55	70	3000	27	1176	5
Polypropylene (fibrillated)	0.9	8	400	8.9	444	7

to 2000 N/mm^2 with a mean strength of about 1000 N/mm^2. Shorter fibres tend to give higher strength. Elastic moduli are also variable, chrysotile having a mean value in the region of 160 kN/mm^2. Fibre diameters are very small, about 1μm, and this may be an important factor in the excellent bonding between asbestos fibres and cement.

Metal fibres
The most common metallic fibres are steel. They are usually relatively coarse – for example, 300μm in diameter – and, since it is unusual for failure of steel fibre-reinforced materials to be caused by failure of the fibres themselves (failure is usually by pull-out of fibres), there is little point in aiming for higher tensile strength than is obtained by drawing ordinary low-carbon steel. Tensile strength is approximately 1100 N/mm^2, though metals are different from ceramic fibres in that failure involves necking and, consequently, larger strains. The 'E' value of steel fibres is similar to that of larger steel components – about 200 kN/mm^2. Fibres may be plated to increase corrosion-resistance.

Organic fibres

Polypropylene fibres This material has great flexibility and toughness, combined with low density, and imparts substantial improvements to the impact strength of materials it reinforces. It is normally manufactured as a film formed by extrusion. This film is then slit and drawn so that spherulites in the partially crystalline polymer are converted into orientated fibrils. The film may, finally, be twisted into twine. The E value is the lowest of any common fibre, approximately 8 kN/mm², so that it would be of no use in increasing pre-cracked strength or stiffening of materials. Tensile strength is approximately 400 N/mm². As would be expected of a non-polar polymer, the fibre has little affinity for water but the fibrillated form produces a good mechanical bond with cement based materials. Polypropylene fibres are resistant to a wide variety of chemicals.

Carbon fibres These are new and highly promising materials based on the strength of the carbon-carbon bond in graphite and the lightness of the carbon atom. Carbon fibres are produced by heat treatment of plastic fibres, such as acrylic fibres, so that the carbon atoms link together to form small graphitic crystallites, which are orientated by stretching while hot. The fibres are about 10 μm in diameter but consist of tiny fibrils stranded together in quantities up to 100 000. There are two chief varieties: high *strength* fibres with ultimate tensile strength of approximately 2400 N/mm² and E value of 240 kN/mm²; and high *modulus* fibres with ultimate tensile strength of 2100 N/mm² and E value of 420 kN/mm². With strengths of this order, it is clearly important that high bond strength with the matrix is essential if the fibres are to be used for reinforcement. Unfortunately, the more perfect the graphitic structure, the less likely the fibre is to bond to other materials, so that treatment, for example, by etching, is required to obtain maximum benefit from this material. The above figures, together with their chemical stability, will give, however, an indication of the importance of the fibres once technological advances result in price reduction though, at present, fibres are very expensive.

Fibre-reinforced cement products

Materials based on Portland cements form a natural choice for application of fibrous materials, since they are cheap, but they leave much to be desired in respect of ductility, impact-resistance and tensile strength, the latter being 3 to 5 N/mm². All the above-named fibres have been used in attempts to improve these properties, though the elastic modulus of the composite is, in most cases, similar to that of the unreinforced material, since the fibres normally form small volume fractions of the total. Table 6.2 summarises properties of typical composites based on Portland cement and, for comparison, glass-reinforced gypsum.

Glass-reinforced cements (GRC)

Glass fibres have been included in certain types of cement product, notably precast units, with a view to increasing flexural strength and impact resistance. Manufacture is often on the lines of asbestos-cement goods – by spraying chopped glass fibres 10 to 50 mm in length on to a perforated base and, at the

Table 6.2 Properties of typical fibre-reinforced cements compared to glass-reinforced gypsum and semi-compressed asbestos-cement sheet.

Material	Modulus of rupture (N/mm^2)	Tensile strength (N/mm^2)	Strain at failure–tension (per cent)	Impact strength
Glass-reinforced cement (5 per cent by volume of alkali-resistant sprayed 40 mm fibres) (air storage, 28 days)	45	17	1	High
Steel fibre-reinforced concrete (2 per cent by volume of 40 mm fibres)	8	4	1	High
Polypropylene fibres in concrete (0.2 per cent by volume of 40 mm fibres)	5	4	High	High
Glass-reinforced gypsum (Class B) (4 per cent by volume sprayed 40 mm fibres)	30	15	0.7	Very high
Semi-compressed asbestos-cement sheet (15 per cent by weight of fibres)	20	14	0.2	Low/medium

same time, spraying on a cement slurry. When a sufficient thickness is built up, excess water is removed by vacuum suction and the flexible composite sheet can be shaped and then cured. Fibres may, alternatively, be introduced by mixing a small percentage of the shorter fibres directly with cement slurry before moulding but, since the resultant orientation is completely random, the tensile strength would only be about half that of products containing fibres orientated in a plane. GRC has very much better impact strength than either unreinforced cement or asbestos cement, 5 per cent by weight of glass fibre giving an impact strength about five times that of the latter. Resistance to fire is much better than that of the unreinforced material, particularly if a proportion of pfa is included. Thermal shocks are also absorbed more satisfactorily.

The main problem with GRC is that ordinary ('E' glass) glass fibres are attacked by the hydrating cement. Figure 6.7 shows that, after a short time in air storage, flexural strength decreases steadily until a low value, about half its previous maximum, is reached. Impact strength is similarly affected. The newer type of glass (Cem-Fil), which includes zirconium oxide ZrO_2, is alkali-resistant and, therefore, not as severely affected as 'E' glass. A typical curve is also shown in Fig. 6.7. It is found, however, that, even with alkali-resistant glass, impact

305

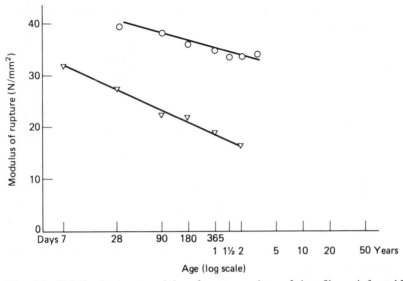

Fig. 6.7 Relation between modulus of rupture and age of glass-fibre reinforced Portland-cement composites. ○ Alkali-resistant glass; △ E-glass. (Courtesy of the Building Research Establishment)

strength reduces with age, especially when the composite is subject to wetting. This is due to an increase of bond strength between fibre and matrix resulting in a higher fracture rate of fibres under impact conditions.

Direct tensile strength is in the region of $17 \, \text{N/mm}^2$ for 5 per cent by volume of alkali-resistant glass and the strain at failure in tension is in the order of 10 000 micro-strain – indicative of the good bonding between fibre and matrix. Tensile strength increases with fibre length and, initially, with fibre-volume fraction, although density reduces with the latter and, with volume fractions of over about 5 per cent, the density effect tends to override the fibre-volume effect, strength falling off as V_f increases above this value. Apparent modulus of rupture is, for reasons stated earlier, much higher than pure tensile strength: values up to $50 \, \text{N/mm}^2$ are attainable.

Glass fibres can also be mixed in situ with concrete, though volume is limited to about 2 per cent maximum, since workability is considerably reduced, especially if long fibres are used. Flexural strength can, nevertheless, be increased up to 4 times with careful mix design.

Applications for GRC are primarily non-structural, in view of the uncertainty in long-term performance even with alkali-resistant fibres. Uses are as follows:

1. In precast pipes, allowing thinner, lighter units to be produced for given strength/impact-resistance properties.
2. In cladding panels and ceiling tiles.
3. Very rapid wall construction has been achieved by assembling dry concrete blocks and then spraying the surfaces with a fibre-mortar mixture. A strong, waterproof structure is formed.

4. Many small precast units, such as manhole covers, ducting, fence posts and garden furniture.
5. A cement and fine-aggregate premix containing alkali-resistant glass fibres is now available for rendering purposes. High impermeability and impact-resistance should be obtainable with correct application.

Steel-fibre-reinforced concrete

Steel is preferable to other metals for fibre reinforcement of concrete on account of its high elastic modulus and reasonable cost.

It would, at first sight, seem reasonable to assume that a good bond would be obtained between steel and concrete in much the same way as in conventional reinforced concrete. However, the bond in the latter is known to be at least partly due to surface irregularities produced by hot-rolling and the presence of thin, adherent rust films. Surface irregularities are virtually absent in steel fibres, which are less than 1 mm in diameter and produced by cold-drawing. This, together with the fact that it is not possible to reproduce the corrosion effect in a fine fibre, results in a relatively poor bond between fibre and matrix in steel-fibre-reinforced concrete (about $5 \, \text{N/mm}^2$ for smooth, single wires). As a result, theoretically, long fibres would be required in order to produce sufficient anchorage to utilise fully, the strength of the steel. There are practical problems here since long fibres tend to 'ball-up', resulting in increased porosity and reduced strength in the final composite. There are, in fact, advantages in having a composite system in which failure occurs by partial pull-out of fibres, since there is often more warning than when it takes place by fracture of fibres (as, for example, in asbestos cement). However, it clearly represents inefficient use of a composite if fibres pull out when well below their yield stress. To this end, many fibres used to reinforce concrete may be deformed (crimped or indented) to increase resistance to pull-out (Fig. 6.8). Alternatively, surface oxidation by heating or controlled acid attack may be used to increase the bond.

Design and mixing of fibre-reinforced concrete require careful attention. 'Balling-up' of fibres is likely to occur if more than 2 per cent by volume of fibres

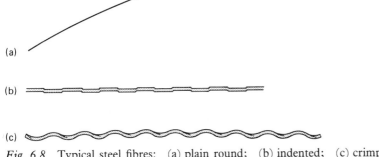

(a)

(b)

(c)

Fig. 6.8 Typical steel fibres: (a) plain round; (b) indented; (c) crimped

is used or if fibres are not added gradually to the mix (for example, through a coarse-mesh sieve). Long, thin fibres (for example, 50 mm in length and 150 μm in diameter) aggravate the situation. The fibres themselves make the concrete unpleasant to handle, due to their stiff, prickly nature. A high proportion by volume of mortar is necessary for incorporation of fibres, hence, rich mixes with a preponderance of fine aggregate are normally used.

Compaction is best achieved by vibration though, with higher fibre concentrations, pokers are not suitable since, on withdrawal, it is difficult to fill the cavity that remains. Table vibration tends to orientate the fibres parallel to the plane of the slab, which is not always advantageous, though the precise effect – especially on more complex shapes – has not been fully investigated.

Properties of the hardened composite
Impact and flexural strengths of concretes are increased considerably by incorporation of steel fibres. Figure 6.9 shows, for example, the approximate relationship between flexural strength and per cent by volume of fibres and indicates that, assuming full compaction can be achieved, flexural strengths will be doubled by incorporation of 2 per cent by volume of certain fibres. An important advantage is that failure is much more gradual than in unreinforced concrete,

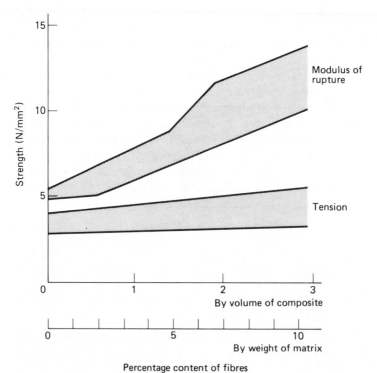

Fig. 6.9 Flexural and direct tensile strengths of steel-fibre reinforced mortar and concrete

with ample visual warning. Increasing fibre aspect ratio increases flexural strength but decreases the percentage fibre content at which balling-up in the mixer occurs, so that, in practice, aspect ratios greater than about 100 are not normally used.

Deformed or treated fibres would be unlikely to improve pre-cracked strength but quite substantial improvements in ultimate strength can be achieved (hence, the bands in Fig. 6.9). The effect is, however, complex: for example, indenting of wires may reduce their strength, while crimping may produce bursting stresses in the concrete, especially if fibres are close together, as would be the case when high-volume fractions are employed.

It is important to appreciate that the action of steel fibres in increasing flexural strength of concrete is different from that by which conventional reinforcement works. The latter is not designed primarily to prevent cracking: it carries the tensile load when cracking has occurred. Fibres, on the other hand, do not carry all the tensile load in concrete – they tend to bridge the microcracks which, under tension, grow to form observable cracks. However, as in the case of conventional reinforced concrete, they do carry some of the load after cracking has taken place, so that a cracked fibre-reinforced concrete may be stressed further before failure occurs.

In order to utilise the fibres more efficiently to improve flexural strength, experiments have been carried out in which fibres have been concentrated at positions of highest tensile stress. This could be by placing of fibres separately during pouring of concrete or by post-treatment, such as is used for gunite (a cement mortar sprayed on to a solid background). The latter could be very effective, provided safety precautions are taken against injury by the steel fibres.

Tensile strength is increased much less than flexural strength, increases of more than 30 per cent being difficult to achieve. Impact properties are considerably improved, particularly in thin slabs, due to post-cracking ductility. Figure 6.10 indicates that high tensile crimped fibres give much higher toughness than indented varieties, presumably due to increased friction during pull-out.

When used in exposed situations, the steel fibres which are adjacent to the surface inevitably corrode, owing to exposure or carbonation of the concrete surface. Such exposure does not affect the mechanical properties of the uncracked composite, though it results in rust-staining, which might be unacceptable if appearance is important.

When concrete becomes cracked, carbonation reaches much greater depths and, although short-term strength may not be affected, long-term strength would be expected to decrease as the effective fibre diameter is reduced. Corrosion of fibres can, of course, be prevented by use of stainless steel or coated fibres: brass may be used for the latter.

Uses

Most applications are based on situations which require a greater degree of impact and flexural strength than can be provided by ordinary concrete. Examples are in

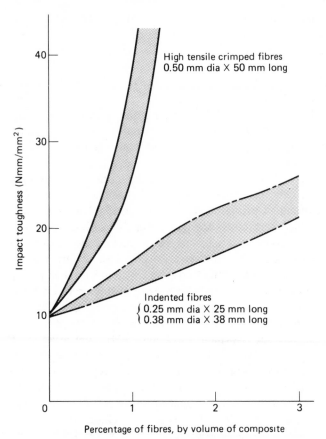

Fig. 6.10 Impact toughness of steel-fibre-reinforced mortar and concrete

factory floor-slabs, aircraft aprons or runways, and surface screeds. The durability of the concrete and, particularly, resistance to extended cracking are considerably improved. Further possible applications include precast units, such as pipes or panels, and the control of cracking in structural concrete.

The high cost of steel has been a drawback in the use of steel fibres in concrete – a concrete containing, for example, 2 per cent by volume of fibres is likely to cost up to six times as much as an ordinary mix. Such a figure could, on the other hand, be misleading, since the material cost is usually a fairly small fraction of the cost of the structure, which might be only slightly increased. Also, the enhanced properties of the concrete may allow the use of thinner sections for a given specification, enabling some saving to be made on the quantity of concrete. Since a wide variety of fibre types is available, it is important to evaluate these for the particular use, as the optimum type and volume fraction of fibres will depend on the precise performance requirements of individual applications.

Polypropylene fibres in concrete

It might seem surprising that polypropylene is used in concrete at all, since its modulus of elasticity is only about 8 kN/mm^2, compared to at least three times this figure for most concretes, so that uncracked tensile or flexural properties are unlikely to be improved. These fibres are, however, cheap and have marked effects on the plastic properties and on post-cracking behaviour of hardened concrete.

Plastic properties
A system has been devised commercially to improve the properties of concrete in the plastic stage. The addition of about 0.1 per cent by volume of short fibres, less than 20 mm in length, in monofilament form (diameter 0.15 mm) leads to a heavily air-entrained mix, containing up to 45 per cent air. This gives the fresh concrete thixotropic properties having, perhaps, zero slump, and yet flowing and compacting readily under vibration. At the same time, it is resistant to bleeding and segregation, which would normally occur in concrete mixes with such high quantities of air. The mix appears 'fatty' so that finishing is easily carried out and textured finishes with fine detail can be achieved, one method being to use patterned rollers. Mixes of varying strength and density can be produced, using dense or lightweight aggregates. The hardened material is said to have improved frost-resistance (due to the entrained air), lower permeability to water, and increased resistance to surface crazing and impact, compared to normal concretes. This type of concrete is likely to have particular application in precast products, such as cladding panels, though wider use in pre-finished flooring and walling units, or structural concrete, may arise.

Hardened properties
Fibrillated polypropylene fibres form an excellent mechanical bond with concrete, so that, although pre-cracked strength is not improved, substantial ultimate stresses in flexure and tension can be obtained. Highest strengths are obtained with flat open continuous networks of polypropylene film, moduli of rupture of over 30 N/mm^2 being possible, with fibre volume fractions in the region of 6 per cent. Cracking of such composites takes the form of fine cracks, often at spacings of less than 10 mm, which are invisible, except at high loads – the failed composite ultimately acquires a leathery consistency. This behaviour is much less marked at small volume fractions or when monofilaments are used – the latter tend to pull out, due to lateral Poisson's ratio contraction. At fibre-volume fractions of 1 per cent or less, the first crack load is also likely to be the ultimate load, although another important property – impact-resistance – is still greatly improved, even at such low volume concentrations. This is due to the greatly increased area under the stress/strain diagram, resulting from the inclusion of polypropylene fibres (Fig. 6.6).

The widest current use of fibres is based on their impact-resistance, impact strengths similar to or slightly greater than conventional steel reinforcing

311

techniques having been obtained by incorporation of approximately 0.4 per cent by volume of fibrillated film fibres about 40 mm in length. Such concrete has been used in a patented system for circular pile shells, 50 mm thick.

A further possible application of composites with higher volume fractions is in corrugated roofing, as a substitute for asbestos-cement sheeting. Clearly, the brittleness associated with asbestos-cement sheets would be overcome, though the latter may be more resistant to high temperatures caused by fire – the post-cracked strength of polypropylene-fibre-reinforced cement would fall dramatically at temperatures above 165 °C, the melting point of polypropylene.

When used in cladding panels, a further advantage, in addition to those given above, is that thickness could be reduced, the minimum thickness of conventionally reinforced panels often being dictated by cover requirements for the steel reinforcement.

Glass-reinforced gypsum (GRG)

A brief description of gypsum is first given. Gypsum is the common name for calcium sulphate, $CaSO_4$, which is the material normally used for plastering. In the natural state, it exists as the dihydrate $CaSO_4.2H_2O$ but, in the manufacture of plasters, some or all of the water is removed by heating. If three-quarters of the water is removed, the hemihydrate, $CaSO_4.\frac{1}{2}H_2O$ (more strictly, $2CaSO_4.H_2O$), is formed, commonly known as plaster of Paris. On mixing with water, this powder sets quickly by crystallisation to form the dihydrate again. It is known as Class A plaster. On addition of a retarder such as keratin, a slower-setting plaster (Class B) is obtained, widely used for undercoat and lightweight plasters. If all the original water is removed, anhydrite – Classes C and D – are obtained, the former being used for finishing-coat plaster and the latter, which is burnt harder, for projections such as arrises, where a harder surface is essential.

The most suitable plaster for reinforcement is Class B, retarded hemihydrate. This material may have a high compressive strength, up to $50\,N/mm^2$ or more at low water content, with an elastic modulus of about $20\,kN/mm^2$, though tensile strength is low, approximately $6\,N/mm^2$. Fibres can, therefore, be profitably used: they will not contribute significantly to stiffness but will considerably improve tensile, flexural, impact and fire-resistance properties. The cheaper 'E' glass fibres can be also used in GRG, since the matrix is of a non-alkaline nature. Mixing methods are as for GRC, maximum flexural strength occurring with about 7 per cent by volume for sprayed fibres. Impact strength is improved remarkably – over twenty times – while flexural strength increases to approximately $30\,N/mm^2$ for 4 per cent by volume of fibres, though the flexural stress at the elastic limit is only $10\,N/mm^2$ approximately. Compressive strength decreases as fibre content increases, probably because fibre interference causes reductions in density. The bond strength between fibre and matrix in GRG is known to be lower than that in GRC, and this is the likely reason for the improved impact strength of the former, especially at high fibre contents. Impacts are absorbed by causing partial bond failure between fibre and matrix.

Higher bond strength produced by better compaction is known to result in lower impact strength.

One most important property of gypsum is its high content of water of crystallisation. As a result, in the form of GRG, it has a high specific heat and very good fire-resistance.

The material has almost no shrinkage, though gypsum is slightly soluble in water, so that GRG could not be used externally unless adequately protected.

Possible applications include:

For fire-resistant partitions. A 10 mm thickness has a fire-resistance of approximately 1 hour. Ceiling tiles of Class 0 (The Building Regulations) have been produced.

In precast flooring units: strength and fire resistance are both satisfactory.

For precast components, such as ducts. GRG could be used in similar situations to asbestos cement (internally only) but without the health hazard associated with the latter on drilling or cutting.

In sandwich construction, for example, timber doors to improve fire-resistance, or with foamed plastics to give fire-resistant partitions with good heat-insulation properties.

Glass-fibre-reinforced polyester resin (GRP)

Great advances have been made in recent years in reinforcement of plastics and, at present, GRP forms the largest bulk of these materials. The mechanical properties of polyester resins are dependent on the polymerisation process, on the presence of plasticisers and fillers, and on the temperature. The tensile strength of polyester resins lies in the range 40 to $100 \, \text{N/mm}^2$ and the tensile modulus of elasticity varies between 1 and $4 \, \text{kN/mm}^2$, too low for efficient structural use. The E value of glass fibre is about $70 \, \text{kN/mm}^2$ in tension, so that considerable improvements in stiffness can be obtained by incorporation of glass fibres, the chief reason for their use. A property of glass which must be considered in the context of reinforcing resins is its high affinity for water. Water is adsorbed in a thickness of twenty or more molecules to the surface of glass on account of its polar bonding: indeed, experiments have shown that water is partly responsible for their low tensile strength. Hence, if a tensile stress is applied to glass, fracture will occur over a period of time unless the glass is completely dry, presumably by the action of stress corrosion due to water in flaws. The exact nature of the glass/resin bond is not fully understood, though water appears to affect the bond even when keying agents are used, since these rarely cover the whole surface and must, in any case, penetrate adsorbed water layers. Fibres are covered with a protective size after manufacture, which is generally removed before keying agents are applied. An exception is PVA size, in which keying agents can be incorporated.

It is found that relatively high aspect ratios, for example 2000, are required to utilise most efficiently the tensile properties of glass fibres. For example, a 10 μm diameter fibre should be at least 20 mm in length to obtain sufficient stress transfer. Fibres in chopped-strand mat generally have lengths in the range 20 to 50 mm.

Manufacture of GRP

Hand lay-up   The laminate is produced by building up layers of resin and fibre in an open mould, often itself made of GRP. A gel coat may then be added, which will improve appearance and weathering performance. Hand lay-up produces only one smooth face. It may be used for small numbers of mouldings or for very large products.

Pressure moulding   The composite is built up on one-half of the mould and then a second matching mould is applied, which presses the composite into shape. A higher proportion of fibre can be used, giving greater strength than in lay-up processes. Two smooth surfaces are obtained.

Continuous processes   These can be used for such products as corrugated sheeting.

Properties of GRP

Large-volume fractions of fibres can be incorporated in the polyester resin by the techniques described above. When continuous rovings or fabrics are employed, volume fractions of about 0.4 are possible, resulting in E values of 20 kN/mm^2 or more and short-term flexural strength over 200 N/mm^2. When the more common chopped-strand mat is used, volume fractions in the region of 0.2 can be incorporated, giving E values of about 8 kN/mm^2 and short-term flexural strength in the region of 100 N/mm^2. On stressing of composites containing discontinuous fibres, plastic deformation, together with reduction in E value, can occur at quite small loads, due to adhesion failure at the end of fibres. The gel coat usually cracks at about 80 per cent of ultimate stress and crazing of the resin matrix further reduces stiffness before failure. Figure 6.11 shows a typical stress/strain curve which is representative of curves for reinforced ductile materials. On loading in flexure, the neutral axis moves towards the compression zone, giving apparently higher flexural strength than is obtained in direct tension. It might be expected that, since the stiffness of a resin is increased significantly by fibre reinforcement, the impact strength would be reduced. In fact, impact strength is increased and this is due to the increase in tensile strength that can be obtained even after crazing in the resin matrix has commenced. Although creep properties of resins are improved by fibre reinforcement, creep is still a significant phenomenon and E values taken over long periods of time are inevitably less than those obtained by short-term measurements. Failure stresses given above may also be reduced substantially in long-term loading, especially in moist conditions.

A most important property of GRP is its low density compared to other similar materials (approximately 1600 kg/m^3). Light transmission of the composite is

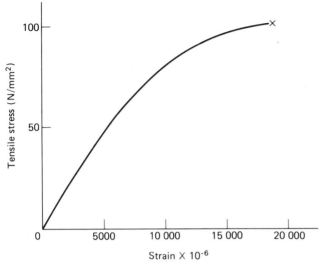

Fig. 6.11 Typical stress/strain graph for glass-reinforced polyester using chopped-strand mat, loaded in tension. The exact relationship depends on the rate of loading

about 85 per cent when new, slightly lower than that of glass, but GRP is stronger and tougher than the latter.

Weathering-resistance depends on the type of resin used, the proportion of resin and the nearness of fibres to the surface. Resins shrink on curing (this is, in fact, thought to be, at least, partly responsible for the glass/resin bond), tending to leave fibres standing on the surface so that water may penetrate by capillarity, destroying the resin/fibre bond. Some resins, themselves, are able to absorb water, resulting in the same effect. Alternatively, weather may erode the surface of the resin, exposing the fibres. The ingress of moisture may be prevented by use of gel coats on the surface of laminates, though these should be lightly reinforced with glass monofilaments to prevent cracking. Acrylic resins are often used as gel coatings. If, after a time, fibres become exposed, it is best to rub the surface down and apply a sealer resin. The procedure should then be repeated periodically. Lives of 30 years or more may be obtained in this way.

Application
GRP is the most important plastic composite in the field of structures. Although the stiffness of the material is not high, the production of the complex shapes which are, therefore, essential for rigidity is easily and cheaply carried out. A multitude of three-dimensional shapes has been produced, some of which have considerable architectural merit. Small, lightweight buildings, such as filling station canopies, shelters and even domestic dwellings, have been constructed from GRP mouldings and, on account of the low density of the material, allow substantial savings in foundation costs. The use of sandwich constructions containing cellular plastics increases stiffness where necessary. The design of all

315

structures requires careful attention to stress transfer at fixings to avoid local failure of GRP.

Roofing The translucency of GRP makes it an attractive material for roofing for buildings which have a daylight requirement. The simplest form is corrugated sheeting, which can be used in place of single sheets in an ordinary corrugated roof. Specially designed dome-lights are now often used and, by fabrication of sections, large spans, such as over swimming pools, warehouses and arcades, can be obtained without the need for a supporting frame. Light-transmission qualities deteriorate over a number of years.

Concrete moulds Concrete is being used increasingly as a facing material for structures and the high quality of patterned finishes that can be obtained with GRP moulds can be a major contribution. For small numbers of units, moulds may be hand-made while, for a larger number of slabs or columns, it may be worthwhile to use presses. Moulds may be used many times over, though choice of release agent is important and moulds may require stiffeners, especially if large components are involved. A further possibility is the use of GRP moulded units as permanent shuttering for concrete. Units containing locating ducts for reinforcement are assembled, and concrete is then poured in and compacted. This provides perfect curing conditions and eliminates formwork removal. This method is most likely to be used for large numbers of *in-situ* units – for example, columns, where the mould would also make some contribution to strength.

Other applications GRP is used in a large number of products in building. Plumbing applications include tanks and cisterns and even hot-water cylinders. In all cases, stresses due to inadequate support or poorly-aligned pipework should be avoided. Other uses include window frames, cladding panels, garage doors and ventilators.

Fire resistance of GRP
In some of the above applications, fire-resistance may be important. All grades of GRP will be destroyed by severe fire, though chlorinated polyester-resin composites are available with the 'P60' rating of BS 476: Part 3. These, however, have been shown to have somewhat inferior weathering resistance. Where fire-resistance for elements of building construction is required (BS 476: Part 8) GRP could be used as a sandwich material with asbestos or concrete.

Uses of glass fibre in other forms of plastics
Epoxy resins have also been used in reinforced form: they adhere well to glass fibres and produce a composite of superior strength and chemical-resistance to GRP. They also shrink less on curing so that initial stresses in composites are reduced. They are, however, more expensive then polyester resins. Typical applications include moulds for concrete products, such as posts, when the moulds, on account of their toughness and strength, can be used time after time.

Resin concretes

These have been introduced in an attempt to improve the tensile properties of concrete and have also permitted the use of very thin sections of concrete, well bonded to their background.

Polyester and, particularly, epoxy resins bond well with most aggregates either by adhesion, or by penetration in the case of porous aggregates, and this is probably the mechanism by which tensile properties are improved – the weakness of ordinary concrete in this respect is due chiefly to failure of the aggregate/cement interface. On account of the lower stiffness of resins compared to concretes (approximately 3 kN/mm² compared to 20 kN/mm² in tension), the stiffness of the composite is likely to be, if anything, less than that of ordinary concretes. Flexural strength has, however, been increased up to four times, though deflections at failure will clearly be relatively larger and failures are usually sudden.

Experiments have been carried out on beams using ordinary concrete for compression zones, bonded to resin concrete in tensile zones, and improved performance is obtained. Disadvantages of resin concretes in structural situations are their susceptibility to fire and their high thermal movement.

Perhaps, the most important uses of resin cements are in surfacing and repair work. Epoxy resin-based floors have long been used in situations where impact- and abrasion-resistance, combined with chemical durability, are required. Epoxy resins are also used for repair work to existing concrete structures damaged by weathering or fire. Extremely good bonds to concrete and steel are obtained, even when wet and when small thicknesses are used. Resins are available in water-dispersable forms that can be mixed in with water in a normal concrete mixer. Resulting properties are intermediate between ordinary concrete and those containing 100 per cent resin binder. Such mixes may be used in thicker sections, for example, granolithic toppings, improving wearing qualities and crack-resistance. Resins containing Portland cement have been produced: these contain a dispersed catalyst which, like the cement, is activated by water, so that the whole sets. Curing times are much reduced and tensile strength is much better than for ordinary concretes, while compressive strength is better than that of either Portland cement concretes or neat resin. These types of cement are also likely to be useful for floor finishes, repair work or other situations where good bond to substrate is essential. More general use of resin cements is at present unlikely, since they are, at least, one order of magnitude more costly than ordinary cements.

Theoretical strength

There is, theoretically, no limit to stresses which could be imposed in compression, although, in practice, compressive stresses give rise to tensile or shear stresses which may, in some cases, lead to their destruction. Even in such cases, very high strength could be obtained if a triaxial compression system could be devised (Fig. 6.12). For example, concrete has been made to withstand compressive stresses of over $200\,N/mm^2$ by enclosing in a steel cylinder, which provides the necessary lateral restraint. Such a system could conceivably be used in concrete columns, though lateral stability would, of course, still have to be satisfactory.

In tension, the theoretical strength must be related to the stress at which crystal slip or bond failure occurs. Theoretical calculations show that, in ceramic-type materials, fracture due to bond failure should not occur until quite large strains are encountered, corresponding to the maximum value of the bonding force of Fig. 1.14 – the order of 20 per cent. Hence, the theoretical strength should be in the region of 20 per cent of their E value. Such strength requires flawless crystals and these can be produced, though they are normally in the form of very thin single-crystal fibres or 'whiskers'. Aluminium oxide whiskers have been produced having, for example, tensile strength over $20\,kN/mm^2$. Iron whiskers may give a strength of $10\,kN/mm^2$ (cf. tensile strength of prestressing wires: Table 4.10), though their elastic modulus is unchanged from that of pure iron.

The above will give some indication of ceiling strengths of materials but, although in the future such materials may find application for specialised purposes, they are unlikely, on account of cost, to be used in constructional engineering or building, where structural problems are usually on a relatively large scale.

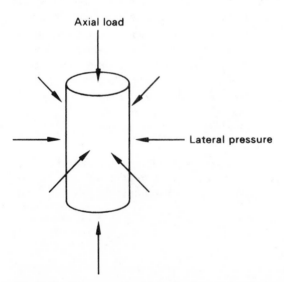

Fig. 6.12 Increase of axial load when a simultaneous lateral pressure is applied. The increase is equal to three times the lateral pressure. For example, concrete of axial strength $50\,N/mm^2$, and subject to a lateral pressure of $50\,N/mm^2$, would fail at a stress of about $200\,N/mm^2$

Problems

6.1 Explain the purpose of incorporating fibres in (a) brittle materials and (b) ductile materials. Give, in each case, requirements of fibres and the volume fractions necessary to achieve the desired effects. Illustrate by reference to actual composites.

6.2 Steel fibres with an elastic modulus of $200 \, \text{kN/mm}^2$ and tensile strength $1000 \, \text{N/mm}^2$ are to be incorporated in a cement based matrix with an elastic modulus of $30 \, \text{kN/mm}^2$ and tensile strength $4 \, \text{N/mm}^2$. A fibre volume fraction of 0.03 is to be used, fibres having a bond strength with the matrix of $5 \, \text{N/mm}^2$. If the fibres have a diameter of 0.25 mm, calculate the critical fibre length. Supposing fibres of this length can be incorporated in a two-dimensional plane, estimate:
(a) first crack strength
(b) pre-cracked elastic modulus
(c) ultimate strength
(d) post-cracked elastic modulus before fibre pull-out occurs.

6.3 A thin strip of resin having a Young's modulus of $2 \, \text{kN/mm}^2$, loaded uniformly, undergoes a deflection of 10 mm when a certain load is applied. What deflection would be obtained if 30 per cent by volume of glass fibres with an E value of $70 \, \text{kN/mm}^2$ were incorporated randomly in the plane of the strip? (Efficiency factor $\frac{1}{3}$).

6.4 A certain fibre of diameter of $10 \, \mu\text{m}$ has an ultimate tensile strength of $1200 \, \text{N/mm}^2$ and a bond strength with the matrix of $10 \, \text{N/mm}^2$. What minimum aspect ratio would theoretically be required to prevent pull-out of the fibre? Give reasons why, in practice, higher values might be required.

6.5 Compare the properties of glass-reinforced gypsum and glass-reinforced cement, in situations where: impact strength, fire-resistance, long-term strength, weather-resistance, are required. Suggest applications of each for general building purposes.

6.6 Discuss the following in relation to fibre-reinforced concretes:
(a) Aspect ratio
(b) Fibre orientation
(c) Volume fraction.

Show how these affect, or are affected by, formation technique (that is, conventional mixing and lay- or spray-up methods).

6.7 Give reasons why glass should be the fibre type normally incorporated with polyester resins. Describe the properties of GRP, comparing with those of competitive materials.

6.8 Discuss the properties and applications of cements reinforced with:
(a) glass
(b) steel
(c) polypropylene.

References

1. 'Prospects for Fibre Reinforced Construction Materials' *Proceedings of the International Building Exhibition Conference, 1971.* Building Research Establishment.
2. G. S. Hollister and C. Thomas, *Fibre Reinforced Materials.* Elsevier, 1966.

3. A. Kelly, *Strong Solids*. Oxford, 1966.
4. L. Holliday, Ed. *Composite Materials*. Elsevier, 1966.
5. D. J. Hannant, *Fibre Cements and Fibre Concretes*. Wiley 1978.
6. 'Fibre Reinforced Concrete', *Concrete Building and Concrete Products*, Vol. XLIV, No. 10, 1969.
7. B. Parkyn, *Glass Reinforced Plastics*. Iliffe.
8. R. J. Towler and R. I. T. Williams, 'Resin Concrete', *Construction Research and Development Journal*, Vol. 1, No. 4.
9. *Polypropylene Fibres in Concrete*. Patent: Shell International Chemical Company.
10. *Use of Polypropylene in Pile Shells*. West's Piling and Construction Company Limited.
11. *Polypropylene Fibres in Concrete: Faircrete*. John Laing Research and Development Ltd.
12. *Building Research Establishment Digests* – several.
13. *Building Research Establishment Current Papers* – several.
14. Rilem Symposium 1975. *Fibre Reinforced Cement and Concrete*. Construction Press Ltd.
15. BS 476: Part 3 1975 External fire exposure roof test.
16. BS 476: Part 8 1972 Text methods and criteria for the fire resistance of elements for building construction.

Bibliography

1. L. Holliday (ed.), *Composite Materials*. Elsevier, 1966.
2. J. B. Moss, *Engineering Materials*. Butterworth, 1971.
3. L. Addleson, *Materials for Building*. Iliffe, 1972.
4. R. M. E. Diamant, *Chemistry of Building Materials*. Business Books, 1970.
5. J. C. Anderson and K. D. Leaver, *Materials Science*. Nelson, 1969.
6. T. J. Lewis and P. E. Secker, *Science of Materials*. Harrap, 1965.
7. BRE Digests, published by HMSO.
8. R. A. Burgess, P. J. Horrobin, Norman McKee and J. W. Simpson (eds), *The Construction Industry Handbook*. Medical and Technical Publish Co. Ltd, 1974.
9. J. W. Simpson and P. J. Horrobin, *Weathering and Performance of Building Materials*. Medical and Technical Publishing Co. Ltd, 1970.
10. R. A. Burgess, P. J. Horrobin and J. W. Simpson (eds), *Progress in Constuction Science and Technology*. Medical and Technical Publishing Co. Ltd, 1971.
11. N. Jackson (ed.), *Civil Engineering Materials*. Macmillan, 1978.
12. J. M. Illston, J. M. Dinwoodie, A. A. Smith, *Concrete, Timber and Metals*. Van Nostrand Reinhold, 1979.
13. C. A. Ragsdale, E. A. Raynham, *Building Materials Technology*, 1972.
14. J.E. Gordon, *The New Science of Strong Materials* Penguin, 1976.

Index